Bilingual Dictionary

English-Bosnian
Bosnian-English
Dictionary

Compiled by

Boris Kažanegra

STAR Foreign Language BOOKS

55, Warren Street, LONDON W1T 5NW (UK)

© Publishers

First Edition: 2011

Published
STAR Foreign Language BOOKS
55, Warren Street, LONDON W1T 5NW (UK)
E-mail : starbooksuk@aol.com
www.foreignlanguagebooks.co.uk

Printed in India at
Star Print-O-Bind, New Delhi-110020

About this Dictionary

Developments in science and technology today have narrowed down distances between countries, and have made the world a small place. A person living thousands of miles away can learn and understand the culture and lifestyle of another country with ease and without travelling to that country. Languages play an important role as facilitators of communocation in this respect.

To promote such an understanding, STAR Foreign Language BOOKS has planned to bring out a series of bilingual dictionaries in which important English words have been translated into other languages, with Roman transliteration in case of languages that have different scripts. This is a humble attempt to bring people of the word closer through the medium of language, thus making communication esay and convenient.

These dictionaries have been compiled and edited by teachers and scholars of relative languages.

Bilingual Dictionaries in this Series

English-Amharic / Amharic-English	Aschalew Mekonnen Bekele
English-Arabic / Arabic-English	Rania-al-Qass
English-Bengali / Bengali-English	Amit Majumdar
English-Bosnian / Bosnian-English	Boris Kazanegra
English-Cantonese / Cantonese-English	Nisa Yang
English-Chinese (Mandarin) / Chinese (Mandarin)-Eng	Y. Shang & R. Yao
English-Croatian / Croatain-English	Vesna Kazanegra
English-Dari / Dari-English	Amir Khan
English-Estonian / Estonian-English	Lana Haleta
English-Farsi / Farsi-English	Maryam Zaman Khani
English-Gujarati / Gujarati-English	Sujata Basaria
English-Hindi / Hindi-English	Sudhakar Chaturvedi
English-Hungarian / Hungarian-English	Lucy Mallows
English-Latvian / Latvian-English	Julija Baranovska
English-Lithuanian / Lithuanian-English	Regina Kazakeviciute
English-Marathi / Marathi-English	Sahard Thackerey
English-Nepali / Nepali-English	Anil Mandal
English-Pashto / Pashto-English	Amir Khan
English-Polish / Polish-English	Magdalena Herok
English-Punjabi / Punjabi-English	Teja Singh Chatwal
English-Romanian / Romanian-English	Georgeta Laura Dutulescu
English-Serbian / Serbian-English	Vesna Kazanegra
English-Slovak / Slovak-English	Zozana Horvathova
English-Somali / Somali-English	Ali Mohamud Omer
English-Tamil / Tamil-English	Sandhya Mahadevan
English-Thai / Thai-English	Suwan Kaewkongpan
English-Turkish / Turkish-English	Nagme Yazgin
English-Urdu / Urdu-English	S. A. Rahman
English-Vietnamese / Vietnamese-English	Hoa Hoang

More languages in print

STAR Foreign Language BOOKS

55, Warren Street, LONDON W1T 5NW (UK)

ENGLISH-BOSNIAN

A

aback *adv.* unazad
abaction *n* krađa stoke
abactor *n* kradljivac stoke
abandon *v.t.* napustiti
abase *v.t.* poniziti
abasement *n* poniženje
abash *v.t.* posramiti
abate *v.t.* smanjiti
abatement *n.* smanjenje
abbey *n.* opatija
abbreviate *v.t.* skratiti
abbreviation *n* kratica
abdicate *v.t,* abdicirati
abdication *n* abdikacija
abdomen *n* stomak
abdominal *a.* stomačni
abduct *v.t.* oteti
abduction *n* otmica
abed *adv. u* postelji
aberrance *n.* nenormalnost
abet *v.t.* potaknuti
abetment *n.* nagovaranje
abeyance *n.* neizvesnost
abhor *v.t.* gnušati se
abhorrence *n.* gnušanje
abide *v.i* trpeti
abiding *a* trajan
ability *n* sposobnost
abject *a.* bijedan
ablaze *adv.* plameno
ablactate *v. t* odbiti dojenče
ablactation *n* odbijanje dojenčeta
able *a* moguć
ablepsy *n* slepilo
ablush *adv* pocrvenio
ablution *n* pranje

abnegate *v. t* poricati
abnegation *n* poricanje
abnormal *a* nenormalan
aboard *adv* ukrcano
abode *n* boravište
abolish *v.t* ukinuti
abolition *v* ukidanje
abominable *a* gnusan
aboriginal *a* starosjedilački
aborigines *n. pl* starosjedioci
abort *v.i* prekinuti
abortion *n* pobačaj
abortive *adv* neuspio
abound *v.i.* obilovati
about *adv* otprilike
about *prep* o
above *adv* povrh
above *prep.* gornji
abreast *adv* usporedo
abridge *v.t* skratiti
abridgement *n* skraćivanje
abroad *adv u* inozemstvu
abrogate *v. t.* poništiti
abrupt *a* naglo
abruption *n* prekid
abscess *n* apsces
absonant *adj* neskladan
abscond *v.i* pobjeći od zakona
absence *n* odsustvo
absent *a* odsutan
absent *v.t* biti odsutan
absolute *a* potpun
absolutely *adv* potpuno
absolve *v.t* osloboditi
absorb *v.t* upiti
abstain *v.i.* suzdržati se
abstract *a* apstraktan
abstract *n* rezime
abstract *v.t* sažeti
abstraction *n.* apstrakcija

absurd *a* apsurdan
absurdity *n* apsurd
abundance *n* obilje
abundant *a* obilan
abuse *v.t.* zlostavljati
abuse *n* zlostavljanje
abusive *a* uvredljiv
abutted *v* naslanjati se
abyss *n* ponor
academic *a* akademski
academy *n* akademija
acarpous *adj.* jalovo
accede *v.t.* pristupiti
accelerate *v.t* ubrzati
acceleration *n* ubrzanje
accent *n* naglasak
accent *v.t* naglasiti
accept & prihvatiti
acceptable *a* prihvatljiv
acceptance *n* prihvaćanje
access *n* pristup
accession *n* pristupanje
accessory *n* pribor
accident *n* nesreća
accidental *a* slučajan
accipitral *adj* sokolovski
acclaim *v.t* odobriti
acclaim *n* odobravanje
acclamation *n* klicanje
acclimatise *v.t* prilagoditi se
accommodate *v.t* smjestiti
accommodation *n.* smještaj
accompaniment *n* pratnja
accompany *v.t.* pratiti
accomplice *n* saučesnik
accomplish *v.t.* ostvariti
accomplished *a* ostvaren
accomplishment *n.* dostignuće
accord *v.t. slagati* se
accord *n.* suglasnost

accordingly *adv.* prema tome
account *n.* račun
account *v.t.* izvjestiti
accountable *a* odgovoran
accountancy *n.* računovodstvo
accountant *n.* računovođa
accredit *v.t.* opunomoćiti
accrete *v.t.* srasti
accrue *v.i.* nagomilati se
accumulate *v.t.* akumulirati
accumulation *n* akumulacija
accuracy *n.* točnost
accurate *a.* točan
accursed *a.* proklet
accusation *n* optužba
accuse *v.t.* optužiti
accused *n.* optuženik
accustom *v.t.* privići se
accustomed *a.* naviknut
ace *n* as
acentric *adj* bezsredišnji
acephalous *adj.* bezglav
acephalus *n.* bezglavi fetus
acetify *v.* oksidisati
ache *n.* bol
ache *v.i.* boljeti
achieve *v.t.* postići
achievement *n.* uspjeh
achromatic *adj* bezbojan
acid *a* kiseo
acid *n* kiselina
acidity *n.* kiselost
acknowledge *v.* priznati
acknowledgement *n.* priznanje
acne *n* bubuljice
acorn *n.* žir
acoustic *a* akustično
acoustics *n.* akustika
acquaint *v.t.* upoznati
acquaintance *n.* poznanstvo

9

acquest *n* tekovina
acquiesce *v.i.* prećutna saglasnost
acquiescence *n.* pomirenje
acquire *v.t.* steći
acquirement *n.* postizanje
acquisition *n.* akvizicija
acquit *v.t.* osloboditi
acquittal *n.* oslobađajuća presuda
acre *n.* jutro (jedinica za površinu)
acreage *n.* površina u jutrima
acrimony *n* ljutina
acrobat *n.* akrobata
across *adv.* preko
across *prep.* preko puta
act *n.* djelo
act *v.i.* postupati
acting *n.* djelovanje
action *n.* akcija
activate *v.t.* aktivirati
active *a.* aktivan
activity *n.* djelatnost
actor *n.* glumac
actress *n.* glumica
actual *a.* stvaran
actually *adv.* zapravo
acumen *n.* sposobnost
acute *a.* oštar
adage *n.* poslovica
adamant *a.* nepopustljiv
adamant *n.* tvrdoća
adapt *v.t.* prilagoditi
adaptation *n.* prilagođavanje
adays *adv.* danju
add *v.t.* dodati
addict *v.t.* biti ovistan
addict *n.* ovisnik
addiction *n.* ovisnost
addition *n.* dodatak
additional *a.* dodatni
addle *adj.* pokvareno

address *v.t.* obratiti se
address *n.* adresa
addressee *n.* primatelj
adduce *v.t.* navesti
adept *n.* vještina
adept *a.* vješt
adequacy *n.* adekvatnost
adequate *a.* adekvatan
adhere *v.i.* držati se
adherence *n.* privrženost
adhesion *n.* adhezija
adhesive *n.* ljepljiva materija
adhesive *a.* ljepljiva materija
adhibit *v.t.* dopustiti
adieu *n.* pozdraviti se
adieu *interj.* zbogom
adjacent *a.* susjedni
adjective *n.* pridev
adjoin *v.t.* graničiti se
adjourn *v.t.* odgoditi
adjournment *n.* odlaganje
adjudge *v.t.* dosuditi
adjunct *n.* dodatak
adjuration *n* preklinjanje
adjust *v.t.* prilagoditi
adjustment *n.* prilagodba
administer *v.t.* upravljati
administration *n.* uprava
administrative *a.* upravni
administrator *n.* administrator
admirable *a.* za divljenje
admiral *n.* admiral
admiration *n.* divljenje
admire *v.t.* diviti se
admissible *a.* prihvatljiv
admission *n.* pristup
admit *v.t.* priznati
admittance *n.* pristupanje
admonish *v.t.* upozoriti
admonition *n.* upozorenje

ado *n.* buka
adobe *n.* čerpić
adolescence *n.* mladost
adolescent *a.* mlad
adopt *v.t.* usvojiti
adoption *n* usvajanje
adorable *a.* neodoljiv
adoration *n.* obožavanje
adore *v.t.* obožavati
adorn *v.t.* uljepšavati
adscititious *adj* dopunski
adulation *n* pretjerano laskanje
adult *a* odrastao
adult *n.* odrasla osoba
adulterate *v.t.* falsifikovati
adulteration *n.* kvarenje
adultery *n.* preljuba
advance *v.t.* unaprijediti
advance *n.* predujam
advancement *n.* napredovanje
advantage *n.* prednost
advantage *v.t.* iskoristiti
advantageous *a.* povoljan
advent *n.* pojava
adventure *n* avantura
adventurous *a.* pustolovan
adverb *n.* prilog
adverbial *a.* priložni
adversary *n.* protivnik
adverse *a* suprotan
adversity *n.* nesreća
advert *v.* skrenuti pažnju
advertise *v.t.* oglašavati
advertisement *n* oglas
advice *n* savjet
advisable *a.* preporučiv
advisability *n* preporučivost
advise *v.t.* savjetovati
advocacy *n.* advokatura
advocate *n* advokat

advocate *v.t.* zastupati
aerial *a.* zračni
aerial *n.* antena
aeriform *adj.* vazdušast
aerify *v.t.* isparavati
aerodrome *n* aerodrom
aeronautics *n.pl.* aeronautika
aeroplane *n.* avion
aesthetic *a.* estetski
aesthetics *n.pl.* estetika
aestival *adj* ljetni
afar *adv.* izdaleka
affable *a.* ljubazan
affair *n.* afera
affect *v.t.* utjecati
affectation *n* prenemaganje
affection *n.* naklonjenost
affectionate *a.* nežan
affidavit *n* pismena izjava
affiliation *n.* pridruženje
affinity *n* sklonost
affirm *v.t.* potvrditi
affirmation *n* potvrda
affirmative *a* potvrdan
affix *v.t.* pričvrstiti
afflict *v.t.* ožalostiti
affliction *n.* žalost
affluence *n.* bogatstvo
affluent *a.* bogat
afford *v.t.* priuštiti
afforest *v.t.* pošumiti
affray *n* kavga
affront *v.t.* uvrijediti
affront *n* uvreda
afield *adv.* vani
aflame *adv.* zapaljeno
afloat *adv.* ploveći
afoot *adv.* pješice
afore *prep.* prije
afraid *a.* uplašen

afresh *adv.* ponovo
after *prep.* nakon
after *adv* nakon
after *conj.* pošto
after *a* poslednji
afterwards *adv.* kasnije
again *adv.* opet
against *prep.* nasuprot
agamist *n* neženja
agape *adv.* zapanjeno
agaze *adv.* zagledano
age *n.* doba
aged *a.* ostario
agency *n.* agencija
agenda *n.* dnevni red
agent *n* agent
aggravate *v.t.* pogoršati
aggravation *n.* pogoršavanje
aggregate *v.t.* nagomilati
aggression *n* agresija
aggressive *a.* agresivan
aggressor *n.* agresor
aggrieve *v.t.* ožalostiti
aghast *a.* prestravljen
agile *a.* agilan
agility *n.* agilnost
agitate *v.t.* uzrujati
agitation *n* uzrujanost
agist *v.t.* iznajmiti pašnjak
aglow *adv.* užaren
agnus *n* jagnje
ago *adv.* prije
agog *adj.* nestrpljiv
agonist *n* natjecatelj
agonize *v.t.* mučiti
agony *n.* agonija
agronomy *n.* agronomija
agrarian *a.* agrarni
agree *v.i.* složiti se
agreeable *a.* suglasan

agreement *n.* sporazum
agricultural *a.* poljoprivredni
agriculture *n.* poljoprivreda
agriculturist *n.* poljoprivrednik
ague *n.* malarična groznica
ahead *adv.* ispred
aheap *adv.* u gomili
aid *n.* pomoć
aid *v.t* pomagati
aigrette *n.* kresta
ail *v.t.* bolovati
ailment *n.* oboljenje
aim *n.* cilj
aim *v.i.* ciljati
air *n.* zrak
aircraft *n.* letjelica
airy *a.* vazdušast
ajar *adv.* pritvoren
akin *a.* srodan
alacrious *adj* živahan
alacrity *n.* živahnost
alamort *adj.* smrtno
alarm *n* uzbuna
alarm *v.t* uzbuniti
alas *interj.* avaj
albeit *conj.* iako
albion *n* albion
album *n.* album
albumen *n* bjelančevina
alchemy *n.* alkemija
alcohol *n* alkohol
ale *n* pivo
alegar *n* ocat
alert *a.* oprezan
alertness *n.* opreznost
algebra *n.* algebra
alias *n.* pseudonim
alias *adv.* zvano
alibi *n.* alibi
alien *a.* stranac

alienate v.t. otuđiti
aliferous adj. krilat
alight v.i. osvijetljen
align v.t. poravnati
alignment n. poravnanje
alike a. nalik
alike adv. jednako
aliment n. izdržavanje
alimony n. alimentacija
aliquot n. delilac bez ostatka
alive a. živ
alkali n. baza
all a. sav
all n. cijeli
all adv. svo
all pron. svi
allay v.t. ublažiti
allegation n. navod
allege v.t. izjaviti
allegiance n. vjernost
allegorical a. alegorijski
allegory n. alegorija
allergy n. alergija
alleviate v.t. olakšati
alleviation n. olakšanje
alley n. uska ulica
alliance n. savez
alligator n aligator
alliterate v. koristiti aliteraciju
alliteration n. aliteracija
allocate v.t. dodijeliti
allocation n. raspodjela
allot v.t. odrediti
allotment n. dodjeljivanje
allow v.t. dopustiti
allowance n. dozvola
alloy n. legura
allude v.i. aludirati
allure v.t. privlačiti
allurement n privlačnost

allusion n nagovještaj
allusive a. skriven
ally v.t. ujediniti se
ally n. saveznik
almanac n. almanah
almighty a. svemoguć
almond n. badem
almost adv. umalo
alms n. milostinja
aloft adv. visoko
alone a. sam
along adv. uzduž
along prep. duž
aloof adv. daleko
aloud adv. naglas
alp n. planinski vrh
alpha n. alfa
alphabet n. abeceda
alphabetical a. abecedno
alpinist n. alpinista
already adv. već
also adv. također
altar n. oltar
alter v.t. izmijeniti
alteration n izmjena
altercation n. prepirka
alternate a. naizmjenično
alternate v.t. zamjenjivati
alternative n. alternativa
alternative a. alternativan
although conj. iako
altimeter n visinomjer
altitude n. visina
alto n alt
altogether adv. sveukupno
aluminium n. aluminij
alumna n svršena učenica
always adv. uvijek
am sam
amalgam n legura žive

amalgamate v.t. miješati sa živom
amalgamation n miješanje
amass v.t. nagomilati
amateur n. amater
amatory adj ljubavni
amaze v.t. zadiviti
amazement n. zadivljenost
ambassador n. veleposlanik
amberite n. vrsta baruta
ambient adj. ambijent
ambiguity n. dvosmislenost
ambiguous a. dvosmislen
ambition n. ambicija
ambitious a. ambiciozan
ambry n. ormar
ambulance n. hitna pomoć
ambulant adj putujući
ambulate v.t kretati se
ambush n. zasjeda
ameliorate v.t. poboljšati
amelioration n. poboljšanje
amen interj. amin
amenable a nadležan
amend v.t. popraviti
amendment n. amandman
amends n.pl. odšteta
amenorrhoea n amenoreja
amiability n. ljubaznost
amiable a. ljubazan
amicable adj. prijateljski
amid prep. među
amiss adv. loše
amity n. prijateljstvo
ammunition n. municija
amnesia n amnezija
amnesty n. amnestija
among prep. među
amongst prep. između
amoral a. nemoralan
amount n iznos

amount v.i iznositi
amount v. iznos
amorous a. zaljubljiv
amour n l jubavna afera
ampere n amper
amphibious adj amfibijski
amphitheatre n amfiteatar
ample a. opsežan
amplification n pojačanje
amplifier n pojačalo
amplify v.t. pojačati
amuck adv. bjesomučno
amulet n. amajlija
amuse v.t. zabavljati
amusement n zabava
an art neodređeni član
anabaptism n anabaptizam
anachronism n anakronizam
anaclisis n ovisnost od drugih
anadem n vijenac za glavu
anaemia n malokrvnost
anaesthesia n anestezija
anaesthetic n. anestetik
anal adj. analni
analogous a. analogan
analogy n. analogija
analyse v.t. analizirati
analysis n. analiza
analyst n analitičar
analytical a analitički
anamnesis n anamneza
anamorphous adj anamorfan
anarchism n. anarhizam
anarchist n anarhista
anarchy n anarhija
anatomy n. anatomija
ancestor n. predak
ancestral a. naslijeđen
ancestry n. porijeklo
anchor n. sidro

anchorage *n* usidrenje
ancient *a.* drevni
ancon *n* konzola
and *conj.* i
androphagi *n.* ljudožderi
anecdote *n.* anegdota
anemometer *n* anemometar
anew *adv.* iznova
anfractuous *adj* krivudav
angel *n* anđeo
anger *n.* bijes
angina *n* angina
angle *n.* kut
angle *n* stanovište
angry *a.* ljut
anguish *n.* bol
angular *a.* kutni
anigh *adv.* blizu
animal *n.* životinja
animate *v.t.* oživjeti
animate *a.* živahan
animation *n* animacija
animosity *n* neprijateljstvo
animus *n* zlonamjernost
aniseed *n* anisovo seme
ankle *n.* članak
anklet *n* ukras za nogu
annalist *n.* ljetopisac
annals *n.pl.* ljetopisi
annectant *adj.* spojni
annex *v.t.* dodati
annexation *n* pripajanje
annihilate *v.t.* uništiti
annihilation *n* uništenje
anniversary *n.* godišnjica
announce *v.t.* objaviti
announcement *n.* objava
annoy *v.t.* dosađivati
annoyance *n.* dosađivanje
annual *a.* godišnji

annuitant *n* rentijer
annuity *n.* renta
annul *v.t.* poništiti
annulet *n* prstenčić
anoint *v.t.* mazati
anomalous *a* nepravilan
anomaly *n* nepravilnost
anon *adv.* odmah
anonymity *n.* anonimnost
anonymity *n.* bezimenost
anonymous *a.* nepoznat
another *a* drugi
answer *n* odgovor
answer *v.t* odgovoriti
answerable *a.* odgovorljiv
ant *n* mrav
antacid *adj.* antacid
antagonism *n.* protivljenje
antagonist *n.* protivnik
antagonize *v.t.* protiviti se
antarctic *a.* antarktički
antecede *v.t.* prethoditi
antecedent *n.* prošlost
antecedent *a.* prethodni
antedate *n.* raniji datum
antelope *n.* antilopa
antenatal *adj.* prenatalni
antennae *n.* antene
antenuptial *adj.* predbračni
anthem *n.* himna
anthology *n.* antologija
anthropoid *adj.* čovjekoliki
anti *pref.* anti
anti-aircraft *a.* protuavionski
antic *n* lakrdijaš
anticipate *v.t.* predvidjeti
anticipation *n.* predviđanje
antidote *n.* protuotrov
antinomy *n.* kontradikcija
antipathy *n.* antipatija

antiphony *n.* antifonija
antipodes *n.* antipodi
antiquarian *a.* starinski
antiquarian *n* antikvar
antiquary *n.* starinar
antiquated *a.* zastario
antique *a.* starinski
antiquity *n.* antika
antiseptic *n.* antiseptik
antiseptic *a.* antiseptički
antithesis *n.* antiteza
antitheist *n* ateist
antler *n.* rog
antonym *n.* antonim
anus *n.* čmar
anvil *n.* nakovanj
anxiety *a* uznemiren
anxious *a.* zabrinut
any *a.* svaki
any *adv.* ma koji
anyhow *adv.* u svakom slučaju
apace *adv.* hitro
apart *adv.* odvojeno
apartment *n.* stan
apathy *n.* apatija
ape *n* majmun
ape *v.t.* oponašati
aperture *n.* otvor
apex *n.* vrh
aphorism *n* aforizam
apiary *n.* pčelinjak
apiculture *n.* pčelarstvo
apish *a.* majmunski
apnoea *n* dišne smetnje
apologize *v.i.* izviniti se
apologue *n* basna
apology *n.* izvinjenje
apostle *n.* apostol
apostrophe *n.* apostrofiranje
apotheosis *n.* obožavanje

apparatus *n.* aparat
apparel *n.* odjeća
apparel *v.t.* obući
apparent *a.* prividan
appeal *n.* žalba
appeal *v.t.* žaliti se
appear *v.i.* pojaviti se
appearance *n* izgled
appease *v.t.* umiriti
appellant *n.* apelant
append *v.t.* dodati
appendage *n.* dodatak
appendicitis *n.* upala slijepog creva
appendix *n.* slijepo crevo
appendix *n.* dodatak
appetence *n.* požuda
appetent *adj.* željno
appetite *n.* apetit
appetite *n.* nagon
appetizer *n* predjelo
applaud *v.t.* aplaudirati
applause *n.* aplauz
apple *n.* jabuka
appliance *n.* uređaj
applicable *a.* primjenjiv
applicant *n.* kandidat
application *n.* primjena
apply *v.t.* primjeniti
appoint *v.t.* imenovati
appointment *n.* imenovanje
apportion *v.t.* raspodijeliti
apposite *adj* prikladan
apposite *a.* primjeran
appositely *adv* prikladno
approbate *v.t* odobriti
appraise *v.t.* procijeniti
appreciable *a.* primjetan
appreciate *v.t.* cijeniti
appreciation *n.* zahvalnost
apprehend *v.t.* shvatiti

apprehension n. razumijevanje
apprehensive a. pronicljiv
apprentice n. šegrt
apprise v.t. obavijestiti
approach v.t. pristupiti
approach n. pristup
approbation n. odobrenje
appropriate v.t. primijeniti
appropriate a. prikladan
appropriation n. prisvajanje
approval n. odobrenje
approve v.t. odobriti
approximate a. približan
apricot n. kajsija
appurtenance n pripadanje
apron n. kecelja
apt a. sposoban
aptitude n. sposobnost
aquarium n. akvarij
aquarius n. vodolija
aqueduct n. akvadukt
arable adj. obradiv
arbiter n. sudija
arbitrary a. proizvoljno
arbitrate v.t. presuditi
arbitration n. arbitraža
arbitrator n. arbiter
arc n. luk
arcade n svod
arch n. svod
arch v.t. zasvoditi
arch a prepreden
archaic a. drevan
archangel n arhanđeo
archbishop n. arhiepiskop
archer n. strijelac
architect n. arhitekt
architecture n. arhitektura
archives n.pl. arhive
Arctic n Arktik

ardent a. užaren
ardour n. vrućina
arduous a. energičan
area n područje
areca n ukrasna palma
arena n arena
argil n glina
argue v.t. raspravljati
argument n. rasprava
argute adj. oštrouman
arid adj. suh
aries n. ovan
aright adv pravilno
aright adv. pravedno
arise v.i. ustati
aristocracy n. plemstvo
aristocrat n. aristokrata
aristophanic adj. aristofanski
arithmetic n. aritmetika
arithmetical a. aritmetički
ark n. kovčeg
arm n. ruka
arm v.t. naoružati
armada n. armada
armament n. naoružanje
armature n. armatura
armistice n. primirje
armlet a. narukvica
armour n. oklop
armoury n. oružarnica
army n. vojska
around prep. oko
around adv. okolo
arouse v.t. pobuditi
arraign v. optužiti
arrange v.t. urediti
arrangement n. uređenje
arrant n. opak
array v.t. rasporediti
array n. red

arrears n.pl. dugovi
arrest v.t. uhititi
arrest n. uhićenje
arrival n. dolazak
arrive v.i. doći
arrogance n. oholost
arrogant a. ohol
arrow n. strela
arrowroot n. strelast koren
arsenal n. arsenal
arsenic n arsen
arson n palež
art n. umejtnost
artery n. arterija
artful a. vješt
arthritis n artritis
artichoke n. artičoka
article n članak
articulate a. raščlanjen
artifice n. smicalica
artificial a. umjetni
artillery n. artiljerija
artisan n. zanatlija
artist n. umjetnik
artistic a. umjetnički
artless a. neumjetnički
as adv. tako
as conj. kao
as pron. koji
asbestos n. azbest
ascend v.t. penjati se
ascent n. uspon
ascertain v.t. utvrditi
ascetic n. asket
ascetic a. asketski
ascribe v.t. pripisati
ash n. pepeo
ashamed a. posramljen
ashore adv. na kopnu
aside adv. po strani

aside n. strana
asinine adj. tvrdoglav
ask v.t. pitati
asleep adv. u snu
aspect n. aspekt
asperse v. ukaljati
aspirant n. pretendent
aspiration n. težnja
aspire v.t. težiti
ass n. magarac
assail v. nasrnuti
assassin n. ubojica
assassinate v.t. ubiti
assassination n atentat
assault n. napad
assault v.t. napasti
assemble v.t. sastaviti
assembly n. zbor
assent v.i. pristati
assent n. pristanak
assert v.t. tvrditi
assess v.t. procijeniti
assessment n. procjena
asset n. imovina
assibilate v. asibilant
assign v.t. dodijeliti
assignee n. opunomoćenik
assimilate v. izjednačiti
assimilation n izjednačavanje
assist v.t. pomoći
assistance n. pomoć
assistant n. asistent
associate v.t. sarađivati
associate a. udružen
associate n. suradnik
association n. udruženje
assoil v.t. oprostiti
assort v.t. svrstavati
assuage v.t. ublažiti
assume v.t. pretpostaviti

assumption n. pretpostavka
assurance n. uverenje
assure v.t. uveriti
astatic adj. nestabilan
asterisk n. zvjezdica
asterism n. sazvježđe
asteroid adj. zvjezdolik
asthma n. astma
astir adv. u pokretu
astonish v.t. začuditi
astonishment n. čuđenje
astound v.t zapanjiti
astray adv. zalutao
astrologer n. astrolog
astrology n. astrologija
astronaut n. astronaut
astronomer n. astronom
astronomy n. astronomija
asunder adv. nadvoje
asylum n azil
at prep. u
atheism n ateizam
atheist n ateista
athirst adj. žedan
athlete n. sportaš
athletic a. atletski
athletics n. atletika
athwart prep. poprijeko
atlas n. atlas
atmosphere n. atmosfera
atoll n. koralno ostrvo
atom n. atom
atomic a. atomski
atone v.i. popraviti
atonement n. pokajanje
atrocious a. okrutan
atrocity n okutnost
attach v.t. pričvrstiti
attache n. ataše
attachment n. prilog

attack n. napad
attack v.t. napasti
attain v.t. postići
attainment n. dostignuće
attaint v.t. osramotiti
attempt v.t. pokušati
attempt n. pokušaj
attend v.t. prisustvovati
attendance n. pohađanje
attendant n. pratilac
attention n. pozornost
attentive a. pažljiv
attest v.t. potvrditi
attire n. ruho
attire v.t. odenuti
attitude n. stav
attorney n. odvjetnik
attract v.t. privući
attraction n. privlačnost
attractive a. privlačan
attribute v.t. dodeliti
attribute n. karakteristika
auction n licitacija
auction v.t. licitirati
audible a glasan
audience n. gledalište
audit n. revizija
audit v.t. revidirati
auditive adj. slušni
auditor n. revizor
auditorium n. gledalište
auger n. svrdlo
aught n. išta
augment v.t. povećati
augmentation n. povećanje
August n. kolovoz
august n kolovoz
aunt n. tetka, strina, ujna
auriform adj. u obliku uha
aurora n zora

auspicate *v.t.* proricati
auspice *n.* proricanje
auspicious *a.* povoljan
austere *a.* strog
authentic *a.* autentičan
author *n.* autor
authoritative *a.* zapovednički
authority *n.* vlast
authorize *v.t.* ovlastiti
autobiography *n.* autobiografija
autocracy *n* autokracija
autocrat *n* autokrata
autocratic *a* autokratski
autograph *n.* autogram
automatic *a.* automatski
automobile *n.* automobil
autonomous *a* autonoman
autumn *n.* jesen
auxiliary *a.* pomoćni
auxiliary *n.* pomoćnik
avale *v.t.* umanjiti
avail *v.t.* pomoći
available *a* raspoloživ
avarice *n.* škrtost
avenge *v.t.* svetiti se
avenue *n.* avenija
average *n.* prosjek
average *a.* prosječan
average *v.t.* naći prosjek
averse *a.* protivan
aversion *n.* averzija
avert *v.t.* sprečiti
aviary *n.* kavez za ptice
aviation *n.* zrakoplovstvo
aviator *n.* avijatičar
avid *adj.* pohlepan
avidity *adv.* pohlepno
avidly *adv* lakomo
avoid *v.t.* izbjegavati
avoidance *n.* izbjegavanje

avow *v.t.* ispovjediti
avulsion *n.* nasilno odvajanje
await *v.t.* čekati
awake *v.t.* probuditi
awake *a* budan
award *v.t.* nagraditi
award *n.* nagrada
aware *a.* svjestan
away *adv.* daleko
awe *n.* strahopoštovanje
awful *a.* neugodan
awhile *adv.* časkom
awkward *a.* nezgodan
axe *n.* sjekira
axis *n.* osovina
axle *n.* osovina

B

babble *n.* brbljanje
babble *v.i.* brbljati
babe *n.* dete
babel *n* metež
baboon *n.* babun
baby *n.* beba
bachelor *n.* neženja
back *n.* nazad
back *adv.* unazad
backbite *v.t.* ogovaranje
backbone *n.* oslonac
background *n.* pozadina
backhand *n.* bekhend
backslide *v.i.* ponovo zapasti u grijeh
backward *a.* unazad
backward *adv.* unazad
bacon *n.* slanina
bacteria *n.* bakterija
bad *a.* loše
badge *n.* značka

badger *n.* jazavac
badly *adv.* gore
badminton *n.* badminton
baffle *v. t.* zbuniti
bag *n.* torba
bag *v. i.* nateći
baggage *n.* prtljag
bagpipe *r.* gajde
bail *n.* jamstvo
bail *v. t.* jamčiti
bailable *a.* sposoban za jemstvo
bailiff *n.* ovršitelj
bait *n* mamac
bait *v.t.* namamiti
bake *v.t.* ispeći
baker *n.* pekar
bakery *n* pekara
balance *n.* ravnoteža
balance *v.t.* uravnotežiti
balcony *n.* balkon
bald *a.* ćelav
bale *n.* bala
bale *v.t.* pakirati u bale
baleful *a.* poguban
baleen *n.* kitova kost
ball *n.* lopta
ballad *n.* balada
ballet *sn.* balet
balloon *n.* balon
ballot *n* glasovanje
ballot *v.i.* glasovati
balm *n.* melem
balsam *n.* balzam
bam *n.* prevara
bamboo *n.* bambus
ban *n.* zabrana
ban *n* anatema
banal *a.* banalan
banana *n.* banana
band *n.* grupa

bandage *n.* zavoj
bandage *v.t* zaviti
bandit *n.* razbojnik
bang *v.t.* lupiti
bang *n.* prasak
bangle *n.* narukvica
banish *v.t.* protjerati
banishment *n.* protjerivanje
banjo *n.* bendžo
bank *n.* banka, nasip
bank *v.t.* nagomilati
banker *n.* bankar
bankrupt *n.* bankrot
bankruptcy *n.* stečaj
banner *n.* zastava
banquet *n.* banket
banquet *v.t.* ugostiti
bantam *n.* kokoška
banter *v.t.* zadirkivati
banter *n.* zadirkivanje
bantling *n.* dijete
banyan *n.* indijska smokva
baptism *n.* krštenje
baptize *v.t.* krstiti
bar *n.* šipka
bar *v.t* zabraniti
barb *n.* bodlja
barbarian *a.* divljački
barbarian *n.* divljak
barbarism *n.* barbarizam
barbarity *n.* barbarstvo
barbarous *a.* barbarski
barbed *a.* bodljikav
barber *n.* brijač
bard *n.* bard
bare *a.* nag
bare *v.t.* razgolititi
barely *adv.* jedva
bargain *n.* cenkanje
bargain *v.t.* cenkati se

barge *n.* teglenica
bark *n.* kora
bark *v.t.* lajati
barley *n.* ječam
barn *n.* štala
barnacles *n* školjke
barometer *n* barometar
barouche *n.* fijaker
barrack *n.* kasarna
barrage *n.* brana
barrator *ns.* podstrekač
barrel *n.* bačva
barren *n* nerotkinja
barricade *n.* barikada
barrier *n.* barijera
barrister *n.* odvjetnik
barter1 *v.t.* trampiti
barter2 *n.* trampa
barton *n.* seosko dvorište
basal *adj.* osnovni
base *n.* baza
base *a.* osnovni
base *v.t.* zasnovati
baseless *a.* neosnovan
basement *n.* podrum
bashful *a.* stidljiv
basic *a.* osnovni
basil *n.* bosiljak
basin *n.* bazen
basis *n.* osnova
bask *v.i.* uživati
basket *n.* korpa
baslard *n.* ornamentni nož
bass *n.* bas
bastard *n.* kopile
bastard *a* vanbračan
bat *n* šišmiš
bat *n* motka
bat *v. i* udariti motkom
batch *n* serija

bath *n* kupanje
bathe *v. t* kupati se
baton *n* palica
batsman *n.* udarač u kriketu
battalion *n* bataljun
battery *n* baterija
battle *n* bitka
battle *v. i.* boriti se
bawd *n.* podvodačica
bawl *n.i.* vika
bawn *n.* štala
bay *n* zaliv
bayard *n.* vrsta konja
bayonet *n* bajonet
be *v.t.* biti
be *pref.* biti
beach *n* plaža
beacon *n* svjetionik
bead *n* perla
beadle *n.* poslužitelj
beak *n* kljun
beaker *n* pehar
beam *n* snop
beam *v. i* zračiti
bean *n.* grah
bear *n* medvjed
bear *v.t* nositi
beard *n* brada
bearing *n* ležaj
beast *n* zvijer
beastly *a* zvjerski
beat *v. t.* udarati
beat *n* udarac
beautiful *a* lep
beautify *v. t* ulepšati
beauty *n* lepota
beaver *n* dabar
because *conj.* jer
beck *n.* mig
beckon *v.t.* zvat

beckon v. t dati znak
become v. i postati
becoming a pristojan
bed n krevet
bedevil v. t opčiniti
bedding n. posteljina
bedight v.t. ukrasiti
bed-time n. vreme za spavanje
bee n. pčela
beech n. bukva
beef n govedina
beehive n. košnica
beer n pivo
beet n repa
beetle n buba
befall v. t zadesiti
before prep prije
before adv. ranije
before conj prije nego
beforehand adv. unaprijed
befriend v. t. sprijateljiti se
beg v. t. moliti
beget v. t začeti
beggar n prosjak
begin n početi
beginning n. početak
begird v.t. opasati
beguile v. t obmanuti
behalf n korist
behave v. i. ponašati se
behaviour n ponašanje
behead v. t. odsjeći glavu
behind adv iza
behind prep iza
behold v. t opaziti
being n postojeći
belabour v. t izlupati
belated adj. zakašnjeli
belch v. t podrigivanje
belch n podrignuti

belief n uvjerenje
believe v. t vjerovati
bell n zvono
belle n lepotica
bellicose a ratoboran
belligerency n zaraćenost
belligerent a ratoboran
belligerent n zaraćena strana
bellow v. i urlati
bellows n. mjeh
belly n trbuh
belong v. i pripadati
belongings n. svojina
beloved a drag
beloved n dragi
below adv dolje
below prep ispod
belt n pojas
belvedere n vidikovac
bemask v. t maskirati se
bemire v. t smutiti
bemuse v. t zbuniti
bench n klupa
bend n savijanje
bend v. t saviti
beneath adv niže
beneath prep ispod
benefaction n. dobročinstvo
benefice n dar
beneficial a koristan
benefit n korist
benefit v. t. imati korist
benevolence n blagonaklonost
benevolent a blagonaklon
benight v. t biti neprosvetljen
benign adj blag
benignly adv dobroćudno
benison n blagoslov
bent n sklonost
bequeath v. t. zaviještati

23

bereave v. t. ucvijeliti
bereavement n ucvijeljenost
berth n vez
beside prep. pored
besides prep u poređenju sa
besides adv sem toga
beslaver v. t balaviti
besiege v. t opsedati
bestow v. t zbrinuti
bestrew v. t zasipati
bet v.i kladiti se
bet n oklada
betel n betel
betray v.t. izdati
betrayal n izdaja
betroth v. t zaručiti
betrothal n. zaruka
better a bolji
better adv. bolje
better v. t poboljšati
betterment n poboljšanje
between prep između
beverage n napitak
bewail v. t oplakivati
beware v.i. čuvati se
bewilder v. t zbuniti
bewitch v.t začarati
beyond prep. izvan
beyond adv. dalje
biangular adj. dvokuti
bias n kosina
bias v. t naginjati ukoso
biaxial adj dvoosni
bibber n pijanac
bible n biblija
bibliography n bibliografija
bibliographer n bibliograf
bicentenary adj dvestogodišnji
biceps n biceps
bicker v. t prepirati se

bicycle n. bicikl
bid v.t ponuditi
bid n ponuda
bidder n ponuditelj
bide v. t čekati
biennial adj dvogodišnji
bier n mrtvačka nosila
big a velik
bigamy n bigamija
bight n omča
bigot n pobornik
bigotry n revnost
bile n žuč
bilingual a dvojezični
bill n priznanica
billion n milijarda
billow n val
billow v.i talasati se
biliteral adj biliteralan
bilk v. t. prevariti
bimonthly adj. dvomjesečni
binary adj binarni
bind v.t vezati
binding a obvezujuć
binocular n. dvogled
biographer n biograf
biography n biografija
biologist n biolog
biology n biologija
bioscope n životopisac
biped n dvonožac
birch n. breza
bird n ptica
birdlime n lepak za ptice
birth n. rođenje
biscuit n keks
bisect v. t prepoloviti
bisexual adj. biseksualan
bishop n biskup
bison n bizon

bisque *n* porcelan
bit *n* komadić
bitch *n* kuja
bite *v. t.* ugristi
bite *n* ugriz
bitter *a* gorak
bi-weekly *adj* dvotjedni
bizarre *adj* bizaran
blab *v. t. & i* izbrbljati
black *a* crno
blacken *v. t.* pocrniti
blackmail *n* ucjena
blackmail *v.t* ucjeniti
blacksmith *n* kovač
bladder *n* mjehur
blade *n.* oštrica
blain *n* plik
blame *v. t* kriviti
blame *n* odgovornost
blanch *v. t. & i* blanširati
bland *adj.* blag
blank *a* prazan
blank *n* praznina
blanket *n* pokrivač
blare *v. t* trubiti
blast *n* eksplozija
blast *v.i* razoriti
blaze *n* blast
blaze *v.i* goreti
bleach *v. t* izbeleti
blear *v. t* zamagliti
bleat *n* blejanje
bleat *v. i* blejati
bleb *n* plik
bleed *v. i* krvariti
blemish *n* mana
blend *v. t* umješati
blend *n* mješavina
bless *v. t* blagosloviti
blether *v. i* besmislica

blight *n* štetan uticaj
blind *a* slijep
blindage *n* bunker
blindfold *v. t* staviti povez preko očiju
blindness *n* sljepoća
blink *v. t. & i* treptati
bliss *n* blaženstvo
blister *n* žulj
blizzard *n* mećava
bloc *n* blok
block *n* panj
block *v.t* blokirati
blockade *n* blokada
blockhead *n* glupan
blood *n* krv
bloodshed *n* krvoproliće
bloody *a* krvav
bloom *n* cvat
bloom *v.i.* cvati
blossom *n* procvat
blossom *v.i* cvati
blot *n.* mrlja
blot *v. t* umrljati
blouse *n* bluza
blow *v.i.* puhati
blow *n* puhanje
blue *n.* plava boja
blue *a.* plav
bluff *v. t* blefirati
bluff *n* strmina
blunder *n* omaška
blunder *v.i* omašiti
blunt *a* tup
blur *n* mrlja
blurt *v. t* izbrbljati
blush *n* rumenilo
blush *v.i* porumeneti
boar *n* vepar
board *n* odbor
board *v. t.* ukrcati

boast v.i hvaliti se
boast n hvalisanje
boat n brod
boat v.i ploviti
bodice n prsluk
bodily a tjelesni
bodily adv. u celosti
body n telo
bodyguard n. tjelohranitelj
bog n močvara
bog v.i zaglibiti
bogle n sablast
bogus a prividan
boil n ključanje
boil v.i. ključati
boiler n bojler
bold a. hrabar
boldness n smjelost
bolt n reza
bolt v. t zabraviti
bomb n bomba
bomb v. t bombardirati
bombard v. t bombardirati
bombardment n bombardiranje
bomber n bombarder
bonafide adv dobronamerno
bonafide a. u dobroj nameri
bond n veza
bondage n ropstvo
bone n. kost
bonfire n krijes
bonnet n kapa
bonus n bonus
book n knjiga
book v. t. uknjižiti
book-keeper n knjigovođa
book-mark n. oznaka
book-seller n prodavac knjiga
book-worm n knjiški moljac
bookish n. knjiški

booklet n brošura
boon n blagodat
boor n gedža
boost n podizanje
boost v. t pojačati
boot n čizma
booth n kabina
booty n plijen
booze v. i pijančiti
border n granica
border v.t graničiti
bore v. t bušiti
bore n bušotina
born v. roditi
born rich adj. rođen bogat
borne adj. nošen
borrow v. t pozajmiti
bosom n grudi
boss n šef
botany n botanika
botch v. t zakrpiti
both a oba
both pron oba
both conj oba
bother v. t gnjaviti
botheration n dosađivanje
bottle n boca
bottler n punionica
bottom n dno
bough n grana
boulder n stena
bouncer n izbacivač
bound n. granica
boundary n međa
bountiful a darežljiv
bounty n darežljivost
bouquet n buket
bout n nastup
bow v. t pokloniti se
bow n luk

bow *n* naklon
bowel *n.* crijevo
bower *n* sjenica
bowl *n* zdjela
bowl *v.i* kuglati se
box *n* kutija
boxing *n* boks
boy *n* dječak
boycott *v. t.* bojkotovati
boycott *n* bojkot
boyhood *n* djetinjstvo
brace *n* spona
bracelet *n* narukvica
brag *v. i* hvalisati se
brag *n* hvalisanje
braille *n* brajeva azbuka
brain *n* mozak
brake *n* kočnica
brake *v. t* kočiti
branch *n* grana
brand *n* marka
brandy *n* rakija
brangle *v. t* prepirka
brass *n.* mesing
brave *a* hrabar
bravery *n* hrabrost
brawl *v. i. & n* svađa
bray *n* njakanje
bray *v. i* njakati
breach *n* prodor
bread *n* kruh
breaden *v. t. & i* napraviti od kruha
breadth *n* širina
break *v. t* prekinuti
break *n* odmor
breakage *n* lom
breakdown *n* slom
breakfast *n* doručak
breakneck *n* opasan
breast *n* grudi

breath *n* dah
breathe *v. i.* disati
breeches *n.* pantalone
breed *v.t* roditi
breed *n* pasmina
breeze *n* povjetarac
breviary *n.* brevijar
brevity *n* sažetost
brew *v. t.* variti
brewery *n* pivovara
bribe *n* mito
bribe *v. t.* podmiti
brick *n* opeka
bride *n* mladenka
bridegroom *n.* mladoženja
bridge *n* most
bridle *n* uzda
brief *a.* kratak
brigade *n.* brigada
brigadier *n* brigadir
bright *a* svijetao
brighten *v. t* razvedriti
brilliance *n* blistavost
brilliant *a* blistav
brim *n* obod
brine *n* rasol
bring *v. t* doneti
brink *n.* rub
brisk *adj* žustar
bristle *n* čekinja
british *adj* britanski
brittle *a.* krhk
broad *a* širok
broadcast *n* emisija
broadcast *v. t* emitirati
brocade *n* brokat
broccoli *n.* brokoli
brochure *n* prospekt
brochure *n* brošura
broker *n* broker

brood *n* leglo
brook *n.* potok
broom *n* metla
bronze *n. & adj* bronza
broth *n* juha
brothel *n* bordel
brother *n* brat
brotherhood *n* bratstvo
brow *n* obrva
brown *a* braon
brown *n* braon boja
browse *n* pregledavanje
bruise *n* modrica
bruit *n* glasina
brush *n* četka
brustle *v. t* pucketati
brutal *a* brutalan
brute *n* nečovek
bubble *n* mehurić
bucket *n* kanta
buckle *n* kopča
bud *n* pupoljak
budge *v. i. & n* mrdnuti
budget *n* budžet
buff *n volovska* koža
buffalo *n.* bizon
buffoon *n* lakrdijaš
bug *n.* kukac
bugle *n* lovački rog
build *v. t* graditi
build *n* građa
building *n* zgrada
bulb *n.* žarulja
bulk *n* hrpa
bulky *a* pozamašan
bull *n* bik
bulldog *n* buldog
bull's eye *n* meta
bullet *n* metak
bulletin *n* bilten

bullock *n* june
bully *n* siledžija
bully *v. t.* zastrašivati
bulwark *n* bedem
bumper *n.* branik
bumpy *adj* neravan
bunch *n* hrpa
bundle *n* snop
bungalow *n* bungalov
bungle *v. t* pobrkati
bungle *n* petljanje
bunk *n* kat
bunker *n* bunker
buoy *n* plutača
buoyancy *n* uzgon
burden *n* teret
burden *v. t* natovariti
burdensome *a* tegoban
bureau *n.* zavod
Bureacuracy *n.* birokratija
bureaucrat *n* birokrata
burglar *n* provalnik
burglary *n* provala
burial *n* pokop
burn *v. t* gorjeti
burn *n.* opekotina
burrow *n.* jazbina
burst *v. i.* prasnuti
burst *n* praska
bury *v. t.* riti
bus *n* autobus
bush *n* grm
business *n* posao
businessman *n* poduzetnik
bustle *v. t* žuriti
busy *a* zauzet
but *prep* ali
but *conj.* osim da
butcher *n* mesar
butcher *v. t* klati

butter *n* maslac
butter *v. t* namazati maslacem
butterfly *n* leptir
buttermilk *n* mlaćenica
buttock *n* stražnjica
button *n* gumb
button *v. t.* zakopčati
buy *v. t.* kupiti
buyer *n.* kupac
buzz *v. i* zujati
buzz *n.* zujanje
by *prep* kod
by *adv* blizu
bye-bye *interj.* zbogom
by-election *n* naknadni izbori
bylaw, bye-law *n.* lokalni akt
bypass *n* zaobilaznica
by-product *n* nusproizvod
byre *n* štala
byword *n* uzrečica

C

cab *n.* taksi
cabaret *n.* kabare
cabbage *n.* kupus
cabin *n.* koliba
cabinet *n.* kabinet
cable *n.* kabel
cable *v. t.* vezati kablom
cache *n* skladište
cachet *n* pečat
cackle *v. i* kokodakati
cactus *n.* kaktus
cad *n* nitkov
cadet *n.* kadet
cadge *v. i* prosjačiti
cadmium *n* kadmij
cafe *n.* kafić

cage *n.* kavez
cain *n* bratoubica
cake *n.* torta
calamity *n.* nesreća
calcium *n* kalcij
calculate *v. t.* izračunati
calculator *n* kalkulator
calculation *n.* proračun
calendar *n.* kalendar
calf *n.* tele
call *v. t.* pozvati
call *n.* poziv
caller *n* pozivatelj
calligraphy *n* kaligrafija
calling *n.* poziv
callow *adj* nezreo
callous *a.* okoreo
calm *n.* mir
calm *n.* spokoj
calm *v. t.* smiriti
calmative *adj* sredstvo za umirenje
calorie *n.* kalorija
calumniate *v. t.* klevetati
camel *n.* deva
camera *n.* kamera
camlet *n* kamelot
camp *n.* kamp
camp *v. i.* kampovati
campaign *n.* kampanja
camphor *n.* kamfor
can *n.* limenka
can *v. t.* konzervirati
can *v.* moći
canal *n.* kanal
canard *n* lažna vest
cancel *v. t.* otkazati
cancellation *n* otkazivanje
cancer *n.* rak
candid *a.* iskren
candidate *n.* kandidat

candle *n.* svijeća
candour *n.* iskrenost
candy *n.* slatkiš
candy *v. t.* zasladiti
cane *n.* trska
cane *v. t.* šibati
canister *n.* kanister
cannon *n.* top
cannonade *n. v. & t* kanonada
canon *n* kanon
canopy *n.* baldahin
canteen *n.* kantina
canter *n laki* galop
canton *n* kanton
cantonment *n.* naselje od baraka
canvas *n.* platno
canvass *v. t.* raspraviti
cap *n.* kapa
cap *v. t.* poklopiti
capability *n.* sposobnost
capable *a.* sposoban
capacious *a.* prostran
capacity *n.* kapacitet
cape *n.* rt
capital *n.* kapital
capital *a.* glavni
capitalist *n.* kapitalista
capitulate *v. t* kapitulirati
caprice *n.* kapric
capricious *a.* kapriciozan
Capricorn *n* jarac
capsicum *n* paprika
capsize *v. i.* prevrnuti
capsular *adj* čaurast
captain *n.* kapetan
captaincy *n.* čin kapetana
caption *n.* naslov
captivate *v. t.* zarobiti
captive *n.* zatočenik
captive *a.* zatočen

captivity *n.* zatočeništvo
capture *v. t.* uhvatiti
capture *n.* hvatanje
car *n.* automobil
carat *n.* karat
caravan *n.* karavan
carbide *n.* karbid
carbon *n.* ugljik
card *n.* kartica
cardamom *n.* vrsta biljke
cardboard *n.* karton
cardiacal *adjs* srčani
cardinal *a.* kardinalan
cardinal *n.* kardinal
care *n.* briga
care *v. i.* brinuti
career *n.* karijera
careful *a* oprezan
careless *a.* neoprezan
caress *v. t.* milovati
cargo *n.* teret
caricature *n.* karikatura
carious *adj* truo
carl *n* momak
carnage *n* pokolj
carnival *n* karneval
carol *n* pjesma
carpal *adj* koji se tiče zapešća
carpenter *n.* stolar
carpentry *n.* stolarija
carpet *n.* tepih
carriage *n.* kočija
carrier *n.* nosač
carrot *n.* mrkva
carry *v. t.* nositi
cart *n.* kolica
cartage *n.* putarina
carton *n* karton
cartoon *n.* crtani film
cartridge *n.* patrona

carve v. t. rezbariti
cascade n. kaskada
case n. slučaj
cash n. gotovina
cash v. t. unovčiti
cashier n. blagajnik
casing n. kućište
cask n bačva
casket n kovčeg
cassette n. kaseta
cast v. t. baciti
cast n. bacanje
caste n kasta
castigate v. t. kazniti
casting n bacanje
cast-iron n izdržljiv
castle n. dvorac
castor oil n. ricinusovo ulje
casual a. ležeran
casualty n. žrtva nesreće
cat n. mačka
catalogue n. katalog
cataract n. katarakt
catch v. t. uloviti
catch n. ulov
categorical a. kategoričan
category n. kategorija
cater v. i. snabdevati hranom
caterpillar n gusenica
cathedral n. katedrala
catholic a. katolički
cattle n. goveda
cauliflower n. karfiol
causal adj. kauzalan
causality n uzročnost
cause n. uzrok
cause v.t uzrokovati
causeway n nasip
caustic a. oštar
caution n. oprez

caution v. t. upozoriti
cautious a. oprezan
cavalry n. konjica
cave n. špilja
cavern n. špilja
cavil v. t cjepidlačiti
cavity n. duplja
caw n. gakanje
caw v. i. gakati
cease v. i. prestati
ceaseless a. neprestan
cedar n. cedar
ceiling n. plafon
celebrate v. t. & i. slaviti
celebration n. slavlje
celebrity n slavna osoba
celestial adj nebeski
celibacy n. celibat
celibacy n. celibat
cell n. stanica
cellar n podrum
cellular adj celularni
cement n. cement
cement v. t. cementirati
cemetery n. groblje
cense v. t kaditi
censer n kadionik
censor n. cenzor
censor v. t. cenzurisati
censorious adj kritičan
censorship n. cenzura
censure n. kritika
censure v. t. kritikovati
census n. cenzus
cent n cent
centenarian n stogodišnjak
centenary n. stogodišnjica
centennial adj. stogodišnji
center n centar
centigrade a. sto stepeni

centipede n. stonoga
central a. centralni
centre n centar
centrifugal adj. centrifugalni
centuple n. & adj stostruk
century n. stoljeće
ceramics n keramika
cerated adj. voštana mast
cereal n. žitarica
cereal a žitni
cerebral adj moždani
ceremonial a. svečan
ceremonious a. obredni
ceremony n. ceremonija
certain a određeni
certainly adv. sigurno
certainty n. izvesnost
certificate n. uvjerenje
certify v. t. potvrditi
cerumen n ušna mast
cesspool n. septička jama
chain n lanac
chair n. stolica
chairman n predsjedatelj
chaise n stolica
challenge n. izazov
challenge v. t. izazvati
chamber n. komora
chamberlain n kancelar
champion n. prvak
champion v. t. braniti
chance n. šansa
chancellor n. kancelar
chancery n arhiv
change v. t. promijeniti
change n. promijena
channel n kanal
chant n pjesma
chaos n. kaos
chaotic adv. kaotičan

chapel n. kapela
chapter n. poglavlje
character n. karakter
charge v. t. puniti
charge n. punjenje
chariot n kočija
charitable a. dobrotvorno
charity n. milosrđe
charm1 n. šarm
charm2 v. t. šarmirati
chart n. grafikon
charter n povelja
chase1 v. t. juriti
chase2 n. potera
chaste a. nevin
chastity n. nevinost
chat1 n. čavrljanje
chat2 v. i. čavrljati
chatter v. t. brbljati
chauffeur n. šofer
cheap a jeftin
cheapen v. t. pojeftiniti
cheat v. t. varati
cheat n. varanje
check v. t. proveriti
check n provera
checkmate n mat
cheek n obraz
cheep v. i pijukati
cheer n. bodrenje
cheer v. t. bodriti
cheerful a. veseo
cheerless a neveseo
cheese n. sir
chemical a. kemijski
chemical n. kemikalija
chemise n ženska košulja
chemist n. hemičar
chemistry n. hemija
cheque n. ček

cherish v. t. negovati
cheroot n vrsta cigare
chess n. šah
chest n prsa
chestnut n. kesten
chew v. t žvakati
chevalier n konjanik
chicken n. kokoš
chide v. t. psovati
chief a. glavni
chieftain n. poglavica
child n dijete
childhood n. djetinjstvo
childish a. djetinjast
chill n. jeza
chilli n. čili
chilly a prohladno
chiliad n. tisuća
chimney n. dimnjak
chimpanzee n. čimpanza
chin n. brada
china n. Kina
chirp v.i. cvrkutati
chirp n cvrkut
chisel n dlijeto
chisel v. t. klesati
chit n. klica
chivalrous a. viteški
chivalry n. viteštvo
chlorine n klor
chloroform n kloroform
choice n. izbor
choir n hor
choke v. t. gušiti se
cholera n. kolera
chocolate n čokolada
choose v. t. izabrati
chop v. t seći
chord n. akord
chorus n. refren

Christ n. hrist
Christendom n. hrišćanstvo
Christian n hrišćanin
Christian a. hrišćanski
Christianity n. hrišćanstvo
Christmas n Božić
chrome n krom
chronic a. kroničan
chronicle n. letopis
chronology n. kronologija
chronograph n kronograf
chuckle v. i prigrušeno se smijati
chum n pobratim
church n. crkva
churchyard n. groblje
churl n grubijan
churn v. t. & i. mućkalica
churn n. mućkati
cigar n. cigara
cigarette n. cigareta
cinema n. kino
cinnabar n cinober
cinnamon n cimet
cipher, cipher n. cifra
circle n. krug
circuit n. kruženje
circumspect adj. obazriv
circular a kružni
circular n. cirkular
circulate v. i. cirkulirati
circulation n cirkulacija
circumference n. raspon
circumstance n okolnost
circus n. cirkus
cist n kripta
citadel n. tvrđava
cite v. t citirati
citizen n građanin
citizenship n državljanstvo
citric adj. limunski

city n grad
civic a građanski
civics n građansko pravo
civil a civilni
civilian n civil
civilization n. civilizacija
civilize v. t civilizovati
clack n. & v. i klopotati
claim n potraživanje
claim v. t zahtijevati
claimant n tužitelj
clamber v. i pentrati se
clamour n galama
clamour v. i. galamiti
clamp n stega
clandestine adj. tajan
clap v. i. pljeskati
clap n pljeskanje
clarify v. t razjasniti
clarification n razjašnjenje
clarion n. zvuk trube
clarity n jasnoća
clash n. sudar
clash v. t. sudariti se
clasp n kopča
class n klasa
classic a klasičan
classic n. klasik
classical a klasičan
classification n klasifikacija
classify v. t razvrstati
clause n klauzula
claw n kandža
clay n glina
clean adj. čist
clean v. t čistiti
cleanliness n čistoća
cleanse v. t očistiti
clear a jasno
clear v. t razjasniti

clearance n čišćenje
clearly adv očigledno
cleft n rascjep
clergy n svećenstvo
clerical a svećenički
clerk n službenik
clever a. pametan
clew n. klupko
click n. škljocaj
client n. klijent
cliff n. litica
climate n. klima
climax n. vrhunac
climb1 n. penjanje
climb v.i penjati se
cling v. i. prilijepiti se
clinic n. klinika
clink n. zveket
cloak n. ogrtač
clock n. sat
clod n. gruda
cloister n. samostan
close n. ograda
close a. zatvoren
close v. t zatvoriti
closet n. plakar
closure n. zatvaranje
clot n. ugrušak
clot v. t zgrušati
cloth n tkanina
clothe v. t obući
clothes n. odjeća
clothing n odjeća
cloud n. oblak
cloudy a oblačno
clove n češanj
clown n klaun
club n klub
clue n indicija
clumsy a nespretan

cluster *n* skupina
cluster *v. i.* nagomilati
clutch *n* kvačilo
clutter *v. t* zakrčiti
coach *n* kočija, trener
coachman *n* kočijaš
coal *n* ugljen
coalition *n* koalicija
coarse *a* grub
coast *n* obala
coat *n* kaput
coating *n* oblaganje
coax *v. t* navesti
cobalt *n* kobalt
cobbler *n* obućar
cobra *n* kobra
cobweb *n* paučina
cocaine *n* kokain
cock *n* pijetao
cocker *v. t* maziti
cockle *v. i* kukolj
cock-pit *n.* kokpit
cockroach *n* bubašvaba
coconut *n* kokos
code *n* kod
co-education *n.* koedukacija
coefficient *n.* koeficijent
co-exist *v. i* koegzistirati
co-existence *n* koegzistencija
coffee *n* kava
coffin *n* mrtvački sanduk
cog *n* zubac
cogent *adj.* ubedljiv
cognate *adj* krvni srodnik
cognizance *n* spoznaja
cohabit *v. t* zajedno živjeti
coherent *a* dosljedan
cohesive *adj* priljubljen
coif *n* kapa
coin *n* novčić

coinage *n* kovanica
coincide *v. i* podudarati
coir *n kokosovo* vlakno
coke *v. t* koks
cold *a* hladan
cold *n* hladnoća
collaborate *v. i* surađivati
collaboration *n* suradnja
collapse *v. i* kolabirati
collar *n* okovratnik
colleague *n* kolega
collect *v. t* prikupiti
collection *n* kolekcija
collective *a* kolektivno
collector *n* kolekcionar
college *n* koledž
collide *v. i.* sudariti se
collision *n* sudar
collusion *n* tajni sporazum
colon *n* debelo crijevo
colon *n* dvotačka
colonel *n.* pukovnik
colonial *a* kolonijalan
colony *n* kolonija
colour *n* boja
colour *v. t* bojiti
colter *n* nož pluga
column *n* kolona
coma *n.* koma
comb *n* češalj
combat1 *n* borba
combat *v. t.* boriti se
combatant1 *n* borac
combatant *a.* pobornik
combination *n* kombinacija
combine *v. t* kombinirati
come *v. i.* doći
comedian *n.* komičar
comedy *n.* komedija
comet *n* kometa

comfit n. poslastica
comfort n. utjeha
comfort v. t utješiti
comfortable a udoban
comic a komičan
comic n komičar
comical a duhovit
comma n zarez
command n naredba
command v. t narediti
commandant n zapovjednik
commander n komandant
commemorate v. t. pomen
commemoration n. komemoracija
commence v. t početi
commencement n početak
commend v. t pohvaliti
commendable a. uzoran
commendation n pohvala
comment v. i komentirati
comment n komentar
commentary n komentar
commentator n komentator
commerce n trgovina
commercial a trgovački
commiserate v. t suosjećati
commission n. provizija
commissioner n. povjerenik
commit v. t. obavezati se
committee n odbor
commodity n. roba
common a. zajednički
commoner n. prost čovjek
commonplace a. svakidašnji
commonwealth n. komonvelt
commotion n metež
commove v. t uznemiriti
communal a komunalan
commune v. t komuna
communicate v. t komunicirati

communication n. komunikacija
communiqué n. priopćenje
communism n komunizam
community n. zajednica
commute v. t zamijeniti
compact a. kompaktan
compact n. sporazum
companion n. suradnik
company n. tvrtka
comparative a komparativno
compare v. t usporediti
comparison n usporedba
compartment n. odjel
compass n kompas
compassion n suosećanje
compel v. t prisiliti
compensate v. t nadoknaditi
compensation n kompenzacija
compete v. i natjecati se
competence n sposobnost
competent a. sposoban
competition n. natjecanje
competitive a konkurentan
compile v. t sastaviti
complacent adj. samozadovoljan
complain v. i žaliti se
complaint n žalba
complaisance n. uslužnost
complaisant adj. uslužan
complement n dopuna
complementary a dopunski
complete a kompletan
complete v. t kompletirati
completion završetak
complex a složen
complex n kompleks
complexion n ten
compliance n. udovoljavanje
compliant adj. popustljiv
complicate v. t komplicirati

complication n. komplikacija
compliment n. kompliment
compliment v. t dati kompliment
comply v. i udovoljiti
component adj. sastavni
compose v. t sastaviti
composition n sastav
compositor n. skladatelj
compost n gnojivo
composure n. pribranost
compound n sastav
compound a složen
compound n mješavina
compound v. i sastaviti
compounder n. sastavljač
comprehend v. t obuhvatiti
comprehension n obuhvaćanje
comprehensive a sveobuhvatan
compress v. t. sažeti
compromise n nagodba
compromise v. t nagoditi se
compulsion n prinuda
compulsory a obavezan
compunction n. griža savjesti
computation n. računanje
compute v.t. računati
comrade n. drug
conation n. aspekt ponašanja
concave adj. udubljen
conceal v. t. prikriti
concede v.t. ustupiti
conceit n uobraženost
conceive v. t začeti
concentrate v. t usredtočiti
concentration n. usredotočenost
concept n koncept
conception n koncepcija
concern v. t brinuti
concern n briga
concert n. koncert

concert2 v. t dogovoriti se
concession n olakšica
conch n. školjka
conciliate v.t. pomiriti se
concise a koncizan
conclude v. t zaključiti
conclusion n. zaključak
conclusive a zaključni
concoct v. t izmisliti
concoction n. izmišljotina
concord n. sloga
concrescence n. srastanje
concrete n beton
concrete a konkretan
concrete v. t betonirati
concubinage n. konkubinat
concubine n konkubina
conculcate v.t. gaziti
condemn v. t. osuditi
condemnation n osuda
condense v. t kondenzirati
condite v.t. vrsta ponošanja
condition n uvjet, stanje
conditional a uvjetni
condole v. i. izjaviti saučešće
condolence n saučešće
condonation n. oproštenje
conduct n upravljanje
conduct v. t upravljati
conductor n kondukter
cone n. šišarka
confectioner n slastičar
confectionery n slastičarnica
confer v. i dodijeliti
conference n konferencija
confess v. t. priznati
confession n priznanje
confidant n povjerenik
confide v. i povjeriti
confidence n povjerenje

confident *a.* samouvjeren
confidential *a.* povjerljiv
confine *v. t* ograničiti
confinement *n.* ograničenje
confirm *v. t* potvrditi
confirmation *n* potvrda
confiscate *v. t* konfiskovati
confiscation *n* konfiskacija
conflict *n.* konflikt
conflict *v. i* sukobiti se
confluence *n* ušće
confluent *adj.* koji se sastavlja
conformity *n.* suglasnost
conformity *n.* sklad
confraternity *n.* bratstvo
confrontation *n.* suočenje
confuse *v. t* zbunjenost
confusion *n* zabuna
confute *v.t.* opovrgnuti
conge *n.* otpust
congenial *a* srodan
conglutinate *v.t.* slijepiti
congratulate *v. t* čestitati
congratulation *n* čestitanje
congress *n* kongres
conjecture *n* pretpostavka
conjecture *v. t* pretpostavljati
conjugal *a* bračni
conjugate *v.t. & i.* sjediniti
conjunct *adj.* združeno
conjunctiva *n.* sluznica
conjuncture *n.* konjukcija
conjure *v.t.* prizivati
conjure *v.i.* bajati
connect *v. t.* povezati
connection *n* veza
connivance *n.* popustljivost
conquer *v. t* osvojiti
conquest *n* osvajanje
conscience *n* savjest

conscious *a* svjestan
consecrate *v.t.* posvetiti
consecutive *adj.* uzastopni
consecutively *adv* uzastopno
consensus *n.* konsenzus
consent *n.* pristanak
consent *v. i* pristati
consent3 *v.t.* privoljeti
consequence *n* posljedica
consequent *a* dosljedan
conservative *a* konzervativan
conservative *n* konzervativnost
conserve *v. t* očuvati
consider *v. t* razmotriti
considerable *a* važan
considerate *a.* promišljen
consideration *n* razmatranje
considering *prep.* uzimajući u obzir
consign *v.t.* izručiti
consign *v. t.* povjeriti
consignment *n.* pošiljka
consist *v. i* sastojati se
consistence,-cy *n.* dosljednost
consistent *a* dosljedan
consolation *n* utjeha
console *v. t* konzola
consolidate *v. t.* konsolidirati
consolidation *n* konsolidacija
consonance *n.* sklad
consonant *n.* suglasnik
consort *n.* bračni drug
conspectus *n.* pregled
conspicuous *a.* upadljiv
conspiracy *n.* zavjera
conspirator *n.* konspirator
conspire *v. i.* kovati zavjeru
constable *n* policajac
constant *a* stalan
constellation *n.* zviježđe
constipation *n.* zatvor

constituency *n* izborna jedinica
constituent *n.* birač
constituent *adj.* sastavni
constitute *v. t* ustanoviti
constitution *n* ustav
constrict *v.t.* stegnuti
construct *v. t.* konstruirati
construction *n* konstrukcija
consult *v. t* konzultirati
consultation *n* konzultacije
consume *v. t* trošiti
consumption *n* potrošnja
consumption *n* konzumacija
contact *n.* kontakt
contact *v. t* kontaktirati
contagious *a* zarazan
contain *v.t.* sadržati
contaminate *v.t.* kontaminirati
contemplate *v. t* razmišljati
contemplation *n* razmišljanje
contemporary *a* suvremen
contempt *n* prezir
contemptuous *a* prezriv
contend *v. i* boriti se
content *a.* zadovoljan
content *v. t* zadovoljiti
content *n* sadržaj
content *n.* zadovoljstvo
contention *n* tvrdnja
contentment *n* zadovoljstvo
contest *v. t* natjecati se
contest *n.* natjecanje
context *n* kontekst
continent *n* kontinent
continental *a* kontinentalni
contingency *n.* slučajnost
continual *adj.* neprestan
continuation *n.* nastavljanje
continue *v. i.* nastaviti
continuity *n* kontinuitet

continuous *a* neprekidan
contour *n* kontura
contra *pref.* protiv
contraception *n.* kontracepcija
contract *n* ugovor
contract *v. t* ugovoriti
contrapose *v.t.* suprotstaviti
contractor *n* izvođač radova
contradict *v. t* proturječiti
contradiction *n* kontradikcija
contrary *a* suprotno
contrast *v. t* suprotstaviti
contrast *n* kontrast
contribute *v. t* doprinijeti
contribution *n* doprinos
control *n* kontrola
control *v. t* kontrolirati
controller *n.* kontrolor
controversy *n* polemika
contuse *v.t.* kontuzovati
conundrum *n.* pitalica
convene *v. t* sazvati
convener *n* sazivač
convenience *n.* pogodnost
convenient *a* pogodan
convent *n* ženski manastir
convention *n.* konvencija
conversant *a* upoznat
conversant *adj.* upućen
conversation *n* razgovor
converse *v.t.* razgovarati
conversion *n* pretvorbe
convert *v. t* pretvoriti
convert *n* preobraćenik
convey *v. t.* prenositi
conveyance *n* prijenos
convict *v. t.* osuditi
convict *n* osuđenik
conviction *n* osuda
convince *v. t* ubediti

convivial adj. druželjubiv
convocation n. sazivanje
convoke v.t. sazivati
convolve v.t. namotati
coo n gukanje
coo v. i gukati
cook v. t kuhati
cook n kuhar
cooker n štednjak
cool a hladan
cool v. i. hladiti
cooler n hladnjak
coolie n nosač
co-operate v. i surađivati
co-operation n suradnja
co-operative a zadružni
co-ordinate a. usklađen
co-ordinate v. t rasporediti
co-ordination n koordinacija
coot n. glupan
co-partner n partner
cope v. i dorasti
coper n. trgovac konjima
copper n bakar
coppice n. šumarak
coprology n. koprologija
copulate v.i. pariti se
copy n kopija
copy v. t kopirati
coral n koral
cord n kabel
cordial a srdačan
corbel n. podupirač
cordate adj. srcolik
core n. jezgro
coriander n. korijander
Corinth n. Korint
cork n. pluta
cormorant n. kormoran
corn n kukuruz

cornea n rožnica
corner n kut
cornet n. kornet
cornicle n. vrsta organa
coronation n krunisanje
coronet n. vijenac
corporal a tjelesni
corporate adj. poduzeća
corporation n korporacija
corps n korpus
corpse n leš
correct a točan
correct v. t ispraviti
correction n korekcija
correlate v.t. poklapati se
correlation n. korelacija
correspond v. i odgovarati
correspondence n. prepiska
correspondent n. dopisnik
corridor n. koridor
corroborate v.t. potkrijepiti
corrosive adj. korozivan
corrupt v. t. korumpirati
corrupt a. korumpiran
corruption n. korupcija
cosier n. vrsta krojača
cosmetic a. kozmetički
cosmetic n. kozmetika
cosmic adj. kozmički
cost v.t. koštati
cost n. cijena
costal adj. rebreni
cote n. staja
costly a. skupo
costume n. kostim
cosy a. udoban
cot n. krevetac
cottage n koliba
cotton n. pamuk
couch n. kauč

cough n. kašalj
cough v. i. kašljati
council n. savjet
councillor n. vijećnik
counsel n. savjet
counsel v. t. savjetovati
counsellor n. savjetnik
count n. račun
count v. t. računati
countenance n. izraz lica
counter n. brojilac
counter v. t uzvratiti
counteract v.t. suprotstaviti
countercharge n. protutužba
counterfeit a. krivotvoren
counterfeiter n. falsifikator
countermand v.t. opozvati
counterpart n. duplikat
countersign v. t. lozinka
countess n. grofica
countless a. bezbrojan
country n. zemlja
county n. kotar
coup n. udar
couple n par
couple v. t spojiti
couplet n. kuplet
coupon n. kupon
courage n. hrabrost
courageous a. hrabar
courier n. kurir
course n. tečaj
court n. sud
court v. t. udvarati se
courteous a. uljudan
courtesan n. kurtizana
courtesy n. učtivost
courtier n. dvoranin
courtship n. udvaranje
courtyard n. dvorište

cousin n. rođak
covenant n. ugovor
cover v. t. pokriti
cover n. poklopac
coverlet n. prekrivač
covet v.t. žudjeti
cow n. krava
cow v. t. zastrašiti
coward n. kukavica
cowardice n. kukavičluk
cower v.i. sakriti se
cozy adj. udoban
crab n kraba
crack n prasak
crack v. i pucketati
cracker n kreker
crackle v.t. pucketati
cradle n kolijevka
craft n zanat
craftsman n zanatlija
crafty a lukav
cram v. t natrpati
crambo n. igra stihovima
crane n dizalica
crankle v.t. savijati
crash v. i sudariti se
crash n sudar
crass adj. potpun
crate n. sanduk
crave v.t. žudjeti
craw n. guša
crawl v. t puziti
crawl n puzanje
craze n pomama
crazy a lud
creak v. i škripati
creak n škripanje
cream n krema
crease n brazda
create v. t kreirati

creation *n* stvaranje
creative *adj.* kreativan
creator *n* tvorac
creature *n* stvorenje
credible *a* vjerodostojan
credit *n* kredit
creditable *a* zaslužan
creditor *n* vjerovnik
credulity *adj.* lakovjernost
creed *n.* vjera
creed *n* kredo
creek *n.* potok
creep *v. i* puzati
creeper *n* puzavac
cremate *v. t* kremirati
cremation *n* kremiranje
crest *n* grb
crevet *n.* retorta
crew *n.* posada
crib *n.* krevetac
cricket *n* cvrčak
crime *n* zločin
crimp *n* vrbovnik
crimple *v.t.* naborati
criminal *n* kriminal
criminal *a* krivično
crimson *n* tamno-crven
cringe *v. i.* puzati
cripple *n* bogalj
crisis *n* kriza
crisp *a* hrskav
criterion *n* kriterij
critic *n* kritičar
critical *a* kritičan
criticism *n* kritika
criticize *v. t* kritizirati
croak *n.* graktanje
crockery *n.* zemljano posuđe
crocodile *n* krokodil
croesus *n.* krez

crook *a* prevarantski
crop *n* usjev
cross *v. t* prekrstiti
cross *n* križ
cross *a* ukršten
crossing *n.* prijelaz
crotchet *n.* kuka
crouch *v. i.* čučnuti
crow *n* vrana
crow *v. i* graktati
crowd *n* gomila
crown *n* kruna
crown *v. t* krunisati
crucial *adj.* presudan
crude *a* sirov
cruel *a* okrutan
cruelty *n* okrutnost
cruise *v.i.* krstariti
cruiser *n* krstarica
crumb *n* mrvica
crumble *v. t* izmrviti
crump *adj.* hrskav
crusade *n* križarski pohod
crush *v. t* gnječiti
crust *n.* kora
crutch *n* štaka
cry *n* uzvik
cry *v. i* vikati
cryptography *n.* kriptografija
crystal *n* kristal
cub *n* mladunče
cube *n* kocka
cubical *a* kockast
cubiform *adj.* cilindričnog oblika
cuckold *n.* rogonja
cuckoo *n* kukavica
cucumber *n* krastavac
cudgel *n* toljaga
cue *n* tak
cuff *n* manžeta

cuff v. t ćušnuti
cuisine n. kuhinja
cullet n. otpaci stakla
culminate v.i. kulminirati
culpable a kriv
culprit n krivac
cult n kult
cultivate v. t obrađivati
cultrate adj. šiljat
cultural a kulturni
culture n kultura
culvert n. odvodni kanal
cunning a lukav
cunning n lukavost
cup n. šolja
cupboard n orman
Cupid n kupidon
cupidity n pohlepa
curable a izlječiv
curative a ljekovit
curb n ivičnjak
curb v. t obuzdatu
curcuma n. egzotična biljka
curd n surutka
cure n lijek
cure v. t. liječiti
curfew n policijski sat
curiosity n radoznalost
curious a radoznao
curl n. uvojak
currant n. ribizla
currency n valuta
current n struja
current a trenutni
curriculum n nastavni plan
curse n kletva
curse v. t prokleti
cursory a površan
curt a odsečan
curtail v. t skratiti

curtain n zavjesa
curve n krivina
curve v. t kriva
cushion n jastuk
cushion v. t obložiti jastucima
custard n fil
custodian n staratelj
custody v starateljstvo
custom n. običaj
customary a uobičajen
customer n kupac
cut v. t rezati
cut n rez
cutis n. koža
cuvette n. laboratorijska posuda
cycle n krug
cyclic a kružni
cyclist n biciklista
cyclone n. ciklon
cyclostyle n ciklostil
cyclostyle v. t umnožavati na ciklostilu
cylinder n cilindar
cynic n cinik
cypher n cifra
cypress čempres

D

dabble v. i. umakati
dacoit n. razbojnik
dacoity n. razbojništvo
dad, daddy n tata
daffodil n. zelenkada
daft adj. lud
dagger n. bodež
daily a dnevni
daily adv. dnevno
daily n. dnevnik
dainty a nježan

dainty *n.* poslastica
dairy *n* mljekara
dais *n.* podijum
daisy *n* krasuljak
dale *n* dolina
dam *n* brana
damage *n.* šteta
damage *v. t.* oštetiti
dame *n.* dama
damn *v. t.* prokleti
damnation *n.* prokletstvo
damp *a* vlažan
damp *n* vlaga
damp *v. t.* vlažiti
damsel *n.* gospođica
dance *n* ples
dance *v. t.* plesati
dandelion *n.* maslačak
dandle *v.t.* ljuljati
dandruff *n* perut
dandy *n* kicoš
danger *n.* opasnost
dangerous *a* opasan
dangle *v. t* klatiti
dank *adj.* vlažan
dap *v.i.* pecati
dare *v. i.* usuditi se
daring *n.* smelost
daring *a* smio
dark *a* taman
dark *n* mrak
darkle *v.i.* sakriti se
darling *n* dragi
darling *a* drag
dart *n.* strelica
dash *v. i.* jurnuti
dash *n* navala
date *n* datum
date *v. t* datirati
daub *n.* mazarija

daub *v. t.* zamazati
daughter *n* ćerka
daunt *v. t* uplašiti
dauntless *a* neustrašiv
dawdle *v.i.* dagubiti
dawn *n* zora
dawn *v. i.* svitati
day *n* dan
daze *n* zapanjenost
daze *v. t* zapanjiti
dazzle *n* blesak
dazzle *v. t.* zasjeniti
deacon *n.* đakon
dead *a* mrtav
deadlock *n* ćorsokak
deadly *a* smrtonosan
deaf *a* gluh
deal *n* dogovor
deal *v. i* dogovoriti se
dealer *n* trgovac
dealing *n.* poslovanje
dean *n.* dekan
dear *a* drag
dearth *n* nestašica
death *n* smrt
debar *v. t.* uskratiti
debase *v. t.* osramotiti
debate *n.* debata
debate *v. t.* debatirati
debauch *v. t.* pijančiti
debauch *n* pijančenje
debauchee *n* razvratnik
debauchery *n* razvrat
debility *n* iznurenost
debit *n* zaduženje
debit *v. t* zadužiti
debris *n* ruševina
debt *n* dug
debtor *n* dužnik
decade *n* desetljeća

decadent *a* dekadentan
decamp *v. i* napustiti logor
decay raspadanje
decay *v. i* raspadati
decease *n* smrt
decease *v. i* preminuti
deceit *n* prijevara
deceive *v. t* obmanuti
december *n* prosinac
decency *n* pristojnost
decennary *n.* desetogodišnjica
decent *a* pristojan
deception *n* prevara
decide *v. t* odlučiti
decimal *a* decimal
decimate *v.t.* desetkovati
decision *n* odluka
decisive *a* odlučujući
deck *n* paluba
deck *v. t* ukrasiti
declaration *n* deklaracija
declare *v. t.* proglasiti
decline *n* propadanje
decline *v. t.* propadati
declivous *adj.* strm
decompose *v. t.* razložiti
decomposition *n.* rastavljanje
decontrol *v.t.* ukinuti ograničenje
decorate *v. t* ukrasiti
decoration *n* dekoracija
decorum *n* pristojnost
decrease *v. t* smanjiti
decrease *n* smanjenje
decree *n* dekret
decree *v. i* narediti
decrement *n.* opadanje
dedicate *v. t.* posvetiti
dedication *n* posveta
deduct *v.t.* odbiti
deed *n* djelo

deem *v.i.* smatrati
deep *a.* duboko
deer *n* jelen
defamation *n* kleveta
defame *v. t.* klevetati
default *n.* prekršaj
defeat *n* poraz
defeat *v. t.* poraziti
defect *n* nedostatak
defence *n* odbrana
defend *v. t* braniti
defendant *n* optuženi
defensive *adv.* odbrambeno
deference *n* priklanjanje
defiance *n* prkos
deficit *n* deficit
deficient *adj.* nedovoljan
defile *n.* tjesnac
define *v. t* definirati
definite *a* određen
definition *n* definicija
deflation *n.* deflacija
deflect *v.t. & i.* odvratiti
deft *adj.* spretan
degrade *v. t* degradirati
degree *n* stupanj
dehort *v.i.* obeshrabriti
deist *n.* deist
deity *n.* božanstvo
deject *v. t* oneraspoložiti
dejection *n* utučenost
delay *v.t. & i.* odložiti
delibate *v.t.* gucnuti
deligate1 *n* vezivanje
delegate *v. t* delegat
delegation *n* delegacija
delete *v. t* izbrisati
deliberate *v. i* razmatrati
deliberate *a* namjeran
deliberation *n* razmatranje

delicate *a* delikatan
delicious *a* ukusan
delight *n* uživanje
delight *v. t.* uživati
deliver *v. t* dostaviti
delivery *n* isporuka
delta *n* delta
delude *n.t.* obmanuti
delusion *n.* obmana
demand *n* zahtjev
demand *v. t* zahtjevati
demarcation *n.* razgraničenje
dement *v.t* izludjeti
demerit *n* nedostatak
democracy *n* demokracija
democratic *a* demokratski
demolish *v. t.* demolirati
demon *n.* demon
demonetize *v.t.* demonetizirati
demonstrate *v. t* pokazati
demonstration *n.* pokazivanje
demoralize *v. t.* demoralisati
demur *n* oklijevanje
demur *v. t* oklijevati
demurrage *n.* prekoračenje
den *n* jazbina
dengue *n.* denga
denial *n* poricanje
denote *v. i* označavati
denounce *v. t* oglasiti
dense *a* gust
density *n* gustoća
dentist *n* stomatolog
denude *v.t.* ogoliti
denunciation *n.* potkazivanje
deny *v. t.* poricati
depart *v. i.* otići
department *n* odjel
departure *n* odlazak
depauperate *v.t.* nedovoljno razviti

depend *v. i.* ovisiti
dependant *n* ovisnik
dependence *n* ovisnost
dependent *a* ovisan
depict *v. t.* prikazivati
deplorable *a* jadan
deploy *v.t.* pregrupisati
deponent *n.* svjedok
deport *v.t.* deportirati
depose *v. t* svrgnuti
deposit *n.* depozit
deposit *v. t* založiti
depot *n* stovarište
depreciate *v.t.i.* obezvrijediti
depredate *v.t.* opljačkati
depress *v. t* pritisnuti
depression *n* depresija
deprive *v. t* lišiti
depth *n* dubina
deputation *n* ovlaštenje
depute *v. t* ovlastiti
deputy *n* zamjenik
derail *v. t.* izbaciti iz kolosijeka
derive *v. t.* izvesti
descend *v. i. spuštati* se
descendant *n* potomak
descent *n.* silazak
describe *v. t* opisati
description *n* opis
descriptive *a* opisni
desert *v. t.* napustiti
desert *n* pustinja
deserve *v. t.* zaslužiti
design *v. t.* dizajnirati
design *n.* dizajn
desirable *a* poželjan
desire *n* želja
desire *v.t* željeti
desirous *a* željan
desk *n* radni sto

despair *n* očajanje
despair *v. i* očajavati
desperate *a* očajan
despicable *a.* dostojan prezira
despise *v. t* prezirati
despot *n* despot
destination *n* destinacija
destiny *n* sudbina
destroy *v. t* uništiti
destruction *n* razaranje
detach *v. t* odvojiti
detachment *n* odvajanje
detail *n* detalj
detail *v. t* detaljisati
detain *v. t* zadržati
detect *v. t* otkriti
detective *a* detektivski
detective *n.* detektiv
determination *n.* odlučnost
determine *v. t* odrediti
dethrone *v. t* zbaciti
develop *v. t.* razviti
development *n.* razvoj
deviate *v. i* odstupati
deviation *n* odstupanje
device *n* uređaj
devil *n* đavo
devise *v. t* izmisliti
devoid *a* lišen
devote *v. t* posvetiti
devotee *n* privrženik
devotion *n* privrženost
devour *v. t* proždirati
dew *n.* rosa
diabetes *n* dijabetes
diagnose *v. t* postaviti dijagnozu
diagnosis *n* dijagnoza
diagram *n* dijagram
dial *n.* brojčanik
dialect *n* dijalekt

dialogue *n* dijalog
diameter *n* promjer
diamond *n* dijamant
diarrhoea *n* dijareja
diary *n* dnevnik
dice *n.* kocke
dice *v. i.* kockati se
dictate *v. t* diktirati
dictation *n* diktiranje
dictator *n* diktator
diction *n* dikcija
dictionary *n* rečnik
dictum *n* izreka
didactic *a* didaktički
die *v. i* umreti
die *n* umiranje
diet *n* dijeta
differ *v. i* razlikovati se
difference *n* razlika
different *a* različit
difficult *a* težak
difficulty *n* teškoća
dig *n* kopanje
dig *v.t.* kopati
digest *v. t.* svariti
digest *n.* pregled
digestion *n* varenje
digit *n* cifra
dignify *v.t* udostojiti
dignity *n* dostojanstvo
dilemma *n* dilema
diligence *n* marljivost
diligent *a* marljiv
dilute *v. t* razvodniti
dilute *a* razvodnjen
dim *a* nejasan
dim *v. t* potamnjeti
dimension *n* dimenzija
diminish *v. t* smanjiti
din *n* buka

47

dine v. t. večerati
dinner n večera
dip n. umakanje
dip v. t umočiti
diploma n diploma
diplomacy n diplomacija
diplomat n diplomat
diplomatic a diplomatski
dire a strašan
direct a direktan
direct v. t usmjeriti
direction n pravac
director n. direktor
directory n direktorij
dirt n nečistoća
dirty a prljav
disability n nesposobnost
disable v. t onesposobiti
disabled a nesposoban
disadvantage n nedostatak
disagree v. i ne slagati se
disagreeable a. neprijatan
disagreement n. nesporazum
disappear v. i nestati
disappearance n nestanak
disappoint v. t. razočarati
disapproval n neodobravanje
disapprove v. t neodobravati
disarm v. t razoružati
disarmament n. razoružanje
disaster n katastrofa
disastrous a katastrofalan
disc n. disk
discard v. t odbaciti
discharge v. t prazniti
discharge n. pražnjenje
disciple n učenik
discipline n disciplina
disclose v. t otkriti
discomfort n nelagodnost

disconnect v. t isključiti
discontent n nezadovoljstvo
discontinue v. t prekinuti
discord n nesloga
discount n popust
discourage v. t. obeshrabriti
discourse n diskurs
discourteous a neučtiv
discover v. t otkriti
discovery n. otkriće
discretion n diskrecija
discriminate v. t. razlikovati
discrimination n diskriminacija
discuss v. t. diskutirati
disdain n prezir
disdain v. t. prezirati
disease n bolest
disguise n prerušen
disguise v. t prerušiti se
dish n jelo
dishearten v. t obeshrabriti
dishonest a nepošten
dishonesty n. nepoštenje
dishonour v. t osramotiti
dishonour n sramota
dislike v. t ne voleti
dislike n antipatija
disloyal a nelojalan
dismiss v. t. odbaciti
dismissal n otpuštanje
disobey v. t biti neposlušan
disorder n poremećaj
disparity n nejednakost
dispensary n ambulanta
disperse v. t rasuti
displace v. t pomaknuti
display v. t pokazati
display n pokazivanje
displease v. t ne sviđati se
displeasure n nezadovoljstvo

disposal n raspolaganje
dispose v. t raspolagati
disprove v. t opovrgnuti
dispute n spor
dispute v. i prepirati se
disqualification n diskvalifikacija
disqualify v. t. diskvalificirati
disquiet n uznemirenost
disregard n potcjenjivanje
disregard v. t potcjenjivati
disrepute n ozloglašenost
disrespect n nepoštivanje
disrupt v. t prekinuti
dissatisfaction n nezadovoljstvo
dissatisfy v. t. ne zadovoljiti
dissect v. t secirati
dissection n seciranje
dissimilar a različit
dissolve v.t rastvoriti
dissuade v. t odvratiti
distance n rastojanje
distant a udaljen
distil v. t destilovati
distillery n destilerija
distinct a poseban
distinction n razlika
distinguish v. i razlikovati
distort v. t izobličiti
distress n bol
distress v. t ožalostiti
distribute v. t distribuirati
distribution n distribucija
district n kotar
distrust n nepovjerenje
distrust v. t. sumnjati
disturb v. t uznemiravati
ditch n jarak
ditto n. isto
dive v. i roniti
dive n ronjenje

diverse a različit
divert v. t skrenuti
divide v. t podijeliti
divine a božanski
divinity n božanstvenost
division n podjela
divorce n razvod
divorce v. t razvesti
divulge v. t otkriti
do v. t činiti
docile a poslušan
dock n. pristanište
doctor n liječnik
doctorate n doktorat
doctrine n doktrina
document n dokument
dodge n izmicanje
dodge v. t izmicati
doe n srna
dog n pas
dog v. t pratiti
dogma n dogma
dogmatic a dogmatski
doll n lutka
dollar n dolar
domain n domen
dome n kupola
domestic a domaći
domestic n posluga
domicile n prebivalište
dominant a dominantan
dominate v. t dominirati
domination n dominacija
dominion n vlast
donate v. t pokloniti
donation n. donacija
donkey n magarac
donor n davalac
doom n propast
doom v. t. osuditi

door *n* vrata
dose *n* doza
dot *n* tačka
dot *v. t* istačkati
double *a* dvostruko
double *v. t.* udvostručiti
double *n* dvostrukost
doubt *v. i* sumnjati
doubt *n* sumnja
dough *n* tijesto
dove *n* golub
down *adv* dolje
down *prep* niz
down *v. t* baciti
downfall *n* slom
downpour *n* pljusak
downright *adv* potpuno
downright *a* potpun
downward *a* nagnut
downward *adv* dolje
downwards *adv* dolje
dowry *n* miraz
doze *n.* drijemanje
doze *v. i* drijemati
dozen *n* tuce
draft *v. t* skicirati
draft *n* skica
draftsman *a* crtač
drag *n* povlačenje
drag *v. t* povlačiti
dragon *n* zmaj
drain *n* odvod
drain *v. t* odvoditi
drainage *n* drenaža
dram *n* gutljaj
drama *n* drama
dramatic *a* dramatičan
dramatist *n* dramaturg
draper *n* suknar
drastic *a* drastičan

draught *n* nacrt
draw *v.t* vući
draw *n* izvlačenje
drawback *n* smetnja
drawer *n* ladica
drawing *n* crtanje
drawing-room *n* salon
dread *n* strah
dread *v.t* strahovati
dread *a* strašan
dream *n* san
dream *v. i.* sanjati
drench *v. t* pokvasiti
dress *n* haljina
dress *v. t* oblačiti
dressing *n* oblačenje
drill *n* bušilica
drill *v. t.* bušenje
drink *n* piće
drink *v. t* piti
drip *n* kapanje
drip *v. i* kapati
drive *v. t* voziti
drive *n* vožnja
driver *n* vozač
drizzle *n* izmaglica
drizzle *v. i* rominjati
drop *n* kap
drop *v. i* kapati
drought *n* suša
drown *v.i* utopiti
drug *n* lijek
druggist *n* apotekar
drum *n* bubanj
drum *v.i.* udarati u bubanj
drunkard *n* pijanica
dry *a* suho
dry *v. i.* osušiti
dual *a* dvostruk
duck *n.* patka

duck *v.i.* zaroniti
due *a* dužan
due *n* dug
due *adv* točno
duel *n* dvoboj
duel *v. i* boriti se
duke *n* vojvoda
dull *a* tup
dull *v. t.* tupiti
duly *adv* propisno
dumb *a* glup
dunce *n* glupan
dung *n* đubre
duplicate *a* dvostruk
duplicate *n* duplikat
duplicate *v. t* udvostručiti
duplicity *n* dvoličnost
durable *a* izdržljiv
duration *n* trajanje
during *prep* za vrijeme
dusk *n* suton
dust *n* prašina
dust *v.t.* zaprašiti
duster *n* pajalica
dutiful *a* savjestan
duty *n* dužnost
dwarf *n* patuljak
dwell *v. i* stanovati
dwelling *n* prebivalište
dwindle *v. t* nestajati
dye *v. t* bojiti
dye *n* boja
dynamic *a* dinamičan
dynamics *n.* dinamika
dynamite *n* dinamit
dynamo *n* generator
dynasty *n* dinastija
dysentery *n* dizenterija

E

each *a* svaki
each *pron.* svaki
eager *a* željan
eagle *n* orao
ear *n* uvo
early *adv* ran
early *a* rano
earn *v. t* zaslužiti
earnest *a* ozbiljan
earth *n* zemlja
earthen *a* zemljan
earthly *a* zemaljski
earthquake *n* potres
ease *n* jednostavnost
ease *v. t* pojednostaviti
east *n* istok
east *adv* istočno
east *a* istočni
easter *n* uskrs
eastern *a* istočni
easy *a* lako
eat *v. t* jesti
eatable *n.* jestivost
eatable *a* jestiv
ebb *n* oseka
ebb *v. i* opadati
ebony *n* abonos
echo *n* odjek
echo *v. t* odjekivati
eclipse *n* pomračenje
economic *a* ekonomski
economical *a* ekonomičan
economics *n.* ekonomija
economy *n* ekonomija
edge *n* ivica
edible *a* jestivo

edifice *n* građevina
edit *v. t* urediti
edition *n* izdanje
editor *n* urednik
editorial *a* urednički
editorial *n* uvodnik
educate *v. t* obrazovati
education *n* obrazovanje
efface *v. t* izbrisati
effect *n* efekat
effect *v. t* djelovanje
effective *a* učinkovit
effeminate *a* ženstven
efficacy *n* djelotvornost
efficiency *n* učinkovitost
efficient *a* efikasan
effigy *n* slika
effort *n* napor
egg *n* jaje
ego *n* ego
egotism *n* egoizam
eight *n* osam
eighteen *a* osamnaest
eighty *n* osamdeset
either *a.* oba
either *adv.* niti
eject *v. t.* izbaciti
elaborate *v. t* razraditi
elaborate *a* razrađen
elapse *v. t* prolaziti
elastic *a* elastičan
elbow *n* lakat
elder *a* stariji
elder *n* starješina
elderly *a* starije
elect *v. t* izabrati
election *n* izbor
electorate *n* biračko tijelo
electric *a* električni
electricity *n* elektricitet

electrify *v. t* naelektrisati
elegance *n* elegancija
elegant *adj* elegantan
elegy *n* elegija
element *n* element
elementary *a* elementarni
elephant *n* slon
elevate *v. t* podići
elevation *n* uzdignuće
eleven *n* jedanaest
elf *n* patuljak
eligible *a* poželjan
eliminate *v. t* eliminirati
elimination *n* eliminacija
elope *v. i* pobeći
eloquence *n* rječitost
eloquent *a* rječit
else *a* drugi
else *adv* drugo
elucidate *v. t* objasniti
elude *v. t* izbjegavati
elusion *n* izbjegavanje
elusive *a* nedostižan
emancipation *n.* emancipacija
embalm *v. t* balsamovati
embankment *n* nasip
embark *v. t* ukrcati
embarrass *v. t* posramiti
embassy *n* ambasada
embitter *v. t* zagorčati
emblem *n* amblem
embodiment *n* utjelovljenje
embody *v. t.* utjeloviti
embolden *v. t.* ohrabriti
embrace *v. t.* zagrliti
embrace *n* zagrljaj
embroidery *n* vez
embryo *n* embrij
emerald *n* smaragd
emerge *v. i* pojaviti se

emergency *n* hitan slučaj
eminence *n* eminencija
eminent *a* eminentni
emissary *n* izaslanik
emit *v. t* emitirati
emolument *n* prihod
emotion *n* emocija
emotional *a* emotivan
emperor *n* imperator
emphasis *n* naglasak
emphasize *v. t* naglasiti
emphatic *a* izrazit
empire *n* carstvo
employ *v. t* zaposliti
employee *n* službenik
employer *n* poslodavac
employment *n* zaposlenje
empower *v. t* osposobiti
empress *n* carica
empty *a* prazan
empty *v* prazniti
emulate *v. t* natjecati se
enable *v. t* omogućiti
enact *v. t* ozakoniti
enamel *n* emajl
enamour *v. t* zaljubiti se
encase *v. t* spakovati
enchant *v. t* opčiniti
encircle *v. t.* okružiti
enclose *v. t* priložiti
enclosure *n.* prilog
encompass *v. t* opkoliti
encounter *n.* susret
encounter *v. t* susresti
encourage *v. t* ohrabriti
encroach *v. i* zadirati
encumber *v. t.* opteretiti
encyclopaedia *n.* enciklopedija
end *v. t* završiti
end *n.* kraj

endanger *v. t.* ugroziti
endear *v.t* učiniti dragim
endearment *n.* nježnost
endeavour *n* nastojanje
endeavour *v.i* nastojati
endorse *v. t.* odobriti
endow *v. t* obdariti
endurable *a* izdržljiv
endurance *n.* izdržljivost
endure *v.t.* izdržati
enemy *n* neprijatelj
energetic *a* energičan
energy *n.* energija
enfeeble *v. t.* oslabiti
enforce *v. t.* primijeniti
enfranchise *v.t.* dati pravo glasa
engage *v. t* angažirati
engagement *n.* angažiranje
engine *n* motor
engineer *n* inženjer
English *n* engleski jezik, Englez
engrave *v. t* ugravirati
engross *v.t* zaokupiti
engulf *v.t* progutati
enigma *n* enigma
enjoy *v. t* uživati
enjoyment *n* uživanje
enlarge *v. t* uvećanje
enlighten *v. t.* prosvijetliti
enlist *v. t* regrutirati
enliven *v. t.* oživjeti
enmity *n* neprijateljstvo
ennoble *v. t.* oplemeniti
enormous *a* ogroman
enough *a* dovoljan
enough *adv* dovoljno
enrage *v. t* razbesneti
enrapture *v. t* ushititi
enrich *v. t* obogatiti
enrol *v. t* upisati

enshrine v. t zatvoriti u svetilište
enslave v.t. zarobiti
ensue v.i proizilaziti
ensure v. t obezbediti
entangle v. t upetljati
enter v. t ulaziti
enterprise n poduzeće
entertain v. t zabaviti
entertainment n. zabava
enthrone v. t ustoličiti
enthusiasm n entuzijazam
enthusiastic a oduševljen
entice v. t. namamiti
entire a čitav
entirely adv potpuno
entitle v. t. ovlastiti
entity n entitet
entomology n. entomologija
entrails n. utroba
entrance n ulaz
entrap v. t. zarobiti
entreat v. t. preklinjati
entreaty n. preklinjanje
entrust v. t povjeriti
entry n ulazak
enumerate v. t. nabrajati
envelop v. t zamotati
envelope n koverat
enviable a zavidan
envious a zavidljiv
environment n. okruženje
envy v biti zavidan
envy v. t zavidjeti
epic n ep
epidemic n epidemija
epigram n epigram
epilepsy n epilepsija
epilogue n epilog
episode n epizoda
epitaph n epitaf

epoch n epoha
equal a jednako
equal v. t izjednačiti
equal n ravnopravnost
equality n jednakost
equalize v. t. izjednačiti
equate v. t uskladiti
equation n jednačina
equator n ekvator
equilateral a jednakostranični
equip v. t opremiti
equipment n oprema
equitable a pravedan
equivalent a ekvivalent
equivocal a dvosmislen
era n doba
eradicate v. t iskorijeniti
erase v. t brisati
erect v. t uspraviti
erect a uspravljen
erection n erekcija
erode v. t erodirati
erosion n erozija
erotic a erotski
err v. i pogriješiti
errand n zadatak
erroneous a pogrešan
error n greška
erupt v. i buknuti
eruption n erupcija
escape n bijeg
escape v.i pobjeći
escort n pratnja
escort v. t pratiti
especial a poseban
essay n. esej
essay v. t. ustanoviti
essayist n esejista
essence n suština
essential a suštinski

establish v. t. uspostaviti
establishment n osnivanje
estate n imanje
esteem n poštovanje
esteem v. t poštovati
estimate n. procjena
estimate v. t procjeniti
estimation n procjena
etcetera i tako dalje
eternal adj. vječan
eternity n vječnost
ether n eter
ethical a etički
ethics n. etika
etiquette n etiketa
etymology n. etimologija
eunuch n evnuh
evacuate v. t evakuirati
evacuation n evakuacija
evade v. t izbeći
evaluate v. t ocijeniti
evaporate v. i ispariti
evasion n izbjegavanje
even a ravan
even v. t izravnati
even adv čak
evening n večer
event n događaj
eventually adv. konačno
ever adv ikad
evergreen a zimzelen
evergreen n evergrin
everlasting a. vječan
every a svaki
evict v. t protjerati
eviction n protjerivanje
evidence n dokaz
evident a. očigledan
evil n zlo
evil a zao

evoke v. t evocirati
evolution n evolucija
evolve v.t evoluirati
ewe n ovca
exact a točan
exaggerate v. t. preuveličavati
exaggeration n. preuveličavanje
exalt v. t veličati
examination n. ispitivanje
examine v. t ispitati
examinee n ispitanik
examiner n ispitivač
example n primjer
excavate v. t. iskopavati
excavation n. iskopavanje
exceed v.t prekoračiti
excel v.i nadmašiti
excellence n. izvrsnost
excellency n ekselencija
excellent a. odličan
except v. t izuzeti
except prep osim
exception n iznimka
excess n višak
excess a suvišan
exchange n razmjena
exchange v. t razmeniti
excise n trošarina
excite v. t uzbuditi
exclaim v.i uzviknuti
exclamation n uzvik
exclude v. t isključiti
exclusive a isključiv
excommunicate v. t. ekskomunicirati
excursion n. ekskurzija
excuse v.t opravdati
excuse n izgovor
execute v. t izvršiti
execution n izvršenje
executioner n. izvršitelj

exempt v. t. osloboditi
exempt adj. oslobođen
exercise n. vježba
exercise v. t vježbati
exhaust v. t. ispuhati
exhibit n. eksponat
exhibit v. t izložiti
exhibition n. Izložba
exile n. progonstvo
exile v. t prognati
exist v.i postojati
existence n postojanje
exit n. izlaz
expand v.t. proširiti
expansion n. proširenje
ex-parte a jednostran
ex-parte adv jednostrano
expect v. t očekivati
expectation n. očekivanje
expedient a prikladan
expedite v. t. požuriti
expedition n ekspedicija
expel v. t. isključiti
expend v. t potrošiti
expenditure n rashod
expense n. trošak
expensive a skup
experience n iskustvo
experience v. t. iskusiti
experiment n eksperiment
expert a stručan
expert n stručnjak
expire v.i. isteći
expiry n istek
explain v. t. objasniti
explanation n objašnjenje
explicit a. eksplicitan
explode v. t. eksplodirati
exploit n eksploatacija
e· ᴥʈt v. t eksploatirati

exploration n istraživanje
explore v.t istražiti
explosion n. eksplozija
explosive n. eksploziv
explosive a eksplozivan
exponent n tumač
export n izvoz
export v. t. izvoziti
expose v. t izložiti
express v. t. izraziti
express a određen
express n ekpres
expression n. izraz
expressive a. izražajan
expulsion n. isključenje
extend v. t proširiti
extent n. opseg
external a vanjski
extinct a izumro
extinguish v.t ugasiti
extol v. t. veličati
extra a dodatni
extra adv ekstra
extract n ekstrakt
extract v. t izdvojiti
extraordinary a. izvanredan
extravagance n ekstravagancija
extravagant a ekstravagantan
extreme a ekstreman
extreme n ekstrem
extremist n ekstremista
exult v. i likovati
eye n oko
eyeball n očna jabučica
eyelash n trepavica
eyelet n rupica
eyewash n prevara

F

fable n. basna
fabric n tkanina
fabricate v.t proizvoditi
fabrication n proizvodnja
fabulous a nevjerojatan
facade n fasada
face n lice
face v.t suočiti se
facet n aspekt
facial a osobni
facile a lak
facilitate v.t olakšati
facility n postrojenje
facsimile n faksimil
fact n činjenica
faction n frakcija
factious a stranački
factor n faktor
factory n tvornica
faculty n fakultet
fad n hir
fade v.i izblijedeti
faggot n naramak pruća
fail v.i ne uspjeti
failure n neuspjeh
faint a slab
faint v.i onesvijestiti se
fair a lijep
fair n. sajam
fairly adv. pošteno
fairy n vila
faith n vjera
faithful a vjeran
falcon n soko
fall v.i. pasti
fall n jesen

fallacy n zabluda
fallow n ugar
false a lažan
falter v.i posrnuti
fame n slava
familiar a poznat
family n porodica
famine n glad
famous a poznat
fan n blag vetar
fanatic a fanatičan
fanatic n fanatik
fancy n mašta
fancy v.t zamisliti
fantastic a fantastičan
far adv. daleko
far a dalek
far n daljina
farce n farsa
fare n karta
farewell n oproštaj
farewell interj. zbogom
farm n farma
farmer n poljoprivrednik
fascinate v.t fascinirati
fascination n. fascinacija
fashion n moda
fashionable a moderan
fast a brz
fast adv brzo
fast n post
fast v.i postiti
fasten v.t pričvrstiti
fat a gojazan
fat n mast
fatal a fatalan
fate n sudbina
father n otac
fathom v.t proniknuti
fathom n hvat

fatigue *n* umor
fatigue *v.t* umarati
fault *n* greška
faulty *a* neispravan
fauna *n* fauna
favour1 *n* naklonost
favour *v.t* pomagati
favourable *a* povoljan
favourite *a* omiljen
favourite *n* favorit
fear *n* strah
fear *v.i* plašiti se
fearful *a.* strašno
feasible *a* izvodljiv
feast *n* gozba
feast *v.i* gostiti se
feat *n* podvig
feather *n* pero
feature *n* odlika
February *n* veljača
federal *a* federalni
federation *n* federacija
fee *n* honorar
feeble *a* slab
feed *v.t* hraniti
feed *n* hranjenje
feel *v.t* osjećati
feeling *n* osjećaj
feign *v.t* pretvarati se
felicitate *v.t* čestitati
felicity *n* blaženstvo
fell *v.t* pasti
fellow *n* kolega
female *a* ženski
female *n* žena
feminine *a* ženskog roda
fence *n* ograda
fence *v.t* ograditi
fend *v.t* braniti se
ferment *n* kvasac

ferment *v.t* ključati
fermentation *n* fermentacija
ferocious *a* svirep
ferry *n* trajekt
ferry *v.t* prevoziti
fertile *a* plodan
fertility *n* plodnost
fertilize *v.t* oploditi
fertilizer *n* gnojivo
fervent *a* vatren
fervour *n* žestina
festival *n* festival
festive *a* svečan
festivity *n* svečanost
festoon *n* vijenac
fetch *v.t* donijeti
fetter *n* karika
fetter *v.t* sputati
feud *n.* zavada
feudal *a* feudalni
fever *n* groznica
few *a* malo
fiasco *n* fijasko
fibre *n* vlakno
fickle *a* promjenljiv
fiction *n* fikcija
fictitious *a* fiktivan
fiddle *n* violina
fiddle *v.i* gudit
fidelity *n* vjernost
fie *interj* fuj
field *n* polje
fiend *n* đavo
fierce *a* žestok
fiery *a* užaren
fifteen *n* petnaest
fifty *n.* pedeset
fig *n* smokva
fight *n* borba
fight *v.t* boriti se

figment *n* izmišljotina
figurative *a* figurativan
figure *n* figura
figure *v.t* uobličiti
file *n* arhiva
file *v.t* arhivirati
file *n* fascikla
file *v.t* ubilježiti
file *n* dosije
file *v.i.* nizati
fill *v.t* popuniti
film *n* film
film *v.t* snimati
filter *n* filter
filter *v.t* čistiti
filth *n* nečistoća
filthy *a* prljav
fin *n* peraje
final *a* konačan
finance *n* finansije
finance *v.t* financirati
financial *a* financijski
financier *n* financijer
find *v.t* kazniti
fine *n* kazna
fine *v.t* čistiti
fine *a* dobar
finger *n* prst
finger *v.t* dodirivati
finish *v.t* završiti
finish *n* završetak
finite *a* konačan
fir *n* jela
fire *n* vatra
fire *v.t* zapaliti
firm *a* čvrst
firm *n.* tvrtka
first *a* prvi
first *n* prvi
first *adv* prvo

fiscal *a* fiskalni
fish *n* riba
fish *v.i* pecati
fisherman *n* ribar
fissure *n* pukotina
fist *n* pesnica
fistula *n* fistula
fit *v.t* podesiti
fit prikladan
fit *n* napad
fitful *a* grčevit
fitter *n* monter
five *n* pet
fix *v.t* popraviti
fix *n* neprilika
flabby *a* mlitav
flag *n* zastava
flagrant *a* sramotan
flame *n* plamen
flame *v.i* plamtjeti
flannel *n* flanel
flare *v.i* planuti
flare *n* bljesak
flash *n* bljeskalica
flash *v.t* zasijati
flask *n* pljoska
flat *a* ravan
flat *n* ravnina
flatter *v.t* laskati
flattery *n* laskanje
flavour *n* okus
flaw *n* mana
flea *n.* buha
flee *v.i* pobeći
fleece *n* runo
fleece *v.t* ošišati
fleet *n* flota
flesh *n* meso
flexible *a* fleksibilan
flicker *n* treperenje

flicker v.t treperiti
flight n let
flimsy a tanak
fling v.t baciti
flippancy n lakomislenost
flirt n flertovanje
flirt v.i flertovati
float v.i ploviti
flock n stado
flock v.i gomilati
flog v.t šibati
flood n poplava
flood v.t poplaviti
floor n pod
floor v.t popločati
flora n flora
florist n cvećar
flour n brašno
flourish v.i cvjetati
flow n protok
flow v.i teći
flower n cvijet
flowery a cvijetni
fluent a tečan
fluid a tekući
fluid n tekućina
flush v.i sprati
flush n rumenilo
flute n flauta
flute v.i svirati flautu
flutter n lepršanje
flutter v.t lepršati
fly n muha
fly v.i letjeti
foam n pjena
foam v.t pjeniti se
focal a žarišni
focus n fokus
focus v.t izoštriti
fodder n stočna hrana

foe n neprijatelj
fog n magla
foil v.t folija
fold n nabor
fold v.t saviti
foliage n lišće
follow v.t pratiti
follower n sljedbenik
folly n glupost
foment v.t izazivati
fond a naklonjen
fondle v.t milovati
food n hrana
fool n budala
foolish a budalast
foolscap n tabak za pisanje
foot n stopalo
for prep za
for conj. jer
forbid v.t zabraniti
force n sila
force v.t siliti
forceful a snažan
forcible a prisilan
forearm n podlaktica
forearm v.t unaprijed oružati
forecast n predviđanje
forecast v.t predviđati
forefather n praotac
forefinger n kažiprst
forehead n čelo
foreign a strani
foreigner n stranac
foreknowledge n. predviđanje
foreleg n prednja noga
forelock n uvojak
foreman n nadzornik
foremost a prednji
forenoon n pre podne
forerunner n prethodnik

foresee *v.t* predvidjeti
foresight *n* predviđanje
forest *n* šuma
forestall *v.t* preduhitriti
forester *n* šumar
forestry *n* šumarstvo
foretell *v.t* proreći
forethought *n* promišljenost
forever *adv* zauvijek
forewarn *v.t* upozoriti
foreword *n* predgovor
forfeit *v.t* izgubiti
forfeit *n* gubitak
forfeiture *n* gubitak prava
forge *n* kovačnica
forge *v.t* falsificirati
forgery *n* falsifikat
forget *v.t* zaboraviti
forgetful *a* zaboravan
forgive *v.t* oprostiti
forgo *v.t* odreći se
forlorn *a* usamljen
form *n* forma
form *v.t.* formirati
formal *a* formalan
format *n* format
formation *n* formacija
former *a* prethodni
former *pron* bivši
formerly *adv* ranije
formidable *a* znatan
formula *n* formula
formulate *v.t* formulirati
forsake *v.t.* napustiti
forswear *v.t.* prekršiti zakletvu
fort *n.* utvrda
forte *n.* jaka točka
forth *adv.* naprijed
forthcoming *a.* predstojeći
forthwith *adv.* odmah

fortify *v.t.* utvrditi
fortitude *n.* hrabrost
fort-night *n.* dva tjedna
fortress *n.* tvrđava
fortunate *a.* sretan
fortune *n.* sreća
forty *n.* četrdeset
forum *n.* forum
forward *a.* prednji
forward *adv* naprijed
forward *v.t* poslati
fossil *n.* fosil
foster *v.t.* odgajati
foul *a.* prekršaj
found *v.t.* utemeljiti
foundation *n.* utemeljenje
founder *n.* osnivač
foundry *n.* livnica
fountain *n.* fontana
four *n.* četiri
fourteen *n.* četrnaest
fowl *n.* živina
fowler *n.* ptičar
fox *n.* lisica
fraction *n.* frakcija
fracture *n.* prijelom
fracture *v.t* polomiti
fragile *a.* krhak
fragment *n.* fragment
fragrance *n.* miris
fragrant *a.* mirisan
frail *a.* slab
frame *v.t.* uramiti
frame *n* okvir
frachise *n.* franšiza
frank *a.* iskren
frantic *a.* pomaman
fraternal *a.* bratski
fraternity *n.* bratstvo
fratricide *n.* bratoubojstvo

fraud *n.* prevara
fraudulent *a.* nepošten
fraught *a.* ispunjen
fray *n* tuča
free *a.* slobodan
free *v.t* osloboditi
freedom *n.* sloboda
freeze *v.i.* zamrznuti
freight *n.* tovar
French *a.* francuski
French *n* francuski jezik, Francuz
frenzy *n.* pomama
frequency *n.* frekvencija
frequent *n.* učestalost
fresh *a.* svjež
fret *n.* uzrujanost
fret *v.t.* uzrujati se
friction *n.* trenje
Friday *n.* petak
fridge *n.* hladnjak
friend *n.* prijatelj
fright *n.* strah
frighten *v.t.* uplašiti
frigid *a.* frigidan
frill *n.* nabor
fringe *n.* resa
fringe *v.t* obrubiti
frivolous *a.* neozbiljan
frock *n.* haljina
frog *n.* žaba
frolic *n.* zabava
frolic *v.i.* veseliti se
from *prep.* od
front *n.* front
front *a* prednji
front *v.t* gledati
frontier *n.* granica
frost *n.* mraz
frown *n.* mrštenje
frown *v.i* mrštiti se

frugal *a.* štedljiv
fruit *n.* voće
fruitful *a.* plodan
frustrate *v.t.* frustrirati
frustration *n.* frustracija
fry *v.t.* pržiti
fry *n* ikra
fuel *n.* gorivo
fugitive *a.* odbegao
fugitive *n.* bjegunac
fulfil *v.t.* ispuniti
fulfilment *n.* ispunjenje
full *a.* pun
full *adv.* puno
fullness *n.* punoća
fully *adv.* potpuno
fumble *v.i.* preturati
fun *n.* zabava
function *n.* funkcija
function *v.i* funkcionirati
functionary *n.* funkcioner
fund *n.* fond
fundamental *a.* osnovni
funeral *n.* sahrana
fungus *n.* gljiva
funny *n.* smiješan
fur *n.* krzno
furious *a.* bijesan
furl *v.t.* smotati
furlong *n.* osmina milje
furnace *n.* peć
furnish *v.t.* opremiti
furniture *n.* namještaj
furrow *n.* brazda
further *adv.* dalje
further *a* daljnji
further *v.t* unaprijediti
fury *n.* bijes
fuse *v.t.* rastopiti
fuse *n* osigurač

fusion *n.* fuzija
fuss *n.* komešanje
fuss *v.i* uznemiriti se
futile *a.* uzaludan
futility *n.* uzaludnost
future *a.* budući
future *n* budućnost

G

gabble *v.i.* blebetati
gadfly *n.* obad
gag *v.t.* geg, čep
gag *n.* začepiti
gaiety *n.* veselost
gain *v.t.* dobiti
gain *n* dobit
gainsay *v.t.* poricati
gait *n.* hod
galaxy *n.* galaksija
gale *n.* oluja
gallant *a.* galantan
gallant *n* kavaljer
gallantry *n.* hrabrost
gallery *n.* galerija
gallon *n.* galon
gallop *n.* galop
gallop *v.t.* galopirati
gallows *n.* . vješala
galore *adv.* u izobilju
galvanize *v.t.* podstaći
gamble *v.i.* kockati se
gamble *n* kockanje
gambler *n.* kockar
game *n.* igra
game *v.i* igrati
gander *n.* glupan
gang *n.* banda
gangster *n.* gangster

gap *n* pukotina
gape *v.i.* zijevati
garage *n.* garaža
garb *n.* odeća
garb *v.t* obući
garbage *n.* smeće
garden *n.* bašta
gardener *n.* baštovan
gargle *v.i.* ispirati grlo
garland *n.* vijenac
garland *v.t.* ovenčati
garlic *n.* češnjak
garment *n.* odeća
garter *n.* podvezica
gas *n.* gas
gasket *n.* zaptivač
gasp *n.* dahtanje
gasp *v.i* dahtati
gassy *a.* gasni
gastric *a.* želudačni
gate *n.* kapija
gather *v.t.* okupiti
gaudy *a.* kitnjast
gauge *n.* kolosijek
gauntlet *n.* oklopna rukavica
gay *a.* veseo
gaze *v.t.* zuriti
gaze *n* zurenje
gazette *n.* novine
gear *n.* oprema
geld *v.t.* kastrirati
gem *n* dragulj
gender *n.* pol
general *a.* opći
generally *adv.* uglavnom
generate *v.t.* generirati
generation *n.* generacija
generator *n.* generator
generosity *n.* velikodušnost
generous *a.* velikodušan

genius *n.* genije
gentle *a.* nježno
gentleman *n.* gospodin
gentry *n.* niže plemstvo
genuine *a.* pravi
geographer *n.* geograf
geographical *a.* geografski
geography *n.* geografija
geological *a.* geološki
geologist *n.* geolog
geology *n.* geologija
geometrical *a.* geometrijski
geometry *n.* geometrija
germ *n.* klica
germicide *n.* germicid
germinate *v.i.* klijati
germination *n.* klijanje
gerund *n.* gerund
gesture *n.* gest
get *v.t.* dobiti
ghastly *a.* jeziv
ghost *n.* duh
giant *n.* džin
gibbon *n.* gibon
gibe *v.i.* rugati se
gibe *n* ruganje
giddy *a.* vrtoglav
gift *n.* poklon
gifted *a.* nadaren
gigantic *a.* gigantski
giggle *v.i.* kikotati se
gild *v.t.* pozlatiti
gilt *a.* pozlata
ginger *n.* đumbir
giraffe *n.* žirafa
gird *v.t.* opasati
girder *n.* nosač
girdle *n.* pojas
girdle *v.t* opasivati
girl *n.* djevojka

girlish *a.* djevojački
gist *n.* suština
give *v.t.* dati
glacier *n.* glečer
glad *a.* radostan
gladden *v.t.* obradovati
glamour *n.* blistavost
glance *n.* pogled
glance *v.i.* pogledati
gland *n.* žlijezda
glare *n.* bleštanje
glare *v.i* bleštati
glass *n.* staklo
glaucoma *n.* glaukom
glaze *v.t.* glačati
glaze *n* glazura
glazier *n.* staklorezac
glee *n.* radost
glide *v.t.* kliziti
glider *n.* jedrilica
glimpse *n.* letimičan pogled
glitter *v.i.* sijati
glitter *n* sjaj
global *a.* globalni
globe *n.* svijet
gloom *n.* sumornost
gloomy *a.* sumoran
glorification *n.* slavljenje
glorify *v.t.* veličati
glorious *a.* slavan
glory *n.* slava
gloss *n.* sjaj
glossary *n.* rječnik
glossy *a.* sjajan
glove *n.* rukavica
glow *v.i.* sijati
glow *n* sjaj
glucose *n.* glukoza
glue *n.* ljepilo
glut *v.t.* prezasititi

glut *n* prezasićenost
glutton *n.* proždrljivac
gluttony *n.* proždrljivost
glycerine *n.* glicerin
go *v.i.* ići
goad *n.* poticaj
goad *v.t* poticati
goal *n.* cilj
goat *n.* koza
gobble *n.* utjerivanje u rupu
goblet *n.* pehar
god *n.* Bog
goddess *n.* boginja
godhead *n.* božanstvo
godly *a.* božji
godown *n.* skladište
godsend *n.* neočekivana sreća
goggles *n.* zaštitne naočale
gold *n.* zlato
golden *a.* zlatan
goldsmith *n.* zlatar
golf *n. golf,* zaljev
gong *n.* gong
good *a.* dobar
good *n* valjanost
good-bye *interj.* zbogom
goodness *n.* dobrota
goodwill *n.* dobra volja
goose *n.* guska
gooseberry *n.* ogrozd
gorgeous *a.* divan
gorilla *n.* gorila
gospel *n.* evanđelje
gossip *n.* ogovaranje
gourd *n.* tikva
gout *n.* giht
govern *v.t.* upravljati
governance *n.* uprava
governess *n.* guvernanta
government *n.* Vlada

governor *n.* guverner
gown *n.* haljina
grab *v.t.* zgrabiti
grace *n.* milost
grace *v.t.* ukrasiti
gracious *a.* milostiv
gradation *n.* gradacija
grade *n.* razred
grade *v.t* oceniti
gradual *a.* postepen
graduate *v.i.* diplomirati
graduate *n* diplomirani đak/student
graft *n.* kalem
graft *v.t* kalemiti
grain *n.* zrno
grammar *n.* gramatika
grammarian *n.* gramatičar
gramme *n.* gram
gramophone *n.* gramofon
granary *n.* ambar
grand *a.* velik
grandeur *n.* veličanstvenost
grant *v.t.* odobriti
grant *n* odobrenje
grape *n.* grožđe
graph *n.* grafikon
graphic *a.* grafički
grapple *n.* rvanje
grapple *v.i.* rvati se
grasp *v.t.* sčepati
grasp *n* zahvat
grass *n* trava
grate *n.* rešetka
grate *v.t* strugati
grateful *a.* zahvalan
gratification *n.* zadovoljstvo
gratis *adv.* besplatno
gratitude *n.* zahvalnost
gratuity *n.* napojnica
grave *n.* grob

grave *a.* ozbiljan
gravitate *v.i.* težiti ka
gravitation *n.* gravitacija
gravity *n.* ozbiljnost
graze *v.i.* pasti
graze *n* lagan dodir
grease *n* mast
grease *v.t* podmazati
greasy *a.* mastan
great *a* velik
greed *n.* pohlepa
greedy *a.* pohlepan
Greek *n.* grčki jezik, Grk
Greek *a* grčki
green *a.* zelen
green *n* zelena boja
greenery *n.* zelenilo
greet *v.t.* pozdraviti
grenade *n.* granata
grey *a.* siva
greyhound *n.* hrt
grief *n.* žalost
grievance *n.* tuga
grieve *v.t.* tugovati
grievous *a.* žalostan
grind *v.i.* mljeti
grinder *n.* mlin
grip *v.t.* stisnuti
grip *n* stisak
groan *v.i.* stenjanje
groan *n* stenjati
grocer *n.* bakalin
grocery *n.* bakalnica
groom *n.* mladoženja
groom *v.t* timariti
groove *n.* žlijeb
groove *v.t* užlebiti
grope *v.t.* pipati
gross *n.* bruto
gross *a* težak

grotesque *a.* groteskan
ground *n.* tlo
group *n.* grupa
group *v.t.* grupirati
grow *v.t.* rasti
grower *n.* uzgajivač
growl *v.i.* režati
growl *n* režanje
growth *n.* rast
grudge *v.t.* gunđati
grudge *n* zavidnik
grumble *v.i.* zanovetati
grunt *n.* roktati
grunt *v.i.* roktanje
guarantee *n.* garancija
guarantee *v.t* jamčiti
guard *v.i.* čuvati
guard *n.* stražar
guardian *n.* čuvar
guerilla *n.* gerila
guess *n.* pretpostavka
guess *v.i* pretpostaviti
guest *n.* gost
guidance *n.* vođstvo
guide *v.t.* voditi
guide *n.* vodič
guild *n.* esnaf
guile *n.* lukavstvo
guilt *n.* krivica
guilty *a.* kriv
guise *n.* izgled
guitar *n.* gitara
gulf *n.* zaljev
gull *n.* galeb
gull *n* glupan
gull *v.t* nadmudriti
gulp *n.* gutljaj
gum *n.* guma
gun *n.* vatreno oružje
gust *n.* nalet

gutter *n.* oluk
guttural *a.* grlen
gymnasium *n.* gimnazija
gymnast *n.* gimnastičar
gymnastic *a.* gimnastički
gymnastics *n.* gimnastika

H

habit *n.* navika
habitable *a.* pogodan za stanovanje
habitat *n.* stanište
habitation *n.* stanovanje
habituate *v. t.* naviknuti
hack *v.t.* pijuk
hag *n.* vještica
haggard *a.* unezveren
haggle *v.i.* iseckati
hail *n.* grad
hail *v.i* padati
hail *v.t* pozdraviti
hair *n* kosa
hale *a.* čio
half *n.* polovina
half *a* pola
hall *n.* hol
hallmark *n.* žig
hallow *v.t.* posvetiti
halt *v. t.* oklijevati
halt *n* zastoj
halve *v.t.* prepoloviti
hamlet *n.* seoce
hammer *n.* čekić
hammer *v.t* čekićati
hand *n* šaka
hand *v.t* uručiti
handbill *n.* oglas
handbook *n.* priručnik
handcuff *n.* lisice

handcuff *v.t* staviti lisice
handful *n.* pregršt
handicap *v.t.* hendikepirati
handicap *n* hendikep
handicraft *n.* rukotvorina
handiwork *n.* ručni rad
handkerchief *n.* maramica
handle *n.* ručka
handle *v.t* rukovati
handsome *a.* zgodan
handy *a.* pogodan
hang *v.t.* objesiti
hanker *v.i.* žudjeti
haphazard *a.* slučajan
happen *v.t.* desiti
happening *n.* događaj
happiness *n.* sreća
happy *a.* srećan
harass *v.t.* uznemiravati
harassment *n.* uznemiravanje
harbour *n.* luka
harbour *v.t* pružiti utočište
hard *a.* težak
harden *v.t.* stvrdnuti
hardihood *n.* hrabrost
hardly *adv.* jedva
hardship *n.* teškoća
hardy *adj.* izdržljiv
hare *n.* zec
harm *n.* šteta
harm *v.t* oštetiti
harmonious *a.* harmoničan
harmonium *n.* harmonij
harmony *n.* harmonija
harness *n.* am
harness *v.t* upregnuti
harp *n.* harfa
harsh *a.* grub
harvest *n.* žetva
haverster *n.* žetelac

haste n. žurba
hasten v.i. ubrzati
hasty a. užurban
hat n. šešir
hatchet n. sjekira
hate n. mržnja
hate v.t. mrziti
haughty a. ohol
haunt v.t. progoniti
haunt n utočište
have v.t. imati
haven n. luka
havoc n. pustoš
hawk n jastreb
hawker n sokolar
hawthorn n. glog
hay n. seno
hazard n. rizik
hazard v.t riskirati
haze n. izmaglica
hazy a. maglovit
he pron. on
head n. glava
head v.t voditi
headache n. glavobolja
heading n. naslov
headlong adv. strmoglav
headstrong a. tvrdoglav
heal v.i. liječiti
health n. zdravlje
healthy a. zdrav
heap n. gomila
heap v.t gomilati
hear v.t. čuti
hearsay n. rekla-kazala
heart n. srce
hearth n. ognjište
heartily adv. srdačno
heat n. toplota
heat v.t zagrijati

heave v.i. dignuti
heaven n. nebo
heavenly a. nebeski
hedge n. živa ograda
hedge v.t ograditi
heed v.t. paziti
heed n pažnja
heel n. peta
hefty a. snažan
height n. visina
heighten v.t. povisiti
heinous a. gnusan
heir n. nasljednik
hell a. pakao
helm n. kormilo
helmet n. kaciga
help v.t. pomoći
help n pomoć
helpful a. koristan
helpless a. bespomoćan
helpmate n. pomoćnik
hemisphere n. hemisfera
hemp n. konoplja
hen n. kokoška
hence adv. otud
henceforth adv. od sada
henceforward adv. ubuduće
henchman n. sljedbenik
henpecked a. papučar
her pron. njoj
her a njen
herald n. glasnik
herald v.t najaviti
herb n. biljka
herculean a. herkulski
herd n. stado
herdsman n. pastir
here adv. ovdje
hereabouts adv. ovdje u okolini
hereafter adv. od sada

hereditary *n.* nasleđenost
heredity *n.* nasljednost
heritable *a.* nasljedan
heritage *n.* nasljeđe
hermit *n.* pustinjak
hermitage *n.* pustinjačka stanica
hernia *n.* hernija
hero *n.* heroj
heroic *a.* herojski
heroine *n.* heroina
heroism *n.* junaštvo
herring *n.* haringa
hesitant *a.* neodlučan
hesitate *v.i.* oklijevati
hesitation *n.* oklijevanje
hew *v.t.* tesati
heyday *n.* vrhunac
hibernation *n.* hibernacija
hiccup *n.* štucanje
hide *n.* sakrivanje
hide *v.t* sakriti
hideous *a.* odvratan
hierarchy *n.* hijerarhija
high *a.* visok
highly *adv.* visoko
Highness *n.* Visost
highway *n.* autoput
hilarious *a.* smiješan
hilarity *n.* veselje
hill *n.* brdo
hillock *n.* breg
him *pron.* njega
hinder *v.t.* ometati
hindrance *n.* prepreka
hint *n.* nagovještaj
hint *v.i* nagovjestiti
hip *n* kuk
hire *n.* najam
hire *v.t* zaposliti
hireling *n.* najamnik

his *pron.* njegov
hiss *n* siktanje
hiss *v.i* siktati
historian *n.* povijesničar
historic *a.* povijesni
historical *a.* povijesni
history *n.* povijest
hit *v.t.* pogoditi
hit *n* pogodak
hitch *n.* zapreka
hither *adv.* ovamo
hitherto *adv.* do sada
hive *n.* košnica
hoarse *a.* promukao
hoax *n.* podvala
hoax *v.t* podvaliti
hobby *n.* hobi
hobby-horse *n.* drveni konjić
hockey *n.* hokej
hoist *v.t.* dizati
hold *n.* držanje
hold *v.t* držati
hole *n* rupa
hole *v.t* probušiti
holiday *n.* odmor
hollow *a.* šupalj
hollow *n.* šupljina
hollow *v.t* izdupsti
holocaust *n.* holokaust
holy *a.* sveti
homage *n.* omaž
home *n.* dom
homicide *n.* ubojstvo
homoeopath *n.* homeopata
homeopathy *n.* homeopatija
homogeneous *a.* homogen
honest *a.* pošten
honesty *n.* poštenje
honey *n.* med
honeycomb *n.* saće

honeymoon *n.* medeni mjesec
honorarium *n.* honorar
honorary *a.* počasni
honour *n.* čast
honour *v. t* poštovati
honourable *a.* častan
hood *n.* hauba
hoodwink *v.t.* prevariti
hoof *n.* kopito
hook *n.* kuka
hooligan *n.* huligan
hoot *n.* trubljenje
hoot *v.i* trubiti
hop *v. i* skočiti
hop *n* skakanje
hope *v.t.* nadati se
hope *n* nada
hopeful *a.* pun nade
hopeless *a.* beznadežan
horde *n.* horda
horizon *n.* horizont
horn *n.* rog
hornet *n.* stršljen
horrible *a.* strašan
horrify *v.t.* zaprepastiti
horror *n.* užas
horse *n.* konj
horticulture *n.* hortikultura
hose *n.* crijevo
hosiery *n.* čarape
hospitable *a.* gostoprimljiv
hospital *n.* bolnica
hospitality *n.* gostoprimstvo
host *n.* domaćin
hostage *n.* talac
hostel *n.* hostel
hostile *a.* neprijateljski
hostility *n.* neprijateljstvo
hot *a.* vreo
hotchpotch *n.* papazjanija

hotel *n.* hotel
hound *n.* lovački pas
hour *n.* sat
house *n* kuća
house *v.t* smjestiti
how *adv.* kako
however *adv.* ma kako
however *conj* ipak
howl *v.t.* zavijati
howl *n* zavijanje
hub *n.* čvor
hubbub *n.* graja
huge *a.* ogroman
hum *v. i* zujati
hum *n* zujanje
human *a.* čovek
humane *a.* human
humanitarian *a* humanitarno
humanity *n.* čovječanstvo
humanize *v.t.* počovječiti
humble *a.* skroman
humdrum *a.* jednoličan
humid *a.* vlažan
humidity *n.* vlažnost
humiliate *v.t.* poniziti
humiliation *n.* poni* ponižavanje
humility *n.* poniznost
humorist *n.* humorista
humorous *a.* humorističan
humour *n.* humor
hunch *n.* slutnja
hundred *n.* sto
hunger *n* glad
hungry *a.* gladan
hunt *v.t.* loviti
hunt *n* lov
hunter *n.* lovac
huntsman *n.* lovac
hurdle1 *n.* ograda
hurdle2 *v.t* ograditi

hurl *v.t.* baciti
hurrah *interj.* ura
hurricane *n.* uragan
hurry *v.t.* žuriti
hurry *n* žurba
hurt *v.t.* povrijediti
hurt *n* povreda
husband *n* muž
husbandry *n.* ratarstvo
hush *n* tišina
hush *v.i* utišati
husk *n.* ljuska
husky *a.* hrapav
hut *n.* koliba
hyaena, hyena *n.* hijena
hybrid *a.* hibridan
hybrid *n* hibrid
hydrogen *n.* vodik
hygiene *n.* higijena
hygienic *a.* higijenski
hymn *n.* himna
hyperbole *n.* hiperbola
hypnotism *n.* hipnotizam
hypnotize *v.t.* hipnotisati
hypocrisy *n.* licemerje
hypocrite *n.* licemjer
hypocritical *a.* licemjeran
hypothesis *n.* hipoteza
hypothetical *a.* hipotetički
hysteria *n.* histerija
hysterical *a.* histeričan

I

I *pron.* ja
ice *n.* led
iceberg *n.* santa leda
icicle *n.* ledenica

icy *a.* leden
idea *n.* ideja
ideal *a.* idealan
ideal *n* ideal
idealism *n.* idealizam
idealist *n.* idealista
idealistic *a.* idealistički
idealize *v.t.* idealizirati
identical *a.* identičan
indentification *n.* identifikacija
identify *v.t.* identifikovati
identity *n.* identitet
ideocy *n.* idiotizam
idiom *n.* idiom
idiomatic *a.* idiomatski
idiot *n.* idiot
idiotic *a.* idiotski
idle *a.* besposlen
idleness *n.* besposlica
idler *n.* besposličar
idol *n.* idol
idolater *n.* obožavalac
if *conj.* ako
ignoble *a.* koji nije plemenit
ignorance *n.* neznanje
ignorant *a.* neobrazovan
ignore *v.t.* ignorirati
ill *a.* bolestan
ill *adv.* loše
ill *n* nevolja
illegal *a.* nezakonit
illegibility *n.* nečitkost
illegible *a.* nečitak
illegitimate *a.* nezakonit
illicit *a.* protuzakonit
illiteracy *n.* nepismenost
illiterate *a.* nepismen
illness *n.* bolest
illogical *a.* nelogičan
illuminate *v.t.* osvijetliti

illumination *n.* osvijetljenje
illusion *n.* iluzija
illustrate *v.t.* ilustrirati
illustration *n.* ilustracija
image *n.* slika
imagery *n.* slikovito izlaganje
imaginary *a.* izmišljen
imagination *n.* mašta
imaginative *a.* maštovit
imagine *v.t.* zamisliti
imitate *v.t.* imitirati
imitation *n.* imitacija
imitator *n.* imitator
immaterial *a.* nematerijalni
immature *a.* nezreo
immaturity *n.* nezrelost
immeasurable *a.* nemjerljiv
immediate *a* neposredan
immemorial *a.* prastari
immense *a.* ogroman
immensity *n.* beskrajnost
immerse *v.t.* utonuti
immersion *n.* potapanje
immigrant *n.* imigrant
immigrate *v.i.* imigrirati
immigration *n.* imigracija
imminent *a.* predstojeći
immodest *a.* neskroman
immodesty *n.* neskromnost
immoral *a.* nemoralan
immorality *n.* nemoralnost
immortal *a.* besmrtan
immortality *n.* besmrtnost
immortalize *v.t.* obesmrtiti
immovable *a.* nepokretan
immune *a.* imun
immunity *n.* imunitet
immunize *v.t.* učiniti imunim
impact *n.* udar
impart *v.t.* priopćiti

impartial *a.* nepristran
impartiality *n.* nepristranost
impassable *a.* neprohodan
impasse *n.* ćorsokak
impatience *n.* nestrpljenje
impatient *a.* nestrpljiv
impeach *v.t.* okriviti
impeachment *n.* optužba
impede *v.t.* ometati
impediment *n.* prepreka
impenetrable *a.* neprobojan
imperative *a.* imperativ
imperfect *a.* nesavršen
imperfection *n.* nesavršenost
imperial *a.* carski
imperialism *n.* imperijalizam
imperil *v.t.* ugroziti
imperishable *a.* neprolazan
impersonal *a.* bezličan
impersonate *v.t.* oličavati
impersonation *n.* predstavljanje
impertinence *n.* drskost
impertinent *a.* drzak
impetuosity *n.* plahovitost
impetuous *a.* nagao
implement *n.* implementacija
implement *v.t.* implementirati
implicate *v.t.* obuhvatati
implication *n.* implikacija
implicit *a.* indirektan
implore *v.t.* preklinjati
imply *v.t.* podrazumijevati
impolite *a.* neljubazan
import *v.t.* uvoziti
import *n.* uvoz
importance *n.* značaj
important *a.* važno
impose *v.t.* nametati
imposing *a.* impozantan
imposition *n.* nametanje

72

impossibility *n.* nemogućnost
impossible *a.* nemoguć
impostor *n.* varalica
imposture *n.* podvala
impotence *n.* impotencija
impotent *a.* impotentan
impoverish *v.t.* osiromašiti
impracticability *n.* neizvodljivost
impracticable *a.* neizvršiv
impress *v.t.* impresionirati
impression *n.* dojam
impressive *a.* impresivan
imprint *v.t.* utisnuti
imprint *n.* otisak
imprison *v.t.* uhapsiti
improper *a.* nepriklada n
impropriety *n.* neprikladnost
improve *v.t.* poboljšati
improvement *n.* poboljšanje
imprudence *n.* nesmotrenost
imprudent *a.* nepromišljen
impulse *n.* impuls
impulsive *a.* impulsivan
impunity *n.* nekažnjivost
impure *a.* nečist
impurity *n.* nečistoća
impute *v.t.* pripisati
in *prep.* u
inability *n.* nesposobnost
inaccurate *a.* netočan
inaction *n.* neaktivnost
inactive *a.* neaktivan
inadmissible *a.* nedopustiv
inanimate *a.* neživ
inapplicable *a.* neprimjenjiv
inattentive *a.* nepažljiv
inaudible *a.* nečujan
inaugural *a.* uvodni
inauguration *n.* inauguracija
inauspicious *a.* zlokoban

inborn *a.* urođen
incalculable *a.* neizračunljiv
incapable *a.* nesposoban
incapacity *n.* nesposobnost
incarnate *a.* utjelovljen
incarnate *v.t.* ovaplotiti
incarnation *n.* ovaploćenje
incense *v.t.* kaditi tamjanom
incense *n.* tamjan
incentive *n.* poticaj
inception *n.* početak
inch *n.* inč
incident *n.* incident
incidental *a.* slučajan
incite *v.t.* huškati
inclination *n.* sklonost
incline *v.i.* nagnuti se
include *v.t.* uključivati
inclusion *n.* uključivanje
inclusive *a.* uključivo
incoherent *a.* nepovezan
income *n.* prihod
incomparable *a.* neuporediv
incompetent *a.* nesposoban
incomplete *a.* nepotpun
inconsiderate *a.* nepromišljen
inconvenient *a.* nepriklada n
incorporate *v.t.* priključiti
incorporate *a.* uključen
incorporation *n.* priključenje
incorrect *a.* netočan
incorrigible *a.* nepopravljiv
incorruptible *a.* nepodmitljiv
increase *v.t.* porasti
increase *n* porast
incredible *a.* nevjerojatan
increment *n.* priraštaj
incriminate *v.t.* okriviti
incubate *v.i.* izleći
inculcate *v.t.* utuviti

incumbent n. koji je obavezan
incumbent a obavezan
incur v.t. natovariti
incurable a. neizlječiv
indebted a. zadužen
indecency n. nepristojnost
indecent a. nepristojan
indecision n. neodlučnost
indeed adv. zaista
indefensible a. neodbranjiv
indefinite a. neodređen
indemnity n. odšteta
independence n. neovisnost
independent a. neovisan
indescribable a. neopisiv
index n. indeks
Indian a. indijski
indicate v.t. ukazati
indication n. indikacija
indicative a. indikativan
indicator n. indikator
indict v.t. optužiti
indictment n. optužnica
indifference n. ravnodušnost
indifferent a. ravnodušan
indigenous a. urođenički
indigestible a. neprobavljiv
indigestion n. loše varenje
indignant a. ozlojeđen
indignation n. ozlojeđenost
indigo n. indigo
indirect a. indirektan
indiscipline n. nedisciplina
indiscreet a. indiskretan
indiscretion n. indiskrecija
indiscriminate a. nekritički
indispensable a. neophodan
indisposed a. neraspoložen
indisputable a. neosporan
indistinct a. nejasan

individual a. pojedinačni
individualism n. individualizam
individuality n. individualnost
indivisible a. nedjeljiv
indolent a. lijen
indomitable a. nesavladiv
indoor a. unutarnji
indoors adv. unutra
induce v.t. navesti
inducement n. navođenje
induct v.t. uvesti
induction n. uvođenje
indulge v.t. ugađati
indulgence n. ugađanje
indulgent a. popustljiv
industrial a. industrijski
industrious a. vrijedan
industry n. industrija
ineffective a. neefikasan
inert a. inertan
inertia n. inercija
inevitable a. neizbježan
inexact a. netočan
inexorable a. neumoljiv
inexpensive a. jeftin
inexperience n. neiskustvo
inexplicable a. neobjašnjiv
infallible a. nepogrešiv
infamous a. ozloglašen
infamy n. sramota
infancy n. rano djetinjstvo
infant n. dojenče
infanticide n. čedomorstvo
infantile a. infantilan
infantry n. pješadija
infatuate v.t. zaluđivati
infatuation n. zaslijepljenost
infect v.t. inficirati
infection n. infekcija
infectious a. zarazan

infer *v.t.* zaključiti
inference *n.* zaključivanje
inferior *a.* inferioran
inferiority *n.* inferiornost
infernal *a.* paklen
infinite *a.* beskonačan
infinity *n.* beskonačnost
infirm *a.* slab
infirmity *n.* nemoć
inflame *v.t.* raspaliti
inflammable *a.* zapaljiv
inflammation *n.* zapaljenje
inflammatory *a.* raspaljiv
inflation *n.* inflacija
inflexible *a.* nefleksibilan
inflict *v.t.* nanijeti
influence *n.* uticaj
influence *v.t.* utjecaj
influential *a.* utjecati
influenza *n.* grip
influx *n.* priliv
inform *v.t.* obavijestiti
informal *a.* neformalan
information *n.* informacija
informative *a.* informativan
informer *n.* izvjestitelj
infringe *v.t.* narušiti
infringement *n.* narušivanje
infuriate *v.t.* razbjesneti
infuse *v.t.* uliti
infusion *n.* infuzija
ingrained *a.* ukorijenjen
ingratitude *n.* nezahvalnost
ingredient *n.* sastojak
inhabit *v.t.* nastaniti
inhabitable *a.* naseljiv
inhabitant *n.* stanovnik
inhale *v.i.* udisati
inherent *a.* inherentan
inherit *v.t.* naslijediti

inheritance *n.* nasljeđe
inhibit *v.t.* inhibirati
inhibition *n.* inhibicija
inhospitable *a.* negostoljubiv
inhuman *a.* nehuman
inimical *a.* neprijateljski
inimitable *a.* jedinstven
initial *a.* početni
initial *n.* inicijal
initial *v.t* obilježiti inicijalima
initiate *v.t.* započeti
initiative *n.* inicijativa
inject *v.t.* ubrizgati
injection *n.* ubrizgavanje
injudicious *a.* nerazborit
injunction *n.* sudski nalog
injure *v.t.* povrijediti
injurious *a.* štetan
injury *n.* povreda
injustice *n.* nepravda
ink *n.* mastilo
inkling *n.* nagoveštaj
inland *a.* u unutrašnjosti
inland *adv.* unutarnji
in-laws *n.* srodnik
inmate *n.* stanar
inmost *a.* najskriveniji
inn *n.* krčma
innate *a.* urođen
inner *a.* unutarnji
innermost *a.* u samoj unutrašnjosti
innings *n.* razdoblje
innocence *n.* nevinost
innocent *a.* nevin
innovate *v.t.* inovirati
innovation *n.* inovacija
innovator *n.* inovator
innumerable *a.* bezbrojan
inoculate *v.t.* kalemiti
inoculation *n.* kalemljenje

inoperative *a.* nedjelotvoran
inopportune *a.* u krivi čas
input *n.* ulazni
inquest *n.* istraga
inquire *v.t.* raspitati se
inquiry *n.* ispitivanje
inquisition *n.* inkvizicija
inquisitive *a.* radoznao
insane *a.* lud
insanity *n.* ludilo
insatiable *a.* nezasit
inscribe *v.t.* upisati
inscription *n.* natpis
insect *n.* insekt
insecticide *n.* insekticid
insecure *a.* nesiguran
insecurity *n.* nesigurnost
insensibility *n.* neosjetljivost
insensible *a.* neosjetljiv
inseparable *a.* neodvojiv
insert *v.t.* umetnuti
insertion *n.* umetanje
inside *n.* unutrašnjost
inside *prep.* unutar
inside *a* unutrašnji
inside *adv.* unutra
insight *n.* uvid
insignificance *n.* beznačajnost
insignificant *a.* beznačajan
insincere *a.* neiskren
insincerity *n.* neiskrenost
insinuate *v.t.* insinuirati
insinuation *n.* insinuacija
insipid *a.* bljutav
insipidity *n.* bljutavost
insist *v.t.* insistirati
insistence *n.* insistiranje
insistent *a.* uporan
insolence *n.* bezobrazluk
insolent *a.* drzak

insoluble *n.* nerastvoriv
insolvency *n.* insolventnost
insolvent *a.* insolventan
inspect *v.t.* pregledati
inspection *n.* inspekcija
inspector *n.* inspektor
inspiration *n.* inspiracija
inspire *v.t.* inspirisati
instability *n.* nestabilnost
install *v.t.* instalirati
installation *n.* instalacija
instalment *n.* otplata
instance *n.* primjer
instant *n.* trenutak
instant *a.* trenutni
instantaneous *a.* istovremen
instantly *adv.* odmah
instigate *v.t.* podstaći
instigation *n.* podstrekivanje
instil *v.t.* ulijevati
instinct *n.* instinkt
instinctive *a.* instinktivan
institute *n.* institut
institution *n.* institucija
instruct *v.t.* narediti
instruction *n.* instrukcija
instructor *n.* instruktor
instrument *n.* instrument
instrumental *a.* instrumentalni
instrumentalist *n.* instrumentalista
insubordinate *a.* neposlušan
insubordination *n.* neposlušnost
insufficient *a.* nedovoljan
insular *a.* otočni
insularity *n.* ograničenost
insulate *v.t.* izolirati
insulation *n.* izolacija
insulator *n.* izolator
insult *n.* uvreda
insult *v.t.* uvrijediti

insupportable a. nesnosan
insurance n. osiguranje
insure v.t. osigurati
insurgent a. buntovnički
insurgent n. buntovnik
insurmountable a. nepremostiv
insurrection n. pobuna
intact a. netaknut
intangible a. neopipljiv
integral a. integralan
integrity n. integritet
intellect n. intelekt
intellectual a. intelektualni
intellectual n. intelektualac
intelligence n. inteligencija
intelligent a. inteligentan
intelligentsia n. inteligencija
intelligible a. shvatljiv
intend v.t. namjeravati
intense a. napregnut
intensify v.t. pojačati
intensity n. intenzitet
intensive a. intenzivan
intent n. napet
intent a. namjerni
intention n. namjera
intentional a. namjeran
intercept v.t. presresti
interception n. presretanje
interchange n. razmjena
interchange v. razmijeniti
intercourse n. odnos
interdependence n. međuzavisnost
interdependent a. međuzavisan
interest n. interes
interested a. zainteresiran
interesting a. zanimljiv
interfere v.i. uplitati se
interference n. uplitanje
interim n. međuvrijeme

interior a. unutrašnji
interior n. unutrašnjost
interjection n. uzvik
interlock v.t. spojiti se
interlude n. interludij
intermediary n. posrednik
intermediate a. srednji
interminable a. beskrajan
intermingle v.t. pomiješati
intern v.t. stažirati
internal a. interni
international a. internacionalni
interplay n. uzajamno djelovanje
interpret v.t. protumačiti
interpreter n. prevodilac
interrogate v.t. saslušavati
interrogation n. saslušavanje
interrogative a. upitni
interrogative n upitnik
interrupt v.t. prekinuti
interruption n. prekid
intersect v.t. seći
intersection n. raskrsnica
interval n. interval
intervene v.i. intervenirati
intervention n. intervencija
interview n. intervju
interview v.t. intervjuirati
intestinal a. crijevni
intestine n. crijevo
intimacy n. intimnost
intimate a. intiman
intimate v.t. nagovijestiti
intimation n. nagovještaj
intimidate v.t. zastrašiti
intimidation n. zastrašivanje
into prep. u
intolerable a. nepodnošljiv
intolerance n. nepodnošljivost
intolerant a. netolerantan

intoxicant *n.* opojno sredstvo
intoxicate *v.t.* otrovati
intoxication *n.* intoksikacija
intransitive *a.* neprelazni
interpid *a.* neustrašiv
intrepidity *n.* neustrašivost
intricate *a.* zapetljan
intrigue *v.t.* intrigirati
intrigue *n* intriga
intrinsic *a.* unutarnji
introduce *v.t.* uvesti
introduction *n.* uvod
introductory *a.* uvodni
introspect *v.i.* preispitivati se
introspection *n.* samoispitivanje
intrude *v.t.* upasti
intrusion *n.* upad
intuition *n.* intuicija
intuitive *a.* intuitivan
invade *v.t.* napasti
invalid *a.* nevažeći
invalid *a.* onesposobljen
invalid *n* invalid
invalidate *v.t.* poništiti
invaluable *a.* neprocjenjiv
invasion *n.* invazija
invective *n.* grdnja
invent *v.t.* izumiti
invention *n.* pronalazak
inventive *a.* pronalazački
inventor *n.* pronalazač
invert *v.t.* obrnuti
invest *v.t.* investirati
investigate *v.t.* istražiti
investigation *n.* istraga
investment *n.* investicija
invigilate *v.t.* nadzirati
invigilation *n.* nadgledanje
invigilator *n.* nadzornik
invincible *a.* nepobjediv

inviolable *a.* neprikosnoven
invisible *a.* nevidljiv
invitation *v.* poziv
invite *v.t.* pozvati
invocation *n.* prizivanje
invoice *n.* faktura
invoke *v.t.* prizivati
involve *v.t.* uključiti
inward *a.* unutarnji
inwards *adv.* unutra
irate *a.* srdit
ire *n.* ljutnja
Irish *a.* Irski
Irish *n.* irski jezik, Irac
irksome *a.* zamoran
iron *n.* željezo
iron *v.t.* okovati
ironical *a.* ironičan
irony *n.* ironija
irradiate *v.i.* ozračiti
irrational *a.* iracionalan
irreconcilable *a.* nepomirljiv
irrecoverable *a.* nepovrativ
irrefutable *a.* nepobitan
irregular *a.* nepravilan
irregularity *n.* nepravilnost
irrelevant *a.* nebitan
irrespective *a.* bez obzira na
irresponsible *a.* neodgovoran
irrigate *v.t.* navodnjavati
irrigation *n.* navodnjavanje
irritable *a.* razdražljiv
irritant *a.* koji draži
irritant *n.* iritiranje
irritate *v.t.* dražiti
irritation *n.* iritacija
irruption *n.* provala
island *n.* otok
isle *n.* otok
isobar *n.* izobara

isolate *v.t.* izolirati
isolation *n.* izolacija
issue *v.i.* izadati
issue *n.* pitanje
it *pron.* to
Italian *a.* Talijanski
Italian *n.* talijanski jezik, Talijan
italic *a.* kurzivan
italics *n.* kurziv
itch *n.* svrab
itch *v.i.* svrbeti
item *n.* stavka
ivory *n.* slonovača
ivy *n* bršljan

J

jab *v.t.* probosti
jabber *v.t.* blebetati
jack *n.* utičnica
jack *v.t.* utaknuti
jackal *n.* šakal
jacket *n.* jakna
jade *n.* žad
jail *n.* zatvor
jailer *n.* tamničar
jam *n.* džem
jam *v.t.* zakucati
jar *n.* tegla
jargon *n.* žargon
jasmine, jessamine *n.* jasmin
jaundice *n.* žutica
jaundice *v.t.* izazvati žuticu
javelin *n.* koplje
jaw *n.* vilica
jay *n.* sojka
jealous *a.* ljubomoran
jealousy *n.* ljubomora
jean *n.* jaka pamučna tkanina

jeer *v.i.* rugati se
jelly *n.* žele
jeopardize *v.t.* ugroziti
jeopardy *n.* opasnost
jerk *n.* trzaj
jerkin *n.* kožuh
jerky *a.* grčevit
jersey *n.* dres
jest *n.* šala
jest *v.i.* šaliti se
jet *n.* mlaznjak
Jew *n.* Židov
jewel *n.* dragulj
jewel *v.t.* ukrasiti draguljima
jeweller *n.* juvelir
jewellery *n.* nakit
jingle *n.* zveckanje
jingle *v.i.* zveckati
job *n.* posao
jobber *n.* nadničar
jobbery *n.* korupcija
jocular *a.* duhovit
jog *v.t.* džogirati
join *v.t.* pridružiti
joiner *n.* stolar
joint *n.* članak
jointly *adv.* zajedničko
joke *n.* vic
joke *v.i.* zbijati šalu
joker *n.* džoker
jollity *n.* veselje
jolly *a.* radostan
jolt *n.* drmusanje
jolt *v.t.* drmati
jostle *n.* udarac
jostle *v.t.* udariti o
jot *n.* sitnica
jot *v.t.* zabilježiti
journal *n.* časopis
journalism *n.* novinarstvo

journalist *n.* novinar
journey *n.* putovanje
journey *v.i.* putovati
jovial *a.* veseo
joviality *n.* veselost
joy *n.* radost
joyful, joyous *n.* radostan
jubilant *a.* ushićen
jubilation *n.* slavlje
jubilee *n.* jubilej
judge *n.* sudac
judge *v.i.* suditi
judgement *n.* presuda
judicature *n.* pravosuđe
judicial *a.* sudski
judiciary *n.* sudstvo
judicious *a.* razborit
jug *n.* krčag
juggle *v.t.* žonglirati
juggler *n.* žongler
juice *n* sok
juicy *a.* sočan
jumble *n.* zbrka
jumble *v.t.* zbrkati
jump *n.* skok
jump *v.i* skočiti
junction *n.* raskrsnica
juncture *n.* spoj
jungle *n.* džungla
junior *a.* mlađi
junior *n.* junior
junk *n.* đubre
jupiter *n.* jupiter
jurisdiction *n.* nadležnost
jurisprudence *n.* jurisprudencija
jurist *n.* pravnik
juror *n.* porotnik
jury *n.* porota
juryman *n.* porotnik
just *a.* pravedan

just *adv.* upravo
justice *n.* pravda
justifiable *a.* opravdan
justification *n.* opravdanje
justify *v.t.* opravdati
justly *adv.* pravedno
jute *n.* juta
juvenile *a.* maloljetnik

K

keen *a.* bodar
keenness *n.* bodrost
keep *v.t.* držati
keeper *n.* čuvar
keepsake *n.* uspomena
kennel *n.* štenara
kerchief *n.* marama
kernel *n.* koštica
kerosene *n.* kerozin
ketchup *n.* kečap
kettle *n.* čajnik
key *n.* ključ
key *v.t* pričvrstiti
kick *n.* šut
kick *v.t.* šutirati
kid *n.* dijete
kidnap *v.t.* kidnapovati
kidney *n.* bubreg
kill *v.t.* ubiti
kill *n.* ubijanje
kiln *n.* sušara
kin *n.* rodbina
kind *n.* vrsta
kind *a* prijatan
kindergarten *n.* obdanište
kindle *v.t.* potpaliti
kindly *adv.* ljubazno
king *n.* kralj

kingdom *n.* kraljevina
kinship *n.* srodstvo
kiss *n.* poljubac
kiss *v.t.* poljubiti
kit *n.* oprema
kitchen *n.* kuhinja
kite *n.* zmaj
kith *n.* poznanici
kitten *n.* mačić
knave *n.* podlac
knavery *n.* podlost
knee *n.* koljeno
kneel *v.i.* klečati
knife *n.* nož
knight *n.* vitez
knight *v.t.* učiniti vitezom
knit *v.t.* plesti
knock *v.t.* kucati
knot *n.* čvor
knot *v.t.* vezati
know *v.t.* znati
knowledge *n.* znanje

L

label *n.* etiketa
label *v.t.* etiketirati
labial *a.* labijalni
laboratory *n.* laboratorija
laborious *a.* mučan
labour *n.* rad
labour *v.i.* raditi
laboured *a.* naporan
labourer *n.* radnik
labyrinth *n.* labirint
lac, lakh *n* lak
lace *n.* čipka
lace *v.t.* vezati
lacerate *v.t.* rastrgnuti

lachrymose *a.* plačljiv
lack *n.* nedostatak
lack *v.t.* nedostajati
lackey *n.* lakej
lacklustre *a.* mutan
laconic *a.* lakonski
lactate *v.i.* dojiti
lactometer *n.* mlekomer
lactose *n.* laktoza
lacuna *n.* praznina
lacy *a.* čipkast
lad *n.* momak
ladder *n.* ljestve
lade *v.t.* natovariti
ladle *n.* kutlača
ladle *v.t.* crpsti
lady *n.* dama
lag *v.i.* uhapsiti
laggard *n.* trom
lagoon *n.* laguna
lair *n.* jazbina
lake *n.* jezero
lama *n.* lama
lamb *n.* jagnje
lambaste *v.t.* izgrditi
lame *a.* krom
lame *v.t.* osakatiti
lament *v.i.* oplakivati
lament *n* oplakivanje
lamentable *a.* žalostan
lamentation *n.* naricanje
lambkin *n.* jagnješce
laminate *v.t.* spljoštiti
lamp *n.* lampa
lampoon *n.* satira
lampoon *v.t.* izrugivati se
lance *n.* koplje
lance *v.t.* ubosti
lancer *n.* kopljanik
lancet *a.* lanceta

land *n.* zemljište
land *v.i.* iskrcati
landing *n.* pristajanje
landscape *n.* pejzaž
lane *n.* sokak
language *n.* jezik
languish *v.i.* čeznuti
lank *a.* mršav
lantern *n.* fenjer
lap *n.* skut
lapse *v.i.* propustiti
lapse *n* propust
lard *n.* salo
large *a.* velik
largesse *n.* darežljivost
lark *n.* ševa
lascivious *a.* lascivan
lash *a.* bičevan
lash *n* udarac bičem
lass *n.* draga
last1 *a.* poslednji
last *adv.* najzad
last *v.i.* trajati
last *n* izdržljivost
lastly *adv.* na kraju
lasting *a.* trajan
latch *n.* kvaka
late *a.* kasno
late *adv.* nedavno
lately *adv.* u posljednje vrijeme
latent *a.* prikriven
lath *n.* letva
lathe *n.* strug
lathe *n.* čekrk
lather *n.* pjena
latitude *n.* širina
latrine *n.* nužnik
latter *a.* kasniji
lattice *n.* rešetka
laud *v.t.* pohvaliti

laud *n* pohvala
laudable *a.* pohvalan
laugh *n.* smijanje
laugh *v.i* smijati se
laughable *a.* smiješan
laughter *n.* smijeh
launch *v.t.* lansirati
launch *n.* lansiranje
launder *v.t.* oprati
laundress *n.* pralja
laundry *n.* rublje
laurel *n.* lovor
laureate *a.* ovjenčan lovorom
laureate *n* laureat
lava *n.* lava
lavatory *n.* toalet
lavender *n.* lavanda
lavish *a.* raskošan
lavish *v.t.* obasipati
law *n.* zakon
lawful *a.* zakonit
lawless *a.* nezakonit
lawn *n.* travnjak
lawyer *n.* odvjetnik
lax *a.* labav
laxative *n.* laksativ
laxative *a* pročišćavajući
laxity *n.* labavost
lay *v.t.* položiti
lay *a.* nestručan
lay *n* smjer
layer *n.* sloj
layman *n.* laik
laze *v.i.* dangubiti
laziness *n.* lijenost
lazy *n.* lijen
lea *n.* ledina
leach *v.t.* navlažiti
lead *n.* olovo
lead *v.t.* plombirati

lead *n.* visak
leaden *a.* olovni
leader *n.* vođa
leadership *n.* vođstvo
leaf *n.* list
leaflet *n.* letak
leafy *a.* lisnat
league *n.* liga
leak *n.* curenje
leak *v.i.* curiti
leakage *n.* curenje
lean *n.* mršavo
lean *v.i.* nasloniti
leap *v.i.* skočiti
leap *n* skok
learn *v.i.* naučiti
learned *a.* učen
learner *n.* učenik
learning *n.* učenje
lease *n.* zakup
lease *v.t.* zakupiti
least *a.* najmanji
least *adv.* najmanje
leather *n.* koža
leave *n.* dopuštenje
leave *v.t.* ostaviti
lecture *n.* predavanje
lecture *v* predavati
lecturer *n.* predavač
ledger *n.* glavna knjiga
lee *n.* zaklon
leech *n.* pijavica
leek *n.* praziluk
left *a.* lijevo
left *n.* ljevica
leftist *n* ljevičar
leg *n.* noga
legacy *n.* nasljeđe
legal *a.* pravni
legality *n.* zakonitost

legalize *v.t.* legalizovati
legend *n.* legenda
legendary *a.* legendaran
legible *a.* čitljiv
legibly *adv.* čitko
legion *n.* legija
legionary *n.* legionar
legislate *v.i.* donositi zakon
legislation *n.* donošenje zakona
legislative *a.* zakonodavan
legislator *n.* zakonodavac
legislature *n.* zakonodavstvo
legitimacy *n.* legitimitet
legitimate *a.* legitiman
leisure *n.* slobodno vrijeme
leisure *a* slobodan
leisurely *a.* ležerno
leisurely *adv.* lagano
lemon *n.* limun
lemonade *n.* limunada
lend *v.t.* posuditi
length *n.* duljina
lengthen *v.t.* produljiti
lengthy *a.* podugačak
lenience, leniency *n.* popustljivost
lenient *a.* popustljiv
lens *n.* objektiv
lentil *n.* leća
Leo *n.* lav
leonine *a* lavovski
leopard *n.* leopard
leper *n.* gubavac
leprosy *n.* lepra
leprous *a.* gubav
less *a.* manji
less *n* ono što je manje
less *adv.* manje
less *prep.* manje
lessee *n.* zakupac
lessen *v.t* smanjiti

lesser *a.* manji
lesson *n.* lekcija
lest *conj.* da ne bi
let *v.t.* dozvoliti
lethal *a.* smrtonosan
lethargic *a.* letargičan
lethargy *n.* letargija
letter *n* pismo
level *n.* razina
level *a* izjednačen
level *v.t.* izjednačiti
lever *n.* poluga
lever *v.t.* služiti se polugom
leverage *n.* moć
levity *n.* lakomislenost
levy *v.t.* nametnuti
levy *n.* nametanje
lewd *a.* razvratan
lexicography *n.* leksikografija
lexicon *n.* leksikon
liability *n.* odgovornost
liable *a.* odgovoran
liaison *n.* veza
liar *n.* lažov
libel *n.* kleveta
libel *v.t.* oklevetati
liberal *a.* liberalan
liberalism *n.* liberalizam
liberality *n.* velikodušnost
liberate *v.t.* osloboditi
liberation *n.* oslobođenje
liberator *n.* oslobodilac
libertine *n.* slobodoumnik
liberty *n.* sloboda
librarian *n.* bibliotekar
library *n.* biblioteka
licence *n.* dozvola
license *v.t.* dozvoliti
licensee *n.* onaj koji ima licencu
licentious *a.* raspojasan

lick *v.t.* lizati
lick *n* lizanje
lid *n.* poklopac
lie *v.i.* lagati
lie *v.i* ležati
lie *n* laž
lien *n.* pravo zaloge
lieu *n.* umjesto
lieutenant *n.* poručnik
life *n* život
lifeless *a.* beživotan
lifelong *a.* doživotni
lift *n.* podizanje
lift *v.t.* podizati
light *n.* svjetlo
light *a* lako
light *v.t.* osvijetliti
lighten *v.i.* olakšati
lighter *n.* upaljač
lightly *adv.* olako
lightening *n.* munja
lignite *n.* lignit
like *a.* sličan
like *n.* naklonost
like *v.t.* kao što
like *prep* poput
likelihood *n.* vjerojatnost
likely *a.* vjerojatno
liken *v.t.* porediti
likeness *n.* sličnost
likewise *adv.* također
liking *n.* dopadanje
lilac *n.* jorgovan
lily *n.* ljiljan
limb *n.* ud
limber *v.t.* pričvrstiti
limber *n* prednjak
lime *n.* limeta
lime *v.t* namazati
lime *n.* vapno

limelight *n.* centar pažnje
limit *n.* granica
limit *v.t.* ograničiti
limitation *n.* ograničenje
limited *a.* ograničen
limitless *a.* neograničen
line *n.* linija
line *v.t.* iscrtati
line *v.t.* poređati
lineage *n.* loza
linen *n.* platno
linger *v.i.* odugovlačiti
lingo *n.* žargon
lingua franca *n.* mješovit žargon
lingual *a.* jezični
linguist *n.* lingvista
linguistic *a.* jezički
linguistics *n.* lingvistika
lining *n* postava
link *n.* spona
link *v.t* spojiti
linseed *n.* laneno sjeme
lintel *n.* nadvratink
lion *n* lav
lioness *n.* lavica
lip *n.* usna
liquefy *v.t.* rastopiti
liquid *a.* tečan
liquid *n* tekućina
liquidate *v.t.* likvidirati
liquidation *n.* likvidacija
liquor *n.* alkoholno piće
lisp *v.t.* šuškati
lisp *n* šuškanje
list *n.* rub
list *v.t.* obrubiti
listen *v.i.* slušati
listener *n.* slušalac
listless *a.* trom
lists *n.* borilište

literacy *n.* pismenost
literal *a.* doslovan
literary *a.* književni
literate *a.* pismen
literature *n.* književnost
litigant *n.* parničar
litigate *v.t.* parničiti
litigation *n.* parničenje
litre *n.* litar
litter *n.* slama
litter *v.t.* pokriti slamom
litterateur *n.* literatura
little *a.* malen
little *adv.* malo
little *n.* ono što je malo
littoral *a.* primorski
liturgical *a.* liturgijski
live *v.i.* živjeti
live *a.* živ
livelihood *n.* izdržavanje
lively *a.* živo
liver *n.* jetra
livery *n.* livreja
living *a.* živahan
living *n* život
lizard *n.* gušter
load *n.* teret
load *v.t.* natovariti
loadstar *n.* zvijezda vodilja
loadstone *n.* magnet
loaf *n.* vekna
loaf *v.i.* dangubiti
loafer *n.* danguba
loan *n.* zajam
loan *v.t.* posuditi
loath *a.* nesklon
loathe *v.t.* prezirati
loathsome *a.* gnusan
lobby *n.* predsoblje
lobe *n.* ušna resa

lobster *n.* jastog
local *a.* lokalno
locale *n.* poprište
locality *n.* položaj
localize *v.t.* lokalizirati
locate *v.t.* locirati
location *n.* lokacija
lock *n.* brava
lock *v.t* zaključati
lock *n* uvojak
locker *n.* ormar
locket *n.* medaljon
locomotive *n.* lokomotiva
locus *n.* mjesto
locust *n.* skakavac
locution *n.* izraz
lodge *n.* kućica
lodge *v.t.* ukonačiti
lodging *n.* konačište
loft *n.* potkrovlje
lofty *a.* uzvišen
log *n.* zabilježiti
logarithim *n.* logaritam
loggerhead *n.* tikvan
logic *n.* logika
logical *a.* logičan
logician *n.* logičar
loin *n.* slabina
loiter *v.i.* tumarati
loll *v.i.* zavaliti se
lollipop *n.* lizalica
lone *a.* usamljen
loneliness *n.* usamljenost
lonely *a.* usamljen
lonesome *a.* usamljen
long *a.* dug
long *adv* dugo
long *v.i* čeznuti
longevity *n.* dugovječnost
longing *n.* čežnja

longitude *n.* duljina
look *v.i* gledati
look *a koji* izgleda
loom *n* razboj
loom *v.i.* nazirati se
loop *n.* petlja
loop-hole *n.* puškarnica
loose *a.* labav
loose *v.t.* odriješiti
loosen *v.t.* olabaviti
loot *n.* pljačka
loot *v.i.* pljačkati
lop *v.t.* rezati
lop *n.* obrezivanje
lord *n.* gospodar
lordly *a.* oholo
lordship *n.* gospodstvo
lore *n.* znanje
lorry *n.* kamion
lose *v.t.* izgubiti
loss *n.* gubitak
lot *n.* mnoštvo
lot *n* gradilište
lotion *n.* losion
lottery *n.* lutrija
lotus *n.* lotos
loud *a.* glasno
lounge *v.i.* šetkati se
lounge *n.* predvorje
louse *n.* vaška
lovable *a.* simpatičan
love *n* ljubav
love *v.t.* voleti
lovely *a.* divan
lover *n.* ljubavnik
loving *a.* voljen
low *a.* nizak
low *adv.* nisko
low *v.i.* mukati
low *n.* nizak položaj

lower *v.t.* niže
lowliness *n.* skromnost
lowly *a.* skroman
loyal *a.* lojalan
loyalist *n.* privrženik
loyalty *n.* lojalnost
lubricant *n.* mazivo
lubricate *v.t.* podmazati
lubrication *n.* podmazivanje
lucent *a.* svijetao
lucerne *n.* djetelina
lucid *a.* bistar
lucidity *n.* lucidnost
luck *n.* sreća
luckily *adv.* srećom
luckless *a.* nesretan
lucky *a.* srećan
lucrative *a.* unosan
lucre *n.* novac
luggage *n.* prtljag
lukewarm *a.* mlak
lull *v.t.* utišati
lull *n.* zatišje
lullaby *n.* uspavanka
luminary *n.* prosvjetitelj
luminous *a.* svjetleći
lump *n.* gruda
lump *v.t.* nagomilati
lunacy *n.* ludilo
lunar *a.* mjesečev
lunatic *n.* ludak
lunatic *a.* lud
lunch *n.* ručak
lunch *v.i.* ručati
lung *n* pluća
lunge *n.* zamah
lunge *v.i* baciti se
lurch *n.* trzaj
lurch *v.i.* zateturati se
lure *n.* mamac

lure *v.t.* namamiti
lurk *v.i.* vrebati
luscious *a.* sočan
lush *a.* bujan
lust *n.* požuda
lustful *a.* pohotan
lustre *n.* sjaj
lustrous *a.* sjajan
lusty *a.* sočan
lute *n.* lauta
luxuriance *n.* raskoš
luxuriant *a.* raskošan
luxurious *a.* luksuzan
luxury *n.* luksuz
lynch *v.t.* linč
lyre *n.* lira
lyric *a.* lirski
lyric *n.* lirika
lyrical *a.* lirski
lyricist *n.* liričar

M

magical *a.* magijski
magician *n.* mađioničar
magisterial *a.* mjerodavan
magistracy *n.* magistrat
magistrate *n.* sudac za prekršaje
magnanimity *n.* velikodušnost
magnanimous *a.* velikodušan
magnate *n.* magnat
magnet *n.* magnet
magnetic *a.* magnetski
magnetism *n.* magnetizam
magnificent *a.* veličanstven
magnify *v.t.* uveličati
magnitude *n.* veličina
magpie *n.* svraka
mahogany *n.* mahagoni

mahout n. čuvar slonova u Indiji
maid n. služavka
maiden n. djevojka
maiden a čedan
mail n. pošta
mail v.t. poslati poštom
mail n oklop
main a glavni
main n snaga
mainly adv. uglavnom
mainstay n. glavna potpora
maintain v.t. održavati
maintenance n. održavanje
maize n. kukuruz
majestic a. veličanstven
majesty n. veličanstvo
major a. glavni
major n major
majority n. većina
make v.t. napraviti
make n tvorevina
maker n. tvorac
maladjustment n. neprilagodljivost
maladministration n. loše poslovanje
malady n. bolest
malaria n. malarija
maladroit a. nespretan
malaise n. slabost
malcontent a. nezadovoljan
malcontent n nezadovoljstvo
male a. muški
male n muški rod
malediction n. prokletstvo
malefactor n. zločinac
maleficent a. škodljiv
malice n. zloba
malicious a. zlonamjeran
malign v.t. klevetati
malign a poguban
malignancy n. opakost

malignant a. zao
malignity n. malignitet
malleable a. prilagodljiv
malmsey n. malvazija
malnutrition n. neuhranjenost
malpractice n. pogrešno liječenje
malt n. slad
mal-treatment n. zlostavljanje
mamma n. vime
mammal n. sisar
mammary a. mliječni
mammon n. mamon
mammoth n. mamut
mammoth a ogroman
man n. čovjek
man v.t. osokoliti
manage v.t. upravljati
manageable a. izvediv
management n. upravljanje
manager n. menadžer
managerial a. menadžerski
mandate n. mandat
mandatory a. obavezan
mane n. griva
manes n. duše pokojnika
manful a. hrabar
manganese n. mangan
manger n. jasle
mangle v.t. valjati rublje
mango n mango
manhandle v.t. maltertirati
manhole n. šaht
manhood n. muškost
mania n manija
maniac n. manijak
manicure n. manikur
manifest a. očevidan
manifest v.t. manifestirati
manifestation n. manifestacija
manifesto n. manifest

manifold a. mnogostruk
manipulate v.t. manipulirati
manipulation n. manipulacija
mankind n. čovječanstvo
manlike a. muževan
manliness n muškost
manly a. muški
manna n. mana
mannequin n. maneken
manner n. način
mannerism n. manirizam
mannerly a. učtiv
manoeuvre n. manevar
manoeuvre v.i. manevrirati
manor n. vlastelinstvo
manorial a. vlastelinski
mansion n. palača
mantel n. okvir kamina
mantle n omotač
mantle v.t pokriti
manual a. ručno
manual n priručnik
manufacture v.t. proizvoditi
manufacture n proizvodnja
manufacturer n proizvođač
manumission n. oslobađanje roba
manumit v.t. osloboditi ropstva
manure n. đubrivo
manure v.t. đubriti
manuscript n. rukopis
many a. mnogo
map n mapa
map v.t. ucrtati
mar v.t. pokvariti
marathon n. maraton
maraud v.i. pljačkati
marauder n. pljačkaš
marble n. mermer
march n ožujak
march n. marš

march v.i marširati
mare n. kobila
margarine n. margarin
margin n. margina
marginal a. marginalni
marigold n. neven
marine a. morski
mariner n. mornar
marionette n. marioneta
marital a. bračni
maritime a. pomorski
mark n. znak
mark v.t označiti
marker n. marker
market n tržište
market v.t trgovati
marketable a. koji se može prodati
marksman n. strijelac
marl n. lapor
marmalade n. marmelada
maroon n. kestenjasta boja
maroon a kestenjast
maroon v.t lutati
marriage n. brak
marriageable a. sposoban za brak
marry v.t. udati
Mars n mars
marsh n. močvara
marshal n maršal
marshal v.t postrojiti
marshy a. močvaran
marsupial n. torbar
mart n. pijaca
marten n. kuna
martial a. vojni
martinet n. starješina
martyr n. mučenik
martyrdom n. mučeništvo
marvel n. čudo
marvel v.i čuditi se

89

marvellous *a.* veličanstven
mascot *n.* maskota
masculine *a.* muški
mash *n.* kaša
mash *v.t* gnječiti
mask *n.* maska
mask *v.t.* maskirati
mason *n.* zidar
masonry *n.* zidarstvo
masquerade *n.* maskarada
mass *n.* masa
mass *v.i* gomilati
massacre *n.* masakr
massacre *v.t.* masakrirati
massage *n.* masaža
massage *v.t.* masirati
masseur *n.* maser
massive *a.* masivan
massy *a.* krupan
mast *n.* jarbol
master *n.* gospodar
master *v.t.* savladati
masterly *a.* majstorski
masterpiece *n.* remek-djelo
mastery *n.* majstorstvo
masticate *v.t.* žvakati
masturbate *v.i.* masturbirati
mat *n.* otirač
matador *n.* matador
match *n.* meč
match *v.i.* odgovarati
match *n* šibica
matchless *a.* bez premca
mate *n.* prijatelj
mate *v.t.* pariti
mate *n* bračni drug
mate *v.t.* matirati
material *a.* materijalan
material *n* materijal
materialism *n.* materijalizam

materialize *v.t.* materijalizovati
maternal *a.* materinski
maternity *n.* materinstvo
mathematical *a.* matematički
mathematician *n.* matematičar
mathematics *n* matematika
matinee *n.* matine
matriarch *n.* matrijarh
matricidal *a.* materoubojstveni
matricide *n.* materoubojstvo
matriculate *v.t.* upisati visoku školu
matriculation *n.* matura
matrimonial *a.* bračni
matrimony *n.* brak
matrix *n* matrica
matron *n.* matrona
matter *n.* stvar
matter *v.i.* mariti
mattock *n.* pijuk
mattress *n.* madrac
mature *a.* zreo
mature *v.i* zreo
maturity *n.* zrelost
maudlin *a* preosjetljiv
maul *n.* malj
maul *v.t* izmlatiti
maulstick *n.* slikarev potporni štap
maunder *v.t.* tromo se kretati
mausoleum *n.* mauzolej
mawkish *a.* sladunjav
maxilla *n.* gornja vilica
maxim *n.* maksima
maximize *v.t.* maksimalno povećati
maximum *a.* maksimalni
maximum *n* maksimum
May *n.* svibanj
may *v* moći
mayor *n.* gradonačelnik
maze *n.* labirint
me *pron.* mene

mead *n.* medovina
meadow *n.* livada
meagre *a.* oskudan
meal *n.* obrok
mealy *a.* brašnjav
mean *a.* značiti
mean *n.* sredina
mean *v.t* značiti
meander *v.i.* meander
meaning *n.* značenje
meaningful *a.* značajan
meaningless *a.* beznačajan
meanness *n.* pakost
means *n* sredstvo
meanwhile *adv.* u međuvremenu
measles *n* male boginje
measurable *a.* mjerljiv
measure *n.* mjera
measure *v.t* mjeriti
measureless *a.* neizmjeran
measurement *n.* mjera
meat *n.* meso
mechanic *n.* mehaničar
mechanic *a* mehanički
mechanical *a.* strojno
mechanics *n.* mehanika
mechanism *n.* mehanizam
medal *n.* medalja
medallist *n.* nositelj medalje
meddle *v.i.* mešati se
medieval *a.* srednjovjekovni
medieval *a.* sredovječan
median *a.* srednji
mediate *v.i.* posredovati
mediation *n.* posredovanje
mediator *n.* posrednik
medical *a.* medicinski
medicament *n.* lijek
medicinal *a.* medicinski
medicine *n.* medicina

medico *n.* student medicine
mediocre *a.* osrednji
mediocrity *n.* osrednjost
meditate *v.t.* meditirati
mediation *n.* posredovanje
meditative *a.* refleksivan
medium *n* medij
medium *a* srednji
meek *a.* krotak
meet *n.* utakmica
meet *v.t.* sresti
meeting *n.* sastanak
megalith *n.* golem kamen
megalithic *a.* megalitski
megaphone *n.* megafon
melancholia *n.* melanholija
melancholic *a.* melanholičan
melancholy *n.* tuga
melancholy *adj* tužan
melee *n.* opšta tuča
meliorate *v.t.* poboljšati
mellow *a.* pripit
melodious *a.* melodičan
melodrama *n.* melodrama
melodramatic *a.* melodramatičan
melody *n.* melodija
melon *n.* dinja
melt *v.i.* rastopiti
member *n.* član
membership *n.* članstvo
membrane *n.* membrana
memento *n.* uspomena
memoir *n.* memoari
memorable *a.* nezaboravan
memorandum *n* memorandum
memorial *n.* komemoracija
memorial *a* komemorativan
memory *n.* memorija
menace *n* prijetnja
menace *v.t* prijetiti

mend v.t. popraviti
mendacious a. lažljiv
menial a. servilan
menial n sluga
meningitis n. meningitis
menopause n. menopauza
menses n. menzis
menstrual a. menstrualni
menstruation n. menstruacija
mental a. mentalni
mentality n. mentalitet
mention n. spominjanje
mention v.t. spominjati
mentor n. mentor
menu n. jelovnik
mercantile a. trgovački
mercenary a. plaćenički
mercerise v.t. mercerizirati
merchandise n. roba
merchant n. trgovac
merciful a. milostiv
merciless adj. nemilosrdan
mercurial a. živin
mercury n. merkur
mercy n. milost
mere a. puki
merge v.t. spojiti
merger n. udruživanje
meridian a. meridijan
merit n. zasluga
merit v.t zaslužiti
meritorious a. zaslužan
mermaid n. sirena
merman n. triton
merriment n. veselje
merry a veseo
mesh n. mreža
mesh v.t uhvatiti u mrežu
mesmerism n. hipnotizam
mesmerize v.t. hipnotizirati

mess n. nered
mess v.i pobrkati
message n. poruka
messenger n. kurir
messiah n. mesija
Messrs n. gospoda
metabolism n. metabolizam
metal n. metal
metallic a. metalni
metallurgy n. metalurgija
metamorphosis n. metamorfoza
metaphor n. metafora
metaphysical a. metafizički
metaphysics n. metafizika
mete v.t odmjeriti
meteor n. meteor
meteoric a. meteorski
meteorologist n. meteorolog
meteorology n. meteorologija
meter n. metar
method n. metod
methodical a. metodičan
metre n. metar
metric a. metrički
metrical a. metarski
metropolis n. metropola
metropolitan a. metropolitski
metropolitan n. metropolit
mettle n. temperament
mettlesome a. odvažan
mew v.i. mjaukati
mew n. galeb
mezzanine n. mezanin
mica n. tinjac
microfilm n. mikrofilm
micrology n. mikrologija
micrometer n. mikrometar
microphone n. mikrofon
microscope n. mikroskop
microscopic a. mikroskopski

microwave *n.* mikrovalna peć
mid *a.* srednji
midday *n.* podne
middle *a.* srednji
middle *n* sredina
middleman *n.* posrednik
middling *a.* osrednji
midget *n.* patuljak
midland *n.* unutrašnjost
midnight *n.* ponoć
mid-off *n.* pozicija u kriketu
mid-on *n.* pozicija u kriketu
midriff *n.* dijafragma
midst *n.* sredina
midsummer *n.* sredina ljeta
midwife *n.* babica
might *n.* moć
mighty *adj.* moćan
migraine *n.* migrena
migrant *n.* migrant
migrate *v.i.* migrirati
migration *n.* migracija
milch *a.* mliječni
mild *a.* blag
mildew *n.* plijesan
mile *n.* milja
mileage *n.* miljaža
milestone *n.* prekretnica
milieu *n.* ambijent
militant *a.* ratoboran
militant *n* militant
military *a.* vojni
military *n* vojska
militate *v.i.* ratovati
militia *n.* milicija
milk *n.* mlijeko
milk *v.t.* musti
milky *a.* mliječan
mill *n.* mlin
mill *v.t.* mljeti

millennium *n.* tisućljeće
miller *n.* mlinar
millet *n.* proso
milliner *n.* modiskinja
milliner *n.* modist
millinery *n.* radnja modistkinje
million *n.* milijun
millionaire *n.* milijuner
millipede *n.* stonoga
mime *n.* mimika
mime *v.i* izraziti mimikom
mimesis *n.* mimikrija
mimic *a.* imitirati
mimic *n* mimičar
mimic *v.t* imitirati
mimicry *n* mimikrija
minaret *n.* minaret
mince *v.t.* ublažiti
mind *n.* um
mind *v.t.* mariti
mindful *a.* pažljiv
mindless *a.* nepromišljen
mine *pron.* moj
mine *n* rudnik
miner *n.* rudar
mineral *n.* mineral
mineral *a* mineralni
mineralogist *n.* mineralog
mineralogy *n.* mineralogija
mingle *v.t.* miješati
miniature *n.* minijaturan
miniature *a.* minijatura
minim *n.* kapljica
minimal *a.* minimalan
minimize *v.t.* umanjivati
minimum *n.* minimum
minimum *a* minimalan
minion *n.* ljubimac
minister *n.* ministar
minister *v.i.* pomagati

ministrant *a.* ministrant
ministry *n.* ministarstvo
mink *n.* kanadska kuna
minor *a.* manji
minor *n* maloljetnik
minority *n.* manjina
minster *n.* katedrala
mint *n.* metvica
mint *n* kovnica
mint *v.t.* kovati
minus *prep.* manje
minus *a* negativan
minus *n* minus
minuscule *a.* beznačajan
minute *a.* minut
minute *n.* unijeti u zapisnik
minutely *adv.* svaki čas
minx *n.* namiguša
miracle *n.* čudo
miraculous *a.* čudesan
mirage *n.* fatamorgana
mire *n.* blato
mire *v.t.* blatiti
mirror *n* ogledalo
mirror *v.t.* odražavati
mirth *n.* razdraganost
mirthful *a.* razdragan
misadventure *n.* nezgoda
misalliance *n.* mezalijansa
misanthrope *n.* mizantrop
misapplication *n.* zloupotreba
misapprehend *v.t.* pogrešno razumjeti
misapprehension *n* nesporazum
misappropriate *v.t.* pronevjeriti
misappropriation *n.* pronevjera
misbehave *v.i.* nedolično se ponašati
misbehaviour *n.* nedolično ponašanje
misbelief *n.* pogrešno vjerovanje
miscalculate *v.t.* loše procijeniti
miscalculation *n.* loša procijena

miscall *v.t.* pogrešno nazvati
miscarriage *n.* pobačaj
miscarry *v.i.* pobaciti
miscellaneous *a.* mješovit
miscellany *n.* zbirka
mischance *n.* nesrećan slučaj
mischief *n* nestašluk
mischievous *a.* vragolast
misconceive *v.t.* pogrešno razumjeti
misconception *n.* pogrešno shvatanje
misconduct *n.* loše vladanje
misconstrue *v.t.* pogrešno razumjeti
miscreant *n.* nitkov
misdeed *n.* nedjelo
misdemeanour *n.* prekršaj
misdirect *v.t.* pogrešno uputiti
misdirection *n.* pogrešno upućivanje
miser *n.* tvrdica
miserable *a.* nesretan
miserly *a.* cicijaški
misery *n.* beda
misfire *v.i.* zatajiti
misfit *n.* loše pristajati
misfortune *n.* nesreća
misgive *v.t.* slutiti
misgiving *n.* slutnja
misguide *v.t.* obmanjivati
mishap *n.* nesrećan slučaj
misjudge *v.t.* pogrešno procijeniti
mislead *v.t.* pogrešno voditi
mismanagement *n.* loše upravljanje
mismatch *v.t.* loše spojiti
misnomer *n.* pogrešan naziv
misplace *v.t.* zagubiti
misprint *n.* štamparska greška
misprint *v.t.* pogrešno odštampati
misrepresent *v.t.* pogrešno predstaviti
misrule *n.* bezakonje
miss *n.* promašaj
miss *v.t.* promašiti

94

missile *n.* projektil
mission *n.* misija
missionary *n.* misionar
missis, *missus n.* gospođa, supruga
missive *n.* poslanica
mist *n.* izmaglica
mistake *n.* greška
mistake *v.t.* pogriješiti
mister *n.* gospodin
mistletoe *n.* imela
mistreat *v.t.* maltretirati
mistress *n.* gospodarica, ljubavnica
mistrust *n.* nepovjerenje
mistrust *v.t.* biti nepovjerljiv
misty *a.* maglovit
misunderstand *v.t.* pogrešno razumjeti
misunderstanding *n.* nesporazum
misuse *n.* zloupotreba
misuse *v.t.* zloupotrebiti
mite *n.* novčić
mite *n* crv
mithridate *n.* protuotrov
mitigate *v.t.* ublažiti
mitigation *n.* ublažavanje
mitre *n.* mitra
mitten *n.* rukavica bez prstiju
mix *v.i* miješati
mixture *n.* mješavina
moan *v.i.* stenjati
moan *n.* stenjanje
moat *n.* šanac
moat *v.t.* opasati šancem
mob *n.* gomila
mob *v.t.* nasrnuti
mobile *a.* pokretan
mobility *n.* pokretnost
mobilize *v.t.* mobilizirati
mock *v.i.* ismijavati
mock *adj* ismijavanje
mockery *n.* izrugivanje

modality *n.* modalitet
mode *n.* način
model *n.* model
model *v.t.* oblikovati
moderate *a.* umjeren
moderate *v.t.* ublažiti
moderation *n.* umjerenost
modern *a.* moderan
modernity *n.* modernost
modernize *v.t.* modernizirati
modest *a.* skroman
modesty *n* skromnost
modicum *n.* malenkost
modification *n.* modifikacija
modify *v.t.* modificirati
modulate *v.t.* modulirati
moil *v.i.* mučiti se
moist *a.* vlažan
moisten *v.t.* vlažiti
moisture *n.* vlaga
molar *n.* kutnjak
molar *a* masivan
molasses *n* melasa
mole *n.* krtica
molecular *a.* molekularni
molecule *n.* molekul
molest *v.t.* zlostavljati
molestation *n.* zlostavljanje
molten *a.* izliven
moment *n.* trenutak
momentary *a.* trenutan
momentous *a.* značajan
momentum *n.* impuls
monarch *n.* monarh
monarchy *n.* monarhija
monastery *n.* manastir
monasticism *n* monaštvo
Monday *n.* ponedjeljak
monetary *a.* monetarni
money *n.* novac

monger *n.* prodavatelj
mongoose *n.* mungos
mongrel *a* melez
monitor *n.* monitor
monitory *a.* koji opominje
monk *n.* monah
monkey *n.* majmun
monochromatic *a.* monokromatski
monocle *n.* monokl
monocular *a.* jednook
monody *n.* monodija
monogamy *n.* monogamija
monogram *n.* monogram
monograph *n.* monografija
monogynous *a.* koji je monogaman
monolith *n.* monolit
monologue *n.* monolog
monopolist *n.* monopolist
monopolize *v.t.* monopolizirati
monopoly *n.* monopol
monosyllable *n.* jedan slog
monosyllabic *a.* jednosložan
monotheism *n.* monoteizam
monotheist *n.* monoteist
monotonous *a.* monoton
monotony *n* monotonija
monsoon *n.* monsun
monster *n.* čudovište
monstrous *a.* monstruozan
monstrous *n.* monstrum
month *n.* mjesec
monthly *a.* mjesečni
monthly *adv* mjesečno
monthly *n* mjesečnik
monument *n.* spomenik
monumental *a.* monumentalan
moo *v.i* mukanje
mood *n.* raspoloženje
moody *a.* ćudljiv
moon *n.* mjesec

moor *n.* vresište
moor *v.t* usidriti brod
moorings *n.* sidrište
moot *n.* sporan
mop *n.* metla
mop *v.t.* brisati
mope *v.i.* biti snužden
moral *a.* moralan
moral *n.* pouka
morale *n.* moral
moralist *n.* moralist
morality *n.* moralnost
moralize *v.t.* moralisati
morbid *a.* morbidan
morbidity *n* morbidnost
more *a.* još
more *adv* više
moreover *adv.* štoviše
morganatic *a.* morgantski
morgue *n.* mrtvačnica
moribund *a.* na umoru
morning *n.* jutro
moron *n.* imbecil
morose *a.* mrzovoljan
morphia *n.* morfij
morrow *n.* jutro
morsel *n.* zalogaj
mortal *a.* smrtan
mortal *n* smrtnik
mortality *n.* mortalitet
mortar *v.t.* žbuka
mortgage *n.* hipoteka
mortgage *v.t.* založiti
mortagagee *n.* založni verovnik
mortgagor *n.* založni dužnik
mortify *v.t.* poniziti
mortuary *n.* mrtvačnica
mosaic *n.* mozaik
mosque *n.* džamija
mosquito *n.* komarac

moss *n.* mahovina
most *a.* većinom
most *adv.* najviše
most *n* većina
mote *n.* trunčica
motel *n.* motel
moth *n.* moljac
mother *n* majka
mother *v.t.* odgajati
motherhood *n.* materinstvo
motherlike *a.* majčinski
motherly *a.* materinski
motif *n.* motiv
motion *n.* kretanje
motion *v.i.* uputiti
motionless *a.* nepokretan
motivate *v* motivirati
motivation *n.* motivacija
motive *n.* motiv
motley *a.* šarolik
motor *n.* motor
motor *v.i.* voziti se
motorist *n.* vozač
mottle *n.* šara
motto *n.* moto
mould *n.* kalup
mould *v.t.* oblikovati
mould *n* humus
mould *n* plijesan
mouldy *a.* ustajao
moult *v.i.* mitariti se
mound *n.* humka
mount *n.* postolje
mount *v.t.* postaviti
mount *n* brdo
mountain *n.* planina
mountaineer *n.* planinar
mountainous *a.* planinski
mourn *v.i.* tugovati
mourner *n.* ožalošćeni

mournful *n.* žalostan
mourning *n.* oplakivanje
mouse *n.* miš
moustache *n.* brkovi
mouth *n.* usta
mouth *v.t.* izustiti
mouthful *n.* zalogaj
movable *a.* pokretan
movables *n.* pokretna imovina
move *n.* potez
move *v.t.* pomaknuti
movement *n.* pokret
mover *n.* pokretač
movies *n.* kino
mow *v.t.* kositi
much *a* mnogo
much *adv* veoma
mucilage *n.* biljno ljepilo
muck *n.* blato
mucous *a.* sluzav
mucus *n.* sluz
mud *n.* blato
muddle *n.* zbrka
muddle *v.t.* zbrkati
muffle *v.t.* prigušiti
muffler *n.* prigušivač
mug *n.* krigla
muggy *a.* sparan
mulatto *n.* mulat
mulberry *n.* dud
mule *n.* mazga
mulish *a.* tvrdoglav
mull *n.* greben
mull *v.t.* zabrljati
mullah *n.* mula
mullion *n.* drveni stup usred prozora
multifarious *a.* raznolik
multiform *n.* raznolik
multilateral *a.* multilateralan
multiparous *a.* multiparan

multiple *a.* mnogostruk
multiple *n* sadržitelj
multiped *n.* mnogonog
multiplex *a.* višestruk
multiplicand *n.* množenik
multiplication *n.* množenje
multiplicity *n.* mnogostrukost
multiply *v.t.* umnožiti
multitude *n.* mnoštvo
mum *a.* miran
mum *n* mama
mumble *v.i.* mrmljati
mummer *n.* pantomimičar
mummy *n.* mumija
mummy *n* mamica
mumps *n.* zauške
munch *v.t.* žvakati
mundane *a.* svjetovni
municipal *a.* općinski
municipality *n.* općina
munificent *a.* darežljiv
muniment *n.* povelja
munitions *n.* municija
mural *a.* zidni
mural *n.* mural
murder *n.* ubojstvo
murder *v.t.* ubiti
murderer *n.* ubojica
murderous *a.* ubilački
murmur *n.* žamor
murmur *v.t.* mrmljati
muscle *n.* mišić
muscovite *n.* moskovljanin
muscular *a.* mišićav
muse *v.i.* razmišljati
muse *n* muza
museum *n.* muzej
mush *n.* kaša
mushroom *n.* gljiva
music *n.* glazba

musical *a.* glazbeni
musician *n.* glazbenik
musk *n.* mošus
musket *n.* mušketa
musketeer *n.* musketar
muslin *n.* muslin
must *v.* morati
must *n.* obaveza
must *n* mošt
mustache *n.* brkovi
mustang *n.* mustang
mustard *n.* senf
muster *v.t.* prikupiti
muster *n* smotra
musty *a.* buđav
mutation *n.* mutacija
mutative *a.* mutativan
mute *a.* nem
mute *n.* nema osoba
mutilate *v.t.* sakatiti
mutilation *n.* sakaćenje
mutinous *a.* buntovan
mutiny *n.* pobuna
mutiny *v. i* pobuniti se
mutter *v.i.* promrmljati
mutton *n.* ovčetina
mutual *a.* zajednički
muzzle *n.* njuška
muzzle *v.t* ušutkati
my *a.* moj
myalgia *n.* mijalgija
myopia *n.* kratkovidost
myopic *a.* kratkovid
myosis *n.* mijoza
myriad *n.* bezbroj
myriad *a* bezbrojan
myrrh *n.* mirisna smola
myrtle *n.* mirta
myself *pron.* sebe
mysterious *a.* misteriozan

mystery n. misterija
mystic a. mističan
mystic n mistik
mysticism n. misticizam
mystify v.t. mistifikovati
myth n. mit
mythical a. mitski
mythological a. mitološki
mythology n. mitologija

N

nab v.t. sčepati
nabob n. nabob
nadir n. nadir
nag n. zanovijetanje
nag v.t. zanovjetalo
nail n. ekser
nail v.t. zabiti
naive a. naivan
naivete n. naivnost
naivety n. naivnost
naked a. nag
name n. ime
name v.t. imenovati
namely adv. naime
namesake n. imenjak
nap v.i. drijemati
nap n. drijemež
nap n riskiranje
nape n. potiljak
napkin n. salveta
narcissism n. narcisizam
narcissus n narcis
narcosis n. narkoza
narcotic n. narkotik
narrate v.t. pripovijedati
narration n. naracija
narrative n. pripovijest

narrative a. pripovjedački
narrator n. pripovjedač
narrow a. uzak
narrow v.t. suziti
nasal a. nazalni
nasal n nazal
nascent a. koji se rađa
nasty a. gadan
natal a. rodni
natant a. plivajući
nation n. nacija
national a. nacionalni
nationalism n. nacionalizam
nationalist n. nacionalista
nationality n. državljanstvo
nationalization n. nacionalizacija
nationalize v.t. nacionalizirati
native a. maternji
native n urođenik
nativity n. rađanje
natural a. prirodni
naturalist n. prirodnjak
naturalize v.t. odomaćiti
naturally adv. prirodno
nature n. priroda
naughty a. nevaljao
nausea n. mučnina
nautic(al) a. nautički
naval a. pomorski
nave n. brod
navigable a. plovan
navigate v.i. upravljati
navigation n. navigacija
navigator n. navigator
navy n. mornarica
nay adv. čak
neap a. najniža plima
near a. blizak
near prep. blizu
near adv. u blizini

near *v.i.* blizu
nearly *adv.* skoro
neat *a.* uredan
nebula *n.* maglina
necessary *n.* potreba
necessary *a* potreban
necessitate *v.t.* zahtijevati
necessity *n.* nužda
neck *n.* vrat
necklace *n.* ogrlica
necklet *n.* ukras za vrat
necromancer *n.* prizivač duhova
necropolis *n.* groblje
nectar *n.* nektar
need *n.* nevolja
need *v.t.* trebati
needful *a.* potreban
needle *n.* igla
needless *a.* nepotreban
needs *adv.* svakako
needy *a.* siromašan
nefandous *a.* neopisiv
nefarious *a.* zao
negation *n.* negacija
negative *a.* negativan
negative *n.* negativ
negative *v.t.* odbiti
neglect *v.t.* zanemariti
neglect *n* zanemarivanje
negligence *n.* nemar
negligent *a.* nemaran
negligible *a.* zanemarljiv
negotiable *a.* premostiv
negotiate *v.t.* pregovarati
negotiation *n.* pregovaranje
negotiator *n.* pregovarač
negress *n.* crnkinja
negro *n.* crnac
neigh *v.i.* rzati
neigh *n.* rzanje

neighbour *n.* komšija
neighbourhood *n.* susjedstvo
neighbourly *a.* susjedski
neither *conj.* ni
nemesis *n.* osvetnik
neolithic *a.* neolitski
neon *n.* neon
nephew *n.* nećak
nepotism *n.* nepotizam
Neptune *n.* neptun
Nerve *n.* živac
nerveless *a.* hladnokrvan
nervous *a.* nervozan
nescience *n.* neznanje
nest *n.* gnijezdo
nest *v.t.* ugnijezditi
nether *a.* niži
nestle *v.i.* gnijezditi se
nestling *n.* goluždravac
net *n.* mreža
net *v.t.* hvatati mrežom
net *a* neto
net *v.t.* zaraditi
nettle *n.* kopriva
nettle *v.t.* opeći koprivom
network *n.* mreža
neurologist *n.* neurolog
neurology *n.* neurologija
neurosis *n.* neuroza
neuter *a.* srednjeg roda
neuter *n* srednji rod
neutral *a.* neutralan
neutralize *v.t.* neutralisati
neutron *n.* neutron
never *adv.* nikada
nevertheless *conj.* ipak
new *a.* nov
news *n.* vijesti
next *a.* sljedeći
next *adv.* potom

nib *n.* pero
nibble *v.t.* grickati
nibble *n* grickanje
nice *a.* lijep
nicety *n.* uglađenost
niche *n.* niša
nick *n.* zerez
nickel *n.* nikl
nickname *n.* nadimak
nickname *v.t.* dati nadimak
nicotine *n.* nikotin
niece *n.* nećaka
niggard *n.* škrtica
niggardly *a.* škrt
nigger *n.* crnac
nigh *adv.* blisko
nigh *prep.* blizu
night *n.* noć
nightingale *n.* slavuj
nightly *adv.* noću
nightmare *n.* noćna mora
nightie *n.* spavaćica
nihilism *n.* nihilizam
nil *n.* nula
nimble *a.* okretni
nimbus *n.* oreol
nine *n.* devet
nineteen *n.* devetnaest
nineteenth *a.* devetnaesti
ninetieth *a.* devedeseti
ninth *a.* deveti
ninety *n.* devedeset
nip *v.t* uštinuti
nipple *n.* bradavica
nitrogen *n.* dušik
no *a.* ni jedan
no *adv.* nikako
no *n* ne
nobility *n.* plemstvo
noble *a.* plemenit

noble *n.* plemenit
nobleman *n.* plemić
nobody *pron.* niko
nocturnal *a.* noćni
nod *v.i.* klimati glavom
node *n.* čvor
noise *n.* buka
noisy *a.* bučan
nomad *n.* nomad
nomadic *a.* nomadski
nomenclature *n.* nomenklatura
nominal *a.* nominalan
nominate *v.t.* nominirati
nomination *n.* imenovanje
nominee *n* kandidat
non-alignment *n.* nesvrstanost
nonchalance *n.* nonšalantnost
nonchalant *a.* nonšalantan
none *pron.* nitko
none *adv.* nikako
nonentity *n.* nepostojanje
nonetheless *adv.* pored toga
nonpareil *a.* neuporediv
nonpareil *n.* nonparel
nonplus *v.t.* zbuniti
nonsense *n.* besmislica
nonsensical *a.* besmislen
nook *n.* kutak
noon *n.* podne
noose *n.* zamka
noose *v.t.* uhvatiti u zamku
nor *conj* niti
norm *n.* norma
norm *n.* obrazac
normal *a.* normalan
normalcy *n.* normalnost
normalize *v.t.* normalizirati
north *n.* sjever
north *a* sjeverni
north *adv.* sjeverno

northerly *a.* sjeverni
northerly *adv.* sjeverno
northern *a.* sjeverni
nose *n.* nos
nose *v.t* njušiti
nosegay *n.* kita cveća
nosey *a.* nosat
nosy *a.* njuškalo
nostalgia *n.* nostalgija
nostril *n.* nozdrva
nostrum *n.* nadrilek
not *adv.* ne
notability *n.* značajnost
notable *a.* značajan
notary *n.* bilježnik
notation *n.* notacija
notch *n.* zarez
note *n.* napomena
note *v.t.* zapisati
noteworthy *a.* vrijedan pažnje
nothing *n.* ništa
nothing *adv.* ništa
notice *a.* primijećen
notice *v.t.* primijetiti
notification *n.* obavijest
notify *v.t.* obavijestiti
notion *n.* pojam
notional *a.* pojmovni
notoriety *n.* ozloglašenost
notorious *a.* ozloglašen
notwithstanding *prep.* unatoč
notwithstanding *adv.* ipak
notwithstanding *conj.* premda
nought *n.* ništa
noun *n.* imenica
nourish *v.t.* hraniti
nourishment *n.* ishrana
novel *a.* nov
novel *n* roman
novelette *n.* novela

novelist *n.* romanopisac
novelty *n.* novost
november *n.* studeni
novice *n.* početnik
now *adv.* sada
now *conj.* sada
nowhere *adv.* nigdje
noxious *a.* štetan
nozzle *n.* mlaznica
nuance *n.* nijansa
nubile *a.* stasala za udaju
nuclear *a.* nuklearna
nucleus *n.* jezgro
nude *a.* akt
nude *n* nagost
nudity *n.* golotinja
nudge *v.t.* gurkati
nugget *n.* grudva
nuisance *n.* neprilika
null *a.* nula
nullification *n.* poništenje
nullify *v.t.* poništiti
numb *a.* ukočen
number *n.* broj
number *v.t.* brojati
numberless *a.* bezbrojan
numeral *a.* brojčani
numerator *n.* brojač
numerical *a.* numerički
numerous *a.* brojni
nun *n.* kaluđerica
nunnery *n.* samostan
nuptial *a.* svadbeni
nuptials *n.* svadba
nurse *n.* medicinska sestra
nurse *v.t* njegovati
nursery *n.* jaslice
nurture *n.* odgoj
nurture *v.t.* negovati
nut *n* orah

nutrition *n.* prehrana
nutritious *a.* hranljiv
nutritive *a.* nutritivan
nuzzle *v.* njuškati
nylon *n.* najlon
nymph *n.* nimfa

O

oak *n.* hrast
oar *n.* veslo
oarsman *n.* veslač
oasis *n.* oaza
oat *n.* zob
oath *n.* zakletva
obduracy *n.* bezdušnost
obdurate *a.* tvrdokoran
obedience *n.* poslušnost
obedient *a.* poslušan
obeisance *n.* naklon
obesity *n.* pretilost
obey *v.t.* pokoravati se
obituary *a.* posmrtni
object *n.* objekat
object *v.t.* prigovoriti
objection *n.* prigovor
objective *n.* cilj
objective *a.* objektivan
oblation *n.* žrtva
obligation *n.* obaveza
obligatory *a.* obavezan
oblige *v.t.* obavezati
oblique *a.* posredan
obliterate *v.t.* uništiti
obliteration *n.* brisanje
oblivion *n.* zaborav
oblivious *a.* nesvjestan
oblong *a.* duguljast

oblong *n.* duguljasta figura
obnoxious *a.* odvratan
obscene *a.* opscen
obscenity *n.* razvratnost
obscure *a.* nejasan
obscure *v.t.* potamnjeti
obscurity *n.* nejasnost
observance *n.* pridržavanje
observant *a.* promatrački
observation *n.* promatranje
observatory *n.* opservatorija
observe *v.t.* promatrati
obsess *v.t.* opsjednuti
obsession *n.* opsesija
obsolete *a.* zastario
obstacle *n.* prepreka
obstinacy *n.* tvrdoglavost
obstinate *a.* tvrdoglav
obstruct *v.t.* ometati
obstruction *n.* opstrukcija
obstructive *a.* opstruktivan
obtain *v.t.* dobiti
obtainable *a.* koji se može dobiti
obtuse *a.* tup
obvious *a.* očigledan
occasion *n.* prilika
occasion *v.t* prouzrokovati
occasional *a.* povremen
occasionally *adv.* povremeno
occident *n.* zapad
occidental *a.* zapadnjački
occult *a.* okultan
occupancy *n.* stanovanje
occupant *n.* stanar
occupation *n.* zanimanje
occupier *n.* okupator
occupy *v.t.* zauzeti
occur *v.i.* desiti se
occurrence *n.* događaj

oceanic *a.* oceanski	**ogle** *v.t.* očijukati
octagon *n.* osmerokut	**ogle** *n* očijukanje
octangular *a.* osmougli	**oil** *n.* ulje
octave *n.* oktava	**oil** *v.t* uljiti
October *n.* listopad	**oily** *a.* mastan
octogenarian *a.* osamdesetogodišnji	**ointment** *n.* mast
octogenarian *a* osamdesetogodišnje	**old** *a.* star
octroi *n.* porez na uvezenu robu	**oligarchy** *n.* oligarhija
ocular *a.* očni	**olive** *n.* maslina
oculist *n.* okular	**olympiad** *n.* olimpijada
odd *a.* neparan	**omega** *n.* omega
oddity *n.* nastranost	**omelette** *n.* omplet
odds *n.* izgledi	**omen** *n.* slutnja
ode *n.* oda	**ominous** *a.* zloslustan
odious *a.* mrzak	**omission** *n.* izostavljanje
odium *n.* mrskost	**omit** *v.t.* izostaviti
odorous *a.* miomirisan	**omnipotence** *n.* svemoć
odour *n.* miris	**omnipotent** *a.* svemoguć
offence *n.* uvreda	**omnipresence** *n.* sveprisutnost
offend *v.t.* uvrijediti	**omnipresent** *a.* sveprisutan
offender *n.* prijestupnik	**omniscience** *n.* sveznanje
offensive *a.* napadački	**omniscient** *a.* sveznajući
offensive *n* napad	**on** *prep.* na
offer *v.t.* ponuditi	**on** *adv.* dalje
offer *n* ponuda	**once** *adv.* jednom
offering *n.* pružanje	**one** *a.* jedan
office *n.* ured	**one** *pron.* neko
officer *n.* časnik	**oneness** *n.* jedinstvo
official *a.* službeni	**onerous** *a.* tegoban
official *n* dužnosnik	**onion** *n.* luk
officially *adv.* službeno	**on-looker** *n.* osmatrač
officiate *v.i.* službovati	**only** *a.* jedini
officious *a.* pretjerano uslužan	**only** *adv.* samo
offing *n.* pučina	**only** *conj.* samo što
offset *v.t.* izjednačiti	**onomatopoeia** *n.* onomatopeja
offset *n* izdanak	**onrush** *n.* nadiranje
offshoot *n.* mladica	**onset** *n.* početak
offspring *n.* potomak	**onslaught** *n.* juriš
oft *adv.* često	**onus** *n.* teret
often *adv.* često	**onward** *a.* naprijed

onwards *adv.* nadalje
ooze *n.* glib
ooze *v.i.* curiti
opacity *n.* neprozirnost
opal *n.* opal
opaque *a.* neproziran
open *a.* otvoren
open *v.t.* otvoriti
opening *n.* otvaranje
openly *adv.* otvoreno
opera *n.* opera
operate *v.t.* raditi
operation *n.* operacija
operative *a.* operativan
operator *n.* operator
opine *v.t.* misliti
opinion *n.* mišljenje
opium *n.* opijum
opponent *n.* protivnik
opportune *a.* prikladan
opportunism *n.* oportunizam
opportunity *n.* prilika
oppose *v.t.* suprotstaviti
opposite *a.* suprotan
opposition *n.* oporba
oppress *v.t.* ugnjetavati
oppression *n.* ugnjetavanje
oppressive *a.* tiranski
oppressor *n.* tlačitelj
opt *v.i.* odlučiti se
optic *a.* optički
optician *n.* optičar
optimism *n.* optimizam
optimist *n.* optimista
optimistic *a.* optimistički
optimum *n.* optimum
optimum *a* optimalan
option *n.* opcija
optional *a.* neobavezan
opulence *n.* bogatstvo

opulent *a.* bogat
oracle *n.* proročanstvo
oracular *a.* proročanski
oral *a.* usmen
orally *adv.* usmeno
orange *n.* naranča
orange *a* narandžast
oration *n.* govor
orator *n.* govornik
oratorical *a.* govornički
oratory *n.* oratorij
orb *n.* nebesko tijelo
orbit *n.* orbita
orchard *n.* voćnjak
orchestra *n.* orkestar
orchestral *a.* orkestralni
ordeal *n.* iskušenje
order *n.* red
order *v.t* naručiti
orderly *a.* uredan
orderly *n.* uredno
ordinance *n.* obred
ordinarily *adv.* redovito
ordinary *a.* redovan
ordnance *n.* borbena tehnika
ore *n.* ruda
organ *n.* organ
organic *a.* organski
organism *n.* organizam
organization *n.* organizacija
organize *v.t.* organizirati
orient *n.* Orijent
orient *v.t.* orijentirati
oriental *a.* orijentalan
oriental *n* istočnjak
orientate *v.t.* orijentirati
origin *n.* porijeklo
original *a.* originalan
original *n* original
originality *n.* originalnost

originate *v.t.* voditi porijeklo
originator *n.* tvorac
ornament *n.* ornament
ornament *v.t.* ukrasiti
ornamental *a.* ukrasni
ornamentation *n.* ukrašavanje
orphan *n.* siroče
orphan *v.t* učiniti siročetom
orphanage *n.* sirotište
orthodox *a.* pravoslavan
orthodoxy *n.* pravoslavlje
oscillate *v.i.* oscilirati
oscillation *n.* oscilacija
ossify *v.t.* okoštati
ostracize *v.t.* prognati
ostrich *n.* noj
other *a.* drugi
other *pron.* drugi
otherwise *adv.* inače
otherwise *conj.* inače
otter *n.* vidra
ottoman *n.* otoman
ounce *n.* unca
our *pron.* naš
oust *v.t.* istisnuti
out *adv.* van
out-balance *v.t.* prevagnuti
outbid *v.t.* više ponuditi
outbreak *n.* izbijanje
outburst *n.* izljev
outcast *n.* izgnanik
outcast *a* izgnan
outcome *n.* ishod
outcry *a.* negodovanje
outdated *a.* zastario
outdo *v.t.* nadmašiti
outdoor *a.* vani
outer *a.* vanjski
outfit *n.* oprema
outfit *v.t* otpremiti

outgrow *v.t.* prerasti
outhouse *n.* poljski klozet
outing *n.* izlet
outlandish *a.* čudnovat
outlaw *n.* odmetnik
outlaw *v.t* staviti van zakona
outline *n.* skica
outline *v.t.* skicirati
outlive *v.i.* nadživjeti
outlook *n.* gledište
outmoded *a.* staromodan
outnumber *v.t.* nadmašiti u brojnosti
outpatient *n.* ambulantni bolesnik
outpost *n.* predstraža
output *n.* izlaz
outrage *n.* nasilje
outrage *v.t.* počiniti nasilje
outright *adv.* izravno
outright *a* izravan
outrun *v.t.* nadmašiti u trčanju
outset *n.* polazak
outshine *v.t.* nadsijati
outside *a.* vanjski
outside *n* spoljašnjost
outside *adv* vani
outside *prep* izvan
outsider *n.* autsajder
outsize *a.* prevelik
outskirts *n.pl.* periferija
outspoken *a.* otvoren
outstanding *a.* izvanredan
outward *a.* vanjski
outward *adv* van
outwards *adv* napolje
outwardly *adv.* napolju
outweigh *v.t.* pretegnuti
outwit *v.t.* nadmudriti
oval *a.* ovalan
oval *n* oval
ovary *n.* jajnik

ovation *n.* ovacija
oven *n.* peć
over *prep.* preko
over *adv* više
over *n* višak
overact *v.t.* pretjerivati
overall *n.* ogrtač
overall *a* ukupan
overawe *v.t.* preplašiti
overboard *adv.* preko palube
overburden *v.t.* preopteretiti
overcast *a.* oblačan
overcharge *v.t.* preopteretiti
overcharge *n* preopterećenje
overcoat *n.* kaput
overcome *v.t.* prevazići
overdo *v.t.* pretjerati
overdose *n.* prevelika doza
overdose *v.t.* predozirati
overdraft *n.* prekoračenje računa
overdraw *v.t.* prekoračiti račun
overdue *a.* zakašnjelo
overhaul *v.t.* pregledati
overhaul *n.* pregled
overhear *v.t.* načuti
overjoyed *a* presrećan
overlap *v.t.* preklapati
overlap *n* preklapanje
overleaf *adv.* na drugoj strani
overload *v.t.* preopteretiti
overload *n* preopterećenje
overlook *v.t.* previdjeti
overnight *adv.* preko noći
overnight *a* noćni
overpower *v.t.* nadjačati
overrate *v.t.* precijeniti
overrule *v.t.* nadglasati
overrun *v.t* pretrčati
oversee *v.t.* nadgledati
overseer *n.* nadzornik

overshadow *v.t.* zasjeniti
oversight *n.* nadzor
overt *a.* otvoren
overtake *v.t.* prestići
overthrow *v.t.* srušiti
overthrow *n* rušenje
overtime *adv.* prekovremeno
overtime *n* prekovremeni rad
overture *n.* uvertira
overwhelm *v.t.* savladati
overwork *v.i.* preopteretiti radom
overwork *n.* prekomjeran rad
owe *v.t* dugovati
owl *n.* sova
own *a.* svoje
own *v.t.* posjedovati
owner *n.* vlasnik
ownership *n.* svojstvo
ox *n.* vo
oxygen *n.* kisik
oyster *n.* ostriga

P

pace *n* korak
pace *v.i.* koračati
pacific *a.* miroljubiv
pacify *v.t.* umiriti
pack *n.* paket
pack *v.t.* upakirati
package *n.* paket
packet *n.* zavežljaj
packing *n.* pakiranje
pact *n.* pakt
pad *n.* jastuk
pad *v.t.* obložiti
padding *n.* punjenje
paddle *v.i.* veslati
paddle *n* veslo

paddy *n.* riža
page *n.* strana
page *v.t.* prelomiti
pageant *n.* parada
svečanost *n.* velelepnost
pagoda *n.* pagoda
pail *n.* kanta
pain *n.* bol
pain *v.t.* boljeti
painful *a.* bolan
painstaking *a.* radan
paint *n.* boja
paint *v.t.* bojiti
painter *n.* slikar
painting *n.* slika
pair *n.* par
pair *v.t.* spariti
pal *n.* drug
palace *n.* palača
palanquin *n.* palankin
palatable *a.* ukusan
palatal *a.* nepčano
palate *n.* nepce
palatial *a.* veličanstven
pale *n.* kolac
pale *a* blijed
pale *v.i.* poblijedeti
palette *n.* paleta
palm *n.* palma
palm *v.t.* dodirnuti
palm *n.* dlan
palmist *n.* hiromant
palmistry *n.* hiromantija
palpable *a.* opipljiv
palpitate *v.i.* podrhtavati
palpitation *n.* treperenje
palsy *n.* paraliza
paltry *a.* tričav
pamper *v.t.* razmaziti
pamphlet *n.* pamflet

pamphleteer *n.* pamfletista
panacea *n.* panaceja
pandemonium *n.* urnebes
pane *n.* okno
panegyric *n.* panegirik
panel *n.* tabla
panel *v.t.* oblagati
pang *n.* žiganje
panic *n.* panika
panorama *n.* panorama
pant *v.i.* brektati
pant *n.* brektanje
pantaloon *n.* lakrdijaš
pantheism *n.* panteizam
pantheist *n.* panteista
panther *n.* panter
pantomime *n.* pantomima
pantry *n.* ostava
papacy *n.* papinstvo
papal *a.* papski
paper *n.* papir
par *n.* jednakost
parable *n.* parabola
parachute *n.* padobran
parachutist *n.* padobranac
parade *n.* parada
parade *v.t.* paradirati
paradise *n.* raj
paradox *n.* paradoks
paradoxical *a.* paradoksalan
paraffin *n.* parafin
paragon *n.* uzor
paragraph *n.* paragraf
parallel *a.* paralelan
parallel *v.t.* načiniti paralelnim
parallelism *n.* paralelizam
parallelogram *n.* paralelogram
paralyse *v.t.* paralizirati
paralysis *n.* paraliza
paralytic *a.* paralitički

paramount *n.* ono što je glavno
paramour *n.* ljubavnik
paraphernalia *n. pl* pribor
paraphrase *n.* parafraza
paraphrase *v.t.* parafrazirati
parasite *n.* parazit
parcel *n.* parcela
parcel *v.t.* razdijeliti
parch *v.t.* spržiti
pardon *v.t.* oprostiti
pardon *n.* oproštenje
pardonable *a.* oprostiv
parent *n.* roditelj
parentage *n.* roditeljstvo
parental *a.* roditeljski
parenthesis *n.* umetak
parish *n.* parohija
parity *n.* paritet
park *n.* park
park *v.t.* parkirati
parlance *n.* način govora
parley *n.* pregovaranje
parley *v.i* pregovarati
parliament *n.* parlament
parliamentarian *n.* parlamentarac
parliamentary *a.* parlamentaran
parlour *n.* soba za posjete
parody *n.* parodija
parody *v.t.* parodirati
parole *n.* uvjetni otpust
parole *v.t.* uvjetno otpustiti
parricide *n.* roditeljoubojstvo
parrot *n.* papagaj
parry *v.t.* parirati
parry *n.* pariranje
parson *n.* paroh
part *n.* dio
part *v.t.* dijeliti
partake *v.i.* sudjelovati
partial *a.* djelomičan

partiality *n.* pristrasnost
participate *v.i.* sudjelovati
participant *n.* učesnik
participation *n.* učešće
particle *a.* poput čestice
particular *a.* poseban
particular *n.* pojedinost
partisan *n.* partizan
partisan *a.* partizanski
partition *n.* podjela
partition *v.t.* podjeliti
partner *n.* partner
partnership *n.* partnerstvo
party *n.* stranka
pass *v.i.* proći
pass *n* prolaz
passage *n.* pasus
passenger *n.* putnik
passion *n.* strast
passionate *a.* strastven
passive *a.* pasivan
passport *n.* putovnica
past *a.* prošli
past *n.* prošlost
past *prep.* nakon
paste *n.* pasta
paste *v.t.* ljepiti
pastel *n.* pastel
pastime *n.* razonoda
pastoral *a.* pastirski
pasture *n.* pašnjak
pasture *v.t.* pasti
pat *v.t.* tapkati
pat *n* tapkanje
pat *adv* upravo
patch *v.t.* zakrpiti
patch *n* zakrpa
patent *a.* patentan
patent *n* patent
patent *v.t.* patentni

paternal a. očinski
path n. put
pathetic a. patetičan
pathos n. patos
patience n. strpljenje
patient a. strpljiv
patient n pacijent
patricide n. oceubojstvo
patrimony n. očevina
patriot n. patriota
patriotic a. patriotski
partiotism n. partiotizam
patrol v.i. patrolirati
patrol n patrola
patron n. pokrovitelj
patronage n. pokroviteljstvo
patronize v.t. štititi
pattern n. obrazac
paucity n. malobrojnost
pauper n. siromah
pause n. pauza
pause v.i. zastati
pave v.t. popločati
pavement n. pločnik
pavilion n. paviljon
paw n. šapa
paw v.t. udariti šapom
pay v.t. platiti
pay n plaća
payable a. plativ
payee n. primatelj
payment n. plaćanje
pea n. grašak
peace n. mir
peaceable a. miroljubiv
peaceful a. miran
peach n. breskva
peacock n. paun
peahen n. paunica
peak n. vrh

pear n. kruška
pearl n. biser
peasant n. seljak
peasantry n. seljaštvo
pebble n. šljunak
peck n. kljucanje
peck v.i. kljucati
peculiar a. čudan
peculiarity n. svojstvenost
pecuniary a. novčan
pedagogue n. pedagog
pedagogy n. pedagogija
pedal n. pedala
pedal v.t. voziti bicikl
pedant n. pedant
pedantic n. pedantan
pedantry n. pedanterija
pedestal n. postolje
pedestrian n. pješak
pedigree n. pedigre
peel v.t. oljuštiti
peel n. kora
peep v.i. viriti
peep n virenje
peer n. plemić
peerless a. bez premca
peg n. klin
peg v.t. prikovati
pelf n. dobitak
pell-mell adv. zbrkano
pen n. pero
pen v.t. pisati
penal a. kazneni
penalize v.t. kazniti
penalty n. kazna
pencil n. olovka
pencil v.t. slikati
pending prep. tijekom
pending a neodređen
pendulum n. klatno

penetrate *v.t.* prodrijeti
penetration *n.* penetracija
penis *n.* penis
penniless *a.* bez novca
penny *n.* peni
pension *n.* mirovina
pension *v.t.* umiroviti
pensioner *n.* umirovljenik
pensive *a.* zadubljen *u* misli
pentagon *n.* pentagon
peon *n.* nadničar
people *n.* narod
people *v.t.* naseliti
pepper *n.* biber
pepper *v.t.* biberiti
per *prep.* na, po
perambulator *n.* dječja kolica
perceive *v.t.* opaziti
perceptible *adj* primjetan
per *cent adv.* posto
percentage *n.* postotak
perception *n.* percepcija
perceptive *a.* perceptivan
perch *n.* grgeč
perch *v.i.* spustiti se
perennial *a.* višegodišnji
perennial *n.* trajnica
perfect *a.* savršen
perfect *v.t.* usavršiti
perfection *n.* savršenstvo
perfidy *n.* podmuklost
perforate *v.t.* probušiti
perforce *adv.* silom
perform *v.t.* izvesti
performance *n.* izvođenje
performer *n.* izvođač
perfume *n.* parfem
perfume *v.t.* namirisati
perhaps *adv.* možda
peril *n.* opasnost

peril *v.t.* ugroziti
perilous *a.* opasan
period *n.* period
periodical *n.* časopis
periodical *a.* periodičan
periphery *n.* periferija
perish *v.i.* poginuti
perishable *a.* kvarljiv
perjure *v.i.* lažno se zakleti
perjury *n.* krivokletstvo
permanence *n.* trajnost
permanent *a.* trajan
permissible *a.* dopustiv
permission *n.* dopuštenje
permit *v.t.* dozvoliti
permit *n.* dozvola
permutation *n.* permutacija
pernicious *a.* škodljiv
perpendicular *a.* vertikalan
perpendicular *n.* vertikala
perpetual *a.* večit
perpetuate *v.t.* ovjekovečiti
perplex *v.t.* zbuniti
perplexity *n.* zbunjenost
persecute *v.t.* progoniti
persecution *n.* proganjanje
perseverance *n.* istrajnost
persevere *v.i.* istrajati
persist *v.i.* izdržati
persistence *n.* izdržljivost
persistent *a.* uporan
person *n.* osoba
personage *n.* ugledna ličnost
personal *a.* osobni
personality *n.* ličnost
personification *n.* personifikacija
personify *v.t.* oličavati
personnel *n.* osoblje
perspective *n.* perspektiva
perspiration *n.* znojenje

perspire v.i. znojiti se
persuade v.t. uvjeriti
persuasion n. uvjeravanje
pertain v.i. odnositi se
pertinent a. prigodan
perturb v.t. poremetiti
perusal n. pregled
peruse v.t. pregledati
pervade v.t. prožimati
perverse a. perverzan
perversion n. perverzija
perversity n. izopačenost
pervert v.t. pokvarenjak
pessimism n. pesimizam
pessimist n. pesimista
pessimistic a. pesimističan
pest n. štetočina
pesticide n. pesticid
pestilence n. kuga
pet n. ljubimac
pet v.t. milovati
petal n. latica
petition n. peticija
petition v.t. moliti
petitioner n. molilac
petrol n. benzin
petroleum n. nafta
petticoat n. podsuknja
petty a. sitan
petulance n. nestašnost
petulant a. mrzovoljan
phantom n. fantom
pharmacy n. apoteka
phase n. faza
phenomenal a. fenomenalan
phenomenon n. fenomen
phial n. bočica
philanthropic a. filantropski
philanthropist n. filantrop
philanthropy n. filantropija

philological a. filološki
philologist n. filolog
philology n. filologija
philosopher n. filozof
philosophical a. filozofski
philosophy n. filozofija
phone n. telefon
phonetic a. fonetski
phonetics n. fonetika
phosphate n. fosfat
phosphorus n. fosfor
photo n fotografija
photograph v.t. fotografirati
photograph n fotografija
photographer n. fotograf
photographic a. fotografski
photography n. fotografija
phrase n. fraza
phrase v.t. izraziti
phraseology n. frazeologija
physic n. medicina
physic v.t. liječiti
physical a. fizički
physician n. liječnik
physicist n. fizičar
physics n. fizika
physiognomy n. fizionomija
physique n. stas
pianist n. pijanista
piano n. klavir
pick v.t. izabrati
pick n. izbor
picket n. kolac
picket v.t. ograditi kolcima
pickle n. turšija
pickle v.t ukiseliti
picnic n. piknik
picnic v.i. ići na izlet
pictorical a. slikarski
picture n. slika

picture *v.t.* naslikati
picturesque *a.* slikovit
piece *n.* komad
piece *v.t.* sastaviti
pierce *v.t.* izbosti
piety *n.* pobožnost
pig *n.* svinja
pigeon *n.* golub
pigmy *n.* pigmej
pile *n.* gomila
pile *v.t.* gomilati
piles *n.* hemoroidi
pilfer *v.t.* ukrasti
pilgrim *n.* hodočasnik
pilgrimage *n.* hodočašće
pill *n.* pilula
pillar *n.* stup
pillow *n* jastuk
pillow *v.t.* položiti
pilot *n.* pilot
pilot *v.t.* pilotirati
pimple *n.* bubuljica
pin *n.* čioda
pin *v.t.* pribosti
pinch *v.t.* uštinuti
pinch *v.* stisnuti
pine *n.* bor
pine *v.i.* čeznuti
pineapple *n.* ananas
pink *n.* karanfil, ružičasta boja
pink *a* ružičast
pinkish *a.* ružičast
pinnacle *n.* vrhunac
pioneer *n.* pionir
pioneer *v.t.* krčiti
pious *a.* pobožan
pipe *n.* cijev, lula
pipe *v.i* svirati na fruli
piquant *a.* pikantan
piracy *n.* piratstvo

pirate *n.* gusar
pirate *v.t* izdavati
pistol *n.* pištolj
piston *n.* klip
pit *n.* jama
pit *v.t.* staviti u jamu
pitch *n.* smola
pitch *v.t.* zaliti
pitcher *n.* krčag
piteous *a.* bijedan
pitfall *n.* zamka
pitiable *a.* jadan
pitiful *a.* sažaljiv
pitiless *a.* nemilosrdan
pitman *n.* kopač
pittance *n.* mali dio
pity *n.* sažaljenje
pity *v.t.* sažaljevati
pivot *n.* stožer
pivot *v.t.* okretati se
placard *n.* plakat
place *n.* mjesto
place *v.t.* smjestiti
placid *a.* miran
plague *a.* kuga
plague *v.t.* zaraziti
plain *a.* jednostavan
plain *n.* ravan
plaintiff *n.* tužitelj
plan *n.* plana
plan *v.t.* planirati
plane *n.* ravnica
plane *v.t.* izravnati
plane *a.* ravan
plane *n* platan
planet *n.* planeta
planetary *a.* planetarni
plank *n.* daska
plank *v.t.* obložiti daskama
plant *n.* biljka

plant *v.t.*	saditi	**plunge** *v.t.*	zaroniti
plantain *n.*	bokvice	**plunge** *n*	ronjenje
plantation *n.*	plantaža	**plural** *a.*	množina
plaster *n.*	flaster	**plurality** *n.*	pluralitet
plaster *v.t.*	okrečiti	**plus** *a.*	dodatni
plate *n.*	ploča	**plus** *n*	plus
plate *v.t.*	oklopiti	**ply** *v.t.*	upotrebljavati
plateau *n.*	plato	**ply** *n*	nabor
platform *n.*	platforma	**pneumonia** *n.*	zapaljenje pluća
platonic *a.*	platonski	**pocket** *n.*	džep
platoon *n.*	vod	**pocket** *v.t.*	staviti *u* džep
play *n.*	igra	**pod** *n.*	mahuna
play *v.i.*	igrati se	**poem** *n.*	pjesma
player *n.*	igrač	**poesy** *n.*	poezija
plea *n.*	molba	**poet** *n.*	pjesnik
plead *v.i.*	obraćati se	**poetaster** *n.*	stihoklepac
pleader *n.*	branitelj	**poetess** *n.*	pjesnikinja
pleasant *a.*	prijatan	**poetic** *a.*	poetski
pleasantry *n.*	šala	**poetics** *n.*	poetika
please *v.t.*	ugoditi	**poetry** *n.*	poezija
pleasure *n.*	zadovoljstvo	**poignancy** *n.*	oštrina
plebiscite *n.*	plebiscit	**poignant** *a.*	oštar
pledge *n.*	zaloga	**point** *n.*	točka
pledge *v.t.*	zaloga	**point** *v.t.*	zaoštriti
plenty *n.*	mnogo	**poise** *v.t.*	izbalansirati
plight *n.*	stanje	**poise** *n*	ravnoteža
plod *v.i.*	teško koračati	**poison** *n.*	otrov
plot *n.*	zaplet	**poison** *v.t.*	otrovati
plot *v.t.*	smišljati	**poisonous** *a.*	otrovan
plough *n.*	plug	**poke** *v.t.*	gurati
plough *v.i*	orati	**poke** *n.*	vreća
ploughman *n.*	orač	**polar** *n.*	polarni
pluck *v.t.*	otrgnuti	**pole** *n.*	pol
pluck *n*	trzanje	**police** *n.*	policija
plug *n.*	utikač	**policeman** *n.*	policajac
plug *v.t.*	začepiti	**policy** *n.*	politika
plum *n.*	šljiva	**polish** *v.t.*	polirati
plumber *n.*	vodoinstalater	**polish** *n*	sjaj
plunder *v.t.*	pljačkanje	**polite** *a.*	učtiv
plunder *n*	pljačkati	**politeness** *n.*	učtivost

politic *a.* lukav
political *a.* politički
politician *n.* političar
politics *n.* politika
polity *n.* državno uređenje
poll *n.* anketa
poll *v.t.* seći
pollen *n.* pelud
pollute *v.t.* zagaditi
pollution *n.* zagađenje
polo *n.* polo
polygamous *a.* poligamski
polygamy *n.* poligamija
polyglot1 *n.* poliglota
polyglot2 *a.* poliglotski
polytechnic *a.* politehnički
polytechnic *n.* politehnika
polytheism *n.* politeizam
polytheist *n.* politeista
polytheistic *a.* politeistički
pomp *n.* raskoš
pomposity *n.* pompeznost
pompous *a.* pompezan
pond *n.* ribnjak
ponder *v.t.* razmišljati
pony *n.* poni
poor *a.* jadan
pop *v.i.* pucati
pop *n* prasak
pope *n.* papa
poplar *n.* topola
poplin *n.* puplin
populace *n.* stanovništvo
popular *a.* popularan
popularity *n.* popularnost
popularize *v.t.* popularizirati
populate *v.t.* naseliti
population *n.* stanovništvo
populous *a.* naseljen
porcelain *n.* porculan

porch *n.* veranda
pore *n.* pora
pork *n.* svinjsko meso
porridge *n.* kaša
port *n.* luka
portable *a.* pokretan
portage *n.* nošenje
portal *n.* portal
portend *v.t.* nagovijestiti
porter *n.* vratar
portfolio *n.* portfolio
portico *n.* trijem
portion *n* dio
portion *v.t.* dijeliti
portrait *n.* portret
portraiture *n.* portretisanje
portray *v.t.* oslikati
portrayal *n.* portret
pose *v.i.* pozirati
pose *n.* poza
position *n.* mjesto
position *v.t.* staviti
positive *a.* pozitivan
possess *v.t.* posjedovati
possession *n.* posjedovanje
possibility *n.* mogućnost
possible *a.* moguć
post *n.* sub
post *v.t.* postaviti
post *n* glasnik
post *v.t.* objaviti
post *adv.* nakon
postage *n.* poštarina
postal *a.* poštanski
post-date *v.t.* staviti kasniji datum
poster *n.* plakat
posterity *n.* potomstvo
posthumous *a.* posmrtni
postman *n.* poštar
postmaster *n.* upravnik pošte

post-mortem a. obdukcioni
post-mortem n. obdukcija
post-office n. pošta
postpone v.t. odložiti
postponement n. odlaganje
postscript n. post skriptum
posture n. stavak
pot n. lonac
pot v.t. ostaviti
potash n. potaša
potassium n. kalij
potato n. krumpir
potency n. potentnost
potent a. potentan
potential a. moguć
potential n. mogućnost
pontentiality n. potencijal
potter n. grnčar
pottery n. grnčarija
pouch n. vrećica
poultry n. živina
pounce v.i. zaleteti se
pounce n zalet
pound n. funta
pound v.t. zatvoriti
pour v.i. sipati
poverty n. siromaštvo
powder n. prah
powder v.t. naprašiti
power n. snaga
powerful a. moćan
practicability n. izvodljivost
practicable a. izvodljiv
practical a. praktičan
practice n. praksa
practise v.t. uvježbavati
practitioner n. praktičar
pragmatic a. pragmatičan
pragmatism n. pragmatizam
praise n. pohvala

praise v.t. hvaliti
praiseworthy a. pohvalan
prank n. nestašluk
prattle v.i. brbljati
prattle n. brbljanje
pray v.i. moliti
prayer n. molitva
preach v.i. propovijedati
preacher n. propovjednik
preamble n. predgovor
precaution n. predostrožnost
precautionary a. obazriv
precede v. prethoditi
precedence n. prednost
precedent n. presedan
precept n. pravilo
preceptor n. učitelj
precious a. dragocjen
precis n. izvod
precise n. preciznost
precision n. preciznost
precursor n. prethodnik
predecessor n. prethodnik
predestination n. predodređenje
predetermine v.t. predodrediti
predicament n. neprilika
predicate n. predikat
predict v.t. predvidjeti
prediction n. predviđanje
predominance n. prevlast
predominant a. nadmoćan
predominate v.i. preovlađivati
pre-eminence n. nadmoćnost
pre-eminent a. nadmoćan
preface n. predgovor
preface v.t. opskrbiti predgovorom
prefect n. prefekt
prefer v.t. preferirati
preference n. sklonost
preferential a. povlašten

prefix *n.* prefiks
prefix *v.t.* dodati prefiks
pregnancy *n.* trudnoća
pregnant *a.* trudna
prehistoric *a.* prapovijesni
prejudice *n.* predrasuda
prelate *n.* prelat
preliminary *a.* preliminaran
preliminary *n* priprema
prelude *n.* uvod
prelude *v.t.* uvesti
premarital *a.* predbračni
premature *a.* prevremen
premeditate *v.t.* unaprijed smisliti
premeditation *n.* predumišljaj
premier *a.* premijer
premier *n* premijer
premiere *n.* premijera
premium *n.* premija
premonition *n.* predosećanje
preoccupation *n.* preokupacija
preoccupy *v.t.* zaokupiti
preparation *n.* priprema
preparatory *a.* pripremni
prepare *v.t.* pripremiti
preponderance *n.* prevaga
preponderate *v.i.* premašivati
preposition *n.* prijedlog
prerequisite *a.* preduslovan
prerequisite *n* preduvjet
prerogative *n.* privilegija
prescience *n.* predosećanje
prescribe *v.t.* propisati
prescription *n.* recept
presence *n.* prisustvo
present *a.* prisutan
present *n.* poklon
present *v.t.* predstaviti
presentation *n.* prezentacija
presently *adv.* uskoro

preservation *n.* čuvanje
preservative *n.* prezervativ
preservative *a.* zaštitni
preserve *v.t.* sačuvati
preserve *n.* ukuhano voće
preside *v.i.* predsjedavati
president *n.* predsjednik
presidential *a.* predsjednički
press *v.t.* pritisnite
press *n* štampa
pressure *n.* pritisak
pressurize *v.t.* staviti pod pritisak
prestige *n.* prestiž
prestigious *a.* prestižan
presume *v.t.* pretpostaviti
presumption *n.* pretpostavka
presuppose *v.t.* pretpostaviti
presupposition *n.* pretpostavljanje
pretence *n.* pretvaranje
pretend *v.t.* pretvarati se
pretension *n.* pretenzija
pretentious *a.* pretenciozan
pretext *n* izgovor
prettiness *n.* ljepota
pretty *a* lijep
pretty *adv.* prilično
prevail *v.i.* preovlađivati
prevalence *n.* prevlast
prevalent *a.* preovlađujući
prevent *v.t.* spriječiti
prevention *n.* prevencija
preventive *a.* preventivan
previous *a.* prethodni
prey *n.* plijen
prey *v.i.* vrebati
price *n.* cijena
price *v.t.* cijeniti
prick *n.* ubod
prick *v.t.* ubosti
pride *n.* ponos

pride *v.t.* ponositi se
priest *n.* svećenik
priestess *n.* svećenica
priesthood *n.* svećenstvo
prima facie *adv.* na prvi pogled
primarily *adv.* prvenstveno
primary *a.* osnovni
prime *a.* glavni
prime *n.* početak
primer *n.* bukvar
primeval *a.* prastar
primitive *a.* primitivan
prince *n.* princ
princely *a.* kneževski
princess *n.* princeza
principal *n.* starješina
principal *a* glavni
principle *n.* princip
print *v.t.* tiskati
print *n* otisak
printer *n.* pisač
prior *a.* raniji
prior *n* iguman
prioress *n.* igumanija
priority *n.* prioritet
prison *n.* zatvor
prisoner *n.* zatvorenik
privacy *n.* privatnost
private *a.* privatni
privation *n.* ištanje
privilege *n.* privilegija
prize *n.* nagrada
prize *v.t.* cijeniti
probability *n.* vjerojatnost
probable *a.* vjerojatan
probably *adv.* vjerojatno
probation *n.* proba
probationer *n.* pripravnik
probe *v.t.* istraživati
probe *n* sonda

problem *n.* problem
problematic *a.* problematičan
procedure *n.* procedura
proceed *v.i.* nastaviti
proceeding *n.* postupak
proceeds *n.* dohodak
process *n.* proces
procession *n.* povorka
proclaim *v.t.* proglasiti
proclamation *n.* proglas
proclivity *n.* sklonost
procrastinate *v.i.* odugovlačiti
procrastination *n.* odugovlačenje
proctor *n.* prokurator
procure *v.t.* nabaviti
procurement *n.* nabavka
prodigal *a.* rasipan
prodigality *n.* rasipnost
produce *v.t.* proizvoditi
produce *n.* proizvod
product *n.* produkt
production *n.* proizvodnja
productive *a.* produktivan
productivity *n.* produktivnost
profane *a.* svetovan
profane *v.t.* poštovati
profess *v.t.* ispovedati
profession *n.* profesija
professional *a.* profesionalan
professor *n.* profesor
proficiency *n.* vještina
proficient *a.* vješt
profile *n.* profil
profile *v.t.* prikazati u profilu
profit *n.* profiter
profit *v.t.* profitirati
profitable *a.* ,profitabilan
profiteer *n.* profiter
profiteer *v.i.* nepošteno zarađivati
profligacy *n.* raskalašnost

profligate *a.* rasipan
profound *a.* dubok
profundity *n.* dubina
profuse *a.* obilan
profusion *n.* obilje
progeny *n.* potomstvo
programme *n.* program
programme *v.t.* programirati
progress *n.* napredak
progress *v.i.* napredovati
progressive *a.* progresivan
prohibit *v.t.* zabraniti
prohibition *n.* zabrana
prohibitive *a.* nedopušten
prohibitory *a.* zabranjujući
project *n.* projekat
project *v.t.* projektirati
projectile *n.* projektil
projectile *a* koji se može baciti
projection *n.* projekcija
projector *n.* projektor
proliferate *v.i.* razmnožiti se
proliferation *n.* razmnožavanje
prolific *a.* plodan
prologue *n.* prolog
prolong *v.t.* produžiti
prolongation *n.* produženje
prominence *n.* istaknutost
prominent *a.* istaknut
promise *n* obećanje
promise *v.t* obećati
promising *a.* obećavajući
promissory *a.* koji sadrži obećanje
promote *v.t.* promovirati
promotion *n.* promocija
prompt *a.* brz
prompt *v.t.* potaknuti
prompter *n.* sufler
prone *a.* sklon
pronoun *n.* zamjenica

pronounce *v.t.* izgovarati
pronunciation *n.* izgovor
proof *n.* dokaz
proof *a* otporan
prop *n.* podupirač
prop *v.t.* podupirati
propaganda *n.* propaganda
propagandist *n.* propagator
propagate *v.t.* propagirati
propagation *n.* širenje
propel *v.t.* pokrenuti
proper *a.* pravi
property *n.* imovina
prophecy *n.* proročanstvo
prophesy *v.t.* proreći
prophet *n.* prorok
prophetic *a.* proročki
proportion *n.* proporcija
proportion *v.t.* podesiti
proportional *a.* proporcionalan
proportionate *a.* razmjeran
proposal *n.* prijedlog
propose *v.t.* predložiti
proposition *n.* prijedlog
propound *v.t.* predložiti
proprietary *a.* vlasnički
proprietor *n.* vlasnik
propriety *n.* ispravnost
prorogue *v.t.* raspustiti
prosaic *a.* prozaičan
prose *n.* proza
prosecute *v.t.* goniti
prosecution *n.* sudski progon
prosecutor *n.* tužitelj
prosody *n.* prozodija
prospect *n.* izgled
prospective *a.* potencijalan
prospectus *n.* prospekt
prosper *v.i.* napredovati
prosperity *n.* blagostanje

prosperous a. uspješan
prostitute n. prostitutka
prostitute v.t. prostituirati
prostitution n. prostitucija
prostrate a. iznuren
prostrate v.t. oboriti
prostration n. iznurenost
protagonist n. protagonista
protect v.t. zaštititi
protection n. zaštita
protective a. zaštitni
protector n. zaštitnik
protein n. protein
protest n. protest
protest v.i. protestovati
protestation n. protest
prototype n. prototip
proud a. ponosan
prove v.t. dokazati
proverb n. poslovica
proverbial a. poslovičan
provide v.i. obezbediti
providence n. proviđenje
provident a. oprezan
providential a. povoljan
province n. provincija
provincial a. provincijski
provincialism n. provincijalizam
provision n. odredba
provisional a. privremen
proviso n. uvjet
provocation n. provokacija
provocative a. provokativan
provoke v.t. provocirati
prowess n. junaštvo
proximate a. neposredan
proximity n. blizina
proxy n. zastupnik
prude n. pretjerano čedna žena
prudence n. razboritost

prudent a. razborit
prudential a. promišljen
prune v.t. orezati
pry v.i. zavirivati
psalm n. psalm
pseudonym n. pseudonim
psyche n. psiha
psychiatrist n. psihijatar
psychiatry n. psihijatrija
psychic a. psihički
psychological a. psihološki
psychologist n. psiholog
psychology n. psihologija
psychopath n. psihopata
psychosis n. psihoza
psychotherapy n. psihoterapija
puberty n. pubertet
public a. javni
public n. javnost
publication n. izdanje
publicity n. publicitet
publicize v.t. dati publicitet
publish v.t. objaviti
publisher n. izdavač
pudding n. puding
puddle n. bara
puddle v.t. gacati
puerile a. djetinjast
puff n. dašak
puff v.i. dahtati
pull v.t. povući
pull n. povlačenje
pulley n. kotur
pullover n. pulover
pulp n. pulpa
pulp v.t. pretvoriti u kašu
pulpit a. propovjedaonica
pulpy a. mekan
pulsate v.i. kucati
pulsation n. pulsacija

pulse *n.* puls
pulse *v.i.* pulsirati
pulse *n* puls
pump *n.* pumpa
pump *v.t.* pumpati
pumpkin *n.* bundeva
pun *n.* igra riječima
pun *v.i.* igrati se riječima
punch *n.* punč
punch *v.t.* udariti
punctual *a.* točan
punctuality *n.* točnost
punctuate *v.t.* naglasiti
punctuation *n.* interpunkcija
puncture *n.* rupa
puncture *v.t.* probušiti
pungency *n.* oporost
pungent *a.* opor
punish *v.t.* kazniti
punishment *n.* kazna
punitive *a.* kazneni
puny *a.* slabašan
pupil *n.* učenik
puppet *n.* marioneta
puppy *n.* štene
purblind *n.* poluslep
purchase *n.* kupovina
purchase *v.t.* kupiti
pure *a* čist
purgation *n.* pročišćenje
purgative *n.* purgativ
purgative *a* purgativan
purgatory *n.* čistilište
purge *v.t.* očistiti
purification *n.* prečišćavanje
purify *v.t.* očistiti
purist *n.* purista
puritan *n.* puritanac
puritanical *a.* puritanski
purity *n.* čistoća

purple *adj./n.* ljubičast, ljubičasta
purport *n.* značenje
purport *v.t.* značiti
purpose *n.* svrha
purpose *v.t.* namjeravati
purposely *adv.* namjerno
purr *n.* predenje
purr *v.i.* presti
purse *n.* novčanik
purse *v.t.* namrštiti
pursuance *n.* izvođenje
pursue *v.t.* progoniti
pursuit *n.* potjera
purview *n.* vidokrug
pus *n.* gnoj
push *v.t.* gurnuti
push *n.* guranje
put *v.t.* staviti
puzzle *n.* slagalica
puzzle *v.t.* zbuniti
pygmy *n.* pigmejac
pyorrhoea *n.* gnojna upala
pyramid *n.* piramida
pyre *n.* lomača
python *n.* piton

Q

quack *v.i.* blebetati
quack *n* šarlatan
quackery *n.* nadriliječnišvo
quadrangle *n.* četvorougaonik
quadrangular *a.* četverokutni
quadrilateral *a. & n.* četvorostran
quadruped *n.* četveronožni
quadruple *a.* četverostruk
quadruple *v.t.* učetvorostručiti
quail *n.* prepelica
quaint *a.* čudan

quake *v.i.* tresti se
quake *n* potres
qualification *n.* kvalifikacija
qualify *v.i.* kvalificirati se
qualitative *a.* kvalitativan
quality *n.* kvalitet
quandary *n.* dilema
quantitative *a.* kvantitativan
quantity *n.* količina
quantum *n.* kvant
quarrel *n.* svađa
quarrel *v.i.* svađati se
quarrelsome *a.* svadljiv
quarry *n.* kamenolom
quarry *v.i.* iskopavati
quarter *n.* četvrtina
quarter *v.t.* podijeliti na četiri dijela
quarterly *a.* tromjesečni
queen *n.* kraljica
queer *a.* nastran
quell *v.t.* ugušiti
quench *v.t.* ugasiti
query *n.* pitanje
query *v.t* pitati
quest *n.* traganje
quest *v.t.* tragati
question *n.* pitanje
question *v.t.* pitati
questionable *a.* sumnjiv
questionnaire *n.* upitnik
queue *n.* red
quibble *n.* dosjetka
quibble *v.i.* praviti dosjetke
quick *a.* brz
quick *n* živac
quicksand *n.* živi pijesak
quicksilver *n.* živa
quiet *a.* miran
quiet *n.* mir
quiet *v.t.* umiriti

quilt *n.* jorgan
quinine *n.* kinin
quintessence *n.* suština
quit *v.t.* prestati
quite *adv.* sasvim
quiver *n.* tobolac
quiver *v.i.* drhtati
quixotic *a.* donkihotski
quiz *n.* kviz
quiz *v.t.* ispitivati
quorum *n.* kvorum
quota *n.* kvota
quotation *n.* citat
quote *v.t.* citirati
quotient *n.* količnik

R

rabbit *n.* zec
rabies *n.* bjesnilo
race *n.* utrka
race *v.i* utrkivati se
racial *a.* rasni
racialism *n.* rasizam
rack *v.t.* mučiti
rack *n.* propast
racket *n.* reket
radiance *n.* sjaj
radiant *a.* sjajan
radiate *v.t.* zračiti
radiation *n.* zračenje
radical *a.* radikalan
radio *n.* radio
radio *v.t.* javiti putem radija
radish *n.* rotkvica
radium *n.* radij
radius *n.* polumjer
rag *n.* krpa
rag *v.t.* zadirkivati

rage *n.* bijes
rage *v.i.* bjesniti
raid *n.* racija
raid *v.t.* upasti
rail *n.* šina
rail *v.t.* ograditi
raling *n.* ograda
raillery *n.* zadirkivanje
railway *n.* željeznica
rain *v.i.* padati
rain *n* kiša
rainy *a.* kišovit
raise *v.t.* dići
raisin *n.* grožđice
rally *v.t.* skupljanje
rally *n* zbor
ram *n.* ovan
ram *v.t.* zakrčiti
ramble *v.t.* skitanje
ramble *n* skitati
rampage *v.i.* divljati
rampage *n.* divljanje
rampant *a.* osion
rampart *n.* bedem
rancour *n.* zloba
random *a.* slučajan
range *v.t.* postrojiti
range *n.* domet
ranger *n.* skitnica
rank *n.* rang
rank *v.t.* rangirati
rank *a* bujan
ransack *v.t.* pretresti
ransom *n.* otkup
ransom *v.t.* otkupiti
rape *n.* silovanje
rape *v.t.* silovati
rapid *a.* hitar
rapidity *n.* hitrina
rapier *n.* rapir

rapport *n.* prisnost
rapt *a.* ushićen
rapture *n.* zanesenost
rare *a.* rijedak
rascal *n.* nitkov
rash *a.* osip
rat *n.* štakor
rate *v.t.* procijeniti
rate *n.* stopa
rather *adv.* radije
ratify *v.t.* ratificirati
ratio *n.* odnos
ration *n.* obrok
rational *a.* racionalan
rationale *n.* obrazloženje
rationality *n.* racionalnost
rationalize *v.t.* racionalizirati
rattle *v.i.* zveckati
rattle *n* zvečka
ravage *n.* pustošenje
ravage *v.t.* pustošiti
rave *v.i.* buncati
raven *n.* gavran
ravine *n.* tjesnac
raw *a.* sirov
ray *n.* zrak
raze *v.t.* razrušiti
razor *n.* brijač
reach *v.t.* dostići
react *v.i.* reagirati
reaction *n.* reakcija
reactionary *a.* reakcionaran
read *v.t.* čitati
reader *n.* čitalac
readily *adv.* spremno
readiness *n.* spremnost
ready *a.* spreman
real *a.* pravi
realism *n.* realizam
realist *n.* realista

realistic a. realističan
reality n. realnost
realization n. realizacija
realize v.t. realizirati
really adv. stvarno
realm a. carstvo
ream n. ris papira
reap v.t. žeti
reaper n. žetelac
rear n. pozadina
rear v.t. gajiti
reason n. razlog
reason v.i. misliti
reasonable a. razuman
reassure v.t. uvjeravati
rebate n. rabat
rebel v.i. buniti se
rebel n. buntovnik
rebellion n. pobuna
rebellious a. buntovan
rebirth n. preporod
rebound v.i. odbiti
rebound n. odbijanje
rebuff n. odbacivanje
rebuff v.t. odbaciti
rebuke v.t. koriti
rebuke n. ukor
recall v.t. opozvati
recall n. opoziv
recede v.i. uzmaći
receipt n. račun
receive v.t. dobiti
receiver n. prijemnik
recent a. nedavni
recently adv. nedavno
reception n. prijem
receptive a. prijemčiv
recess n. udubljenje
recession n. recesija
recipe n. recept

recipient n. primatelj
reciprocal a. recipročan
reciprocate v.t. uzvraćati
recital n. recital
recitation n. recitacija
recite v.t. recitovati
reckless a. nemaran
reckon v.t. računati
reclaim v.t. vratiti
reclamation n reklamacija
recluse n. pustinjak
recognition n. prepoznavanje
recognize v.t. prepoznati
recoil v.i. ustuknuti
recoil adv. odbojno
recollect v.t. sjetiti se
recollection n. sjećanje
recommend v.t. preporučiti
recommendation n. preporuka
recompense v.t. nadoknaditi
recompense n. naknada
reconcile v.t. pomiriti
reconciliation n. izmirenje
record v.t. zapisati
record n. zapisnik
recorder n. zapisničar
recount v.t. iznova brojati
recoup v.t. nadoknaditi
recourse n. regres
recover v.t. oporaviti se
recovery n. oporavak
recreation n. rekreacija
recruit n. regrut
recruit v.t. regrutovati
rectangle n. pravoukutnik
rectangular a. pravokutni
rectification n. ispravljanje
rectify v.i. ispraviti
rectum n. rektum
recur v.i. ponavljati se

recurrence *n.* vraćanje
recurrent *a.* povratni
red *a.* crven
red *n.* crvena boja
redden *v.t.* porumeneti
reddish *a.* crvenkast
redeem *v.t.* iskupiti se
redemption *n.* iskupljenje
redouble *v.t.* udvostručiti
redress *v.t.* popraviti
redress *n* obeštećenje
reduce *v.t.* smanjiti
reduction *n.* smanjenje
redundance *n.* obilje
redundant *a.* suvišan
reel *n.* kalem
reel *v.i.* namotati
refer *v.t.* uputiti
referee *n.* sudac
reference *n.* referenca
referendum *n.* referendum
refine *v.t.* preraditi
refinement *n.* prečišćavanje
refinery *n.* rafinerija
reflect *v.t.* odraziti
reflection *n.* odraz
reflective *a.* reflektujuće
reflector *n.* reflektor
reflex *n.* refleks
reflex *a* refleksan
reflexive *a* povratni
reform *v.t.* reformirati
reform *n.* reforma
reformation *n.* reformacija
reformatory *n.* popravni dom
reformatory *a* popravni
reformer *n.* reformator
refrain *v.i.* uzdržavati se
refrain *n* refren
refresh *v.t.* osvježiti

refreshment *n.* osvježenje
refrigerate *v.t.* rashladiti
refrigeration *n.* hlađenje
refrigerator *n.* hladnjak
refuge *n.* utočište
refugee *n.* izbjeglica
refulgence *n.* sjaj
refulgent *a.* sjajan
refund *v.t.* povratiti
refund *n.* povraćaj
refusal *n.* odbijanje
refuse *v.t.* odbiti
refuse *n.* smeće
refutation *n.* pobijanje
refute *v.t.* pobiti
regal *a.* kraljevski
regard *v.t.* cijeniti
regard *n.* poštovanje
regenerate *v.t.* regenerirati
regeneration *n.* regeneracija
regicide *n.* kraljoubojstvo
regime *n.* režim
regiment *n.* puk
regiment *v.t.* rasporediti
region *n.* regij
regional *a.* regionalni
register *n.* registar
register *v.t.* registrirati
registrar *n.* matičar
registration *n.* registracija
registry *n.* registar
regret *v.i.* žaliti
regret *n* žaljenje
regular *a.* redovan
regularity *n.* pravilnost
regulate *v.t.* regulirati
regulation *n.* propis
regulator *n.* regulator
rehabilitate *v.t.* rehabilititati
rehabilitation *n.* rehabilitacija

rehearsal *n.* proba
rehearse *v.t.* probati
reign *v.i.* vladati
reign *n* vladavina
reimburse *v.t.* nadoknaditi
rein *n.* uzda
rein *v.t.* zauzdati
reinforce *v.t.* pojačati
reinforcement *n.* pojačanje
reinstate *v.t.* ponovno postavljanje
reinstatement *n.* ponovno postaviti
reiterate *v.t.* neprestano ponavljati
reiteration *n.* neprestano ponavljanje
reject *v.t.* odbiti
rejection *n.* odbijanje
rejoice *v.i.* radovati se
rejoin *v.t.* ponovno pridružiti
rejoinder *n.* odgovor
rejuvenate *v.t.* podmladiti
rejuvenation *n.* podmlađivanje
relapse *v.i.* vratiti se
relapse *n.* povratak
relate *v.t.* odnositi se
relation *n.* odnos
relative *a.* relativan
relative *n.* rođak
relax *v.t.* opustiti
relaxation *n.* opuštanje
relay *n.* relej
relay *v.t.* prenositi
release *v.t.* pustiti
release *n* puštanje
relent *v.i.* popustiti
relentless *a.* nemilosrdan
relevance *n.* relevantnost
relevant *a.* relevantan
reliable *a.* pouzdan
reliance *n.* pouzdanje
relic *n.* relikvija
relief *n.* reljef

relieve *v.t.* olakšati
religion *n.* religija
religious *a.* vjerski
relinquish *v.t.* odreći se
relish *v.t.* uživati
relish *n* slast
reluctance *n.* opiranje
reluctant *a.* nerad
rely *v.i.* osloniti
remain *v.i.* ostati
remainder *n.* ostatak
remains *n.* ostaci
remand *v.t.* vratiti u pritvor
remand *n* vraćanje *u* pritvor
remark *n.* napomena
remark *v.t.* napomenuti
remarkable *a.* izvanredan
remedial *a.* popravni
remedy *n.* pravni lijek
remedy *v.t* lijek
remember *v.t.* zapamtiti
remembrance *n.* sećanje
remind *v.t.* podsjetiti
reminder *n.* podsjetnik
reminiscence *n.* uspomena
reminiscent *a.* koji podseća
remission *n.* opraštanje
remit *v.t.* oprostiti
remittance *n.* novčana pošiljka
remorse *n.* pokajanje
remote *a.* dalek
removable *a.* prenosiv
removal *n.* uklanjanje
remove *v.t.* ukloniti
remunerate *v.t.* nagraditi
remuneration *n.* plaća
remunerative *a.* unosan
renaissance *n.* renesansa
render *v.t.* učiniti
rendezvous *n.* randevu

renew *v.t.* obnoviti
renewal *n.* obnova
renounce *v.t.* odreći se
renovate *v.t.* renovirati
renovation *n.* obnova
renown *n.* renome
renowned *a.* poznat
rent *n.* iznajmljivanje
rent *v.t.* iznajmljivati
renunciation *n.* odricanje
repair *v.t.* popraviti
repair *n.* popravka
repairable *a.* opravljiv
repartee *n.* duhovit odgovor
repatriate *v.t.* vratiti *u* domovinu
repatriate *n* povratnik
repatriation *n.* povratak *u* domovinu
repay *v.t.* isplatiti
repayment *n.* otplata
repeal *v.t.* opozvati
repeal *n* opozivanje
repeat *v.t.* ponoviti
repel *v.t.* odbiti
repellent *a.* odvratan
repellent *n* sredstvo protiv insekata
repent *v.i.* *pokajati* se
repentance *n.* pokajanje
repentant *a.* pokajnički
repercussion *n.* posljedica
repetition *n.* ponavljanje
replace *v.t.* zamijeniti
replacement *n.* zamjena
replenish *v.t.* napuniti
replete *a.* napunjen
replica *n.* replika
reply *v.i.* odgovoriti
reply *n* odgovor
report *v.t.* izvijestiti
report *n.* izvješće
reporter *n.* novinar

repose *n.* odmor
repose *v.i.* odmarati se
repository *n.* skladište
represent *v.t.* predstavljati
representation *n.* predstavljanje
representative *n.* predstavnik
representative *a.* reprezentativan
repress *v.t.* potisnuti
repression *n.* suzbijanje
reprimand *n.* ukor
reprimand *v.t.* ukoriti
reprint *v.t.* ponovo štampati
reprint *n.* preštampavanje
reproach *v.t.* prigovarati
reproach *n.* prijekor
reproduce *v.t.* reproducirati
reproduction *n* reprodukcija
reproductive *a.* reproduktivan
reproof *n.* ukor
reptile *n.* reptil
republic *n.* republika
republican *a.* republikanski
republican *n* republikanac
repudiate *v.t.* razvesti se
repudiation *n.* razvod
repugnance *n.* odvratnost
repugnant *a.* odvratan
repulse *v.t.* odbiti
repulse *n.* odbijanje
repulsion *n.* odbojnost
repulsive *a.* odbojan
reputation *n.* ugled
repute *v.t.* smatrati za
repute *n.* ugled
request *v.t.* zahtijevati
request *n* zahtjev
requiem *n.* rekvijem
require *v.t.* tražiti
requirement *n.* traženje
requisite *a.* potreban

requisite *n* potreba
requisition *n.* trebovanje
requisition *v.t.* trebovati
requite *v.t.* vratiti
rescue *v.t.* spasiti
rescue *n* spašavanje
research *v.i.* istraživati
research *n* istraživanje
resemblance *n.* sličnost
resemble *v.t.* ličiti
resent *v.t.* vrijeđati
resentment *n.* ozlojeđenost
reservation *n.* rezervat
reserve *v.t.* rezervisati
reservoir *n.* rezervoar
reside *v.i.* boraviti
residence *n.* prebivalište
resident *a.* rezidentan
resident *n* stanovnik
residual *a.* preostali
residue *n.* ostatak
resign *v.t.* dati ostavku
resignation *n.* ostavka
resist *v.t.* odoljeti
resistance *n.* otpor
resistant *a.* otporan
resolute *a.* odlučan
resolution *n.* rezolucija
resolve *v.t.* riješiti
resonance *n.* rezonanca
resonant *a.* rezonantan
resort *v.i.* pribjeći
resort *n* pribježište
resound *v.i.* odjeknuti
resource *n.* resurs
resourceful *a.* snalažljiv
respect *v.t.* poštovati
respect *n.* poštovanje
respectful *a.* pun poštovanja
respective *a.* odnosan

respiration *n.* disanje
respire *v.i.* disati
resplendent *a.* sjajan
respond *v.i.* odgovoriti
respondent *n.* optuženik
response *n.* odgovor
responsibility *n.* odgovornost
responsible *a.* odgovoran
rest *v.i.* odmoriti se
rest *n* odmor
restaurant *n.* restoran
restive *a.* jogunast
restoration *n.* restauracija
restore *v.t.* obnoviti
restrain *v.t.* obuzdati
restrict *v.t.* ograničiti
restriction *n.* ograničenje
restrictive *a.* restriktivan
result *v.i.* proizlaziti
result *n.* rezultat
resume *v.t.* rezimirati
resume *n.* sažetak
resumption *n.* nastavljanje
resurgence *n.* preporod
resurgent *a.* koji oživljava
retail *v.t.* prodavati robu na malo
retail *n.* maloprodaja
retail *adv.* maloprodajno
retail *a* maloprodajni
retailer *n.* trgovac na malo
retain *v.t.* zadržati
retaliate *v.i.* osvetiti se
retaliation *n.* odmazda
retard *v.t.* usporiti
retardation *n.* retardiranost
retention *n.* zadržavanje
retentive *a.* koji zadržava
reticence *n.* povučenost
reticent *a.* povučen
retina *n.* mrežnica

retinue *n.* pratnja
retire *v.i.* umiroviti
retirement *n.* mirovina
retort *v.t.* odgovoriti
retort *n.* odgovor
retouch *v.t.* retuširati
retrace *v.t.* vratiti se istim putem
retread *v.t.* protektirati gumu
retread *n.* protektirana guma
retreat *v.i.* povlačiti se
retrench *v.t.* smanjiti izdatke
retrenchment *n.* štednja
retrieve *v.t.* povratiti
retrospect *n.* retrospektiva
retrospection *n.* retrospekcija
retrospective *a.* retrospektivan
return *v.i.* vratiti se
return *n.* povratak
revel *v.i.* pijančiti
revel *n.* pijanka
revelation *n.* otkrovenje
reveller *n.* mangup
revelry *n.* terevenka
revenge *v.t.* osvetiti
revenge *n.* osveta
revengeful *a.* osvetoljubiv
revenue *n.* prihod
revere *v.t.* duboko poštovati
reverence *n.* poštovanje
reverend *a.* častan
reverent *a.* pun poštovanja
reverential *a.* pun poštovanja
reverie *n.* sanjarenje
reversal *n.* preokret
reverse *a.* suprotan
reverse *n* suprotnost
reverse *v.t.* obrnuti
reversible *a.* povratan
revert *v.i.* vratiti se
review *v.t.* pregledati

review *n* pregled
revise *v.t.* prepraviti
revision *n.* revizija
revival *n.* oživljavanje
revive *v.i.* oživjeti
revocable *a.* opozivan
revocation *n.* opoziv
revoke *v.t.* opozvati
revolt *v.i.* pobuniti se
revolt *n.* pobuna
revolution *n.* revolucija
revolutionary *a.* revolucionaran
revolutionary *n* revolucionar
revolve *v.i.* obrtati se
revolver *n.* revolver
reward *n.* nagrada
reward *v.t.* nagraditi
rhetoric *n.* retorika
rhetorical *a.* retorički
rheumatic *a.* reumatski
rheumatism *n.* reumatizam
rhinoceros *n.* nosorog
rhyme *n.* rima
rhyme *v.i.* rimovati se
rhymester *n.* stihopisac
rhythm *n.* ritam
rhythmic *a.* ritmičan
rib *n.* rebro
ribbon *n.* traka
rice *n.* riža
rich *a.* bogat
riches *n.* izobilje
richness *n.* bogatstvo
rick *n.* plast
rickets *n.* rahitis
rickety *a.* rahitičan
rickshaw *n.* rikša
rid *v.t.* osloboditi
riddle *n.* zagonetka
riddle *v.i.* prosijati

ride v.t. voziti
ride n vožnja
rider n. jahač
ridge n. greben
ridicule v.t. ismijavati
ridicule n. ismijavanje
ridiculous a. smiješan
rifle v.t. opljačkati
rifle n puška
rift n. pukotina
right a. pravi
right adv ispravno
right n pravo
right v.t. postaviti
righteous a. pravedan
rigid a. rigidan
rigorous a. rigorozan
rigour n. strogost
rim n. obod
ring n. prsten
ring v.t. okružiti
ringlet n. prstenčić
ringworm n. lišaj (oboljenje kože)
rinse v.t. ispirati
riot n. pobuna
riot v.t. bjesniti
rip v.t. cijepati
ripe a zreo
ripen v.i. sazrijevati
ripple n. talasanje
ripple v.t. talasati
rise v. dići se
rise n. dizanje
risk v.t. riskirati
risk n. rizik
risky a. rizičan
rite n. obred
ritual n. ritual
ritual a. ritualni
rival n. protivnik

rival v.t. nadmetati se
rivalry n. rivalstvo
river n. rijeka
rivet n. zakovica
rivet v.t. zakovati
rivulet n. potočić
road n. put
roam v.i. lutati
roar n. rika
roar v.i. rikati
roast v.t. peći
roast a pečen
roast n pečenje
rob v.t. opljačkati
robber n. pljačkaš
robbery n. pljačka
robe n. haljina
robe v.t. odjenuti
robot n. robot
robust a. kršan
rock v.t. ljuljati
rock n. stijena
rocket n. raketa
rod n. štap
rodent n. glodar
roe n. srna
rogue n. bitanga
roguery n. nevaljalost
roguish a. lopovski
role n. uloga
roll n. rolna
roll v.i. kotrljati
roll-call n. prozivka
roller n. valjak
romance n. romantika
romantic a. romantičan
romp v.i. skakati
romp n. ludiranje
rood n. raspeće
roof n. krov

roof *v.t.* pokriti krovom
rook *n.* kula
rook *v.t.* varati
room *n.* soba
roomy *a.* prostran
roost *n.* kokošinjac
roost *v.i.* prenoćiti
root *n.* korijen
root *v.i.* ukorijeniti
rope *n.* uže
rope *v.t.* povezati
rosary *n.* ružičnjak, brojanica
rose *n.* ruža
roseate *a.* ružičast
rostrum *n.* govornica
rosy *a.* rumen
rot *n.* trulež
rot *v.i.* truliti
rotary *a.* rotacijski
rotate *v.i.* rotirati
rotation *n.* rotacija
rote *n.* učenje napamet
rouble *n.* rublja
rough *a.* grub
round *a.* okrugao
round *adv.* okolo
round *n.* okruglost
round *v.t.* zaobliti
rouse *v.i.* probuditi se
rout *v.t.* razbiti
rout *n* trupa
route *n.* put
routine *n.* rutina
routine *a* rutinski
rove *v.i.* lunjati
rover *n.* lutalica
row *n.* red
row *v.t.* veslati
row *n* veslanje
row *n.* svađa

rowdy *a.* larmadžija
royal *a.* kraljevski
royalist *n.* rojalistički
royalty *n.* kraljevstvo
rub *v.t.* trljati
rub *n* trljanje
rubber *n.* guma
rubbish *n.* đubre
rubble *n.* krš
ruby *n.* rubin
rude *a.* nepristojan
rudiment *n.* osnov
rudimentary *a.* osnovni
rue *v.t.* žaliti
rueful *a.* žalostan
ruffian *n.* siledžija
ruffle *v.t.* nabrati
rug *n.* ćilim
rugged *a.* neravan
ruin *n.* propast
ruin *v.t.* upropastiti
rule *n.* pravilo
rule *v.t.* vladati
ruler *n.* vladar
ruling *n.* upravljanje
rum *n.* rum
rum *a* čudan
rumble *v.i.* tutnjiti
rumble *n.* tutnjava
ruminant *a.* koji preživa
ruminant *n.* preživač
ruminate *v.i.* preživati
rumination *n.* razmišljanje
rummage *v.i.* preživanje
rummage *n* preturanje
rummy *n.* remi
rumour *n.* glasina
rumour *v.t.* razglasiti
run *v.i.* trčati
run *n.* trčanje

rung *n.* pregača
runner *n.* trkač
rupee *n.* rupija
rupture *n.* raskid
rupture *v.t.* raskinuti
rural *a.* seoski
ruse *n.* prevara
rush *n.* žurba
rush *v.t.* žuriti
rush *n* nalet
rust *n.* rđa
rust *v.i* rđati
rustic *a.* seoski
rustic *n* seljak
rusticate *v.t.* živjeti na selu
rustication *n.* slanje u selo
rusticity *n.* neotesanost
rusty *a.* zarđao
rut *n.* kolosijek
ruthless *a.* nemilosrdan
rye *n.* raž

S

sabbath *n.* sabat
sabotage *n.* sabotaža
sabotage *v.t.* sabotirati
sabre *n.* sablja
sabre *v.t.* posjeći sabljom
saccharin *n.* saharin
saccharine *a.* šećerni
sack *n.* vreća
sack *v.t.* opljačkati
sacrament *n.* sakrament
sacred *a.* svijeti
sacrifice *n.* žrtvovanje
sacrifice *v.t.* žrtvovati
sacrificial *a.* žrtveni
sacrilege *n.* svetogrđe

sacrilegious *a.* svetogrdan
sacrosanct *a.* svijeti
sad *a.* tužan
sadden *v.t.* rastužiti
saddle *n.* sedlo
saddle *v.t.* osedlati
sadism *n.* sadizam
sadist *n.* sadista
safe *a.* siguran
safe *n.* sigurnost
safeguard *n.* zaštita
safety *n.* bezbednost
saffron *n.* šafran
saffron *a* žut poput šafrana
sagacious *a.* mudar
sagacity *n.* mudrost
sage *n.* mudrac
sage *a.* razborit
sail *n.* jedro
sail *v.i.* jedriti
sailor *n.* mornar
saint *n.* svetac
saintly *a.* svetački
sake *n.* korist
salable *a.* koji se može prodati
salad *n.* salata
salary *n.* zarada
sale *n.* prodaja
salesman *n.* prodavatelj
salient *a.* istaknut
saline *a.* slan
salinity *n.* slanoća
saliva *n.* pljuvačka
sally *n.* ispad
sally *v.i.* ispasti
saloon *n.* krčma
salt *n.* so
salt *v.t* soliti
salty *a.* slan
salutary *a.* zdrav

salutation *n.* pozdrav
salute *v.t.* pozdraviti
salute *n* pozdrav
salvage *n.* spasavanje
salvage *v.t.* spasiti
salvation *n.* spasenje
same *a.* isti
sample *n.* uzorak
sample *v.t.* uzorkovati
sanatorium *n.* sanatorij
sanctification *n.* posvećivanje
sanctify *v.t.* osvetiti
sanction *n.* sankcija
sanction *v.t.* sankcionirati
sanctity *n.* svetost
sanctuary *n.* svetište
sand *n.* pijesak
sandal *n.* sandala
sandalwood *n.* sandalovina
sandwich *n.* sendvič
sandwich *v.t.* umetnuti
sandy *a.* pjeskovit
sane *a.* razuman
sanguine *a.* sangviničan
sanitary *a.* sanitarni
sanity *n.* razum
sap *n.* rov
sap *v.t.* potkopavati
sapling *n.* mladica
sapphire *n.* safir
sarcasm *n.* sarkazam
sarcastic *a.* sarkastičan
sardonic *a.* zloban
satan *n.* sotona
satchel *n.* torba
satellite *n.* satelit
satiable *a.* zajažljiv
satiate *v.t.* zasititi
satiety *n.* sitost
satire *n.* satira

satirical *a.* satiričan
satirist *n.* satiričar
satirize *v.t.* satirizovati
satisfaction *n.* zadovoljstvo
satisfactory *a.* zadovoljavajući
satisfy *v.t.* zadovoljiti
saturate *v.t.* zasititi
saturation *n.* zasićenje
Saturday *n.* subota
sauce *n.* sos
saucer *n.* tanjurić
saunter *v.t.* tumarati
savage *a.* divlji
savage *n* divljak
savagery *n.* divljaštvo
save *v.t.* sačuvati
save *prep* izuzev
saviour *n.* spasitelj
savour *n.* miris
savour *v.t.* mirisati
saw *n.* pila
saw *v.t.* piliti
say *v.t.* riječ
say *n.* reći
scabbard *n.* korice
scabies *n.* šuga
scaffold *n.* skele
scale *n.* skala
scale *v.t.* vagati
scalp *n* skalp
scamper *v.i* pobjeći
scamper *n* bježanje
scan *v.t.* skenirati
scandal *n* skandal
scandalize *v.t.* skandalizovati
scant *a.* oskudan
scanty *a.* oskudan
scapegoat *n.* žrtveni jarac
scar *n* ožiljak
scar *v.t.* zaderati

scarce *a.* rijedak
scarcely *adv.* jedva
scarcity *n.* ištanje
scare *n.* strah
scare *v.t.* uplašiti
scarf *n.* šal
scatter *v.t.* rasturiti
scavenger *n.* skupljač trofeja
scene *n.* scena
scenery *n.* pejzaž
scenic *a.* scenski
scent *n.* miris
scent *v.t.* mirisati
sceptic *n.* skeptik
sceptical *a.* skeptičan
scepticism *n.* skepticizam
sceptre *n.* skiptar
schedule *n.* raspored
schedule *v.t.* rasporediti
scheme *n.* shema
scheme *v.i.* spletkariti
schism *n.* raskol
scholar *n.* stipendista
scholarly *a.* znanstveni
scholarship *n.* stipendija
scholastic *a.* skolastičar
school *n.* škola
science *n.* nauka
scientific *a.* znanstveni
scientist *n.* znanstvenik
scintillate *v.i.* svjetlucati
scintillation *n.* svjetlucanje
scissors *n.* škare
scoff *n.* ruganje
scoff *v.i.* rugati se
scold *v.t.* grditi
scooter *n.* skuter
scope *n.* obim
scorch *v.t.* oprljiti
score *n.* brazda

score *v.t.* urezati
scorer *n.* zapisničar
scorn *n.* prezir
scorn *v.t.* prezirati
scorpion *n.* škorpija
Scot *n.* Škot
scotch *a.* škotski
scotch *n.* urez
scot-free *a.* nekažnjen
scoundrel *n.* nitkov
scourge *n.* bič
scourge *v.t.* bičevati
scout *n* izviđač
scout *v.i* izviđati
scowl *v.i.* mrko gledati
scowl *n.* mrk pogled
scramble *v.i.* verati se
scramble *n* penjanje
scrap *n.* otpadak
scratch *n.* grebanje
scratch *v.t.* grebati
scrawl *v.t.* škrabati
scrawl *n* škrabotina
scream *v.i.* vrištati
scream *n* vrisak
screen *n.* ekran
screen *v.t.* zaklanjati
screw *n.* vijak
screw *v.t.* zašrafiti
scribble *v.t.* škrabati
scribble *n.* škrabanje
script *n.* skripte
scripture *n.* biblija
scroll *n.* svitak
scrutinize *v.t.* pregledati
scrutiny *n.* ispitivanje
scuffle *n.* kavga
scuffle *v.i.* tući se
sculptor *n.* vajar
sculptural *a.* vajarski

sculpture *n.* skulptura
scythe *n.* kosa
scythe *v.t.* pokositi
sea *n.* more
seal *n.* pečat
seal *n.* foka
seal *v.t.* zapečatiti
seam *n.* šav
seam *v.t.* šiti
seamy *a.* pun šavova
search *n.* pretraga
search *v.t.* tražiti
season *n.* sezona
season *v.t.* začiniti
seasonable *a.* pravovremen
seasonal *a.* sezonski
seat *n.* sjedište
seat *v.t.* sjesti
secede *v.i.* otcepiti se
secession *n.* odcjepljenje
secessionist *n.* secesionista
seclude *v.t.* osamiti
secluded *a.* osamljen
seclusion *n.* osamljenost
second *a.* drugi
second *n* sekunda
second *v.t.* podupirati
secondary *a.* sekundaran
seconder *n.* podupirač
secrecy *n.* tajnost
secret *a.* tajni
secret *n.* tajna
secretariat *n.* tajništvo
secretary *n.* tajnik
secrete *v.t.* lučiti
secretion *n.* lučenje
secretive *a.* tajanstven
sect *n.* sekta
sectarian *a.* sektaški
section *n.* odjeljak

sector *n.* sektor
secure *a.* siguran
secure *v.t.* osigurati
security *n.* bezbednosti
sedan *n.* nosiljka
sedate *a.* staložen
sedate *v.t.* uravnotežiti
sedative *a.* umirujući
sedative *n* sedativ
sedentary *a.* sjedeći
sediment *n.* talog
sedition *n.* pobuna
seditious *a.* buntovan
seduce *n.* zavoditi
seduction *n.* zavođenje
seductive *a* zavodljiv
see *v.t.* vidjeti
seed *n.* sjeme
seed *v.t.* posaditi
seek *v.t.* tražiti
seem *v.i.* činiti se
seemly *a.* prikladan
seep *v.i.* curiti
seer *n.* vidovnjak
seethe *v.i.* kipeti
segment *n.* segment
segment *v.t.* segmentirati
segregate *v.t.* odvojiti
segregation *n.* segregacija
seismic *a.* seizmički
seize *v.t.* zgrabiti
seizure *n.* napad
seldom *adv.* rijetko
select *v.t.* izabrati
select *a* izabran
selection *n.* izbor
selective *a.* selektivan
self *n.* svoja ličnost
selfish *a.* sebičan
selfless *a.* nesebičan

sell v.t. prodavati
seller n. prodavatelj
semblance n. sličnost
semen n. sjeme
semester n. semestar
seminal a. iskonski
seminar n. seminar
senate n. senat
senator n. senator
senatorial a. senatorski
senatorial a senatski
send v.t. poslati
senile a. senilan
senility n. senilnost
senior a. stariji
senior n. senior
seniority n. starešinstvo
sensation n. senzacija
sensational a. senzacionalan
sense n. osjećaj
sense v.t. osjetiti
senseless a. besmislen
sensibility n. osjetljivost
sensible a. razuman
sensitive a. osjetljiv
sensual a. senzualan
sensualist n. čulna osoba
sensuality n. čulnost
sensuous a. čulni
sentence n. rečenica
sentence v.t. osuditi
sentience n. osjećaj
sentient a. osjećajan
sentiment n. osjećanje
sentimental a. sentimentalan
sentinel n. stražar
sentry n. straža
separable a. separabilan
separate v.t. odvojiv
separate a. odvojen

separation n. razdvajanje
sepsis n. sepsa
September n. rujan
septic a. septičan
sepulchre n. grobnica
sepulture n. sahrana
sequel n. nastavak
sequence n. sekvenca
sequester v.t. zaplijeniti
serene a. spokojan
serenity n. spokoj
serf n. kmet
serge n. serž
sergeant n. narednik
serial a. serijski
serial n. časopis
series n. serija
serious a ozbiljan
sermon n. propovijed
sermonize v.i. propovijedati
serpent n. zmija
serpentine n. serpentina
servant n. sluga
serve v.t. poslužiti
serve n. servis
service n. služba
service v.t servisirati
serviceable a. uslužan
servile a. servilan
servility n. servilnost
session n. sjednica
set v.t postaviti
set a određen
set n zalazak
settle v.i. naseliti
settlement n. naselje
settler n. naseljenik
seven n. sedam
seven a sedmo-
seventeen n., a sedamnaest

seventeenth *a.* sedamnaesti	**shape** *n.* oblik
seventh *a.* sedmi	**shape** *v.t* oblikovati
seventieth *a.* sedamdeseti	**shapely** *a.* skladan
seventy *n.*, *a* sedamdeset	**share** *n.* udio
sever *v.t.* prekinuti	**share** *v.t.* dijeliti
several *a* više	**share** *n* dionica
severance *n.* razdvajanje	**shark** *n.* ajkula
severe *a.* oštar	**sharp** *a.* oštar
severity *n.* ozbiljnost	**sharp** *adv.* oštro
sew *v.t.* šiti	**sharpen** *v.t.* izoštriti
sewage *n.* odvodni sustav	**sharpener** *n.* rezač
sewer *n* odvodni kanal	**sharper** *n.* varalica
sewerage *n.* kanalizacija	**shatter** *v.t.* razbiti
sex *n.* pol	**shave** *v.t.* brijati
sexual *a.* seksualan	**shave** *n* brijanje
sexuality *n.* seksualnost	**shawl** *n.* šal
sexy *n.* privlačan	**she** *pron.* ona
shabby *a.* otrcan	**sheaf** *n.* snop
shackle *n.* okovi	**shear** *v.t.* ošišati
shackle *v.t.* okovati	**shears** *n.* *pl.* škare
shade *n.* hlad	**shed** *v.t.* ispuštati
shade *v.t.* zasjeniti	**shed** *n* hangar
shadow *n.* senka	**sheep** *n.* ovca
shadow *v.t* potamnjeti	**sheepish** *a.* glup
shadowy *a.* sanjalački	**sheer** *a.* potpun
shaft *n.* vratilo	**sheet** *n.* list
shake *v.i.* tresti	**sheet** *v.t.* umotati
shake *n* potres	**shelf** *n.* polica
shaky *a.* drhtav	**shell** *n.* školjka
shallow *a.* plitak	**shell** *v.t.* ljuštiti
sham *v.i.* pretvarati se	**shelter** *n.* sklonište
sham *n* varka	**shelter** *v.t.* štititi
sham *a* lažan	**shelve** *v.t.* staviti na policu
shame *n.* sramota	**shepherd** *n.* pastir
shame *v.t.* sramotiti	**shield** *n.* štit
shameful *a.* sraman	**shield** *v.t.* braniti
shameless *a.* besraman	**shift** *v.t.* mijenjati
shampoo *n.* šampon	**shift** *n* smjena
shampoo *v.t.* šamponirati	**shifty** *a.* snalažljiv
shanty *a.* straćara	**shilling** *n.* šiling

shilly-shally *v.i.* kolebati se
shilly-shally *n.* kolebljiv
shin *n.* golenica
shine *v.i.* penjati se
shine *n* sjaj
shiny *a.* blistav
ship *n.* brod
ship *v.t.* ukrcati
shipment *n.* pošiljka
shire *n.* grofovija
shirk *v.t.* zabušavati
shirker *n.* zabušant
shirt *n.* košulja
shiver *v.i.* drhtati
shoal *n.* plićak
shoal *n* mnoštvo
shock *n.* šok
shock *v.t.* šokirati
shoe *n.* cipela
shoe *v.t.* obuti
shoot *v.t.* pucati
shoot *n* pucanje
shop *n.* prodavnica
shop *v.i.* kupovati
shore *n.* obala
short *a.* kratak
short *adv.* kratko
shortage *n.* manjak
shortcoming *n.* mana
shorten *v.t.* skratiti
shortly *adv.* uskoro
shorts *n. pl.* šorts
shot *n.* hitac
shoulder *n.* rame
shoulder *v.t.* preuzeti
shout *n.* povik
shout *v.i.* vikati
shove *v.t.* gurati
shove *n.* guranje
shovel *n.* lopata

shovel *v.t.* kopati
show *v.t.* prikazati
show *n.* prikazivanje
shower *n.* tuš
shower *v.t.* tuširati
shrew *n.* oštrokondža
shrewd *a.* lukav
shriek *n.* vrisak
shriek *v.i.* vrištati
shrill *a.* piskav
shrine *n.* svetinja
shrink *v.i* smanjiti se
shrinkage *n.* skupljanje
shroud *n.* pokrov
shroud *v.t.* pokriti plaštom
shrub *n.* žbun
shrug *v.t.* slegnuti ramenima
shrug *n* sleganje ramenima
shudder *v.i.* ježiti se
shudder *n* jeza
shuffle *v.i.* vući noge
shuffle *n.* težak hod
shun *v.t.* izbjegavati
shunt *v.t.* skrenuti
shut *v.t.* zatvoriti
shutter *n.* zatvarač
shuttle *n.* čunak
shuttle *v.t.* ići tamo-ovamo
shuttlecock *n.* loptica za badminton
shy *n.* plašenje
shy *v.i.* plašiti se
sick *a.* bolestan
sickle *n.* srp
sickly *a.* bolesno
sickness *n.* bolest
side *n.* strana
side *v.i.* pristati uz jednu stranu
siege *n.* opsada
siesta *n.* popodnevni odmor
sieve *n.* sito

sieve v.t. prosijati
sift v.t. sijati
sigh n. uzdah
sigh v.i. uzdahnuti
sight n. pogled
sight v.t. ugledati
sightly a. naočit
sign n. znak
sign v.t. obilježiti
signal n. signal
signal a. znamenit
signal v.t. signalizirati
signatory n. potpisnik
signature n. potpis
significance n. značaj
significant a. značajan
signification n. značenje
signify v.t. označavati
silence n. tišina
silence v.t. utišati
silencer n. prigušivač
silent a. tih
silhouette n. silueta
silk n. svila
silken a. svilen
silky a. svilenkast
silly a. glup
silt n. mulj
silt v.t. zamuljiti
silver n. srebro
silver a srebrn
silver v.t. posrebriti
similar a. slične
similarity n. sličnost
simile n. poređenje
similitude n. sličnost
simmer v.i. krčkati
simple a. jednostavan
simpleton n. glupak
simplicity n. jednostavnost

simplification n. uprošćavanje
simplify v.t. pojednostaviti
simultaneous a. istovremen
sin n. grijeh
sin v.i. počiniti grijeh
since prep. od
since conj. odkad
since adv. odonda
sincere a. iskren
sincerity n. iskrenost
sinful a. grešan
sing v.i. pjevati
singe v.t. oprljiti
singe n opeklina
singer n. pjevač
single a. jedini
single n. samac
single v.t. singlirati
singular a. pojedinačan
singularity n. pojedinačnost
singularly adv. pojedinačno
sinister a. zlokoban
sink v.i. potonuti
sink n sudopera
sinner n. grešnik
sinuous a. vijugav
sip v.t. gucnuti
sip n. gutljaj
sir n. gospodin
siren n. sirena
sister n. sestra
sisterhood n. sestrinstvo
sisterly a. sestrinski
sit v.i. sjediti
site n. gradilište
situation n. situacija
six n. šest
sixteen n. šesnaest
sixteenth a. šesnaesti
sixth a. šesti

sixtieth *a.* šezdeseti

sixty *n.* šezdeset

sizable *a.* povelik

size *n.* veličina

size *v.t.* sortirati

sizzle *v.i.* cvrčati

sizzle *n.* cvrčanje

skate *n.* klizaljka

skate *v.t.* klizati

skein *n.* jato divljih ptica

skeleton *n.* skelet

sketch *n.* skica

sketch *v.t.* skicirati

sketchy *a.* nedovršen

skid *v.i.* nepovoljnost

skid *n* kočnica

skilful *a.* vješt

skill *n.* vještina

skin *n.* koža

skin *v.t* oderati

skip *v.i.* preskočiti

skip *n* preskakivanje

skipper *n.* kapetan

skirmish *n.* čarka

skirmish *v.t.* čarkati se

skirt *n.* suknja

skirt *v.t.* ići uzduž

skit *n.* skeč

skull *n.* lubanja

sky *n.* nebo

sky *v.t.* udariti da poleti visoko

slab *n.* ploča

slack *a.* nemaran

slacken *v.t.* olabaviti

slacks *n.* hlače

slake *v.t.* utoliti

slam *v.t.* tresnuti

slam *n* tresak

slander *n.* kleveta

slander *v.t.* klevetati

slanderous *a.* klevetnički

slang *n.* sleng

slant *v.t.* nagnuti

slant *n* nagib

slap *n.* šamar

slap *v.t.* ošamariti

slash *v.t.* bičevati

slash *n* udarac bičem

slate *n.* škriljevac

slattern *n.* aljkava žena

slatternly *a.* aljkav

slaughter *n.* pokolj

slaughter *v.t.* zaklati

slave *n.* rob

slave *v.i.* robovati

slavery *n.* ropstvo

slavish *a.* ropski

slay *v.t.* ubiti

sleek *a.* uglađen

sleep *v.i.* spavati

sleep *n.* san

sleeper *n.* spavač

sleepy *a.* pospan

sleeve *n* rukav

sleight *n.* majstorija

slender *n.* vitak

slice *n.* parče

slice *v.t.* seći

slick *a* klizav

slide *v.i.* kliziti

slide *n* slajd

slight *a.* blag

slight *n.* omalovažavanje

slight *v.t.* omalovažavati

slim *a.* vitak

slim *v.i.* *postati* vitak

slime *n.* mulj

slimy *a.* muljav

sling *n.* praćka

slip *v.i.* okliznuti se

slip *n.* okliznuće
slipper *n.* papuča
slippery *a.* klizav
slipshod *a.* nemaran
slit *n.* raspor
slit *v.t.* rasporiti
slogan *n.* parola
slope *n.* nagib
slope *v.i.* nagnuti
sloth *n.* lijenost
slothful *n.* lijen
slough *n.* močvara
slough *n.* košuljica zmije
slough *v.t.* svlačiti
slovenly *a.* aljkav
slow *a* spor
slow *v.i.* usporiti
slowly *adv.* polako
slowness *n.* sporost
sluggard *n.* ljenjivac
sluggish *a.* lijen
sluice *n.* brana
slum *n.* sirotinjski kraj
slumber *v.i.* drijemati
slumber *n.* drijemež
slump *n.* kriza
slump *v.i.* pasti u krizu
slur *n.* uprljati
slush *n.* bljuzgavica
slushy *a.* bljuzgav
slut *n.* kurva
sly *a.* lukav
smack *n.* okus
smack *v.i.* zveknuti
smack *n* šamar
smack *n.* cmok
smack *v.t.* cmoknuti
small *a.* mali
small *n* mali
smallness *adv.* sićušnost

smallpox *n.* velike boginje
smart *a.* pametan
smart *v.i* žacnuti
smart *n* oštar bol
smash *v.t.* razbiti
smash *n* razbijanje
smear *v.t.* zamazati
smear *n.* mrlja
smell *n.* miris
smell *v.t.* mirisati
smelt *v.t.* istopiti
smile *n.* osmijeh
smile *v.i.* smiješiti se
smith *n.* kovač
smock *n.* radno odijelo
smog *n.* smog
smoke *n.* dim
smoke *v.i.* pušiti se
smoky *a.* zadimljen
smooth *a.* gladak
smooth *v.t.* gladiti
smother *v.t.* ugušiti
smoulder *v.i.* tinjati
smug *a.* samozadovoljan
smuggle *v.t.* prokrijumčariti
smuggler *n.* švercer
snack *n.* užina
snag *n.* čvrga
snail *n.* puž
snake *n.* zmija
snake *v.i.* izvijati se
snap *v.t.* ščepati
snap *n* prasak
snap *a* pras
snare *n.* zamka
snare *v.t.* uhvatiti u zamku
snarl *n.* režanje
snarl *v.i.* režati
snatch *v.t.* zgrabiti
snatch *n.* hvatanje

sneak *v.i.* šunjati se
sneak *n* doušnik
sneer *v.i* podrugivati se
sneer *n* podrugivanje
sneeze *v.i.* kihnuti
sneeze *n* kihanje
sniff *v.i.* šmrkati
sniff *n* šmrkanje
snob *n.* snob
snobbery *n.* snobizam
snobbish *v* snobovski
snore *v.i.* hrkati
snore *n* hrkanje
snort *v.i.* frktati
snort *n.* frktanje
snout *n.* rilo
snow *n.* sneg
snow *v.i.* sniježiti
snowy *a.* snežiti
snub *v.t.* izgrditi
snub *n.* grdnja
snuff *n.* burmut
snug *n.* udoban
so *adv.* tako
so *conj.* pa
soak *v.t.* potopiti
soak *n.* kvašenje
soap *n.* sapun
soap *v.t.* nasapunjati
soapy *a.* sapunast
soar *v.i.* vinuti se
sob *v.i.* jecati
sob *n* jecaj
sober *a.* trezan
sobriety *n.* trezvenost
sociability *n.* društvenost
sociable *a.* društven
social *n.* skup
socialism *n* socijalizam
socialist *n,a* socijalistički

society *n.* društvo
sociology *n.* sociologija
sock *n.* čarapa
socket *n.* utičnica
sod *n.* busen
sodomite *n.* sodomit
sodomy *n.* sodomija
sofa *n.* sofa
soft *n.* zvekan
soften *v.t.* ublažiti
soil *n.* tlo
soil *v.t.* kaljati
sojourn *v.i.* boraviti
sojourn *n* boravak
solace *v.t.* utješiti
solace *n.* utjeha
solar *a.* solarni
solder *n.* lemljenje
solder *v.t.* zalemiti
soldier *n.* vojnik
soldier *v.i.* služiti vojsku
sole *n.* đon
sole *v.t* pođoniti
sole *a* jedini
solemn *a.* svečan
solemnity *n.* svečanost
solemnize *v.t.* svetkovati
solicit *v.t.* izazvati
solicitation *n.* pobuđivanje
solicitor *n.* odvjetnik
solicitous *a.* zabrinut
solicitude *n.* zabrinutost
solid *a.* čvrst
solid *n* čvrsto tijelo
solidarity *n.* solidarnost
soliloquy *n.* monolog
solitary *a.* usamljen
solitude *n.* usamljenost
solo *n* solo
solo *a.* sam

solo *adv.* solo
soloist *n.* solista
solubility *n.* rastvorljivost
soluble *a.* topiv
solution *n.* rješenje
solve *v.t.* riješiti
solvency *n.* solventnost
solvent *a.* solventan
solvent *n* otapalo
sombre *a.* tmuran
some *a.* neki
some *pron.* nešto
somebody *pron.* neko
somebody *n.* neko
somehow *adv.* nekako
someone *pron.* neko
somersault *n.* salto
somersault *v.i.* napraviti salto
something *pron.* nešto
something *adv.* nešto
sometime *adv.* jednom
sometimes *adv.* ponekad
somewhat *adv.* nešto
somewhere *adv.* negde
somnambulism *n.* mjesečarenje
somnambulist *n.* mesečar
somnolence *n.* pospanost
somnolent *n.* pospan
son *n.* sin
song *n.* pjesma
songster *n.* pjevač
sonic *a.* zvučni
sonnet *n.* sonet
sonority *n.* zvučnost
soon *adv.* uskoro
soot *n.* čađ
soot *v.t.* čađiti
soothe *v.t.* ublažiti
sophism *n.* sofizam
sophist *n.* sofista

sophisticate *v.t.* sofisticirati
sophisticated *a.* sofisticiran
sophistication *n.* prefinjenost
sorcerer *n.* čarobnjak
sorcery *n.* čarobnjaštvo
sordid *a.* prljav
sore *a.* ranjiv
sore *n* rana
sorrow *n.* tuga
sorrow *v.i.* žaliti
sorry *a.* žalostan
sort *n.* vrsta
sort *v.t* sortirati
soul *n.* duša
sound *a.* zdrav
sound *v.i.* zvučati
sound *n* zvuk
soup *n.* juha
sour *a.* kiseo
sour *v.t.* ukiseliti
source *n.* izvor
south *n.* jug
south *n.* južni krajevi
south *adv* južno
southerly *a.* južni
southern *a.* južni
souvenir *n.* suvenir
sovereign *n.* vladar
sovereign *a* suveren
sovereignty *n.* suverenost
sow *v.t.* sejati
sow *n.* krmača
space *n.* prostor
space *v.t.* ostaviti razmak
spacious *a.* prostran
spade *n.* lopata
spade *v.t.* kopati lopatom
span *n.* raspon
span *v.t.* premostiti
Spaniard *n.* Španjolac

spaniel *n.* španijel
Spanish *a.* španjolski
Spanish *n.* španjloski jezik, Španjolac
spanner *n.* izvijač
spare *v.t.* štedjeti
spare *a* rezervni
spare *n.* rezervni dio
spark *n.* varnica
spark *v.i.* varničiti
spark *n.* veseljak
sparkle *v.i.* sjajiti
sparkle *n.* sjaj
sparrow *n.* vrabac
sparse *a.* oskudan
spasm *n.* grč
spasmodic *a.* grčevit
spate *n.* bujica
spatial *a.* prostorni
spawn *n.* mrijest
spawn *v.i.* mrijestiti se
speak *v.i.* govoriti
speaker *n.* zvučnik, govornik
spear *n.* koplje
spear *v.t.* probosti kopljem
spearhead *n.* *vrh* koplja
spearhead *v.t.* voditi napad
special *a.* poseban
specialist *n.* specijalista
speciality *n.* specijalitet
specialization *n.* specijalizacija
specialize *v.i.* specijalizirati se
species *n.* vrsta
specific *a.* specifičan
specification *n.* specifikacija
specify *v.t.* navesti
specimen *n.* primjerak
speck *n.* čestica
spectacle *n.* spektakl
spectacular *a.* spektakularan
spectator *n.* gledatelj

spectre *n.* avet
speculate *v.i.* spekulirati
speculation *n.* spekulacija
speech *n.* govor
speed *n.* brzina
speed *v.i.* ubrzati
speedily *adv.* brzo
speedy *a.* brz
spell *n.* čarolija
spell *v.t.* spelovati
spell *n* opčinjenost
spend *v.t.* provesti
spendthrift *n.* rasipnik
sperm *n.* sperma
sphere *n.* sfera
spherical *a.* sferni
spice *n.* začin
spice *v.t.* začiniti
spicy *a.* ljut
spider *n.* pauk
spike *n.* šiljak
spike *v.t.* zašiljiti
spill *v.i.* prosuti
spill *n* prolivanje
spin *v.i.* zavrtjeti
spin *n.* okretanje
spinach *n.* spanać
spinal *a.* kičmeni
spindle *n.* vreteno
spine *n.* kičma
spinner *n.* prelja
spinster *n.* usedelica
spiral *n.* spirala
spiral *a.* spiralni
spirit *n.* duh
spirited *a.* živahan
spiritual *a.* duhovni
spiritualism *n.* spiritualizam
spiritualist *n.* spiritista
spirituality *n.* duhovnost

spit *v.i.* pljunuti

spit *n* pljuvačka

spite *n.* inat

spittle *n* ispljuvak

spittoon *n.* pljuvaonica

splash *v.i.* poprskati

splash *n* prskanje

spleen *n.* slezina

splendid *a.* sjajan

splendour *n.* sjaj

splinter *n.* iverica

splinter *v.t.* rascepiti

split *v.i.* rascepiti

split *n* pukotina

spoil *v.t.* pokvariti

spoil *n* plijen

spoke *n.* prečka

spokesman *n.* glasnogovornik

sponge *n.* spužva

sponge *v.t.* obrisati spužvicom

sponsor *n.* sponzor

sponsor *v.t.* sponzorirati

spontaneity *n.* spontanost

spontaneous *a.* spontan

spoon *n.* žlica

spoon *v.t.* uzeti žlicom

spoonful *n.* *puna* žlica

sporadic *a.* sporadičan

sport *n.* sport

sport *v.i.* zabavljati se

sportive *a.* veseo

sportsman *n.* spotraš

spot *n.* mjesto

spot *v.t.* okaljati

spotless *a.* neokaljan

spousal *n.* svadba

spouse *n.* bračni drug

spout *n.* pisak posude

spout *v.i.* izbacivati

sprain *n.* uganuće

sprain *v.t.* uganuti

spray *n.* sprej

spray *n* grančica

spray *v.t.* prskati

spread *v.i.* širiti

spread *n.* širenje

spree *n.* pijanka

sprig *n.* grančica

sprightly *a.* živahan

spring *v.i.* skočiti

spring *n* proleće

sprinkle *v. t.* posipati

sprint *v.i.* sprintati

sprint *n* sprint

sprout *v.i.* nicati

sprout *n* mladica

spur *n.* mamuza

spur *v.t.* podbosti

spurious *a.* lažan

spurn *v.t.* gurnuti nogom

spurt *v.i.* špricati

spurt *n* mlaz

sputnik *n.* sputnik

sputum *n.* ispljuvak

spy *n.* špijun

spy *v.i.* špijunirati

squad *n.* vod

squadron *n.* eskadrila

squalid *a.* bijedan

squalor *n.* bijeda

squander *v.t.* traćiti

square *n.* kvadrat

square *a* četvrtast

square *v.t.* načiniti četvorokutim

squash *v.t.* cijediti

squash *n* bundeva

squat *v.i.* čučati

squeak *v.i.* cičati

squeak *n* priča

squeeze *v.t.* iscijediti

squint *v.i.* razrokost
squint *n* razrokost
squire *n.* vlastelin
squirrel *n.* veverica
stab *v.t.* ubosti
stab *n.* ubod
stability *n.* stabilnost
stabilization *n.* stabilizacija
stabilize *v.t.* stabilizirati
stable *a.* stabilan
stable *n* štala
stable *v.t.* držati u štali
stadium *n.* stadion
staff *n.* osoblje
staff *v.t.* snabdjeti osobljem
stag *n.* jelen
stage *n.* pozornica
stage *v.t.* prirediti
stagger *v.i.* teturati se
stagger *n.* teturanje
stagnant *a.* nepokretan
stagnate *v.i.* stagnirati
stagnation *n.* stagnacija
staid *a.* staložen
stain *n.* mrlja
stain *v.t.* mrljati
stainless *a.* neumrljan
stair *n.* stepenik
stake *n* ulog
stake *v.t.* uložiti
stale *a.* ustajao
stale *v.t.* istrošiti
stalemate *n.* pat
stalk *n.* stabljika
stalk *v.i.* prikradati se
stalk *n* kočoperenje
stall *n.* štala
stall *v.t.* držati u štali
stallion *n.* pastuh
stalwart *a.* odlučan

stalwart *n* odlučan zagovornik
stamina *n.* izdržljivost
stammer *v.i.* mucati
stammer *n* mucanje
stamp *n.* pečat
stamp *v.i.* zapečatiti
stampede *n.* stampedo
stampede *v.i* bježati u panici
stand *v.i.* stajati
stand *n.* štand
standard *n.* standard
standard *a* standardan
standardization *n.* standardizacija
standardize *v.t.* standardizirati
standing *n.* stajanje
standpoint *n.* stanovište
standstill *n.* zastoj
stanza *n.* strofa
staple *n.* spajalica
staple *a* heftati
star *n.* zvijezda
star *v.t.* ukrasiti zvijezdama
starch *n.* škrob
starch *v.t.* štirkati
stare *v.i.* buljiti
stare *n.* buljenje
stark *n.* potpunost
stark *adv.* potpun
starry *a.* zvezdan
start *v.t.* početi
start *n* start
startle *v.t.* iznenaditi
starvation *n.* gladovanje
starve *v.i.* umirati *od* gladi
state *n.* stanje, država
state *v.t* navoditi
stateliness *n.* dostojanstvenost
stately *a.* veličanstven
statement *n.* izjava
statesman *n.* državnik

static *n.* statičnost
statics *n.* statika
station *n.* stanica
station *v.t.* stacionirati
stationary *a.* stacionaran
stationer *n.* trgovac pisaćim priborom
stationery *n.* kancelarijski pribor
statistical *a.* statistički
statistician *n.* statističar
statistics *n.* statistika
statue *n.* statua
stature *n.* stas
status *n.* status
statute *n.* statut
statutory *a.* statutarne
staunch *a.* odan
stay *v.i.* ostati
stay *n* boravak
steadfast *a.* postojan
steadiness *n.* postojanost
steady *a.* čvrst
steady *v.t.* učvrstiti
steal *v.i.* ukrasti
stealthily *adv.* krišom
steam *n* para
steam *v.i.* pariti
steamer *n.* parobrod
steed *n.* konj
steel *n.* čelik
steep *a.* strm
steep *v.t.* močiti
steeple *n.* zvonik
steer *v.t.* upravljati
stellar *a.* zvezdan
stem *n.* stabla
stem *v.i.* zaustaviti
stench *n.* smrad
stencil *n.* matrica
stencil *v.i.* umnožiti matricom
stenographer *n.* stenograf

stenography *n.* stenografija
step *n.* korak
step *v.i.* koračati
steppe *n.* stepa
stereotype *n.* stereotip
stereotype *v.t.* stereotipizirati
stereotyped *a.* ukalupljen
sterile *a.* sterilan
sterility *n.* sterilitet
sterilization *n.* sterilizacija
sterilize *v.t.* sterilizirati
sterling *a.* prvoklasan
sterling *n.* sterling
stern *a.* ozbiljan
stern *n.* krma
stethoscope *n.* stetoskop
stew *n.* paprikaš
stew *v.t.* dinstati
steward *n.* stjuard
stick *n.* štap
stick *v.t.* zabosti
sticker *n.* naljepnica
stickler *n.* pristalica
sticky *n.* ljepljiv
stiff *n.* krut
stiffen *v.t.* ukrutiti
stifle *v.t.* ugušiti
stigma *n.* stigma
still *a.* miran
still *adv.* još uvijek
still *v.t.* umiriti
still *n.* mir
stillness *n.* tišina
stilt *n.* štula
stimulant *n.* stimulans
stimulate *v.t.* stimulisati
stimulus *n.* poticaj
sting *v.t.* ubod
sting *n.* žaoka
stingy *a.* škrt

stink *v.i.* smrdjeti
stink *n* smrad
stipend *n.* plaća
stipulate *v.t.* ustanoviti
stipulation *n.* odredba
stir *v.i.* uskomešati se
stirrup *n.* uzengija
stitch *n.* šav
stitch *v.t.* krpiti
stock *n.* zaliha
stock *v.t.* opskrbiti
stock *a.* spreman
stocking *n.* čarapa
stoic *n.* stoik
stoke *v.t.* ložiti
stoker *n.* ložač
stomach *n.* stomak
stomach *v.t.* podnositi
stone *n.* kamen
stone *v.t.* kamenovati
stony *a.* kamenit
stool *n.* stolica
stoop *v.i.* pognuti se
stoop *n* pognutost
stop *v.t.* zaustaviti
stop *n* obustava
stoppage *n* zastoj
storage *n.* skladištenje
store *n.* prodavaonica
store *v.t.* skladištiti
storey *n.* kat
stork *n.* roda
storm *n.* oluja
storm *v.i.* jurišati
stormy *a.* olujni
story *n.* priča
stout *a.* krupan
stove *n.* peć
stow *v.t.* natovariti
straggle *v.i.* lutati

straggler *n.* lutalica
straight *a.* prav
straight *adv.* pravo
straighten *v.t.* ispraviti
straightforward *a.* iskren
straightway *adv.* smjesta
strain *v.t.* naprezati
strain *n* naprezanje
strait *n.* tjesnac
straiten *v.t.* suziti
strand *v.i.* nasukati
strand *n* obala
strange *a.* čudan
stranger *n.* stranac
strangle *v.t.* ugušiti
strangulation *n.* gušenje
strap *n.* pojas
strap *v.t.* opasati
strategem *n.* lukavstvo
strategic *a.* strateški
strategist *n.* strateg
strategy *n.* strategija
stratum *n.* naslaga
straw *n.* slama
strawberry *n.* jagoda
stray *v.i.* zalutati
stray *a* zalutao
stray *n* lutalice
stream *n.* potok
stream *v.i.* teći
streamer *n.* traka
streamlet *n.* potočić
street *n.* ulica
strength *n.* snaga
strengthen *v.t.* ojačati
strenuous *a.* naporan
stress *n.* stres
stress *v.t* naglašavati
stretch *v.t.* rastezati
stretch *n* rastezanje

stretcher *n.* nosila	**studio** *n.* studio
strew *v.t.* posuti	**studious** *a.* marljiv
strict *a.* strog	**study** *v.i.* učiti
stricture *n.* zamjerka	**study** *n.* radna soba
stride *v.i.* koračati	**stuff** *n.* materijal
stride *n* korak	**stuff 2** *v.t* . napuniti, ispuniti
strident *a.* kreštav	**stuffy** *a.* zagušljiv
strife *n.* sukob	**stumble** *v.i.* spotaći se
strike *v.t.* udariti	**stumble** *n.* spoticanje
strike *n* štrajk	**stump** *n.* panj
striker *n.* štrajkač	**stump** *v.t* tabati
string *n.* vrpca	**stun** *v.t.* ošamutiti
string *v.t.* nategnuti	**stunt** *v.t.* praviti akrobacije
stringency *n.* ištanje	**stunt** *n* majstorija
stringent *a.* strog	**stupefy** *v.t.* omamiti
strip *n.* traka	**stupendous** *a.* čudesan
strip *v.t.* svlačiti	**stupid** *a* glup
stripe *n.* pruga	**stupidity** *n.* glupost
stripe *v.t.* isprugati	**sturdy** *a.* čvrst
strive *v.i.* težiti	**sty** *n.* svinjac
stroke *n.* udarac	**stye** *n.* čmičak
stroke *v.t.* milovati	**style** *n.* stil
stroke *n* milovanje	**subdue** *v.t.* obuzdati
stroll *v.i.* tumarati	**subject** *n.* subjekat
stroll *n* tumaranje	**subject** *a* podložan
strong *a.* jak	**subject** *v.t.* podvrgnuti
stronghold *n.* uporište	**subjection** *n.* potčinjenje
structural *a.* strukturni	**subjective** *a.* subjektivan
structure *n.* struktura	**subjugate** *v.t.* potčiniti
struggle *v.i.* boriti se	**subjugation** *n.* pokoravanje
struggle *n* borba	**sublet** *v.t.* dati u podzakup
strumpet *n.* uličarka	**sublimate** *v.t.* sublimirati
strut *v.i.* razmetati se	**sublime** *a.* uzvišen
strut *n* razmetanje	**sublime** *n* uzvišenost
stub *n.* panj	**sublimity** *n.* otmjenost
stubble *n.* strnjika	**submarine** *n.* podmornica
stubborn *a.* tvrdoglav	**submarine** *a* podmorski
stud *n.* ergela	**submerge** *v.i.* potopiti
stud *v.t.* odbiti	**submission** *n.* pokornost
student *n.* student	**submissive** *a.* pokoran

submit *v.t.* podnijeti
subordinate *a.* podređen
subordinate *n* podređeni
subordinate *v.t.* potčiniti
subordination *n.* podređenost
subscribe *v.t.* potpisati
subscription *n.* pretplata
subsequent *a.* sledeći
subservience *n.* korist
subservient *a.* koristan
subside *v.i.* opasti
subsidiary *a.* podružnica
subsidize *v.t.* subvencionirati
subsidy *n.* subvencija
subsist *v.i.* opstajati
subsistence *n.* opstanak
substance *n.* supstanca
substantial *a.* znatan
substantially *adv.* bitno
substantiate *v.t.* potvrditi
substantiation *n.* potvrđivanje
substitute *n.* zamjena
substitute *v.t.* zamijeniti
substitution *n.* zamjena
subterranean *a.* podzemni
subtle *n.* suptilan
subtlety *n.* suptilnost
subtract *v.t.* oduzeti
subtraction *n.* oduzimanje
suburb *n.* predgrađe
suburban *a.* prigradski
subversion *n.* subverzija
subversive *a.* subverzivan
subvert *v.t.* podriti
succeed *v.i.* uspjeti
success *n.* uspjeh
successful *a* uspješan
succession *n.* nasljedstvo
successive *a.* uzastopan
successor *n.* nasljednik

succour *n.* pomoć
succour *v.t.* pomoći
succumb *v.i.* podleći
such *a.* ovakav
such *pron.* takav
suck *v.t.* sisati
suck *n.* sisanje
suckle *v.t.* dojiti
sudden *n.* iznenadnost
suddenly *adv.* iznenada
sue *v.t.* tužiti
suffer *v.t.* patiti
suffice *v.i.* zadovoljavati
sufficiency *n.* dostatnost
sufficient *a.* dovoljan
suffix *n.* sufiks
suffix *v.t.* dodati
suffocate *v.t* ugušiti
suffocation *n.* gušenje
suffrage *n.* *pravo* glasa
sugar *n.* šećer
sugar *v.t.* zasladiti
suggest *v.t.* predložiti
suggestion *n.* prijedlog
suggestive *a.* sugestivan
suicidal *a.* samoubilački
suicide *n.* samoubojstvo
suit *n.* odijelo
suit *v.t.* odgovarati
suitability *n.* podobnost
suitable *a.* pogodan
suite *n.* apartman
suitor *n.* prosilac
sullen *a.* sumoran
sulphur *n.* sumpor
sulphuric *a.* sumporni
sultry *a.* sparan
sum *n.* suma
sum *v.t.* sumirati
summarily *adv.* ukratko

summarize *v.t.* rezimirati

summary *n.* sažetak

summary *a* sažet

summer *n.* ljeto

summit *n.* vrh

summon *v.t.* pozvati

summons *n.* poziv

sumptuous *a.* raskošan

sun *n.* sunce

sun *v.t.* sunčati

Sunday *n.* nedjelja

sunder *v.t.* rastaviti

sunny *a.* sunčan

sup *v.i.* gucnuti

superabundance *n.* preobilje

superabundant *a.* preobilan

superb *a.* izvanredan

superficial *a.* površan

superficiality *n.* površnost

superfine *a.* najfiniji

superfluity *n.* višak

superfluous *a.* suvišno

superhuman *a.* nadljudski

superintend *v.t.* rukovoditi

superintendence *n.* vrhovni nadzor

superintendent *n.* nadzornik

superior *a.* nadmoćan

superiority *n.* superiornost

superlative *a.* superlativan

superlative *n.* superlativ

superman *n.* nadčovjek

supernatural *a.* natprirodan

supersede *v.t.* zamijeniti

supersonic *a.* supersoničan

superstition *n.* praznovjerje

superstitious *a.* praznovjeran

supertax *n.* poseban porez na dohodak

supervise *v.t.* nadgledati

supervision *n.* nadzor

supervisor *n.* nadzornik

supper *n.* večera

supple *a.* savitljiv

supplement *n.* dopuna

supplement *v.t.* dopuniti

supplementary *a.* dopunski

supplier *n.* dobavljač

supply *v.t.* opskrbljivati

supply *n* opskrba

support *v.t.* podržati

support *n.* podrška

suppose *v.t.* pretpostaviti

supposition *n.* pretpostavka

suppress *v.t.* suzbijati

suppression *n.* suzbijanje

supremacy *n.* prevlast

supreme *a.* vrhovni

surcharge *n.* preopterećenje

surcharge *v.t.* preopteretiti

sure *a.* siguran

surely *adv.* sigurno

surety *n.* izvjesnost

surf *n.* surf

surface *n.* površina

surface *v.i* poravnati

surfeit *n.* prezasićenost

surge *n.* val

surge *v.i.* val

surgeon *n.* kirurg

surgery *n.* kirurgija

surmise *n.* pretpostavka

surmise *v.t.* pretpostaviti

surmount *v.t.* savladati

surname *n.* prezime

surpass *v.t.* nadmašiti

surplus *n.* višak

surprise *n.* iznenađenje

surprise *v.t.* iznenaditi

surrender *v.t.* predati se

surrender *n* predaja

surround *v.t.* okruživati

surroundings n. okruženje
surtax n. dopunski porez
surveillance n. nadzor
survey n. pregled
survey v.t. pregledati
survival n. opstanak
survive v.i. opstati
suspect v.t. osumnjičiti
suspect a. osumnjičen
suspect n osumnjičeni
suspend v.t. suspendirati
suspense n. neizvjesnost
suspension n. obustava
suspicion n. sumnja
suspicious a. sumnjiv
sustain v.t. održati
sustenance n. izdržavanje
swagger v.i. šepuriti se
swagger n šepurenje
swallow v.t. progutati
swallow n. gutljaj
swallow n. lasta
swamp n. močvara
swamp v.t. poplaviti
swan n. labud
swarm n. roj
swarm v.i. rojiti se
swarthy a. crnpurast
sway v.i. njihati
sway n njihanje
swear v.t. psovati
sweat n. znoj
sweat v.i. kleti se
sweater n. džemper
sweep v.i. čistiti
sweep n. zamah
sweeper n. čistač
sweet a. sladak
sweet n slatkiš
sweeten v.t. zašećeriti

sweetmeat n. slatkiš
sweetness n. slatkoća
swell v.i. nabreknuti
swell n oteklina
swift a. brz
swim v.i. plivati
swim n plivanje
swimmer n. plivač
swindle v.t. prevariti
swindle n. prijevara
swindler n. varalica
swine n. svinja
swing v.i. ljuljati
swing n ljuljaška
swiss n. švicarska
swiss a švicarski
switch n. prekidač
switch v.t. skrenuti
swoon n. nesvijest
swoon v.i onesvijestiti se
swoop v.i. kidisati
swoop n prepad
sword n. mač
sycamore n. javor
sycophancy n. ulizivanje
sycophant n. ulizica
syllabic n. slogovni
syllable n. slog
syllabus n. pregled
sylph n. zračni duh
sylvan a. pošumljen
symbol n. simbol
symbolic a. simboličan
symbolism n. simbolizam
symbolize v.t. simbolizirati
symmetrical a. simetričan
symmetry n. simetrija
sympathetic a. saosećajan
sympathize v.i. suosjećati
sympathy n. simpatija

symphony n. simfonija
symposium n. simpozijum
symptom n. simptom
symptomatic a. simptomatičan
synonym n. sinonim
synonymous a. sinoniman
synopsis n. sinopsis
syntax n. sintaksa
synthesis n. sinteza
synthetic a. sintetički
synthetic n sintetika
syringe n. špric
syringe v.t. štrcnuti
syrup n. sirup
system n. sistem
systematic a. sistematičan
systematize v.t. sistematizirati

T

table n. sto
table v.t. izložiti
tablet n. tableta
taboo n. tabu
taboo a zabranjen
taboo v.t. zabraniti
tabular a. tabelarni
tabulate v.t. poređati
tabulation n. tabelisanje
tabulator n. tabulator
tacit a. prećutan
taciturn a. suzdržan
tackle n. pribor
tackle v.t. prionuti
tact n. takt
tactful a. taktičan
tactician n. taktičar
tactics n. taktika
tactile a. taktilni

tag n. oznaka
tag v.t. označiti
tail n. rep
tailor n. krojač
tailor v.t. krojiti
taint n. mrlja
taint v.t. uprljati
take v.t uzeti
tale n. priča
talent n. talenat
talisman n. talisman
talk v.i. pričati
talk n razgovor
talkative a. pričljiv
tall a. visok
tallow n. loj
tally n. evidencija
tally v.t. podudarati
tamarind n. indijska urma
tame a. pitom
tame v.t. pripitomiti
tamper v.i. pokvariti
tan v.i. preplanuti
tan n., a. preplanulost
tangent n. tangenta
tangible a. opipljiv
tangle n. zaplet
tangle v.t. zamrsiti
tank n. rezervoar
tanker n. tanker
tanner n. kožar
tannery n. kožara
tantalize v.t. mučiti
tantamount a. jednake vrijednosti
tap n. slavina
tap v.t. tapkati
tape n. traka
tape v.t svezati trakom
taper v.i. zašiljiti
taper n tanka voštana svijeća

tapestry *n.* tapiserija
tar *n.* katran
tar *v.t.* premazati katranom
target *n.* cilj
tariff *n.* tarifa
tarnish *v.t.* gubiti boju
task *n.* zadatak
task *v.t.* uposliti
taste *n.* okus
taste *v.t.* okusiti
tasteful *a.* ukusan
tasty *a.* ukusan
tatter *n.* dronjak
tatter *v.t* pocepati u dronjke
tattoo *n.* tetoviranje
tattoo *v.i.* tetovirati
taunt *v.t.* podrugivati se
taunt *n* podrugivanje
tavern *n.* krčma
tax *n.* porez
tax *v.t.* oporezovati
taxable *a.* oporeziv
taxation *n.* oporezivanje
taxi *n.* taksi
taxi *v.i.* Taksirati
tea *n* čaj
teach *v.t.* učiti
teacher *n.* učitelj
teak *n.* tik
team *n.* tim
tear *v.t.* poderati
tear *n.* suza
tear *n.* poderotina
tearful *a.* suzan
tease *v.t.* zadirkivati
teat *n.* sisa
technical *n.* tehnički
technicality *n.* formalnost
technician *n.* tehničar
technique *n.* tehnika

technological *a.* tehnološki
technologist *n.* tehnolog
technology *n.* tehnologija
tedious *a.* dosadan
tedium *n.* dosada
teem *v.i.* vrveti
teenager *n.* tinejdžer
teens *n. pl.* omladina
teethe *v.i.* dobiti zube
teetotal *a.* trezvenjački
teetotaller *n.* trezvenjak
telecast *n.* prijenos
telecast *v.t.* prenositi
telegram *n.* telegram
telegraph *n.* telegraf
telegraph *v.t.* telegrafisati
telegraphic *a.* telegrafski
telegraphist *n.* telegrafista
telegraphy *n.* telegrafija
telepathic *a.* telepatski
telepathist *n.* telepata
telepathy *n.* telepatija
telephone *n.* telefon
telephone *v.t.* telefonirati
telescope *n.* teleskop
telescopic *a.* teleskopski
televise *v.t.* emitirati preko televizije
television *n.* televizija
tell *v.t.* reći
teller *n.* blagajnik
temper *n.* temperament
temper *v.t.* miješati
temperament *n.* temperament
temperamental *a.* temperamentan
temperance *n.* umjerenost
temperate *a.* umjeren
temperature *n.* temperatura
tempest *n.* oluja
tempestuous *a.* buran
temple *n.* hram

temple *n* sljepoočnica
temporal *a.* vremenski
temporary *a.* privremen
tempt *v.t.* dovesti u iskušenje
temptation *n.* iskušenje
tempter *n.* iskušavač
ten *n.*, *a* deset
tenable *a.* održiv
tenacious *a.* uporan
tenacity *n.* istrajnost
tenancy *n.* zakup
tenant *n.* stanar
tend *v.i.* biti sklon
tendency *n.* tendencija
tender *n* ponuda
tender *v.t.* ponuditi
tender *n* njegovatelj
tender *a* nježan
tenet *n.* načelo
tennis *n.* tenis
tense *n.* glagolsko vrijeme
tense *a.* napet
tension *n.* tenzija
tent *n.* šator
tentative *a.* probni
tenure *n.* mandat
term *n.* rok
term *v.t.* nazvati
terminable *a.* ograničen
terminal *a.* konačni
terminal *n* terminal
terminate *v.t.* okončati
termination *n.* završetak
terminological *a.* terminološki
terminology *n.* terminologija
terminus *n.* kraj
terrace *n.* terasa
terrible *a.* užasan
terrier *n.* terijer
terrific *a.* strašan

terrify *v.t.* prestraviti
territorial *a.* teritorijalni
territory *n.* teritorija
terror *n.* teror
terrorism *n.* terotizam
terrorist *n.* terorista
terrorize *v.t.* terorisati
terse *a.* sažet
test *v.t.* testirati
test *n* test
testament *n.* testament
testicle *n.* testis
testify *v.i.* svjedočiti
testimonial *n.* uvjerenje
testimony *n.* svjedočanstvo
tete-a-tete *n.* sastanak u četiri oka
tether *n.* lanac
tether *v.t.* privezati
text *n.* tekst
textile *a.* tekstilni
textile *n* tekstil
textual *n.* tekstualni
texture *n.* sastav
thank *v.t.* zahvaliti
thanks *n.* zahvalnost
thankful *a.* zahvalan
thankless *a.* nezahvalan
that *a.* taj
that *dem. pron.* onaj
that *rel. pron.* koji
that *adv.* tako
that *conj.* da
thatch *n.* slama
thatch *v.t.* pokriti krov
thaw *v.i* topiti se
thaw *n* topljenje
theatre *n.* kazalište
theatrical *a.* kazališni
theft *n.* krađa
their *a.* njihov

theirs *pron.* njihov
theism *n.* teizam
theist *n.* teista
them *pron.* njih
thematic *a.* tematski
theme *n.* tema
then *adv.* onda
then *a* tadašnji
thence *adv.* odande
theocracy *n.* teokracija
theologian *n.* teolog
theological *a.* teološki
theology *n.* teologija
theorem *n.* teorema
theoretical *a.* teorijski
theorist *n.* teoretičar
theorize *v.i.* teoretizirati
theory *n.* teorija
therapy *n.* terapija
there *adv.* tamo
thereabouts *adv.* otprilike
thereafter *adv.* posle toga
thereby *adv.* time
therefore *adv.* dakle
thermal *a.* termalni
thermometer *n.* termometar
thermos (flask) *n.* termos (boca)
thesis *n.* teza
thick *a.* debeo
thick *n.* najgušći dio
thick *adv.* debelo
thicken *v.i.* zgusnuti
thicket *n.* gustiš
thief *n.* lopov
thigh *n.* bedro
thimble *n.* naprstak
thin *a.* tanak
thin *v.t.* tanjiti
thing *n.* stvar
think *v.t.* misliti

thinker *n.* mislilac
third *a.* treći
third *n.* trećina
thirdly *adv.* treće
thirst *n.* žeđ
thirst *v.i.* biti žedan
thirsty *a.* žedan
thirteen *n.* trinaest
thirteen *a* trinaest
thirteenth *a.* trinaesti
thirtieth *a.* trideseti
thirtieth *n* tridesetina
thirty *n.* trideset
thirty *a* trideset
thistle *n.* čičak
thither *adv.* tamo
thorn *n.* trn
thorny *a.* trnovit
thorough *a* temeljan
thoroughfare *n.* prolaz
though *conj.* premda
though *adv.* ipak
thought *n* misao
thoughtful *a.* pažljiv
thousand *n.* tisuća
thousand *a* tisuću
thrall *n.* rob
thraldom *n.* ropstvo
thrash *v.t.* mlatiti
thread *n.* nit
thread *v.t* udenuti
threadbare *a.* otrcan
threat *n.* prijetnja
threaten *v.t.* prijetiti
three *n.* tri
three *a* tri
thresh *v.t.* vršati
thresher *n.* vršalica
threshold *n.* prag
thrice *adv.* triput

thrift *n.* štednja

thrifty *a.* štedljiv

thrill *n.* uzbuđenje

thrill *v.t.* uzbuditi

thrive *v.i.* napredovati

throat *n.* grlo

throaty *a.* grlen

throb *v.i.* lupati

throb *n.* lupanje

throe *n.* agonija

throne *n.* tron

throne *v.t.* posaditi na prijestolje

throng *n.* gomila

throng *v.t.* gomilati se

throttle *n.* dušnik

throttle *v.t.* gušiti

through *prep.* kroz

through *adv.* skroz

through *a* izravan

throughout *adv.* skroz

throughout *prep.* širom

throw *v.t.* baciti

throw *n.* bacanje

thrust *v.t.* gurati

thrust *n* potisak

thud *n.* tutnjava

thud *v.i.* tutnjiti

thug *n.* razbojnik

thumb *n.* palac

thumb *v.t.* opipati palcem

thump *n.* *tup* udarac

thump *v.t.* lupiti

thunder *n.* grom

thunder *v.i.* grmeti

thunderous *a.* gromovit

Thursday *n.* četvrtak

thus *adv.* stoga

thwart *v.t.* osujetiti

tiara *n.* tijara

tick *n.* otkucaj

tick *v.i.* kucati

ticket *n.* karta

tickle *v.t.* golicati

ticklish *a.* golicljiv

tidal *a.* plimski

tide *n.* plima

tidings *n. pl.* vijesti

tidiness *n.* urednost

tidy *a.* uredan

tidy *v.t.* počistiti

tie *v.t.* vezati

tie *n* kravata

tier *n.* niz

tiger *n.* tigar

tight *a.* čvrst

tighten *v.t.* pritegnuti

tigress *n.* tigrica

tile *n.* crijep

tile *v.t.* pokriti crijepom

till *prep.* do

till *n. conj.* dok

till *v.t.* obrađivati

tilt *v.i.* nagnuti se

tilt *n.* nagib

timber *n.* greda

time *n.* vrijeme

time *v.t.* izabrati vrijeme

timely *a.* na vrijeme

timid *a.* stidljiv

timidity *n.* bojažljivost

timorous *a.* plašljiv

tin *n.* konzerva

tin *v.t.* kalajisati

tincture *n.* boja

tincture *v.t.* obojiti

tinge *n.* nijansa

tinge *v.t.* nijansirati

tinker *n.* kotlar

tinsel *n.* šljokica

tint *n.* boja

tint *v.t.* obojiti
tiny *a.* sićušan
tip *n.* savjet
tip *v.t.* savjetovati
tip *n.* vrh
tip *v.t.* prevrnuti
tip *n.* kraj
tip *v.t.* okovati
tipsy *a.* pripit
tirade *n.* tirada
tire *v.t.* izmoriti
tiresome *a.* zamoran
tissue *n.* tkivo
titanic *a.* titanski
tithe *n.* desetina
title *n.* naslov
titular *a.* titularni
toad *n.* žaba krastača
toast *n.* zdravica
toast *v.t.* nazdraviti
tobacco *n.* duhan
today *adv.* danas
today *n.* današnjica
toe *n.* nožni prst
toe *v.t.* dodirnuti nožnim prstima
toffee *n.* karamela
toga *n.* toga
together *adv.* zajedno
toil *n.* rintanje
toil *v.i.* rintati
toilet *n.* toalet
toils *n. pl.* mreže
token *n.* znak
tolerable *a.* podnošljiv
tolerance *n.* tolerancija
tolerant *a.* tolerantan
tolerate *v.t.* tolerirati
toleration *n.* tolerancija
toll *n.* pristojba
toll *n* zvonjava

toll *v.t.* zvoniti
tomato *n.* paradajz
tomb *n.* grob
tomboy *n.* nestaško
tomcat *n.* mačak
tome *n.* tom
tomorrow *n.* sutrašnji dan
tomorrow *adv.* sutra
ton *n.* tona
tone *n.* zvuk
tone *v.t.* davati ton
tongs *n. pl.* kliješta
tongue *n.* jezik
tonic *a.* toničan
tonic *n.* tonik
to-night *n.* ova noć
tonight *adv.* večeras
tonne *n.* tona
tonsil *n.* krajnik
tonsure *n.* tonzura
too *adv.* suviše
tool *n.* alat
tooth *n.* zub
toothache *n.* zubobolja
toothsome *a.* ukusan
top *n.* vrh
top *v.t.* pokriti
top *n.* čigra
topaz *n.* topaz
topic *n.* tema
topical *a.* tematski
topographer *n.* topograf
topographical *a.* topografski
topography *n.* topografija
topple *v.i.* srušiti se
topsy turvy *a.* pobrkan
topsy turvy *adv* pobrkano
torch *n.* baklja
torment *n.* muka
torment *v.t.* mučiti

tornado *n.* tornado
torpedo *n.* torpedo
torpedo *v.t.* torpedovati
torrent *n.* bujica
torrential *a.* bujan
torrid *a.* suh
tortoise *n.* kornjača
tortuous *a.* kazneni
torture *n.* mučenje
torture *v.t.* mučiti
toss *v.t.* zbaciti
toss *n* zbacivanje
total *a.* ukupan
total *n.* cjelina
total *v.t.* zbrojiti
totality *n.* cjelokupnost
touch *v.t.* dodirnuti
touch *n* dodir
touchy *a.* osjetljiv
tough *a.* težak
toughen *v.t.* očvrsnuti
tour *n.* tura
tour *v.i.* putovati
tourism *n.* turizam
tourist *n.* turista
tournament *n.* turnir
towards *prep.* ka
towel *n.* ručnik
towel *v.t.* brisati ručnikom
tower *n.* toranj
tower *v.i.* dizati se
town *n.* grad
township *a.* općinski
toy *n.* igračka
toy *v.i.* igrati se
trace *n.* trag
trace *v.t.* tragati
traceable *a.* kome se može naći trag
track *n.* staza
track *v.t.* slijediti

tract *n.* trakt
tract *n* traktat
traction *n.* vuča
tractor *n.* traktor
trade *n.* trgovina
trade *v.i* trgovati
trader *n.* trgovac
tradesman *n.* trgovac
tradition *n.* tradicija
traditional *a.* tradicionalan
traffic *n.* saobraćaj
traffic *v.i.* trgovati
tragedian *n.* tragičar
tragedy *n.* tragedija
tragic *a.* tragičan
trail *n.* trag
trail *v.t.* puzati
trailer *n.* prikolica
train *n.* voz
train *v.t.* trenirati
trainee *n.* pripravnik
training *n.* obuka
trait *n.* osobina
traitor *n.* izdajnik
tram *n.* tramvaj
trample *v.t.* pogaziti
trance *n.* trans
tranquil *a.* miran
tranquility *n.* mir
tranquillize *v.t.* stišati
transact *v.t.* obaviti
transaction *n.* transakcija
transcend *v.t.* prekoračiti
transcendent *a.* nenadmašan
transcribe *v.t.* prepisati
transcription *n.* transkripcija
transfer *n.* prijenos
transfer *v.t.* prenositi
transferable *a.* prenosiv
transfiguration *n.* preobraženje

transfigure *v.t.* preobraziti
transform *v.* transformirati
transformation *n.* transformacija
transgress *v.t.* prekršiti
transgression *n.* prijestup
transit *n.* tranzit
transition *n.* prijelaz
transitive *n.* prijelazni
transitory *n.* prolazan
translate *v.t.* prevoditi
translation *n.* prevođenje
transmigration *n.* seoba
transmission *n.* transmisija
transmit *v.t.* prenositi
transmitter *n.* odašiljač
transparent *a.* transparentan
transplant *v.t.* presađivati
transport *v.t.* prevoziti
transport *n.* prijevoz
transportation *n.* transport
trap *n.* zamka
trap *v.t.* uhvatiti u zamku
trash *n.* smeće
travel *v.i.* putovati
travel *n* putovanje
traveller *n.* putnik
tray *n.* pladanj
treacherous *a.* izdajnički
treachery *n.* izdaja
tread *v.t.* koračati
tread *n* hod
treason *n.* izdaja
treasure *n.* blago
treasure *v.t.* čuvati
treasurer *n.* blagajnik
treasury *n.* državna blagajna
treat *v.t.* liječiti
treat *n* čašćenje
treatise *n.* rasprava
treatment *n.* tretman

treaty *n.* pregovor
tree *n.* drvo
trek *v.i.* seliti se
trek *n.* putovanje
tremble *v.i.* drhtati
tremendous *a.* ogroman
tremor *n.* drhtanje
trench *n.* rov
trench *v.t.* rezati
trend *n.* trend
trespass *v.i.* zgriješiti
trespass *n.* prijestup
trial *n.* suđenje
triangle *n.* trokut
triangular *a.* trokutni
tribal *a.* plemenski
tribe *n.* pleme
tribulation *n.* stradanje
tribunal *n.* sud
tributary *n.* pritoka
tributary *a.* dužan da daje danak
trick *n* trik
trick *v.t.* prevariti
trickery *n.* varanje
trickle *v.i.* kapati
trickster *n.* varalica
tricky *a.* lukav
tricolour *a.* trobojni
tricolour *n* trobojnica
tricycle *n.* tricikl
trifle *n.* sitnica
trifle *v.i* igrati se
trigger *n.* okidač
trim *a.* uredan
trim *n* red
trim *v.t.* urediti
trinity *n.* trojstvo
trio *n.* trio
trip *v.t.* poigravati
trip *n.* putovanje

tripartite *a.* trodelan	**trusty** *n.* vjeran
triple *a.* trostruk	**truth** *n.* istina
triple *v.t.*, utrostručiti	**truthful** *a.* istinoljubiv
triplicate *a.* trokratan	**try** *v.i.* pokušati
triplicate *n* triplikat	**try** *n* pokušaj
triplicate *v.t.* potrostručiti	**trying** *a.* težak
triplication *n.* utrostručenje	**tryst** *n.* sastanak
tripod *n.* tronožac	**tub** *n.* kada
triumph *n.* trijumf	**tube** *n.* cijev
triumph *v.i.* trijumfovati	**tuberculosis** *n.* tuberkuloza
triumphal *a.* trijumfalan	**tubular** *a.* cjevasti
triumphant *a.* pobednički	**tug** *v.t.* trzati
trivial *a.* trivijalan	**tuition** *n.* školarina
troop *n.* četa	**tumble** *v.i.* pasti
troop *v.i* skupljati se	**tumble** *n.* pad
trooper *n.* policajac	**tumbler** *n.* akrobata
trophy *n.* trofej	**tumour** *n.* tumor
tropic *n.* tropski pojas	**tumult** *n.* metež
tropical *a.* tropski	**tumultuous** *a.* bučan
trot *v.i.* kasati	**tune** *n.* melodija
trot *n* kas	**tune** *v.t.* ugađati
trouble *n.* nevolja	**tunnel** *n.* tunel
trouble *v.t.* uzburkati	**tunnel** *v.i.* bušiti tunel
troublesome *a.* mučan	**turban** *n.* turban
troupe *n.* glumačka družina	**turbine** *n.* turbina
trousers *n. pl* hlače	**turbulence** *n.* turbulencije
trowel *n.* mistrija	**turbulent** *a.* turbulentan
truce *n.* primirje	**turf** *n.* treset
truck *n.* kamion	**turkey** *n.* ćurka
true *a.* pravi	**turmeric** *n.* kurkuma
trump *n.* adut	**turmoil** *n.* nemir
trump *v.t.* nadmudriti	**turn** *v.i.* okrenuti
trumpet *n.* truba	**turn** *n* okret
trumpet *v.i.* trubiti	**turner** *n.* strugar
trunk *n.* stablo	**turnip** *n.* repa
trust *n.* povjerenje	**turpentine** *n.* terpentin
trust *v.t* vjerovati	**turtle** *n.* kornjača
trustee *n.* povjerenik	**tusk** *n.* kljova
trustful *a.* povjerljiv	**tussle** *n.* borba
trustworthy *a.* pouzdan	**tussle** *v.i.* boriti se

tutor *n.* tutor
tutorial *a.* učiteljski
tutorial *n.* uputa
twelfth *a.* dvanaesti
twelfth *n.* dvanaestina
twelve *n.* dvanaestorica
twelve *n* dvanaest
twentieth *a.* dvadeseti
twentieth *n* dvadesetina
twenty *a.* dvadeset
twenty *n* dvadesetorica
twice *adv.* dvaput
twig *n.* grančica
twilight *n* suton
twin *n.* blizanac
twin *a* dvostruk
twinkle *v.i.* svjetlucati
twinkle *n.* svjetlucanje
twist *v.t.* uviti
twist *n.* obrt
twitter *n.* cvrkut
twitter *v.i.* cvrkutati
two *n.* dva
two *a.* dvoje
twofold *a.* dvostruk
type *n.* tip
type *v.t.* tipkati
typhoid *n.* tifozan
typhoon *n.* tajfun
typhus *n.* tifus
typical *a.* tipičan
typify *v.t.* predstaviti
typist *n.* daktilograf
tyranny *n.* tiranija
tyrant *n.* tiranin
tyre *n.* guma

U

udder *n.* vime
uglify *v.t.* poružnjavati
ugliness *n.* ružnoća
ugly *a.* ružan
ulcer *n.* čir
ulcerous *a.* gnojan
ulterior *a.* prikriven
ultimate *a.* krajnji
ultimately *adv.* na kraju
ultimatum *n.* ultimatum
umbrella *n.* kišobran
umpire *n.* sudac
umpire *v.t.,* osuditi
unable *a.* nemoćan
unanimity *n.* jednoglasnost
unanimous *a.* jednoglasan
unaware *a.* nesvjestan
unawares *adv.* nehotice
unburden *v.t.* rasteretiti
uncanny *a.* neugodan
uncertain *a.* neizvjestan
uncle *n.* stric, tetak, ujak
uncouth *a.* nepoznat
under *prep.* ispod
under *adv* niže
under *a* niži
undercurrent *n.* podvodna struja
underdog *n* gubitnik
undergo *v.t.* pretrpjeti
undergraduate *n.* student
underhand *a.* nepošten
underline *v.t.* podvući
undermine *v.t.* podriti
underneath *adv.* ispod
underneath *prep.* pod
understand *v.t.* razumjeti

undertake v.t. poduzeti
undertone n. prigušen glas
underwear n. donje rublje
underworld n. podzemlje
undo v.t. poništiti
undue a. nepriklada
undulate v.i. talasati se
undulation n. lelujanje
unearth v.t. iskopati
uneasy a. nelagodan
unfair a nepravedan
unfold v.t. otvoriti
unfortunate a. nesrećan
ungainly a. nezgrapan
unhappy a. nesrećan
unification n. ujedinjenje
union n. unija
unionist n. unionista
unique a. jedinstven
unison n. jednoglasje
unit n. jedinica
unite v.t. ujediniti
unity n. jedinstvo
universal a. univerzalan
universality n. univerzalnost
universe n. svemir
university n. sveučilište
unjust a. nepravedan
unless conj. sem ako
unlike a nejednak
unlike prep za razliku od
unlikely a. nevjerojatan
unmanned a. bez posade
unmannerly a nevaspitan
unprincipled a. neprincipijelan
unreliable a. nepouzdan
unrest n nemir
unruly a. jogunast
unsettle v.t. uznemiriti
unsheathe v.t. izvaditi iz korica

until prep. do
until conj dok
untoward a. uporan
unwell a. bolestan
unwittingly adv. nenamjerno
up adv. gore
up prep. prema gore
upbraid v.t kuditi
upheaval n. preokret
uphold v.t podržati
upkeep n održavanje
uplift v.t. podići
uplift n uzdignuće
upon prep na
upper a. gornji
upright a. čestit
uprising n. ustanak
uproar n. metež
uproarious a. bučan
uproot v.t. iskorjeniti
upset v.t. uznemiriti
upshot n. ishod
upstart n. skorojević
up-to-date a. suvremen
upward a. okrenut uvis
upwards adv. nagore
urban a. urbani
urbane a. učtiv
urbanity n. učtivost
urchin n. derište
urge v.t nagnati
urge n nagon
urgency n. hitnost
urgent a. hitan
urinal n. pisoar
urinary a. urinarni
urinate v.i. urinirati
urination n. mokrenje
urine n. urin
urn n urna

usage *n.* primjena
use *n.* upotreba
use *v.t.* upotrijebiti
useful *a.* koristan
usher *n.* vratar
usher *v.t.* uvesti
usual *a.* uobičajen
usually *adv.* obično
usurer *n.* zelenaš
usurp *v.t.* uzurpirati
usurpation *n.* uzurpacija
usury *n.* zelenaštvo
utensil *n.* pribor
uterus *n.* materica
utilitarian *a.* utilitaristički
utility *n.* korisnost
utilization *n.* korišćenje
utilize *v.t.* iskoristiti
utmost *a.* krajnji
utmost *n* krajnost
utopia *n* . utopija
utopian *a.* utopijski
utter *v.t.* izustiti
utter *a* potpun
utterance *n.* iskaz
utterly *adv.* potpuno

V

vacancy *n.* upražnjeno mesto
vacant *a.* prazan
vacate *v.t.* napustiti
vacation *n.* odmor
vaccinate *v.t.* cijepiti
vaccination *n.* cijepljenje
vaccinator *n.* liječnik koji cijepi
vaccine *n.* cjepivo
vacillate *v.i. kolebati* se
vacuum *n.* vakuum

vagabond *n.* skitnica
vagabond *a* skitalački
vagary *n.* lutanje
vagina *n.* vagina
vague *a.* nejasan
vagueness *n.* neodređenost
vain *a.* uzaludan
vainglorious *a.* hvalisav
vainglory *n.* hvalisavost
vainly *adv.* uzalud
vale *n.* dolina
valiant *a.* hrabar
valid *a.* validan
validate *v.t.* potvrditi
validity *n.* pravovaljanost
valley *n.* dolina
valour *n.* junaštvo
valuable *a.* vrijedan
valuation *n.* procjena
value *n.* vrijednost
value *v.t.* cijeniti
valve *n.* ventil
van *n.* kombi
vanish *v.i.* iščeznuti
vanity *n.* sujeta
vanquish *v.t.* pobediti
vaporize *v.t.* isparavati
vaporous *a.* parni
vapour *n.* para
variable *a.* varijabla
variance *n.* promjena
variation *n.* varijacija
varied *a.* raznolik
variety *n.* raznovrsnost
various *a.* različit
varnish *n.* lak
varnish *v.t.* lakirati
vary *v.t.* varirati
vasectomy *n.* vazektomija
vaseline *n.* vazelin

vast *a.* ogroman
vault *n.* svod
vault *n.* skok
vault *v.i.* nadsvoditi
vegetable *n.* povrće
vegetable *a.* povrtni
vegetarian *n.* vegetarijanac
vegetarian *a* vegetarijanski
vegetation *n.* vegetacija
vehemence *n.* žestina
vehement *a.* žestok
vehicle *n.* vozilo
vehicular *a.* automobilski
veil *n.* veo
veil *v.t.* prekriti
vein *n.* vena
velocity *n.* brzina
velvet *n.* somot
velvety *a.* baršunast
venal *a.* podmitljiv
venality *n.* podmitljivost
vendor *n.* prodavatelj
venerable *a.* prečasni
venerate *v.t.* poštovati
veneration *n.* strahopoštovanje
vengeance *n.* osveta
venial *a.* oprostiv
venom *n.* otrov
venomous *a.* otrovan
vent *n.* odušak
ventilate *v.t.* ventilirati
ventilation *n.* ventilacija
ventilator *n.* ventilator
venture *n.* pothvat
venture *v.t.* usuditi se
venturesome *a.* riskantan
venturous *a.* opasan
venue *n.* djelokrug
veracity *n.* istinitost
verendah *n.* veranda

verb *n.* glagol
verbal *a.* verbalni
verbally *adv.* usmeno
verbatim *a.* doslovan
verbatim *adv.* doslovno
verbose *a.* preopširan
verbosity *n.* preopširnost
verdant *a.* zelen
verdict *n.* presuda
verge *n.* rub
verification *n.* verifikacija
verify *v.t.* verificirati
verisimilitude *n.* vjerojatnost
veritable *a.* pravi
vermillion *n.* cinober
vermillion *a.* boje cinobera
vernacular *n.* domaći
vernacular *a.* narodni
vernal *a.* proljetni
versatile *a.* svestran
versatility *n.* svestranost
verse *n.* stih
versed *a.* okretan
versification *n.* stihotvorstvo
versify *v.t.* pretvoriti u stihove
version *n.* verzija
versus *prep.* protiv
vertical *a.* vertikalan
verve *n.* elan
very *a.* veoma
vessel *n.* brod
vest *n.* prsluk
vest *v.t.* obući
vestige *n.* trag
vestment *n.* odežda
veteran *n.* veteran
veteran *a.* veteranski
veterinary *a.* veterinarski
veto *n.* veto
veto *v.t.* staviti veto

vex *v.t.* nasekirati	**violation** *n.* kršenje
vexation *n* sekiracija	**violence** *n.* nasilje
via *prep.* preko	**violent** *a.* nasilan
viable *a.* održiv	**violet** *n.* ljubičica
vial *n.* bočica	**violin** *n.* violina
vibrate *v.i.* vibrirati	**violinist** *n.* violinista
vibration *n.* vibracija	**virgin** *n.* devac
vicar *n.* vikar	**virgin** *n* djevica
vicarious *a.* namjesnički	**virginity** *n.* nevinost
vice *n.* porok	**virile** *a.* muški
viceroy *n.* potkralj	**virility** *n.* muževnost
vice-versa *adv.* obrnuto	**virtual** *a* virtuelan
vicinity *n.* blizina	**virtue** *n.* vrlina
vicious *a.* opak	**virtuous** *a.* vrli
vicissitude *n.* nestalnost	**virulence** *n.* pakost
victim *n.* žrtva	**virulent** *a.* pakostan
victimize *v.t.* žrtvovati	**virus** *n.* virus
victor *n.* pobjednik	**visage** *n.* lice
victorious *a.* pobjedonosan	**visibility** *n.* vidljivost
victory *n.* pobjeda	**visible** *a.* vidljiv
victuals *n. pl* hrana	**vision** *n.* vizija
vie *v.i.* nadmetati se	**visionary** *a.* vizionarski
view *n.* pogled	**visionary** *n.* vizionar
view *v.t.* razgledati	**visit** *n.* posjet
vigil *n.* bdijenje	**visit** *v.t.* posjetiti
vigilance *n.* budnost	**visitor** *n.* posjetitelj
vigilant *a.* oprezan	**vista** *n.* vidik
vigorous *a.* energičan	**visual** *a.* vizualni
vile *a.* loš	**visualize** *v.t.* vizualizovati
vilify *v.t.* sramotiti	**vital** *a.* vitalan
villa *n.* vila	**vitality** *n.* vitalnost
village *n.* selo	**vitalize** *v.t.* oživljavati
villager *n.* seljak	**vitamin** *n.* vitamin
villain *n.* zlikovac	**vitiate** *v.t.* pokvariti
vindicate *v.t.* opravdati	**vivacious** *a.* čio
vindication *n.* opravdanje	**vivacity** *n.* živahnost
vine *n.* vinova loza	**viva-voce** *adv.* usmeno
vinegar *n.* sirće	**viva-voce** *a* usmen
vintage *n.* berba	**viva-voce** *n* usmeni ispit
violate *v.t.* povrijediti	**vivid** *a.* živ

vixen *n.* lisica
vocabulary *n.* rječnik
vocal *a.* vokalni
vocalist *n.* pjevač
vocation *n.* zanimanje
vogue *n.* moda
voice *n.* glas
voice *v.t.* izgovoriti
void *a.* prazan
void *v.t.* poništiti
void *n.* praznina
volcanic *a.* vulkanski
volcano *n.* vulkan
volition *n.* volja
volley *n.* volej
volley *v.t* skresati
volt *n.* volt
voltage *n.* napon
volume *n.* obujam
voluminous *a.* obiman
voluntarily *adv.* dobrovoljno
voluntary *a.* dobrovoljan
volunteer *n.* volonter
volunteer *v.t.* volontirati
voluptuary *n.* pohotljivac
voluptuous *a.* pohotan
vomit *v.t.* povraćati
vomit *n* povraćanje
voracious *a.* proždrljiv
votary *n.* kaluđer
vote *n.* glasovanje
vote *v.i.* glasati
voter *n.* glasač
vouch *v.i.* jamčiti
voucher *n.* vaučer
vouchsafe *v.t.* odobriti
vow *n.* zavjet
vow *v.t.* zavjetovati
vowel *n.* samoglasnik
voyage *n.* putovanje

voyage *v.i.* putovati
voyager *n.* putnik
vulgar *a.* vulgaran
vulgarity *n.* vulgarnost
vulnerable *a.* ranjiv
vulture *n.* lešinar

W

wade *v.i.* gaziti
waddle *v.i.* geganje
waft *v.t.* lebdjeti
waft *n* dah
wag *v.i.* mahati
wag *n* mahanje
wage *v.t.* voditi
wage *n.* plaća
wager *n.* ulog
wager *v.i.* kladiti se
wagon *n.* vagon
wail *v.i.* jadikovati
wail *n* jadikovanje
wain *n.* kola
waist *n.* struk
waistband *n.* opasač
waistcoat *n.* prsluk
wait *v.i.* čekati
wait *n.* čekanje
waiter *n.* konobar
waitress *n.* konobarica
waive *v.t.* odustati
wake *v.t.* probuditi
wake *n* bdijenje
wake *n* daća
wakeful *a.* budan
walk *v.i.* šetati
walk *n* šetnja
wall *n.* zid
wall *v.t.* opasati zidom

wallet *n.* novčanik
wallop *v.t.* istući
wallow *v.i.* valjati se
walnut *n.* orah
walrus *n.* morž
wan *a.* bled
wand *n.* štapić
wander *v.i.* lutati
wane *v.i.* opadati
wane *n* opadanje
want *v.t.* željeti
want *n* potreba
wanton *a.* raskalašan
war *n.* rat
war *v.i.* ratovati
warble *v.i.* treperiti
warble *n* treperenje
warbler *n.* ptica pjevačica
ward *n.* štićenik
ward *v.t.* čuvati
warden *n.* upravitelj zatvora
warder *n.* čuvar
wardrobe *n.* garderoba
wardship *n.* skrbništvo
ware *n.* roba
warehouse *v.t* magacin
warfare *n.* ratovanje
warlike *a.* ratoboran
warm1 *a.* vruć
warm *v.t.* topao
warmth *n.* toplota
warn *v.t.* upozoriti
warning *n.* upozorenje
warrant *n.* nalog
warrant *v.t.* jamčiti
warrantee *n.* opunomoćenik
warrantor *n.* jamac
warranty *n.* jamstvo
warren *n.* odgajivačnica zečeva
warrior *n.* ratnik

wart *n.* bradavica
wary *a.* oprezan
wash *v.t.* prati
wash *n* pranje
washable *a.* koji se može prati
washer *n.* perač
wasp *n.* osa
waspish *a.* naprasit
wassail *n.* pijanka
wastage *n.* rasipanje
waste *a.* pust
waste *n.* otpad
waste *v.t.* pustošiti
wasteful *a.* rasipan
watch *v.t.* gledati
watch *n.* sat
watchful *a.* budan
watchword *n.* lozinka
water *n.* vode
water *v.t.* zalijevati
waterfall *n.* vodopad
water-melon *n.* lubenica
waterproof *a.* vodootporan
waterproof *n* vodootpornost
waterproof *v.t.* učiniti nepromočivim
watertight *a.* nepromočiv
watery *a.* vodeni
watt *n.* vat
wave *n.* val
wave *v.t.* val
waver *v.i.* mahati
wax *n.* vosak
wax *v.t.* rasti
way *n.* način
wayfarer *n.* putnik
waylay *v.t.* napasti iz zasjede
wayward *a.* svojevoljan
weak *a.* slab
weaken *v.t. & i* oslabiti
weakling *n.* slabić

weakness *n.* slabost	**weld** *v.t.* zavarivati
weal *n.* masnica	**weld** *n.* zavarak
wealth *n.* bogatstvo	**welfare** *n.* blagostanje
wealthy *a.* bogat	**well** *a.* dobar
wean *v.t.* odučiti	**well** *adv.* dobro
weapon *n.* oružje	**well** *n.* bunar
wear *v.t.* pohabati	**well** *v.i.* izviriti
weary *a.* umoran	**wellignton** *n.* velington
weary *v.t. & i* umoriti	**well-known** *a.* poznat
weary *a.* dosadan	**well-read** *a.* načitan
weary *v.t.* dosađivati	**well-timed** *a.* blagovremen
weather *n* vrijeme	**well-to-do** *a.* imućan
weather *v.t.* odoljeti	**welt** *n.* porub
weave *v.t.* tkati	**welter** *n.* zbrka
weaver *n.* tkač	**wen** *n.* izraslina
web *n.* mreža	**wench** *n.* djevojka
webby *a.* koji je kao tkivo	**west** *n.* zapad
wed *v.t.* vjenčati	**west** *a.* zapadni
wedding *n.* vjenčanje	**west** *adv.* zapadno
wedge *n.* klin	**westerly** *a.* zapadno
wedge *v.t.* pričvrstiti klinom	**westerly** *adv.* zapadni
wedlock *n.* brak	**western** *a.* vestern
Wednesday *n.* sreda	**wet** *a.* mokar
weed *n.* korov	**wet** *v.t.* pokvasiti
weed *v.t.* pleviti	**wetness** *n.* vlažnost
week *n.* nedjelja	**whack** *v.t.* udariti
weekly *a.* tjedni	**whale** *n.* kit
weekly *adv.* tjedno	**wharfage** *n.* taksa za vezivanje broda
weekly *n.* tjednik	**what** *a.* kakav
weep *v.i.* plakati	**what** *pron.* šta
weevil *n.* žižak	**what** *interj.* šta
weigh *v.t.* vagati	**whatever** *pron.* štagod
weight *n.* težina	**wheat** *n.* pšenica
weighage *n.* pristojba za vaganje	**wheedle** *v.t.* iskamčiti
weighty *a.* važan	**wheel** *a.* kotač
weir *n.* brana	**wheel** *v.t.* kotrljati
weird *a.* čudan	**whelm** *v.t.* poplaviti
welcome *a.* dobrodošao	**whelp** *n.* štene
welcome *n* dobrodošlica	**when** *adv.* kada
welcome *v.t* pozdraviti	**when** *conj.* kad

whence *adv.* odakle
whenever *adv. conj* kad god
where *adv.* gdje
where *conj.* gdje
whereabout *adv.* negdje
whereas *conj.* pošto
whereat *conj.* gdje
wherein *adv. u* kome
whereupon *conj.* nakon čega
wherever *adv. gdje* god
whet *v.t.* brusiti
whether *conj.* bilo da
which *pron.* koji
which *a* koji
whichever *pron* koji god
whiff *n.* dašak
while *n.* vremenski period
while *conj.* dok
while *v.t.* provesti
whim *n.* kapric
whimper *v.i.* cviljenje
whimsical *a.* kapriciozan
whine *v.i.* prenemagati se
whine *n* prenemaganje
whip *v.t.* bičevati
whip *n.* bič
whipcord *n.* uzica biča
whir *n.* zujanje
whirl *n.i.* kovitlac
whirl *n* vrtlog
whirligig *n.* zvrk
whirlpool *n.* vrtlog
whirlwind *n.* vihor
whisk *v.t.* mahati
whisk *n* zamah
whisker *n.* dlaka
whisky *n.* viski
whisper *v.t.* šaputati
whisper *n* šapat
whistle *v.i.* zviždati

whistle *n* zvižduk
white *a.* bijeli
white *n* bijela boja
whiten *v.t.* bijeleti
whitewash *n.* bjelilo
whitewash *v.t.* obijeleti
whither *adv.* kuda
whitish *a.* bjelkast
whittle *v.t.* strugati
whiz *v.i.* zujanje
who *pron.* ko
whoever *pron.* ma ko
whole *a.* cijeli
whole *n* cjelina
whole-hearted *a.* odan
wholesale *n.* veleprodaja
wholesale *a* veleprodajni
wholesale *adv.* veleprodajno
wholesaler *n.* veletrgovac
wholesome *a.* zdrav
wholly *adv. u* potpunosti
whom *pron.* koga
whore *n.* prostitutka
whose *pron.* čiji
why *adv.* zašto
wick *n.* fitilj
wicked *a.* zao
wicker *n.* ispleten od pruća
wicket *n.* vratnice
wide *a.* širok
wide *adv.* široko
widen *v.t.* proširiti
widespread *a.* rasprostranjen
widow *n.* udovica
widow *v.t.* učiniti udovicom
widower *n.* udovac
width *n.* širina
wield *v.t.* rukovati
wife *n.* supruga
wig *n.* perika

wight *n.* stvor
wigwam *n.* vigvam
wild *a.* divlji
wilderness *n.* divljina
wile *n.* lukavstvo
will *n.* volja
will *v.t.* htjeti
willing *a.* voljan
willingness *n.* spremnost
willow *n.* vrba
wily *a.* lukav
wimble *n.* ručna burgija
wimple *n.* kaluđerički veo
win *v.t.* pobijediti
win *n* pobjeda
wince *v.i.* trzati se
winch *n.* čekrk
wind *n.* vjetar
wind *v.t.* navijati
wind *v.t.* namotati
windbag *n.* blebetalo
winder *n.* motač
windlass *v.t.* motovilo
windmill *n.* vjetrenjača
window *n.* prozor
windy *a.* vjetrovit
wine *n.* vino
wing *n.* krilo
wink *v.i.* namigivati
wink *n* mig
winner *n.* pobjednik
winnow *v.t.* razbacati
winsome *a.* dopadljiv
winter *n.* zima
winter *v.i* zimovati
wintry *a.* zimski
wipe *v.t.* brisati
wipe *n.* brisanje
wire *n.* žica
wire *v.t.* svezati žicom

wireless *a.* bežični
wireless *n* radio
wiring *n.* spajanje žicom
wisdom *n.* mudrost
wisdom-tooth *n.* mudrost
wise *a.* mudar
wish *n.* želja
wish *v.t.* željeti
wishful *a.* željan
wisp *n.* čuperak
wistful *a.* zamišljen
wit *n.* duhovitost
witch *n.* vještica
witchcraft *n.* vračanje
witchery *n.* čarolija
with *prep.* sa
withal *adv.* sem toga
withdraw *v.t.* povući
withdrawal *n.* povlačenje
withe *n.* prut
wither *v.i.* uvenuti
withhold *v.t.* zadržati
within *prep.* u
within *adv.* u okviru
within *n.* unutrašnjost
without *prep.* bez
without *adv.* izvan
without *n* bez
withstand *v.t.* izdržati
witless *a.* bezuman
witness *n.* svjedok
witness *v.i.* svjedočiti
witticism *n.* dosjetka
witty *a.* duhovit
wizard *n.* čarobnjak
wobble *v.i* klimati
woe *n.* jad
woebegone *a.* nesrećan
woeful *n.* tužan
wolf *n.* vuk

woman *n.* žena
womanhood *n.* ženstvenost
womanish *n.* ženski
womanize *v.t.* trčati za ženama
womb *n.* maternica
wonder *n* čudo
wonder *v.i.* čuditi se
wonderful *a.* predivan
wondrous *a.* čudesan
wont *a.* naviknut
wont *n* navika
wonted *a.* uobičajen
woo *v.t.* udvarati se
wood *n.* drvo
woods *n.* šuma
wooden *a.* drveni
woodland *n.* šumovit kraj
woof *n.* potka
wool *n.* vuna
woollen *a.* vuneni
woollen *n* vunena tkanina
word *n.* riječ
word *v.t* rijeći
wordy *a.* izraziti
work *n.* rad
work *v.t.* raditi
workable *a.* obradiv
workaday *a.* svakidašnji
worker *n.* radnik
workman *n.* radnik
workmanship *n.* izrada
workshop *n.* radionica
world *n.* svijet
worldling *n.* svjetski čovek
worldly *a.* svjetovni
worm *n.* crv
wormwood *n.* pelen
worn *a.* iznošen
worry *n.* briga
worry *v.i.* brinuti

worsen *v.t.* pogoršati
worship *n.* obožavanje
worship *v.t.* obožavati
worshipper *n.* obožavatelj
worst *n.* ono što je najgore
worst *a* najgori
worst *v.t.* pobijediti
worsted *n.* češljana vuna
worth *n.* vrijednost
worth *a* vrijedan
worthless *a.* bezvijredan
worthy *a.* dostojan
would-be *a.* tobožnji
wound *n.* rana
wound *v.t.* raniti
wrack *n.* olupina
wraith *n.* utvara
wrangle *v.i.* prepirati se
wrangle *n.* prepirka
wrap *v.t.* zamotati
wrap *n* pokrivač
wrapper *n.* omotač
wrath *n.* gnjev
wreath *n.* vijenac
wreathe *v.t.* uplesti
wreck *n.* olupina
wreck *v.t.* uništiti
wreckage *n.* olupina
wrecker *n.* brod za spasavanje
wren *n.* carić
wrench *n.* iščašenje
wrench *v.t.* iščašiti
wrest *v.t.* istrgnuti
wrestle *v.i.* hrvati se
wrestler *n.* hrvač
wretch *n.* bijednik
wretched *a.* bijedan
wrick *n* iščašenje
wriggle *v.i.* vijugati
wriggle *n* vijuganje

wring *v.t* stiskati
wrinkle *n.* bora
wrinkle *v.t.* izborati
wrist *n.* ručni zglob
writ *n.* spis
write *v.t.* napisati
writer *n.* pisac
writhe *v.i.* grčiti se
wrong *a.* pogrešan
wrong *adv.* pogrešno
wrong *v.t.* nanijeti štetu
wrongful *a.* nezakonit
wry *a.* iskrivljen

X

xerox *n.* način fotokopiranja
xerox *v.t.* fotokopirati
Xmas *n.* Božić
x-ray *n.* rendgen
x-ray *a.* rendgenski
x-ray *v.t.* izložiti rendgenskim zrakama
xylophagous *a.* koji se hrani drvetom
xylophilous *a.* koji živi na drvetu
xylophone *n.* ksilofon

Y

yacht *n.* jahta
yacht *v.i* voziti se na jahti
yak *n.* jak
yap *v.i.* lajati
yap *n* lajanje
yard *n.* dvorište
yarn *n.* predivo
yawn *v.i.* zijevati
yawn *n.* zijevanje
year *n.* godina

yearly *a.* godišnji
yearly *adv.* godišnje
yearn *v.i.* žudjeti
yearning *n.* žudnja
yeast *n.* kvasac
yell *v.i.* vikati
yell *n* vikanje
yellow *a.* žut
yellow *n* žuta boja
yellow *v.t.* požutjeti
yellowish *a.* žućkast
Yen *n.* jen
yeoman *n.* slobodnjak
yes *adv.* da
yesterday *n.* jučerašnji dan
yesterday *adv.* jučer
yet *adv.* još
yet *conj.* ipak
yield *v.t.* donijeti
yield *n* prinos
yoke *n.* jaram
yoke *v.t.* ujarmiti
yolk *n.* žumance
yonder *a.* tamošnji
yonder *adv.* tamo
young *a.* mlad
young *n* mladi
youngster *n.* mladić
youth *n.* mladi
youthful *a.* mladalački

Z

zany *a.* smiješan
zeal *n.* revnost
zealot *n.* fanatik
zealous *a.* revnostan
zebra *n.* zebra
zenith *n.* zenit

zephyr *n.* zefir
zero *n.* nula
zest *n.* polet
zigzag *n.* cik-cak
zigzag *a.* vijugav
zigzag *v.i.* vijugati se
zinc *n.* cink
zip *n.* aktivnost
zip *v.t.* oživjeti
zodiac *n* zodijak
zonal *a.* zonski
zone *n.* zona
zoo *n.* zoološki vrt
zoological *a.* zoološki
zoologist *n.* zoolog
zoology *n.* zoologija
zoom *n.* zum
zoom *v.i.* zumirati

BOSNIAN-ENGLISH

A

abdicirati *v.t.* abdicate
abdikacija *n* abdication
abeceda *n.* alphabet
abecedno *a.* alphabetical
abonos *n* ebony
adekvatan *a.* adequate
adekvatnost *n.* adequacy
adhezija *n.* adhesion
administrator *n.* administrator
admiral *n.* admiral
adresa *n.* address
adut *n.* trump
advokat *n* advocate
advokatura *n.* advocacy
aerodrom *n* aerodrome
aeronautika *n.pl.* aeronautics
afera *n.* affair
aforizam *n* aphorism
agencija *n.* agency
agent *n* agent
agilan *a.* agile
agilnost *n.* agility
agonija *n.* throe
agonija *n.* agony
agrarni *a.* agrarian
agresija *n* aggression
agresivan *a.* aggressive
agresor *n.* aggressor
agronomija *n.* agronomy
ajkula *n.* shark
akademija *n* academy
akademski *a* academic
akcija *n.* action
ako *conj.* if
akord *n.* chord
akrobata *n.* tumbler

akrobata *n.* acrobat
akt *a.* nude
aktivan *a.* active
aktivirati *v.t.* activate
aktivnost *n.* zip
akumulacija *n* accumulation
akumulirati *v.t.* accumulate
akustično *a* acoustic
akustika *n.* acoustics
akvadukt *n.* aqueduct
akvarij *n.* aquarium
akvizicija *n.* acquisition
alat *n.* tool
albion *n* albion
album *n.* album
alegorija *n.* allegory
alegorijski *a.* allegorical
alergija *n.* allergy
alfa *n.* alpha
algebra *n.* algebra
ali *prep* but
alibi *n.* alibi
aligator *n* alligator
alimentacija *n.* alimony
aliteracija *n.* alliteration
alkemija *n.* alchemy
alkohol *n* alcohol
alkoholno piće *n.* liquor
almanah *n.* almanac
alpinista *n.* alpinist
alt *n* alto
alternativa *n.* alternative
alternativan *a.* alternative
aludirati *v.i.* allude
aluminij *n.* aluminium
aljkav *a.* slatternly
aljkav *a.* slovenly
aljkava žena *n.* slattern
am *n.* harness
amajlija *n.* amulet

amandman *n.* amendment
amater *n.* amateur
ambar *n.* granary
ambasada *n* embassy
ambicija *n.* ambition
ambiciozan *a.* ambitious
ambijent *n.* milieu
ambijent *adj.* ambient
amblem *n* emblem
ambulanta *n* dispensary
ambulantni bolesnik *n.* outpatient
amenoreja *n* amenorrhoea
amfibijski *adj* amphibious
amfiteatar *n* amphitheatre
amin *interj.* amen
amnestija *n.* amnesty
amnezija *n* amnesia
amper *n* ampere
anabaptizam *n* anabaptism
anakronizam *n* anachronism
analitičar *n* analyst
analitički *a* analytical
analiza *n.* analysis
analizirati *v.t.* analyse
analni *adj.* anal
analogan *a.* analogous
analogija *n.* analogy
anamneza *n* anamnesis
anamorfan *adj* anamorphous
ananas *n.* pineapple
anarhija *n* anarchy
anarhista *n* anarchist
anarhizam *n.* anarchism
anatema *n* ban
anatomija *n.* anatomy
anđeo *n* angel
anegdota *n.* anecdote
anemometar *n* anemometer
anestetik *n.* anaesthetic
anestezija *n* anaesthesia

angažiranje *n.* engagement
angažirati *v. t* engage
angina *n* angina
animacija *n* animation
anisovo seme *n* aniseed
anketa *n.* poll
anonimnost *n.* anonymity
antacid *adj.* antacid
antarktički *a.* antarctic
antena *n.* aerial
antene *n.* antennae
anti *pref.* anti
antifonija *n.* antiphony
antika *n.* antiquity
antikvar *n* antiquarian
antilopa *n.* antelope
antipatija *n* dislike
antipatija *n.* antipathy
antipodi *n.* antipodes
antiseptički *a.* antiseptic
antiseptik *n.* antiseptic
antiteza *n.* antithesis
antologija *n.* anthology
antonim *n.* antonym
aparat *n.* apparatus
apartman *n.* suite
apatija *n.* apathy
apelant *n.* appellant
apetit *n.* appetite
aplaudirati *v.t.* applaud
aplauz *n.* applause
apostol *n.* apostle
apostrofiranje *n.* apostrophe
apoteka *n.* pharmacy
apotekar *n* druggist
apsces *n* abscess
apstrakcija *n.* abstraction
apstraktan *a* abstract
apsurd *n* absurdity
apsurdan *a* absurd

arbiter *n.* arbitrator
arbitraža *n.* arbitration
arena *n* arena
arhanđeo *n* archangel
arhiepiskop *n.* archbishop
arhitekt *n.* architect
arhitektura *n.* architecture
arhiv *n* chancery
arhiva *n* file
arhive *n.pl.* archives
arhivirati *v.t* file
aristofanski *adj.* aristophanic
aristokrata *n.* aristocrat
aritmetički *a.* arithmetical
aritmetika *n.* arithmetic
Arktik *n* Arctic
armada *n.* armada
armatura *n.* armature
arsen *n* arsenic
arsenal *n.* arsenal
arterija *n.* artery
artičoka *n.* artichoke
artiljerija *n.* artillery
artritis *n* arthritis
as *n* ace
asibilant *v.* assibilate
asistent *n.* assistant
asket *n.* ascetic
asketski *a.* ascetic
aspekt *n* facet
aspekt ponašanja *n.* conation
aspekt *n.* aspect
astma *n.* asthma
astrolog *n.* astrologer
astrologija *n.* astrology
astronaut *n.* astronaut
astronom *n.* astronomer
astronomija *n.* astronomy
ataše *n.* attache
ateist *n* antitheist

ateista *n* atheist
ateizam *n* atheism
atentat *n* assassination
atlas *n.* atlas
atletika *n.* athletics
atletski *a.* athletic
atmosfera *n.* atmosphere
atom *n.* atom
atomski *a.* atomic
autentičan *a.* authentic
autobiografija *n.* autobiography
autobus *n* bus
autogram *n.* autograph
autokracija *n* autocracy
autokrata *n* autocrat
autokratski *a* autocratic
automatski *a.* automatic
automobil *n.* automobile
automobil *n.* car
automobilski *a.* vehicular
autonoman *a* autonomous
autoput *n.* highway
autor *n.* author
autsajder *n.* outsider
avaj *interj.* alas
avantura *n* adventure
avenija *n.* avenue
averzija *n.* aversion
avet *n.* spectre
avijatičar *n.* aviator
avion *n.* aeroplane
azbest *n.* asbestos
azil *n* asylum

B

babica *n.* midwife
babun *n.* baboon
bacanje *n.* cast

bacanje *n* casting	**bard** *n.* bard
bacanje *n.* throw	**barijera** *n.* barrier
baciti *v. t* down	**barikada** *n.* barricade
baciti *v.t* fling	**barometar** *n* barometer
baciti *v.t.* hurl	**baršunast** *a.* velvety
baciti *v.t.* throw	**bas** *n.* bass
baciti se *v.i* lunge	**basna** *n* apologue
baciti *v. t.* cast	**basna** *n.* fable
bačva *n.* barrel	**bašta** *n.* garden
bačva *n* cask	**baštovan** *n.* gardener
badem *n.* almond	**bataljun** *n* battalion
badminton *n.* badminton	**baterija** *n* battery
bajati *v.i.* conjure	**baza** *n.* alkali
bajonet *n* bayonet	**baza** *n.* base
bakalin *n.* grocer	**bazen** *n.* basin
bakalnica *n.* grocery	**bdijenje** *n.* vigil
bakar *n* copper	**bdijenje** *n* wake
baklja *n.* torch	**beba** *n.* baby
bakterija *n.* bacteria	**beda** *n.* misery
bala *n.* bale	**bedem** *n.* rampart
balada *n.* ballad	**bedem** *n* bulwark
balaviti *v. t* beslaver	**bedro** *n.* thigh
baldahin *n.* canopy	**bekhend** *n.* backhand
balet *n.* ballet	**bendžo** *n.* banjo
balkon *n.* balcony	**benzin** *n.* petrol
balon *n.* balloon	**berba** *n.* vintage
balsamovati *v. t* embalm	**beskonačan** *a.* infinite
balzam *n.* balsam	**beskonačnost** *n.* infinity
bambus *n.* bamboo	**beskrajan** *a.* interminable
banalan *a.* banal	**beskrajnost** *n.* immensity
banana *n.* banana	**besmislen** *a.* nonsensical
banda *n.* gang	**besmislen** *a.* senseless
banka, nasip *n.* bank	**besmislica** *n.* nonsense
bankar *n.* banker	**besmislica** *v. i* blether
banket *n.* banquet	**besmrtan** *a.* immortal
bankrot *n.* bankrupt	**besmrtnost** *n.* immortality
bara *n.* puddle	**besplatno** *adv.* gratis
barbarizam *n.* barbarism	**bespomoćan** *a.* helpless
barbarski *a.* barbarous	**besposlen** *a.* idle
barbarstvo *n.* barbarity	**besposlica** *n.* idleness

besposličar *n.* idler
besraman *a.* shameless
betel *n* betel
beton *n* concrete
betonirati *v. t* concrete
bez *n* without
bez *prep.* without
bez novca *a.* penniless
bez obzira na *a.* irrespective
bez posade *a.* unmanned
bez premca *a.* matchless
bez premca *a.* peerless
bezakonje *n.* misrule
bezbednost *n.* safety
bezbednosti *n.* security
bezbojan *adj* achromatic
bezbroj *n.* myriad
bezbrojan *a.* countless
bezbrojan *a.* innumerable
bezbrojan *a* myriad
bezbrojan *a.* numberless
bezdušnost *n.* obduracy
bezglav *adj.* acephalous
bezglavi fetus *n.* acephalus
bezimenost *n.* anonymity
bezličan *a.* impersonal
beznačajan *a.* insignificant
beznačajan *a.* meaningless
beznačajan *a.* minuscule
beznačajnost *n.* insignificance
beznadežan *a.* hopeless
bezobrazluk *n.* insolence
bezsredišnji *adj* acentric
bezuman *a.* witless
bezvijredan *a.* worthless
bežični *a.* wireless
beživotan *a.* lifeless
biber *n.* pepper
biberiti *v.t.* pepper
biblija *n.* scripture

biblija *n* bible
bibliograf *n* bibliographer
bibliografija *n* bibliography
biblioteka *n.* library
bibliotekar *n.* librarian
biceps *n* biceps
bicikl *n.* bicycle
biciklista *n* cyclist
bič *n.* scourge
bič *n.* whip
bičevan *a.* lash
bičevati *v.t.* scourge
bičevati *v.t.* slash
bičevati *v.t.* whip
bigamija *n* bigamy
bijeda *n.* squalor
bijedan *a.* abject
bijedan *a.* piteous
bijedan *a.* squalid
bijedan *a.* wretched
bijednik *n.* wretch
bijeg *n* escape
bijela boja *n* white
bijeleti *v.t.* whiten
bijeli *a.* white
bijes *n.* fury
bijes *n.* rage
bijes *n.* anger
bijesan *a.* furious
bik *n* bull
biliteralan *adj* biliteral
bilo *conj.* whether
bilten *n* bulletin
bilježnik *n.* notary
biljka *n.* herb
biljka *n.* plant
biljno ljepilo *n.* mucilage
binarni *adj* binary
biograf *n* biographer
biografija *n* biography

biolog *n* biologist
biologija *n* biology
birač *n.* constituent
biračko tijelo *n* electorate
birokrata *n* bureaucrat
birokratija *n.* Bureacuracy
biseksualan *adj.* bisexual
biser *n.* pearl
biskup *n* bishop
bistar *a.* lucid
bitanga *n.* rogue
biti neposlušan *v. t* disobey
biti nepovjerljiv *v.t.* mistrust
biti neprosvetljen *v. t* benight
biti odsutan *v.t* absent
biti sklon *v.i.* tend
biti snužden *v.i.* mope
biti zavidan *v* envy
biti zavistan *v.t.* addict
biti žedan *v.i.* thirst
biti *pref.* be
biti *v.t.* be
bitka *n* battle
bitno *adv.* substantially
bivši *pron* former
bizaran *adj* bizarre
bizon *n* bison
bizon *n.* buffalo
bjegunac *n.* fugitive
bjelančevina *n* albumen
bjelilo *n.* whitewash
bjelkast *a.* whitish
bjesnilo *n.* rabies
bjesniti *v.i.* rage
bjesniti *v.t.* riot
bjesomučno *adv.* amuck
bježanje *n* scamper
bježati u panici *v.i* stampede
blag *adj* benign
blag *a.* mild

blag *a.* slight
blag vetar *n* fan
blag *adj.* bland
blagajnik *n.* teller
blagajnik *n.* treasurer
blagajnik *n.* cashier
blago *n.* treasure
blagodat *n* boon
blagonaklon *a* benevolent
blagonaklonost *n* benevolence
blagoslov *n* benison
blagosloviti *v. t* bless
blagostanje *n.* prosperity
blagostanje *n.* welfare
blagovremen *a.* well-timed
blanširati *v. t. & i* blanch
blast *n* blaze
blatiti *v.t.* mire
blato *n.* mire
blato *n.* muck
blato *n.* mud
blaženstvo *n* felicity
blaženstvo *n* bliss
blebetalo *n.* windbag
blebetati *v.i.* gabble
blebetati *v.t.* jabber
blebetati *v.i.* quack
bled *a.* wan
blefirati *v. t* bluff
blejanje *n* bleat
blejati *v. i* bleat
blesak *n* dazzle
bleštanje *n.* glare
bleštati *v.i* glare
blijed *a* pale
blisko *adv.* nigh
blistav *a* brilliant
blistav *a.* shiny
blistavost *n* brilliance
blistavost *n.* glamour

blizak *a.* near
blizanac *n.* twin
blizina *n.* proximity
blizina *n.* vicinity
blizu *adv.* anigh
blizu *adv* by
blizu *prep.* near
blizu *v.i.* near
blizu *prep.* nigh
blok *n* bloc
blokada *n* blockade
blokirati *v.t* block
bluza *n* blouse
bljesak *n* flare
bljeskalica *n* flash
bljutav *a.* insipid
bljutavost *n.* insipidity
bljuzgav *a.* slushy
bljuzgavica *n.* slush
boca *n* bottle
bočica *n.* phial
bočica *n.* vial
bodar *a.* keen
bodež *n.* dagger
bodlja *n.* barb
bodljikav *a.* barbed
bodrenje *n.* cheer
bodriti *v. t.* cheer
bodrost *n.* keenness
Bog *n.* god
bogalj *n* cripple
bogat *a.* affluent
bogat *a.* opulent
bogat *a.* rich
bogat *a.* wealthy
bogatstvo *n.* opulence
bogatstvo *n.* richness
bogatstvo *n.* wealth
bogatstvo *n.* affluence
boginja *n.* goddess

boja *n* colour
boja *n* dye
boja *n.* paint
boja *n.* tincture
boja *n.* tint
bojažljivost *n.* timidity
boje cinobera *a.* vermillion
bojiti *v. t* colour
bojiti *v. t* dye
bojiti *v.t.* paint
bojkot *n* boycott
bojkotovati *v. t.* boycott
bojler *n* boiler
boks *n* boxing
bokvice *n.* plantain
bol *n* distress
bol *n.* pain
bol *n.* ache
bol *n.* anguish
bolan *a.* painful
bolesno *a.* sickly
bolest *n* disease
bolest *n.* illness
bolest *n.* malady
bolest *n.* sickness
bolestan *a.* ill
bolestan *a.* sick
bolestan *a.* unwell
bolnica *n.* hospital
bolovati *v.t.* ail
bolje *adv.* better
boljeti *v.t.* pain
boljeti *v.i.* ache
bolji *a* better
bomba *n* bomb
bombarder *n* bomber
bombardiranje *n* bombardment
bombardirati *v. t* bomb
bombardirati *v. t* bombard
bonus *n* bonus

bor *n.* pine
bora *n.* wrinkle
borac *n* combatant1
boravak *n* sojourn
boravak *n* stay
boravište *n* abode
boraviti *v.i.* reside
boraviti *v.i.* sojourn
borba *n* combat
borba *n* fight
borba *n* struggle
borba *n.* tussle
borbena tehnika *n.* ordnance
bordel *n* brothel
borilište *n.* lists
boriti *se v. i.* battle
boriti *se v. t.* combat
boriti *se v. i* contend
boriti *se v. i* duel
boriti *se v.t* fight
boriti *se v.i.* struggle
boriti *se v.i.* tussle
bosiljak *n.* basil
botanika *n* botany
božanski *a* divine
božanstvenost *n* divinity
božanstvo *n.* deity
božanstvo *n.* godhead
Božić *n* Christmas
Božić *n.* Xmas
božji *a.* godly
bračni *a* conjugal
bračni *a.* marital
bračni *a.* matrimonial
bračni drug *n.* consort
bračni drug *n* mate
bračni *i n.* spouse
brada *n* beard
brada *n.* chin
bradavica *n.* nipple

bradavica *n.* wart
brajeva azbuka *n* braille
brak *n.* marriage
brak *n.* matrimony
brak *n.* wedlock
brana *n* dam
brana *n.* sluice
brana *n.* weir
brana *n.* barrage
branik *n.* bumper
branitelj *n.* pleader
braniti *v. t.* champion
braniti *v. t* defend
braniti *v.t.* shield
braniti se *v.t* fend
braon *a* brown
braon boja *n* brown
brašno *n* flour
brašnjav *a.* mealy
brat *n* brother
bratoubica *n* cain
bratoubojstvo *n.* fratricide
bratski *a.* fraternal
bratstvo *n.* confraternity
bratstvo *n.* fraternity
bratstvo *n* brotherhood
brava *n.* lock
brazda *n* crease
brazda *n.* furrow
brazda *n.* score
brbljanje *n.* babble
brbljanje *n.* prattle
brbljati *v.i.* babble
brbljati *v.i.* prattle
brbrljati *v. t.* chatter
brdo *n.* hill
brdo *n* mount
breg *n.* hillock
brektanje *n.* pant
brektati *v.i.* pant

breskva *n.* peach
brevijar *n.* breviary
breza *n.* birch
briga *n* concern
briga *n.* worry
briga *n.* care
brigada *n.* brigade
brigadir *n* brigadier
brijač *n.* barber
brijač *n.* razor
brijanje *n* shave
brijati *v.t.* shave
brinuti *v. t* concern
brinuti *v.i.* worry
brinuti *v. i.* care
brisanje *n.* obliteration
brisanje *n.* wipe
brisati *v. t* erase
brisati *v.t.* mop
brisati *v.t.* wipe
brisati ručnikom *v.t.* towel
britanski *adj* british
brkovi *n.* moustache
brkovi *n.* mustache
brod *n.* nave
brod *n.* ship
brod *n.* vessel
brod za spasavanje *n.* wrecker
brod *n* boat
broj *n.* number
broj delilac bez ostatka *n.* aliquot
brojač *n.* numerator
brojati *v.t.* number
brojčani *a.* numeral
brojčanik *n.* dial
brojilac *n.* counter
brojni *a.* numerous
brokat *n* brocade
broker *n* broker
brokoli *n.* broccoli

bronza *n. & adj* bronze
brošura *n* booklet
brošura *n* brochure
bršljan *n* ivy
brusiti *v.t.* whet
brutalan *a* brutal
bruto *n.* gross
brz *a* fast
brz *a.* prompt
brz *a.* quick
brz *a.* speedy
brz *a.* swift
brzina *n.* speed
brzina *n.* velocity
brzo *adv* fast
brzo *adv.* speedily
buba *n* beetle
bubanj *n* drum
bubašvaba *n* cockroach
bubreg *n.* kidney
bubuljica *n.* pimple
bubuljice *n* acne
bučan *a.* noisy
bučan *a.* tumultuous
bučan *a.* uproarious
budala *n* fool
budalast *a* foolish
budan *a.* wakeful
budan *a.* watchful
budan *a* awake
budnost *n.* vigilance
budući *a.* future
budućnost *n* future
budžet *n* budget
buđav *a.* musty
buha *n.* flea
bujan *a.* lush
bujan *a* rank
bujan *a.* torrential
bujica *n.* spate

bujica *n.* torrent	**carstvo** *n* empire
buka *n.* ado	**carstvo** *a.* realm
buka *n* din	**cedar** *n.* cedar
buka *n.* noise	**celibat** *n.* celibacy
buket *n* bouquet	**celibat** *n.* celibacy
buknuti *v. i* erupt	**celularni** *adj* cellular
bukva *n.* beech	**cement** *n.* cement
bukvar *n.* primer	**cementirati** *v. t.* cement
buldog *n* bulldog	**cenkanje** *n.* bargain
buljenje *n.* stare	**cenkati se** *v.t.* bargain
buljiti *v.i.* stare	**cent** *n* cent
bunar *n.* well	**centar** *n* center
buncati *v.i.* rave	**centar** *n* centre
bundeva *n.* pumpkin	**centar pažnje** *n.* limelight
bundeva *n* squash	**centralni** *a.* central
bungalov *n* bungalow	**centrifugalni** *adj.* centrifugal
buniti *se v.i.* rebel	**cenzor** *n.* censor
bunker *n* blindage	**cenzura** *n.* censorship
bunker *n* bunker	**cenzurisati** *v. t.* censor
buntovan *a.* mutinous	**cenzus** *n.* census
buntovan *a.* rebellious	**ceremonija** *n.* ceremony
buntovan *a.* seditious	**cicijaški** *a.* miserly
buntovnički *a.* insurgent	**ciča** *n* squeak
buntovnik *n.* insurgent	**cičati** *v.i.* squeak
buntovnik *n.* rebel	**cifra** *n.* cipher, cipher
buran *a.* tempestuous	**cifra** *n* cypher
burmut *n.* snuff	**cifra** *n* digit
busen *n.* sod	**cigara** *n.* cigar
bušenje *v. t.* drill	**cigareta** *n.* cigarette
bušilica *n* drill	**cijediti** *v.t.* squash
bušiti *v. t* bore	**cijeli** *n.* all
bušiti tunel *v.i.* tunnel	**cijeli** *a.* whole
bušotina *n* bore	**cijena** *n.* cost
	cijena *n.* price
	cijeniti *v.t.* price
C	**cijeniti** *v.t.* prize
	cijeniti *v.t.* regard
	cijeniti *v.t.* value
carica *n* empress	**cijeniti** *v.t.* appreciate
carić *n.* wren	**cijepati** *v.t.* rip
carski *a.* imperial	

cijepiti *v.t.* vaccinate
cijepljenje *n.* vaccination
cijev *n.* tube
cijev, lula *n.* pipe
cik-cak *n.* zigzag
ciklon *n.* cyclone
ciklostil *n* cyclostyle
cilindar *n* cylinder
cilindričnog oblika *adj.* cubiform
cilj *n.* goal
cilj *n.* objective
cilj *n.* target
cilj *n.* aim
ciljati *v.i.* aim
cimet *n* cinnamon
cinik *n* cynic
cink *n.* zinc
cinober *n* cinnabar
cinober *n.* vermillion
cipela *n.* shoe
cirkulacija *n* circulation
cirkular *n.* circular
cirkulirati *v. i.* circulate
cirkus *n.* circus
citat *n.* quotation
citirati *v. t* cite
citirati *v.t.* quote
civil *n* civilian
civilizacija *n.* civilization
civilizovati *v. t* civilize
civilni *a* civil
cjelina *n.* total
cjelina *n* whole
cjelokupnost *n.* totality
cjepidlačiti *v. t* cavil
cjepivo *n.* vaccine
cjevasti *a.* tubular
cmok *n.* smack
cmoknuti *v.t.* smack
crijep *n.* tile

crijevni *a.* intestinal
crijevo *n.* hose
crijevo *n.* intestine
crijevo *n.* bowel
crkva *n.* church
crnac *n.* negro
crnac *n.* nigger
crnkinja *n.* negress
crno *a* black
crnpurast *a.* swarthy
crpsti *v.t.* ladle
crtač *a* draftsman
crtani film *n.* cartoon
crtanje *n* drawing
crv *n* mite
crv *n.* worm
crven *a.* red
crvena boja *n.* red
crvenkast *a.* reddish
curenje *n.* leak
curenje *n.* leakage
curiti *v.i.* leak
curiti *v.i.* ooze
curiti *v.i.* seep
cvat *n* bloom
cvati *v.i.* bloom
cvati *v.i* blossom
cvećar *n* florist
cvijet *n* flower
cvijetni *a* flowery
cviljenje *v.i.* whimper
cvjetati *v.i* flourish
cvrčak *n* cricket
cvrčanje *n.* sizzle
cvrčati *v.i.* sizzle
cvrkut *n* chirp
cvrkut *n.* twitter
cvrkutati *v.i.* chirp
cvrkutati *v.i.* twitter

Č

čađ *n.* soot
čađiti *v.t.* soot
čaj *n* tea
čajnik *n.* kettle
čak *adv* even
čak *adv.* nay
čarapa *n.* sock
čarapa *n.* stocking
čarape *n.* hosiery
čarka *n.* skirmish
čarkati *se v.t.* skirmish
čarobnjak *n.* sorcerer
čarobnjak *n.* wizard
čarobnjaštvo *n.* sorcery
čarolija *n.* spell
čarolija *n.* witchery
časkom *adv.* awhile
časnik *n.* officer
časopis *n.* journal
časopis *n.* periodical
časopis *n.* serial
čast *n.* honour
častan *a.* honourable
častan *a.* reverend
čašćenje *n* treat
čaurast *adj* capsular
čavrljanje *n.* chat
čavrljati *v. i.* chat2
čedan *a* maiden
čedomorstvo *n.* infanticide
ček *n.* cheque
čekanje *n.* wait
čekati *v.i.* wait
čekati *v.t.* await
čekati *v. t* bide
čekić *n.* hammer

čekićati *v.t* hammer
čekinja *n* bristle
čekrk *n.* lathe
čekrk *n.* winch
čelik *n.* steel
čelo *n* forehead
čempres cypress
čerpić *n.* adobe
čestica *n.* speck
čestit *a.* upright
čestitanje *n* congratulation
čestitati *v. t* congratulate
čestitati *v.t* felicitate
često *adv.* oft
često *adv.* often
češalj *n* comb
češanj *n* clove
češljana vuna *n.* worsted
češnjak *n.* garlic
četa *n.* troop
četiri *n.* four
četka *n* brush
četrdeset *n.* forty
četrnaest *n.* fourteen
četverokutni *a.* quadrangular
četveronožni *n.* quadruped
četverostruk *a.* quadruple
četvorostran *a. & n.* quadrilateral
četvorougaonik *n.* quadrangle
četvrtak *n.* Thursday
četvrtast *a* square
četvrtina *n.* quarter
čeznuti *v.i.* languish
čeznuti *v.i* long
čeznuti *v.i.* pine
čežnja *n.* longing
čičak *n.* thistle
čigra *n.* top
čiji *pron.* whose
čili *n.* chilli

čimpanza *n.* chimpanzee
čin kapetana *n.* captaincy
činiti *v. t* do
činiti se *v.i.* seem
činjenica *n* fact
čio *a.* hale
čio *a.* vivacious
čioda *n.* pin
čipka *n.* lace
čipkast *a.* lacy
čir *n.* ulcer
čist *adj.* clean
čist *a* pure
čistač *n.* sweeper
čistilište *n.* purgatory
čistiti *v. t* clean
čistiti *v.t* filter
čistiti *v.t* fine
čistiti *v.i.* sweep
čistoća *n* cleanliness
čistoća *n.* purity
čišćenje *n* clearance
čitalac *n.* reader
čitati *v.t.* read
čitav *a* entire
čitko *adv.* legibly
čitljiv *a.* legible
čizma *n* boot
član *n.* member
članak *n.* ankle
članak *n.* joint
članak *n* article
članstvo *n.* membership
čmar *n.* anus
čmičak *n.* stye
čokolada *n* chocolate
čovek *a.* human
čovječanstvo *n.* humanity
čovječanstvo *n.* mankind
čovjek *n.* man

čovjekoliki *adj.* anthropoid
čučati *v.i.* squat
čučnuti *v. i.* crouch
čudan *a.* peculiar
čudan *a.* quaint
čudan *a* rum
čudan *a.* strange
čudan *a.* weird
čudesan *a.* miraculous
čudesan *a.* stupendous
čudesan *a.* wondrous
čuditi se *v.i* marvel
čuditi se *v.i.* wonder
čudnovat *a.* outlandish
čudo *n.* marvel
čudo *n.* miracle
čudo *n* wonder
čudovište *n.* monster
čuđenje *n.* astonishment
čulna osoba *n.* sensualist
čulni *a.* sensuous
čulnost *n.* sensuality
čunak *n.* shuttle
čuperak *n.* wisp
čuti *v.t.* hear
čuvanje *n.* preservation
čuvar *n.* guardian
čuvar *n.* keeper
čuvar *n.* warder
čuvar *slonova u Indiji* *n.* mahout
čuvati *v.i.* guard
čuvati *v.t.* treasure
čuvati *v.t.* ward
čuvati se *v.i.* beware
čvor *n.* hub
čvor *n.* knot
čvor *n.* node
čvrga *n.* snag
čvrst *a* firm
čvrst *a.* solid

čvrst *a.* steady
čvrst *a.* sturdy
čvrst *a.* tight
čvrsto tijelo *n* solid

Ć

ćelav *a.* bald
ćerka *n* daughter
ćilim *n.* rug
ćorsokak *n* deadlock
ćorsokak *n.* impasse
ćudljiv *a.* moody
ćurka *n.* turkey
ćušnuti *v. t* cuff

D

da *conj.* that
da *adv.* yes
da ne bi *conj.* lest
dabar *n* beaver
daća *n* wake
dagubiti *v.i.* dawdle
dah *n* waft
dah *n* breath
dahtanje *n.* gasp
dahtati *v.i* gasp
dahtati *v.i.* puff
dakle *adv.* therefore
daktilograf *n.* typist
dalek *a* far
dalek *a.* remote
daleko *adv.* aloof
daleko *adv.* far
daleko *adv.* away
dalje *adv.* beyond
dalje *adv.* further

dalje *adv.* on
daljina *n* far
daljnji *a* further
dama *n.* dame
dama *n.* lady
dan *n* day
danas *adv.* today
današnjica *n.* today
danguba *n.* loafer
dangubiti *v.i.* laze
dangubiti *v.i.* loaf
danju *adv.* adays
dar *n* benefice
darežljiv *a* bountiful
darežljiv *a.* munificent
darežljivost *n* bounty
darežljivost *n.* largesse
daska *n.* plank
dašak *n.* puff
dašak *n.* whiff
dati *v.t.* give
dati kompliment *v. t* compliment
dati nadimak *v.t.* nickname
dati ostavku *v.t.* resign
dati pravo glasa *v.t.* enfranchise
dati publicitet *v.t.* publicize
dati u podzakup *v.t.* sublet
dati znak *v. t* beckon
datirati *v. t* date
datum *n* date
davalac *n* donor
davati ton *v.t.* tone
debata *n.* debate
debatirati *v. t* debate
debelo *adv.* thick
debelo crijevo *n* colon
debeo *a.* thick
decimal *a* decimal
deficit *n* deficit
definicija *n* definition

definirati *v. t* define
deflacija *n.* deflation
degradirati *v. t* degrade
deist *n.* deist
dekadentan *a* decadent
dekan *n.* dean
deklaracija *n* declaration
dekoracija *n* decoration
dekret *n* decree
delegacija *n* delegation
delegat *v. t* delegate
delikatan *a* delicate
delta *n* delta
demokracija *n* democracy
demokratski *a* democratic
demolirati *v. t.* demolish
demon *n.* demon
demonetizirati *v.t.* demonetize
demoralisati *v. t.* demoralize
denga *n.* dengue
deo korena u medicini *n.* asafoetida
deportirati *v.t.* deport
depozit *n.* deposit
depresija *n* depression
derište *n.* urchin
deset *n., a* ten
desetina *n.* tithe
desetkovati *v.t.* decimate
desetljeća *n* decade
desetogodišnjica *n.* decennary
desiti *v.t.* happen
desiti se *v.i.* occur
despot *n* despot
destilerija *n* distillery
destilovati *v. t* distil
destinacija *n* destination
detalj *n* detail
detaljisati *v. t* detail
dete *n.* babe
detektiv *n.* detective

detektivski *a* detective
deva *n.* camel
devac *n.* virgin
devedeset *n.* ninety
devedeseti *a.* ninetieth
devet *n.* nine
deveti *a.* ninth
devetnaest *n.* nineteen
devetnaesti *a.* nineteenth
dići *v.t.* raise
dići se *v.* rise
didaktički *a* didactic
dignuti *v.i.* heave
dijabetes *n* diabetes
dijafragma *n.* midriff
dijagnoza *n* diagnosis
dijagram *n* diagram
dijalekt *n* dialect
dijalog *n* dialogue
dijamant *n* diamond
dijareja *n* diarrhoea
dijeliti *v.t.* part
dijeliti *v.t.* portion
dijeliti *v.t.* share
dijeta *n* diet
dijete *n* child
dijete *n.* kid
dijete *n.* bantling
dikcija *n* diction
diktator *n* dictator
diktiranje *n* dictation
diktirati *v. t* dictate
dilema *n* dilemma
dilema *n.* quandary
dim *n.* smoke
dimenzija *n* dimension
dimnjak *n.* chimney
dinamičan *a* dynamic
dinamika *n.* dynamics
dinamit *n* dynamite

dinastija *n* dynasty	**divlji** *a.* wild
dinstati *v.t.* stew	**divljina** *n.* wilderness
dinja *n.* melon	**dizajn** *n.* design
dio *n.* part	**dizajnirati** *v. t.* design
dio *n* portion	**dizalica** *n* crane
dionica *n* share	**dizanje** *n.* rise
diploma *n* diploma	**dizati** *v.t.* hoist
diplomacija *n* diplomacy	**dizati se** *v.i.* tower
diplomat *n* diplomat	**dizenterija** *n* dysentery
diplomatski *a* diplomatic	**dječak** *n* boy
diplomirani đak/student *n* graduate	**dječja kolica** *n.* perambulator
diplomirati *v.i.* graduate	**djelatnost** *n.* activity
direktan *a* direct	**djelo** *n* deed
direktor *n.* director	**djelo** *n.* act
direktorij *n* directory	**djelokrug** *n.* venue
disanje *n.* respiration	**djelomičan** *a.* partial
disati *v.i.* respire	**djelotvornost** *n* efficacy
disati *v. i.* breathe	**djelovanje** *n.* acting
disciplina *n* discipline	**djelovanje** *v. t* effect
disk *n.* disc	**djetelina** *n.* lucerne
diskrecija *n* discretion	**djetinjast** *a.* childish
diskriminacija *n* discrimination	**djetinjast** *a.* puerile
diskurs *n* discourse	**djetinjstvo** *n* boyhood
diskutirati *v. t.* discuss	**djetinjstvo** *n.* childhood
diskvalificirati *v. t.* disqualify	**djevica** *n* virgin
diskvalifikacija *n* disqualification	**djevojački** *a.* girlish
distribucija *n* distribution	**djevojka** *n.* girl
distribuirati *v. t* distribute	**djevojka** *n.* maiden
dišne smetnje *n* apnoea	**djevojka** *n.* wench
divan *a.* gorgeous	**dlaka** *n.* whisker
divan *a.* lovely	**dlan** *n.* palm
diviti se *v.t.* admire	**dlijeto** *n* chisel
divljački *a.* barbarian	**dnevni** *a* daily
divljak *n* savage	**dnevni red** *n.* agenda
divljak *n.* barbarian	**dnevnik** *n.* daily
divljanje *n.* rampage	**dnevnik** *n* diary
divljaštvo *n.* savagery	**dnevno** *adv.* daily
divljati *v.i.* rampage	**dno** *n* bottom
divljenje *n.* admiration	**do** *prep.* till
divlji *a.* savage	**do** *prep.* until

do sada *adv.* hitherto	**dodijeliti** *v. i* confer
doba *n.* age	**dodijeliti** *v.t.* allocate
doba *n* era	**dodijeliti** *v.t.* assign
dobar *a* fine	**dodir** *n* touch
dobar *a.* good	**dodirivati** *v.t* finger
dobar *a.* well	**dodirnuti** *v.t.* palm
dobavljač *n.* supplier	**dodirnuti** *v.t.* touch
dobit *n* gain	**dodirnuti nožnim prstima** *v.t.* toe
dobitak *n.* pelf	**dodjeljivanje** *n.* allotment
dobiti *v.t.* gain	**događaj** *n* event
dobiti *v.t.* get	**događaj** *n.* happening
dobiti *v.t.* obtain	**događaj** *n.* occurrence
dobiti *v.t.* receive	**dogma** *n* dogma
dobiti zube *v.i.* teethe	**dogmatski** *a* dogmatic
dobra volja *n.* goodwill	**dogovor** *n* deal
dobro *adv.* well	**dogovoriti se** *v. t* concert2
dobročinstvo *n.* benefaction	**dogovoriti se** *v. i* deal
dobroćudno *adv* benignly	**dohodak** *n.* proceeds
dobrodošao *a.* welcome	**dojam** *n.* impression
dobrodošlica *n* welcome	**dojenče** *n.* infant
dobronamerno *adv* bonafide	**dojiti** *v.i.* lactate
dobrota *n.* goodness	**dojiti** *v.t.* suckle
dobrotvorno *a.* charitable	**dok** *n. conj.* till
dobrovoljan *a.* voluntary	**dok** *conj* until
dobrovoljno *adv.* voluntarily	**dok** *conj.* while
doći *v. i.* come	**dokaz** *n* evidence
doći *v.i.* arrive	**dokaz** *n.* proof
dodatak *n.* appendage	**dokazati** *v.t.* prove
dodatak *n.* appendix	**doktorat** *n* doctorate
dodatak *n.* addition	**doktrina** *n* doctrine
dodatak *n.* adjunct	**dokument** *n* document
dodati *v.t.* suffix	**dolar** *n* dollar
dodati prefiks *v.t.* prefix	**dolazak** *n.* arrival
dodati *v.t.* add	**dolina** *n* dale
dodati *v.t.* annex	**dolina** *n.* vale
dodati *v.t.* append	**dolina** *n.* valley
dodatni *a* extra	**dolje** *adv* below
dodatni *a.* plus	**dolje** *adv* down
dodatni *a.* additional	**dolje** *adv* downward
dodeliti *v.t.* attribute	**dolje** *adv* downwards

dom *n.* home
domaći *a* domestic
domaćin *n.* host
domaći *n.* vernacular
domen *n* domain
domet *n.* range
dominacija *n* domination
dominantan *a* dominant
dominirati *v. t* dominate
donacija *n.* donation
doneti *v. t* bring
donijeti *v.t* fetch
donijeti *v.t.* yield
donkihotski *a.* quixotic
donositi zakon *v.i.* legislate
donošenje zakona *n.* legislation
donje rublje *n.* underwear
dopadanje *n.* liking
dopadljiv *a.* winsome
dopisnik *n.* correspondent
doprinijeti *v. t* contribute
doprinos *n* contribution
dopuna *n* complement
dopuna *n.* supplement
dopuniti *v.t.* supplement
dopunski *adj* adscititious
dopunski *a* complementary
dopunski *a.* supplementary
dopunski porez *n.* surtax
dopustiti *v.t.* adhibit
dopustiti *v.t.* allow
dopustiv *a.* permissible
dopuštenje *n.* leave
dopuštenje *n.* permission
dorasti *v. i* cope
doručak *n* breakfast
dosada *n.* tedium
dosadan *a.* tedious
dosadan *a.* weary
dosađivanje *n* botheration

dosađivanje *n.* annoyance
dosađivati *v.t.* annoy
dosađivati *v.t.* weary
dosije *n* file
dosjetka *n.* quibble
dosjetka *n.* witticism
doslovan *a.* literal
doslovan *a.* verbatim
doslovno *adv.* verbatim
dosljedan *a* coherent
dosljedan *a* consequent
dosljedan *a* consistent
dosljednost *n.* consistence,-cy
dostatnost *n.* sufficiency
dostaviti *v. t* deliver
dostići *v.t.* reach
dostignuće *n.* accomplishment
dostignuće *n.* attainment
dostojan *a.* worthy
dostojan *prezira a* despicable
dostojanstvenost *n.* stateliness
dostojanstvo *n* dignity
dosuditi *v.t.* adjudge
doušnik *n* sneak
dovesti u iskušenje *v.t.* tempt
dovoljan *a* enough
dovoljan *a.* sufficient
dovoljno *adv* enough
doza *n* dose
dozvola *n.* allowance
dozvola *n.* licence
dozvola *n.* permit
dozvoliti *v.t.* let
dozvoliti *v.t.* license
dozvoliti *v.t.* permit
doživotni *a.* lifelong
drag *a* beloved
drag *a* darling
drag *a* dear
draga *n.* lass

dragi *n* beloved
dragi *n* darling
dragocjen *a.* precious
dragulj *n* gern
dragulj *n.* jewel
drama *n* drama
dramatičan *a* dramatic
dramaturg *n* dramatist
drastičan *a* drastic
dražiti *v.t.* irritate
drenaža *n* drainage
dres *n.* jersey
drevan *a.* archaic
drevni *a.* ancient
drhtanje *n.* tremor
drhtati *v.i.* quiver
drhtati *v.i.* shiver
drhtati *v.i.* tremble
drhtav *a.* shaky
drijemanje *n.* doze
drijemati *v. i* doze
drijemati *v.i.* nap
drijemati *v.i.* slumber
drijemež *n.* nap
drijemež *n.* slumber
drmati *v.t.* jolt
drmusanje *n.* jolt
dronjak *n.* tatter
drskost *n.* impertinence
drug *n.* comrade
drug *n.* pal
drugi *a* else
drugi *a.* other
drugi *pron.* other
drugi *a.* second
drugi *a* another
drugo *adv* else
društven *a.* sociable
društvenost *n.* sociability
društvo *n.* society

druželjubiv *adj.* convivial
drveni *a.* wooden
drveni *konjić* *n.* hobby-horse
drveni stup usred prozora *n.* mullion
drvo *n.* tree
drvo *n.* wood
drzak *a.* impertinent
drzak *a.* insolent
držanje *n.* hold
držati *v.t* hold
držati *v.t.* keep
držati se *v.i.* adhere
držati u štali *v.t.* stable
držati *u štali* *v.t.* stall
državljanstvo *n* citizenship
državljanstvo *n.* nationality
državna blagajna *n.* treasury
državnik *n.* statesman
državno uređenje *n.* polity
dubina *n* depth
dubina *n.* profundity
dubok *a.* profound
duboko *a.* deep
duboko poštovati *v.t.* revere
dud *n.* mulberry
dug *n* debt
dug *n* due
dug *a.* long
dugo *adv* long
dugovati *v.t* owe
dugovi *n.pl.* arrears
dugovječnost *n.* longevity
duguljast *a.* oblong
duguljasta figura *n.* oblong
duh *n.* ghost
duh *n.* spirit
duhan *n.* tobacco
duhovit *a* comical
duhovit *a.* jocular
duhovit *a.* witty

duhovit odgovor *n.* repartee
duhovitost *n.* wit
duhovni *a.* spiritual
duhovnost *n.* spirituality
duljina *n.* length
duljina *n.* longitude
duplikat *n.* counterpart
duplikat *n* duplicate
duplja *n.* cavity
duša *n.* soul
duše pokojnika *n.* manes
dušik *n.* nitrogen
dušnik *n.* throttle
duž *prep.* along
dužan *a* due
dužan da daje danak *a.* tributary
dužnik *n* debtor
dužnosnik *n* official
dužnost *n* duty
dva *n.* two
dva tjedna *n.* fort-night
dvadeset *a.* twenty
dvadeseti *a.* twentieth
dvadesetina *n* twentieth
dvadesetorica *n* twenty
dvanaest *n* twelve
dvanaesti *a.* twelfth
dvanaestina *n.* twelfth
dvanaestorica *n.* twelve
dvaput *adv.* twice
dvestogodišnji *adj* bicentenary
dvoboj *n* duel
dvogled *n.* binocular
dvogodišnji *adj* biennial
dvoje *a.* two
dvojezični *a* bilingual
dvokuti *adj.* biangular
dvoličnost *n* duplicity
dvomjesečni *adj.* bimonthly
dvonožac *n* biped

dvoosni *adj* biaxial
dvorac *n.* castle
dvoranin *n.* courtier
dvorište *n.* courtyard
dvorište *n.* yard
dvosmislen *a* equivocal
dvosmislen *a.* ambiguous
dvosmislenost *n.* ambiguity
dvostruk *a* dual
dvostruk *a* duplicate
dvostruk *a* twin
dvostruk *a.* twofold
dvostruko *a* double
dvostrukost *n* double
dvotačka *n* colon
dvotjedni *adj* bi-weekly

DŽ

džamija *n.* mosque
džem *n.* jam
džemper *n.* sweater
džep *n.* pocket
džin *n.* giant
džogirati *v.t.* jog
džoker *n.* joker
džungla *n.* jungle

Đ

đakon *n.* deacon
đavo *n* devil
đavo *n* fiend
đon *n.* sole
đubre *n* dung
đubre *n.* junk
đubre *n.* rubbish
đubriti *v.t.* manure

đubrivo *n.* manure
đumbir *n.* ginger

E

efekat *n* effect
efikasan *a* efficient
ego *n* ego
egoizam *n* egotism
egzotična biljka *n.* curcuma
ekonomičan *a* economical
ekonomija *n.* economics
ekonomija *n* economy
ekonomski *a* economic
ekpres *n* express
ekran *n.* screen
ekselencija *n* excellency
ekser *n.* nail
ekskomunicirati *v. t.* excommunicate
ekskurzija *n.* excursion
ekspedicija *n* expedition
eksperiment *n* experiment
eksplicitan *a.* explicit
eksploatacija *n* exploit
eksploatirati *v. t* exploit
eksplodirati *v. t.* explode
eksplozija *n.* explosion
eksplozija *n* blast
eksploziv *n.* explosive
eksplozivan *a* explosive
eksponat *n.* exhibit
ekstra *adv* extra
ekstrakt *n* extract
ekstravagancija *n* extravagance
ekstravagantan *a* extravagant
ekstrem *n* extreme
ekstreman *a* extreme
ekstremista *n* extremist
ekvator *n* equator

ekvivalent *a* equivalent
elan *n.* verve
elastičan *a* elastic
elegancija *n* elegance
elegantan *adj* elegant
elegija *n* elegy
elektricitet *n* electricity
električni *a* electric
element *n* element
elementarni *a* elementary
eliminacija *n* elimination
eliminirati *v. t* eliminate
emajl *n* enamel
emancipacija *n.* emancipation
embrij *n* embryo
eminencija *n* eminence
eminentni *a* eminent
emisija *n* broadcast
emitirati *v. t* broadcast
emitirati *v. t* emit
emitirati preko televizije *v.t.* televise
emocija *n* emotion
emotivan *a* emotional
enciklopedija *n.* encyclopaedia
energičan *a.* arduous
energičan *a* energetic
energičan *a.* vigorous
energija *n.* energy
engleski jezik, Englez *n* English
enigma *n* enigma
entitet *n* entity
entomologija *n.* entomology
entuzijazam *n* enthusiasm
ep *n* epic
epidemija *n* epidemic
epigram *n* epigram
epilepsija *n* epilepsy
epilog *n* epilogue
epitaf *n* epitaph
epizoda *n* episode

epoha *n* epoch
erekcija *n* erection
ergela *n.* stud
erodirati *v. t* erode
erotski *a* erotic
erozija *n* erosion
erupcija *n* eruption
esej *n.* essay
esejista *n* essayist
eskadrila *n.* squadron
esnaf *n.* guild
estetika *n.pl.* aesthetics
estetski *a.* aesthetic
eter *n* ether
etički *a* ethical
etika *n.* ethics
etiketa *n* etiquette
etiketa *n.* label
etiketirati *v.t.* label
etimologija *n.* etymology
evakuacija *n* evacuation
evakuirati *v. t* evacuate
evanđelje *n.* gospel
evergrin *n* evergreen
evidencija *n.* tally
evnuh *n* eunuch
evocirati *v. t* evoke
evolucija *n* evolution
evoluirati *v.t* evolve

F

faksimil *n* facsimile
faktor *n* factor
faktura *n.* invoice
fakultet *n* faculty
falsificirati *v.t* forge
falsifikat *n* forgery
falsifikator *n.* counterfeiter

falsifikovati *v.t.* adulterate
fanatičan *a* fanatic
fanatik *n* fanatic
fanatik *n.* zealot
fantastičan *a* fantastic
fantom *n.* phantom
farma *n* farm
farsa *n* farce
fasada *n* facade
fascikla *n* file
fascinacija *n.* fascination
fascinirati *v.t* fascinate
fatalan *a* fatal
fatamorgana *n.* mirage
fauna *n* fauna
favorit *n* favourite
faza *n.* phase
federacija *n* federation
federalni *a* federal
fenomen *n.* phenomenon
fenomenalan *a.* phenomenal
fenjer *n.* lantern
fermentacija *n* fermentation
festival *n* festival
feudalni *a* feudal
figura *n* figure
figurativan *a* figurative
fijaker *n.* barouche
fijasko *n* fiasco
fikcija *n* fiction
fiktivan *a* fictitious
fil *n* custard
filantrop *n.* philanthropist
filantropija *n.* philanthropy
filantropski *a.* philanthropic
film *n* film
filolog *n.* philologist
filologija *n.* philology
filološki *a.* philological
filozof *n.* philosopher

filozofija *n.* philosophy
filozofski *a.* philosophical
filter *n* filter
financijer *n* financier
financijski *a* financial
financirati *v.t* finance
finansije *n* finance
fiskalni *a* fiscal
fistula *n* fistula
fitilj *n.* wick
fizičar *n.* physicist
fizički *a.* physical
fizika *n.* physics
fizionomija *n.* physiognomy
flanel *n* flannel
flaster *n.* plaster
flauta *n* flute
fleksibilan *a* flexible
flertovanje *n* flirt
flertovati *v.i* flirt
flora *n* flora
flota *n* fleet
foka *n.* seal
fokus *n* focus
folija *v.t* foil
fond *n.* fund
fonetika *n.* phonetics
fonetski *a.* phonetic
fontana *n.* fountain
forma *n* form
formacija *n* formation
formalan *a* formal
formalnost *n.* technicality
format *n* format
formirati *v.t.* form
formula *n* formula
formulirati *v.t* formulate
forum *n.* forum
fosfat *n.* phosphate
fosfor *n.* phosphorus

fosil *n.* fossil
fotograf *n.* photographer
fotografija *n* photo
fotografija *n* photograph
fotografija *n.* photography
fotografirati *v.t.* photograph
fotografski *a.* photographic
fotokopirati *v.t.* xerox
fragment *n.* fragment
frakcija *n* faction
frakcija *n.* fraction
francuski *a.* French
francuski jezik, Francuz *n* French
franšiza *n.* frachise
fraza *n.* phrase
frazeologija *n.* phraseology
frekvencija *n.* frequency
frigidan *a.* frigid
frktanje *n.* snort
frktati *v.i.* snort
front *n.* front
frustracija *n.* frustration
frustrirati *v.t.* frustrate
fuj *interj* fie
funkcija *n.* function
funkcioner *n.* functionary
funkcionirati *v.i* function
funta *n.* pound
fuzija *n.* fusion

G

gacati *v.t.* puddle
gadan *a.* nasty
gajde *n.* bagpipe
gajiti *v.t.* rear
gakanje *n.* caw
gakati *v. i.* caw
galaksija *n.* galaxy

galama *n* clamour
galamiti *v. i.* clamour
galantan *a.* gallant
galeb *n.* gull
galeb *n.* mew
galerija *n.* gallery
galon *n.* gallon
galop *n.* gallop
galopirati *v.t.* gallop
gangster *n.* gangster
garancija *n.* guarantee
garaža *n.* garage
garderoba *n.* wardrobe
gas *n.* gas
gasni *a.* gassy
gavran *n.* raven
gaziti *v.t.* conculcate
gaziti *v.i.* wade
gdje *conj.* where
gdje *adv.* where
gdje *conj.* whereat
gdje *god adv.* wherever
gedža *n* boor
geg, čep *v.t.* gag
geganje *v.i.* waddle
generacija *n.* generation
generator *n* dynamo
generator *n.* generator
generirati *v.t.* generate
genije *n.* genius
geograf *n.* geographer
geografija *n.* geography
geografski *a.* geographical
geolog *n.* geologist
geologija *n.* geology
geološki *a.* geological
geometrija *n.* geometry
geometrijski *a.* geometrical
gerila *n.* guerilla
germicid *n.* germicide

gerund *n.* gerund
gest *n.* gesture
gibon *n.* gibbon
gigantski *a.* gigantic
giht *n.* gout
gimnastičar *n.* gymnast
gimnastički *a.* gymnastic
gimnastika *n.* gymnastics
gimnazija *n.* gymnasium
gitara *n.* guitar
glačati *v.t.* glaze
glad *n* famine
glad *n* hunger
gladak *a.* smooth
gladan *a.* hungry
gladiti *v.t.* smooth
gladovanje *n.* starvation
glagol *n.* verb
glagolsko *vrijeme n.* tense
glas *n.* voice
glasač *n.* voter
glasan *a* audible
glasati *v.i.* vote
glasina *n* bruit
glasina *n.* rumour
glasnik *n.* herald
glasnik *n* post
glasno *a.* loud
glasnogovornik *n.* spokesman
glasovanje *n* ballot
glasovanje *n.* vote
glasovati *v.i.* ballot
glaukom *n.* glaucoma
glava *n.* head
glavna knjiga *n.* ledger
glavna potpora *n.* mainstay
glavni *a.* chief
glavni *a* main
glavni *a.* major
glavni *a.* prime

glavni *a* principal	**gljiva** *n.* mushroom
glavni *a.* capital	**gnijezditi se** *v.i.* nestle
glavobolja *n.* headache	**gnijezdo** *n.* nest
glazba *n.* music	**gnoj** *n.* pus
glazbeni *a.* musical	**gnojan** *a.* ulcerous
glazbenik *n.* musician	**gnojivo** *n* compost
glazura *n* glaze	**gnojivo** *n* fertilizer
glečer *n.* glacier	**gnojna upala** *n.* pyorrhoea
gledalište *n.* audience	**gnusan** *a* abominable
gledalište *n.* auditorium	**gnusan** *a.* heinous
gledatelj *n.* spectator	**gnusan** *a.* loathsome
gledati *v.t* front	**gnušanje** *n.* abhorrence
gledati *v.i* look	**gnušati se** *v.t.* abhor
gledati *v.t.* watch	**gnjaviti** *v.t* bother
gledište *n.* outlook	**gnječiti** *v.t* crush
glib *n.* ooze	**gnječiti** *v.t* mash
glicerin *n.* glycerine	**gnjev** *n.* wrath
glina *n* clay	**godina** *n.* year
glina *n* argil	**godišnje** *adv.* yearly
globalni *a.* global	**godišnji** *a.* annual
glodar *n.* rodent	**godišnji** *a.* yearly
glog *n.* hawthorn	**godišnjica** *n.* anniversary
gluh *a* deaf	**gojazan** *a* fat
glukoza *n.* glucose	**golem kamen** *n.* megalith
glumac *n.* actor	**golenica** *n.* shin
glumačka družina *n.* troupe	**golf, zaljev** *n.* golf
glumica *n.* actress	**golicati** *v.t.* tickle
glup *a* dumb	**golicljiv** *a.* ticklish
glup *a.* sheepish	**golotinja** *n.* nudity
glup *a.* silly	**golub** *n* dove
glup *a* stupid	**golub** *n.* pigeon
glupak *n.* simpleton	**goluždravac** *n.* nestling
glupan *n* blockhead	**gomila** *n* crowd
glupan *n.* coot	**gomila** *n.* heap
glupan *n* dunce	**gomila** *n.* mob
glupan *n.* gander	**gomila** *n.* pile
glupan *n* gull	**gomila** *n.* throng
glupost *n* folly	**gomilati** *v.i* flock
glupost *n.* stupidity	**gomilati** *v.t* heap
gljiva *n.* fungus	**gomilati** *v.i* mass

gomilati *v.t.* pile
gomilati se *v.t.* throng
gong *n.* gong
goniti *v.t.* prosecute
gorak *a* bitter
gore *adv.* badly
gore *adv.* up
goreti *v.i* blaze
gorila *n.* gorilla
gorivo *n.* fuel
gorjeti *v. t* burn
gornja vilica *n.* maxilla
gornji *prep.* above
gornji *a.* upper
gospoda *n.* Messrs
gospodar *n.* lord
gospodar *n.* master
gospodarica, ljubavnica *n.* mistress
gospodin *n.* gentleman
gospodin *n.* mister
gospodin *n.* sir
gospodstvo *n.* lordship
gospođa, supruga *n.* missis, missus
gospođica *n.* damsel
gost *n.* guest
gostiti se *v.i* feast
gostoprimljiv *a.* hospitable
gostoprimstvo *n.* hospitality
gotovina *n.* cash
goveda *n.* cattle
govedina *n* beef
govor *n.* oration
govor *n.* speech
govoriti *v.i.* speak
govornica *n.* rostrum
govornički *a.* oratorical
govornik *n.* orator
gozba *n* feast
grad *n* city
grad *n.* hail

grad *n.* town
gradacija *n.* gradation
gradilište *n* lot
gradilište *n.* site
graditi *v. t* build
gradonačelnik *n.* mayor
građa *n* build
građanin *n* citizen
građanski *a* civic
građansko pravo *n* civics
građevina *n* edifice
grafički *a.* graphic
grafikon *n.* chart
grafikon *n.* graph
grah *n.* bean
graja *n.* hubbub
graktanje *n.* croak
graktati *v. i* crow
gram *n.* gramme
gramatičar *n.* grammarian
gramatika *n.* grammar
gramofon *n.* gramophone
grana *n* bough
grana *n* branch
granata *n.* grenade
grančica *n* spray
grančica *n.* sprig
grančica *n.* twig
granica *n.* frontier
granica *n.* limit
granica *n* border
granica *n.* bound
graničiti se *v.t.* adjoin
graničiti *v.t* border
grašak *n.* pea
gravitacija *n.* gravitation
grb *n* crest
grč *n.* spasm
grčevit *a* fitful
grčevit *a.* jerky

grčevit *a.* spasmodic
grčiti *se v.i.* writhe
grčki *a* Greek
grčki jezik, Grk *n.* Greek
grditi *v.t.* scold
grdnja *n.* invective
grdnja *n.* snub
grebanje *n.* scratch
grebati *v.t.* scratch
greben *n.* mull
greben *n.* ridge
greda *n.* timber
grešan *a.* sinful
greška *n* error
greška *n* fault
greška *n.* mistake
grešnik *n.* sinner
grgeč *n.* perch
grickanje *n* nibble
grickati *v.t.* nibble
grijeh *n.* sin
grip *n.* influenza
griva *n.* mane
griža savjesti *n.* compunction
grlen *a.* guttural
grlen *a.* throaty
grlo *n.* throat
grm *n* bush
grmeti *v.i.* thunder
grnčar *n.* potter
grnčarija *n.* pottery
grob *n.* grave
grob *n.* tomb
groblje *n.* necropolis
groblje *n.* cemetery
groblje *n.* churchyard
grobnica *n.* sepulchre
grofica *n.* countess
grofovija *n.* shire
grom *n.* thunder

gromovit *a.* thunderous
groteskan *a.* grotesque
groznica *n* fever
grožđe *n.* grape
grožđice *n.* raisin
grub *a* coarse
grub *a.* harsh
grub *a.* rough
grubijan *n* churl
gruda *n.* clod
gruda *n.* lump
grudi *n* bosom
grudi *n* breast
grudva *n.* nugget
grupa *n.* group
grupa *n.* band
grupirati *v.t.* group
gubav *a.* leprous
gubavac *n.* leper
gubitak *n* forfeit
gubitak *n.* loss
gubitak prava *n* forfeiture
gubiti boju *v.t.* tarnish
gubitnik *n* underdog
gucnuti *v.t.* delibate
gucnuti *v.t.* sip
gucnuti *v.i.* sup
gudit *v.i* fiddle
gukanje *n* coo
gukati *v. i* coo
guma *n.* gum
guma *n.* rubber
guma *n.* tyre
gumb *n* button
gunđati *v.t.* grudge
guranje *n.* push
guranje *n.* shove
gurati *v.t.* poke
gurati *v.t.* shove
gurati *v.t.* thrust

gurkati *v.t.* nudge
gurnuti *v.t.* push
gurnuti nogom *v.t.* spurn
gusar *n.* pirate
gusenica *n* caterpillar
guska *n.* goose
gust *a* dense
gustiš *n.* thicket
gustoća *n* density
guša *n.* craw
gušenje *n.* strangulation
gušenje *n.* suffocation
gušiti *v.t.* throttle
gušiti se *v. t.* choke
gušter *n.* lizard
gutljaj *n* dram
gutljaj *n.* gulp
gutljaj *n.* sip
gutljaj *n.* swallow
guvernanta *n.* governess
guverner *n.* governor

H

haljina *n* dress
haljina *n.* frock
haljina *n.* gown
haljina *n.* robe
hangar *n* shed
harfa *n.* harp
haringa *n.* herring
harmoničan *a.* harmonious
harmonij *n.* harmonium
harmonija *n.* harmony
hauba *n.* hood
heftati *a* staple
hemičar *n.* chemist
hemija *n.* chemistry
hemisfera *n.* hemisphere

hemoroidi *n.* piles
hendikep *n* handicap
hendikepirati *v.t.* handicap
herkulski *a.* herculean
hernija *n.* hernia
heroina *n.* heroine
heroj *n.* hero
herojski *a.* heroic
hibernacija *n.* hibernation
hibrid *n* hybrid
hibridan *a.* hybrid
higijena *n.* hygiene
higijenski *a.* hygienic
hijena *n.* hyaena, hyena
hijerarhija *n.* hierarchy
himna *n.* hymn
himna *n.* anthem
hiperbola *n.* hyperbole
hipnotisati *v.t.* hypnotize
hipnotizam *n.* hypnotism
hipnotizam *n.* mesmerism
hipnotizirati *v.t.* mesmerize
hipoteka *n.* mortgage
hipotetički *a.* hypothetical
hipoteza *n.* hypothesis
hir *n* fad
hiromant *n.* palmist
hiromantija *n.* palmistry
histeričan *a.* hysterical
histerija *n.* hysteria
hitac *n.* shot
hitan *a.* urgent
hitan slučaj *n* emergency
hitar *a.* rapid
hitna pomoć *n.* ambulance
hitnost *n.* urgency
hitrina *n.* rapidity
hitro *adv.* apace
hlače *n.* slacks
hlače *n. pl* trousers

hlad *n.* shade
hladan *a* cold
hladan *a* cool
hladiti *v. i.* cool
hladnoća *n* cold
hladnokrvan *a.* nerveless
hladnjak *n* cooler
hladnjak *n.* fridge
hladnjak *n.* refrigerator
hlađenje *n.* refrigeration
hobi *n.* hobby
hod *n.* gait
hod *n* tread
hodočasnik *n.* pilgrim
hodočašće *n.* pilgrimage
hokej *n.* hockey
hol *n.* hall
holokaust *n.* holocaust
homeopata *n.* homoeopath
homeopatija *n.* homeopathy
homogen *a.* homogeneous
honorar *n* fee
honorar *n.* honorarium
hor *n* choir
horda *n.* horde
horizont *n.* horizon
hortikultura *n.* horticulture
hostel *n.* hostel
hotel *n.* hotel
hrabar *a.* courageous
hrabar *a.* manful
hrabar *a.* valiant
hrabar *a.* bold
hrabar *a* brave
hrabrost *n.* courage
hrabrost *n.* fortitude
hrabrost *n.* gallantry
hrabrost *n.* hardihood
hrabrost *n* bravery
hram *n.* temple

hrana *n* food
hrana *n. pl* victuals
hraniti *v.t* feed
hraniti *v.t.* nourish
hranljiv *a.* nutritious
hranjenje *n* feed
hrapav *a.* husky
hrast *n.* oak
hrist *n.* Christ
hrišćanin *n* Christian
hrišćanski *a.* Christian
hrišćanstvo *n.* Christendom
hrišćanstvo *n.* Christianity
hrkanje *n* snore
hrkati *v.i.* snore
hrpa *n* bulk
hrpa *n* bunch
hrskav *a* crisp
hrskav *adj.* crump
hrt *n.* greyhound
hrvač *n.* wrestler
hrvati se *v.i.* wrestle
htjeti *v.t.* will
huligan *n.* hooligan
human *a.* humane
humanitarno *a* humanitarian
humka *n.* mound
humor *n.* humour
humorista *n.* humorist
humorističan *a.* humorous
humus *n* mould
huškati *v.t.* incite
hvalisanje *n* boast
hvalisanje *n* brag
hvalisati se *v. i* brag
hvalisav *a.* vainglorious
hvalisavost *n.* vainglory
hvaliti *v.t.* praise
hvaliti se *v.i* boast
hvat *n* fathom

hvatanje *n.* snatch
hvatanje *n.* capture
hvatati mrežom *v.t.* net

I

i *conj.* and
i tako dalje etcetera
iako *conj.* albeit
iako *conj.* although
ići *v.i.* go
ići na izlet *v.i.* picnic
ići tamo-ovamo *v.t.* shuttle
ići uzduž *v.t.* skirt
ideal *n* ideal
idealan *a.* ideal
idealista *n.* idealist
idealistički *a.* idealistic
idealizam *n.* idealism
idealizirati *v.t.* idealize
ideja *n.* idea
identičan *a.* identical
identifikacija *n.* indentification
identifikovati *v.t.* identify
identitet *n.* identity
idiom *n.* idiom
idiomatski *a.* idiomatic
idiot *n.* idiot
idiotizam *n.* ideocy
idiotski *a.* idiotic
idol *n.* idol
igla *n.* needle
ignorirati *v.t.* ignore
igra *n.* game
igra *n.* play
igra riječima *n.* pun
igra stihovima *n.* crambo
igrač *n.* player
igrač udarač u kriketu *n.* batsman

igračka *n.* toy
igrati *v.i* game
igrati se *v.i.* play
igrati se *v.i.* toy
igrati se *v.i* trifle
igrati se riječima *v.i.* pun
iguman *n* prior
igumanija *n.* prioress
ikad *adv* ever
ikra *n* fry
ilustracija *n.* illustration
ilustrirati *v.t.* illustrate
iluzija *n.* illusion
imanje *n* estate
imati *v.t.* have
imati korist *v. t.* benefit
imbecil *n.* moron
ime *n.* name
imela *n.* mistletoe
imenica *n.* noun
imenovanje *n.* nomination
imenovanje *n.* appointment
imenovati *v.t.* name
imenovati *v.t.* appoint
imenjak *n.* namesake
imigracija *n.* immigration
imigrant *n.* immigrant
imigrirati *v.i.* immigrate
imitacija *n.* imitation
imitator *n.* imitator
imitirati *v.t.* imitate
imitirati *a.* mimic
imitirati *v.t* mimic
imovina *n.* asset
imovina *n.* property
imperativ *a.* imperative
imperator *n* emperor
imperijalizam *n.* imperialism
implementacija *n.* implement
implementirati *v.t.* implement

implikacija *n.* implication
impotencija *n.* impotence
impotentan *a.* impotent
impozantan *a.* imposing
impresionirati *v.t.* impress
impresivan *a.* impressive
impuls *n.* impulse
impuls *n.* momentum
impulsivan *a.* impulsive
imućan *a.* well-to-do
imun *a.* immune
imunitet *n.* immunity
inače *conj.* otherwise
inače *adv.* otherwise
inat *n.* spite
inauguracija *n.* inauguration
incident *n.* incident
inč *n.* inch
indeks *n.* index
indicija *n* clue
indigo *n.* indigo
indijska smokva *n.* banyan
indijska urma *n.* tamarind
indijski *a.* Indian
indikacija *n.* indication
indikativan *a.* indicative
indikator *n.* indicator
indirektan *a.* implicit
indirektan *a.* indirect
indiskrecija *n.* indiscretion
indiskretan *a.* indiscreet
individualizam *n.* individualism
individualnost *n.* individuality
industrija *n.* industry
industrijski *a.* industrial
inercija *n.* inertia
inertan *a.* inert
infantilan *a.* infantile
infekcija *n.* infection
inferioran *a.* inferior

inferiornost *n.* inferiority
inficirati *v.t.* infect
inflacija *n.* inflation
informacija *n.* information
informativan *a.* informative
infuzija *n.* infusion
inherentan *a.* inherent
inhibicija *n.* inhibition
inhibirati *v.t.* inhibit
inicijal *n.* initial
inicijativa *n.* initiative
inkvizicija *n.* inquisition
inovacija *n.* innovation
inovator *n.* innovator
inovirati *v.t.* innovate
insekt *n.* insect
insekticid *n.* insecticide
insinuacija *n.* insinuation
insinuirati *v.t.* insinuate
insistiranje *n.* insistence
insistirati *v.t.* insist
insolventan *a.* insolvent
insolventnost *n.* insolvency
inspekcija *n.* inspection
inspektor *n.* inspector
inspiracija *n.* inspiration
inspirisati *v.t.* inspire
instalacija *n.* installation
instalirati *v.t.* install
instinkt *n.* instinct
instinktivan *a.* instinctive
institucija *n.* institution
institut *n.* institute
instrukcija *n.* instruction
instruktor *n.* instructor
instrument *n.* instrument
instrumentalista *n.* instrumentalist
instrumentalni *a.* instrumental
integralan *a.* integral
integritet *n.* integrity

intelekt *n.* intellect

intelektualac *n.* intellectual

intelektualni *a.* intellectual

inteligencija *n.* intelligence

inteligencija *n.* intelligentsia

inteligentan *a.* intelligent

intenzitet *n.* intensity

intenzivan *a.* intensive

interes *n.* interest

interludij *n.* interlude

internacionalni *a.* international

interni *a.* internal

interpunkcija *n.* punctuation

interval *n.* interval

intervencija *n.* intervention

intervenirati *v.i.* intervene

intervju *n.* interview

intervjuirati *v.t.* interview

intiman *a.* intimate

intimnost *n.* intimacy

intoksikacija *n.* intoxication

intriga *n* intrigue

intrigirati *v.t.* intrigue

intuicija *n.* intuition

intuitivan *a.* intuitive

invalid *n* invalid

invazija *n.* invasion

investicija *n.* investment

investirati *v.t.* invest

injenjer *n* engineer

ipak *conj* however

ipak *conj.* nevertheless

ipak *adv.* notwithstanding

ipak *adv.* though

ipak *conj.* yet

iracionalan *a.* irrational

iritacija *n.* irritation

iritiranje *n.* irritant

ironičan *a.* ironical

ironija *n.* irony

Irski *a.* Irish

irski jezik, Irac *n.* Irish

iscijediti *v.t.* squeeze

iscrtati *v.t.* line

iseckati *v.i.* haggle

ishod *n.* outcome

ishod *n.* upshot

ishrana *n.* nourishment

iskamčiti *v.t.* wheedle

iskaz *n.* utterance

isključenje *n.* expulsion

isključiti *v. t* disconnect

isključiti *v. t* exclude

isključiti *v. t.* expel

isključiv *a* exclusive

iskonski *a.* seminal

iskopati *v.t.* unearth

iskopavanje *n.* excavation

iskopavati *v. t.* excavate

iskopavati *v.i.* quarry

iskorijeniti *v. t* eradicate

iskoristiti *v.t.* advantage

iskoristiti *v.t.* utilize

iskorjeniti *v.t.* uproot

iskrcati *v.i.* land

iskren *a.* frank

iskren *a.* sincere

iskren *a.* straightforward

iskren *a.* candid

iskrenost *n.* sincerity

iskrenost *n.* candour

iskrivljen *a.* wry

iskupiti se *v.t.* redeem

iskupljenje *n.* redemption

iskusiti *v. t.* experience

iskustvo *n* experience

iskušavač *n.* tempter

iskušenje *n.* ordeal

iskušenje *n.* temptation

ismijavanje *adj* mock

ismijavanje *n.* ridicule
ismijavati *v.i.* mock
ismijavati *v.t.* ridicule
ispad *n.* sally
isparavati *v.t.* aerify
isparavati *v.t.* vaporize
ispariti *v. i* evaporate
ispasti *v.i.* sally
ispeći *v.t.* bake
ispirati *v.t.* rinse
ispirati grlo *v.i.* gargle
ispitanik *n* examinee
ispitati *v. t* examine
ispitivač *n* examiner
ispitivanje *n.* examination
ispitivanje *n.* inquiry
ispitivanje *n.* scrutiny
ispitivati *v.t.* quiz
isplatiti *v.t.* repay
ispleten od pruća *n.* wicker
ispljuvak *n* spittle
ispljuvak *n.* sputum
ispod *prep.* under
ispod *adv.* underneath
ispod *prep* below
ispod *prep* beneath
isporuka *n* delivery
ispovedati *v.t.* profess
ispovjediti *v.t.* avow
ispraviti *v. t* correct
ispraviti *v.i.* rectify
ispraviti *v.t.* straighten
ispravljanje *n.* rectification
ispravno *adv* right
ispravnost *n.* propriety
ispred *adv.* ahead
isprugati *v.t.* stripe
ispuhati *v. t.* exhaust
ispuniti *v.t.* fulfil
ispunjen *a.* fraught

ispunjenje *n.* fulfilment
ispuštati *v.t.* shed
istačkati *v. t* dot
istaknut *a.* prominent
istaknut *a.* salient
istaknutost *n.* prominence
isteći *v.i.* expire
istek *n* expiry
isti *a.* same
istina *n.* truth
istinitost *n.* veracity
istinoljubiv *a.* truthful
istisnuti *v.t.* oust
isto *n.* ditto
istočni *a* east
istočni *a* eastern
istočno *adv* east
istočnjak *n* oriental
istok *n* east
istopiti *v.t.* smelt
istovremen *a.* instantaneous
istovremen *a.* simultaneous
istraga *n.* inquest
istraga *n.* investigation
istrajati *v.i.* persevere
istrajnost *n.* perseverance
istrajnost *n.* tenacity
istražiti *v.t* explore
istražiti *v.t.* investigate
istraživanje *n* exploration
istraživanje *n* research
istraživati *v.t.* probe
istraživati *v.i.* research
istrgnuti *v.t.* wrest
istrošiti *v.t.* stale
istući *v.t.* wallop
iščašenje *n.* wrench
iščašenje *n* wrick
iščašiti *v.t.* wrench
iščeznuti *v.i.* vanish

išta *n.* aught
ištanje *n.* privation
ištanje *n.* scarcity
ištanje *n.* stringency
iverica *n.* splinter
ivica *n* edge
ivičnjak *n* curb
iza *adv* behind
iza *prep* behind
izabran *a* select
izabrati *v. t.* choose
izabrati *v. t* elect
izabrati *v.t.* pick
izabrati *v.t.* select
izabrati vrijeme *v.t.* time
izadati *v.i.* issue
izaslanik *n* emissary
izazivati *v.t* foment
izazov *n.* challenge
izazvati *v. t.* challenge
izazvati *v.t.* solicit
izazvati žuticu *v.t.* jaundice
izbaciti *v. t.* eject
izbaciti iz kolosijeka *v. t.* derail
izbacivač *n* bouncer
izbacivati *v.i.* spout
izbalansirati *v.t.* poise
izbeći *v. t* evade
izbeleti *v. t* bleach
izbijanje *n.* outbreak
izbjegavanje *n* elusion
izbjegavanje *n* evasion
izbjegavanje *n.* avoidance
izbjegavati *v. t* elude
izbjegavati *v.t.* shun
izbjegavati *v.t.* avoid
izbjeglica *n.* refugee
izblijedeti *v.i* fade
izbor *n.* choice
izbor *n* election

izbor *n.* pick
izbor *n.* selection
izborati *v.t.* wrinkle
izborna jedinica *n* constituency
izbosti *v.t.* pierce
izbrbljati *v. t. & i* blab
izbrbljati *v. t* blurt
izbrisati *v. t* delete
izbrisati *v. t* efface
izdaja *n.* treachery
izdaja *n.* treason
izdaja *n* betrayal
izdajnički *a.* treacherous
izdajnik *n.* traitor
izdaleka *adv.* afar
izdanak *n* offset
izdanje *n* edition
izdanje *n.* publication
izdati *v.t.* betray
izdavač *n.* publisher
izdavati *v.t* pirate
izdržati *v.t.* endure
izdržati *v.i.* persist
izdržati *v.t.* withstand
izdržavanje *n.* aliment
izdržavanje *n.* livelihood
izdržavanje *n.* sustenance
izdržljiv *n* cast-iron
izdržljiv *a* durable
izdržljiv *a* endurable
izdržljiv *adj.* hardy
izdržljivost *n.* endurance
izdržljivost *n* last
izdržljivost *n.* persistence
izdržljivost *n.* stamina
izdupsti *v.t* hollow
izdvojiti *v. t* extract
izgled *n.* guise
izgled *n.* prospect
izgled *n* appearance

izgledi *n.* odds
izgnan *a* outcast
izgnanik *n.* outcast
izgovarati *v.t.* pronounce
izgovor *n* excuse
izgovor *n* pretext
izgovor *n.* pronunciation
izgovoriti *v.t.* voice
izgrditi *v.t.* lambaste
izgrditi *v.t.* snub
izgubiti *v.t* forfeit
izgubiti *v.t.* lose
izjava *n.* statement
izjaviti saučešće *v. i.* condole
izjaviti *v.t.* allege
izjednačavanje *n* assimilation
izjednačen *a* level
izjednačiti *v. t* equal
izjednačiti *v. t.* equalize
izjednačiti *v.t.* level
izjednačiti *v.t.* offset
izjednačiti *v.* assimilate
izlaz *n.* exit
izlaz *n.* output
izleći *v.i.* incubate
izlet *n.* outing
izliven *a.* molten
Izložba *n.* exhibition
izložiti *v. t* exhibit
izložiti *v. t* expose
izložiti *v.t.* table
izložiti rendg. zrakama *v.t.* x-ray
izludjeti *v.t* dement
izlupati *v. t* belabour
izlječiv *a* curable
izljev *n.* outburst
izmaglica *n* drizzle
izmaglica *n.* haze
izmaglica *n.* mist
između *prep.* amongst

između *prep* between
izmicanje *n* dodge
izmicati *v. t* dodge
izmijeniti *v.t.* alter
izmirenje *n.* reconciliation
izmisliti *v. t* concoct
izmisliti *v. t* devise
izmišljen *a.* imaginary
izmišljotina *n.* concoction
izmišljotina *n* figment
izmjena *n* alteration
izmlatiti *v.t* maul
izmoriti *v.t.* tire
izmrviti *v. t* crumble
iznajmiti pašnjak *v.t.* agist
iznajmljivanje *n.* rent
iznajmljivati *v.t.* rent
iznenada *adv.* suddenly
iznenaditi *v.t.* startle
iznenaditi *v.t.* surprise
iznenadnost *n.* sudden
iznenađenje *n.* surprise
iznimka *n* exception
iznos *n* amount
iznos *v.* amount
iznositi *v.i* amount
iznošen *a.* worn
iznova brojati *v.t.* recount
iznova *adv.* anew
iznuren *a.* prostrate
iznurenost *n* debility
iznurenost *n.* prostration
izobara *n.* isobar
izobilje *n.* riches
izobličiti *v. t* distort
izolacija *n.* insulation
izolacija *n.* isolation
izolator *n.* insulator
izolirati *v.t.* insulate
izolirati *v.t.* isolate

izopačenost *n.* perversity
izostaviti *v.t.* omit
izostavljanje *n.* omission
izoštriti *v.t* focus
izoštriti *v.t.* sharpen
izračunati *v. t.* calculate
izrada *n.* workmanship
izraslina *n.* wen
izravan *a* outright
izravan *a* through
izravnati *v. t* even
izravnati *v.t.* plane
izravno *adv.* outright
izraz *n.* expression
izraz *n.* locution
izraz lica *n.* countenance
izrazit *a* emphatic
izraziti *v. t.* express
izraziti *v.t.* phrase
izraziti *a.* wordy
izraziti mimikom *v.i* mime
izražajan *a.* expressive
izreka *n* dictum
izručiti *v.t.* consign
izrugivanje *n.* mockery
izrugivati se *v.t.* lampoon
izumiti *v.t.* invent
izumro *a* extinct
izustiti *v.t.* mouth
izustiti *v.t.* utter
izuzeti *v. t* except
izuzev *prep* save
izvaditi iz korica *v.t.* unsheathe
izvan *prep* outside
izvan *adv.* without
izvan *prep.* beyond
izvanredan *a.* extraordinary
izvanredan *a.* outstanding
izvanredan *a.* remarkable
izvanredan *a.* superb

izvediv *a.* manageable
izvesnost *n.* certainty
izvesti *v. t.* derive
izvesti *v.t.* perform
izviđač *n* scout
izviđati *v.i* scout
izvijač *n.* spanner
izvijati se *v.i.* snake
izvijestiti *v.t.* report
izviniti se *v.i.* apologize
izvinjenje *n.* apology
izviriti *v.i.* well
izvjesnost *n.* surety
izvjestitelj *n.* informer
izvjestiti *v.t.* account
izvješće *n.* report
izvlačenje *n* draw
izvod *n.* precis
izvodljiv *a* feasible
izvodljiv *a.* practicable
izvodljivost *n.* practicability
izvođač *n.* performer
izvođač radova *n* contractor
izvođenje *n.* performance
izvođenje *n.* pursuance
izvor *n.* source
izvoz *n* export
izvoziti *v. t.* export
izvrsnost *n.* excellence
izvršenje *n* execution
izvršitelj *n.* executioner
izvršiti *v. t* execute

J

ja *pron.* I
jabuka *n.* apple
jad *n.* woe
jadan *a* deplorable

jadan *a.* pitiable
jadan *a.* poor
jadikovanje *n* wail
jadikovati *v.i.* wail
jagnje *n* agnus
jagnje *n.* lamb
jagnješce *n.* lambkin
jagoda *n.* strawberry
jahač *n.* rider
jahta *n.* yacht
jaje *n* egg
jajnik *n.* ovary
jak *a.* strong
jak *n.* yak
jaka pamučna tkanina *n.* jean
jaka točka *n.* forte
jakna *n.* jacket
jalovo *adj.* acarpous
jama *n.* pit
jamac *n.* warrantor
jamčiti *v. t.* bail
jamčiti *v.t* guarantee
jamčiti *v.i.* vouch
jamčiti *v.t.* warrant
jamstvo *n.* bail
jamstvo *n.* warranty
jarac *n* Capricorn
jarak *n* ditch
jaram *n.* yoke
jarbol *n.* mast
jasle *n.* manger
jaslice *n.* nursery
jasmin *n.* jasmine, jessamine
jasno *a* clear
jasnoća *n* clarity
jastog *n.* lobster
jastreb *n* hawk
jastuk *n* cushion
jastuk *n.* pad
jastuk *n* pillow

jato divljih ptica *n.* skein
javiti putem radija *v.t.* radio
javni *a.* public
javnost *n.* public
javor *n.* sycamore
jazavac *n.* badger
jazbina *n.* burrow
jazbina *n* den
jazbina *n.* lair
jecaj *n* sob
jecati *v.i.* sob
ječam *n.* barley
jedan *a.* one
jedan slog *n.* monosyllable
jedanaest *n* eleven
jedini *a.* only
jedini *a.* single
jedini *a* sole
jedinica *n.* unit
jedinstven *a.* inimitable
jedinstven *a.* unique
jedinstvo *n.* oneness
jedinstvo *n.* unity
jednačina *n* equation
jednake vrijednosti *a.* tantamount
jednako *a* equal
jednako *adv.* alike
jednakost *n* equality
jednakost *n.* par
jednakostranični *a* equilateral
jednoglasan *a.* unanimous
jednoglasje *n.* unison
jednoglasnost *n.* unanimity
jednoličan *a.* humdrum
jednom *adv.* once
jednom *adv.* sometime
jednook *a.* monocular
jednosložan *a.* monosyllabic
jednostavan *a.* plain
jednostavan *a.* simple

jednostavnost *n* ease
jednostavnost *n.* simplicity
jednostran *a* ex-parte
jednostrano *adv* ex-parte
jedrilica *n.* glider
jedriti *v.i.* sail
jedro *n.* sail
jedva *adv.* hardly
jedva *adv.* scarcely
jedva *adv.* barely
jeftin *a* cheap
jeftin *a.* inexpensive
jela *n* fir
jelen *n* deer
jelen *n.* stag
jelo *n* dish
jelovnik *n.* menu
jen *n.* Yen
jer *conj.* for
jer *conj.* because
jesen *n* fall
jesen *n.* autumn
jesti *v. t* eat
jestiv *a* eatable
jestivo *a* edible
jestivost *n.* eatable
jetra *n.* liver
jeza *n.* chill
jeza *n* shudder
jezero *n.* lake
jezgro *n.* core
jezgro *n.* nucleus
jezički *a.* linguistic
jezični *a.* lingual
jezik *n.* language
jezik *n.* tongue
jeziv *a.* ghastly
ježiti se *v.i.* shudder
jogunast *a.* restive
jogunast *a.* unruly

jorgan *n.* quilt
jorgovan *n.* lilac
još *a.* more
još *adv.* yet
još uvijek *adv.* still
jubilej *n.* jubilee
jučer *adv.* yesterday
jučerašnji dan *n.* yesterday
jug *n.* south
juha *n* broth
juha *n.* soup
junaštvo *n.* heroism
junaštvo *n.* prowess
junaštvo *n.* valour
june *n* bullock
junior *n.* junior
jupiter *n.* jupiter
jurisprudencija *n.* jurisprudence
juriš *n.* onslaught
jurišati *v.i.* storm
juriti *v. t.* chase
jurnuti *v. i.* dash
juta *n.* jute
jutro *n.* morning
jutro *n.* morrow
jutro (jedinica za površinu) *n.* acre
juvelir *n.* jeweller
južni *a.* southerly
južni *a.* southern
južni krajevi *n.* south
južno *adv* south

K

ka *prep.* towards
kabare *n.* cabaret
kabel *n* cord
kabel *n.* cable
kabina *n* booth

kabinet *n.* cabinet
kaciga *n.* helmet
kad *conj.* when
kad god *adv. conj.* whenever
kada *n.* tub
kada *adv.* when
kadet *n.* cadet
kadionik *n* censer
kaditi tamjanom *v.t.* incense
kaditi *v. t* cense
kadmij *n* cadmium
kafić *n.* cafe
kajsija *n.* apricot
kakav *a.* what
kako *adv.* how
kaktus *n.* cactus
kalajisati *v.t.* tin
kalcij *n* calcium
kalem *n.* graft
kalem *n.* reel
kalemiti *v.t* graft
kalemiti *v.t.* inoculate
kalemljenje *n.* inoculation
kalendar *n.* calendar
kaligrafija *n* calligraphy
kalij *n.* potassium
kalkulator *n* calculator
kalorija *n.* calorie
kaluđer *n.* votary
kaluđerica *n.* nun
kaluđerički veo *n.* wimple
kalup *n.* mould
kaljati *v.t.* soil
kamelot *n* camlet
kamen *n.* stone
kamenit *a.* stony
kamenolom *n.* quarry
kamenovati *v.t.* stone
kamera *n.* camera
kamfor *n.* camphor

kamion *n.* lorry
kamion *n.* truck
kamp *n.* camp
kampanja *n.* campaign
kampovati *v. i.* camp
kanadska kuna *n.* mink
kanal *n* channel
kanal *n.* canal
kanalizacija *n.* sewerage
kancelar *n* chamberlain
kancelar *n.* chancellor
kancelarijski pribor *n.* stationery
kandidat *n.* applicant
kandidat *n* nominee
kandidat *n.* candidate
kandža *n* claw
kanister *n.* canister
kanon *n* canon
kanonada *n. v. & t* cannonade
kanta *n.* pail
kanta *n* bucket
kantina *n.* canteen
kanton *n* canton
kao što *v.t.* like
kao *conj* as
kaos *n.* chaos
kaotičan *adv.* chaotic
kap *n* drop
kapa *n* bonnet
kapa *n* coif
kapa *n.* cap
kapacitet *n.* capacity
kapanje *n* drip
kapati *v. i* drip
kapati *v. i* drop
kapati *v.i.* trickle
kapela *n.* chapel
kapetan *n.* skipper
kapetan *n.* captain
kapija *n.* gate

kapital *n.* capital
kapitalista *n.* capitalist
kapitulirati *v. t* capitulate
kapljica *n.* minim
kapric *n.* caprice
kapric *n.* whim
kapriciozan *a.* whimsical
kapriciozan *a.* capricious
kaput *n* coat
kaput *n.* overcoat
karakter *n.* character
karakteristika *n.* attribute
karamela *n.* toffee
karanfil, ružičasta boja *n.* pink
karat *n.* carat
karavan *n.* caravan
karbid *n.* carbide
kardinal *n.* cardinal
kardinalan *a.* cardinal
karfiol *n.* cauliflower
karijera *n.* career
karika *n* fetter
karikatura *n.* caricature
karneval *n* carnival
karta *n* fare
karta *n.* ticket
kartica *n.* card
karton *n.* cardboard
karton *n* carton
kas *n* trot
kasarna *n.* barrack
kasati *v.i.* trot
kaseta *n.* cassette
kaskada *n.* cascade
kasnije *adv.* afterwards
kasniji *a.* latter
kasno *a.* late
kasta *n* caste
kastrirati *v.t.* geld
kaša *n.* mash

kaša *n.* mush
kaša *n.* porridge
kašalj *n.* cough
kašljati *v. i.* cough
kat *n* bunk
kat *n.* storey
katalog *n.* catalogue
katarakt *n.* cataract
katastrofa *n* disaster
katastrofalan *a* disastrous
katedrala *n.* minster
katedrala *n.* cathedral
kategoričan *a.* categorical
kategorija *n.* category
katolički *a.* catholic
katran *n.* tar
kauč *n.* couch
kauzalan *adj.* causal
kava *n* coffee
kavaljer *n* gallant
kavez za ptice *n.* aviary
kavez *n.* cage
kavga *n* affray
kavga *n.* scuffle
kazališni *a.* theatrical
kazalište *n.* theatre
kazna *n* fine
kazna *n.* penalty
kazna *n.* punishment
kazneni *a.* penal
kazneni *a.* punitive
kazneni *a.* tortuous
kazniti *v.t* find
kazniti *v.t.* penalize
kazniti *v.t.* punish
kazniti *v. t.* castigate
kažiprst *n* forefinger
kecelja *n.* apron
kečap *n.* ketchup
keks *n* biscuit

kemijski *a.* chemical
kemikalija *n.* chemical
keramika *n* ceramics
kerozin *n.* kerosene
kesten *n.* chestnut
kestenjast *a* maroon
kestenjasta boja *n.* maroon
kicoš *n* dandy
kičma *n.* spine
kičmeni *a.* spinal
kidisati *v.i.* swoop
kidnapovati *v.t.* kidnap
kihanje *n* sneeze
kihnuti *v.i.* sneeze
kikotati se *v.i.* giggle
Kina *n.* china
kinin *n.* quinine
kino *n.* cinema
kino *n.* movies
kipeti *v.i.* seethe
kirurg *n.* surgeon
kirurgija *n.* surgery
kiselina *n* acid
kiselost *n.* acidity
kiseo *a* acid
kiseo *a.* sour
kisik *n.* oxygen
kiša *n* rain
kišobran *n.* umbrella
kišovit *a.* rainy
kit *n.* whale
kita cveća *n.* nosegay
kitnjast *a.* gaudy
kitova kost *n.* baleen
kladiti se *v.i* bet
kladiti se *v.i.* wager
klasa *n* class
klasičan *a* classic
klasičan *a* classical
klasifikacija *n* classification

klasik *n.* classic
klati *v. t* butcher
klatiti *v. t* dangle
klatno *n.* pendulum
klaun *n* clown
klauzula *n* clause
klavir *n.* piano
klečati *v.i.* kneel
klesati *v. t.* chisel
kleti se *v.i.* sweat
kletva *n* curse
kleveta *n* defamation
kleveta *n.* libel
kleveta *n.* slander
klevetati *v. t.* defame
klevetati *v.t.* malign
klevetati *v.t.* slander
klevetati *v. t.* calumniate
klevetnički *a.* slanderous
klica *n.* chit
klica *n.* germ
klicanje *n* acclamation
klijanje *n.* germination
klijati *v.i.* germinate
klijent *n..* client
kliješta *n. pl.* tongs
klima *n.* climate
klimati *v.i* wobble
klimati glavom *v.i.* nod
klin *n.* peg
klin *n.* wedge
klinika *n.* clinic
klip *n.* piston
klizaljka *n.* skate
klizati *v.t.* skate
klizav *a* slick
klizav *a.* slippery
kliziti *v.t.* glide
kliziti *v.i.* slide
klopotati *n. & v. i* clack

klor *n* chlorine	kočoperenje *n* stalk
kloroform *n* chloroform	kod *prep* by
klub *n* club	kod *n* code
klupa *n* bench	koedukacija *n.* co-education
klupko *n.* clew	koeficijent *n.* coefficient
kljova *n.* tusk	koegzistencija *n* co-existence
kljucanje *n.* peck	koegzistirati *v. i* co-exist
kljucati *v.i.* peck	koga *pron.* whom
ključ *n.* key	koji *pron.* as
ključanje *n* boil	koji *rel. pron.* that
ključati *v.i.* boil	koji *pron.* which
ključati *v.t* ferment	koji *a* which
kljun *n* beak	koji draži *a.* irritant
kmet *n.* serf	koji god *pron* whichever
kneževski *a.* princely	koji izgleda *a* look
knjiga *n* book	koji je kao tkivo *a.* webby
knjigovođa *n* book-keeper	koji je obavezan *n.* incumbent
knjiški moljac *n* book-worm	koji nije plemenit *a.* ignoble
knjiški *n.* bookish	koji opominje *a.* monitory
književni *a.* literary	koji oživljava *a.* resurgent
književnost *n.* literature	koji podseća *a.* reminiscent
ko *pron.* who	koji preživa *a.* ruminant
koalicija *n* coalition	koji sadrži obećanje *a.* promissory
kobalt *n* cobalt	koji se hrani drvetom *a.* xylophagous
kobila *n.* mare	koji se može baciti *a* projectile
kobra *n* cobra	koji se može dobiti *a.* obtainable
kocka *n* cube	koji se može prati *a.* washable
kockanje *n* gamble	koji se može prodati *a.* marketable
kockar *n.* gambler	koji se može prodati *a.* salable
kockast *a* cubical	koji se rađa *a.* nascent
kockati se *v. i.* dice	koji se sastavlja *adj.* confluent
kockati se *v.i.* gamble	koji se tiče zapešća *adj* carpal
kocke *n.* dice	koji zadržava *a.* retentive
kočija *n.* carriage	koji živi na drvetu *a.* xylophilous
kočija *n* chariot	kokain *n* cocaine
kočija, trener *n* coach	kokodakati *v. i* cackle
kočijaš *n* coachman	kokos *n* coconut
kočiti *v. t* brake	kokosovo vlakno *n* coir
kočnica *n* skid	kokoš *n.* chicken
kočnica *n* brake	kokošinjac *n.* roost

kokoška *n.* bantam
kokoška *n.* hen
kokpit *n.* cock-pit
koks *v. t* coke
kola *n.* wain
kolabirati *v. i* collapse
kolac *n.* pale
kolac *n.* picket
kolebati se *v.i.* shilly-shally
kolebati se *v.i.* vacillate
kolebljiv *n.* shilly-shally
koledž *n* college
kolega *n* colleague
kolega *n* fellow
kolekcija *n* collection
kolekcionar *n* collector
kolektivno *a* collective
kolera *n.* cholera
koliba *n.* cabin
koliba *n* cottage
koliba *n.* hut
kolica *n.* cart
količina *n.* quantity
količnik *n.* quotient
kolijevka *n* cradle
kolona *n* column
kolonija *n* colony
kolonijalan *a* colonial
kolosijek *n.* gauge
kolosijek *n.* rut
kolovoz *n.* August
kolovoz *n* august
koljeno *n.* knee
koma *n.* coma
komad *n.* piece
komadić *n* bit
komandant *n* commander
komarac *n.* mosquito
kombi *n.* van
kombinacija *n* combination

kombinirati *v. t* combine
kome se može naći trag *a.* traceable
komedija *n.* comedy
komemoracija *n.* commemoration
komemoracija *n.* memorial
komemorativan *a* memorial
komentar *n* comment
komentar *n* commentary
komentator *n* commentator
komentirati *v. i* comment
komešanje *n.* fuss
kometa *n* comet
komičan *a* comic
komičar *n.* comedian
komičar *n* comic
komonvelt *n.* commonwealth
komora *n.* chamber
kompaktan *a.* compact
komparativno *a* comparative
kompas *n* compass
kompenzacija *n* compensation
kompleks *n* complex
kompletan *a* complete
kompletirati *v. t* complete
komplicirati *v. t* complicate
komplikacija *n.* complication
kompliment *n.* compliment
komšija *n.* neighbour
komuna *v. t* commune
komunalan *a* communal
komunicirati *v. t* communicate
komunikacija *n.* communication
komunizam *n* communism
konačan *a* final
konačan *a* finite
konačište *n.* lodging
konačni *a.* terminal
konačno *adv.* eventually
koncepcija *n* conception
koncept *n* concept

koncert *n.* concert
koncizan *a* concise
kondenzirati *v. t* condense
kondukter *n* conductor
konferencija *n* conference
konfiskacija *n* confiscation
konfiskovati *v. t* confiscate
konflikt *n.* conflict
kongres *n* congress
konkretan *a* concrete
konkubina *n* concubine
konkubinat *n.* concubinage
konkurentan *a* competitive
konobar *n.* waiter
konobarica *n.* waitress
konoplja *n.* hemp
konsenzus *n.* consensus
konsolidacija *n* consolidation
konsolidirati *v. t.* consolidate
konspirator *n.* conspirator
konstruirati *v. t.* construct
konstrukcija *n* construction
kontakt *n.* contact
kontaktirati *v. t* contact
kontaminirati *v.t.* contaminate
kontekst *n* context
kontinent *n* continent
kontinentalni *a* continental
kontinuitet *n* continuity
kontracepcija *n.* contraception
kontradikcija *n.* antinomy
kontradikcija *n* contradiction
kontrast *n* contrast
kontrola *n* control
kontrolirati *v. t* control
kontrolor *n.* controller
kontura *n* contour
kontuzovati *v.t.* contuse
konvencija *n.* convention
konzerva *n.* tin

konzervativan *a* conservative
konzervativnost *n* conservative
konzervirati *v. t.* can
konzola *n* ancon
konzola *v. t* console
konzultacije *n* consultation
konzultirati *v. t* consult
konzumacija *n* consumption
konj *n.* horse
konj *n.* steed
konjanik *n* chevalier
konjica *n.* cavalry
konjukcija *n.* conjuncture
koordinacija *n* co-ordination
kopač *n.* pitman
kopanje *n* dig
kopati *v.t.* dig
kopati *v.t.* shovel
kopati lopatom *v.t.* spade
kopča *n* clasp
kopča *n* buckle
kopija *n* copy
kopile *n.* bastard
kopirati *v. t* copy
kopito *n.* hoof
kopljanik *n.* lancer
koplje *n.* javelin
koplje *n.* lance
koplje *n.* spear
kopriva *n.* nettle
koprologija *n.* coprology
kora *n.* crust
kora *n.* peel
kora *n.* bark
koračati *v.i.* pace
koračati *v.i.* step
koračati *v.i.* stride
koračati *v.t.* tread
korak *n* pace
korak *n.* step

korak *n* stride
koral *n* coral
koralno ostrvo *n.* atoll
korekcija *n* correction
korelacija *n.* correlation
korice *n.* scabbard
koridor *n.* corridor
korijander *n.* coriander
korijen *n.* root
Korint *n.* Corinth
korisnost *n.* utility
korist *n.* sake
korist *n.* subservience
korist *n* behalf
korist *n* benefit
koristan *a* beneficial
koristan *a.* helpful
koristan *a.* subservient
koristan *a.* useful
koristiti aliteraciju *v.* alliterate
korišćenje *n.* utilization
koriti *v.t.* rebuke
kormilo *n.* helm
kormoran *n.* cormorant
kornet *n.* cornet
kornjača *n.* tortoise
kornjača *n.* turtle
korov *n.* weed
korozivan *adj.* corrosive
korpa *n.* basket
korporacija *n* corporation
korpus *n* corps
korumpiran *a.* corrupt
korumpirati *v. t.* corrupt
korupcija *n.* corruption
korupcija *n.* jobbery
kosa *n* hair
kosa *n.* scythe
kosina *n* bias
kositi *v.t.* mow

kost *n.* bone
kostim *n.* costume
košnica *n.* hive
košnica *n.* beehive
koštati *v.t.* cost
koštica *n.* kernel
košulja *n.* shirt
košuljica zmije *n.* slough
kotač *a.* wheel
kotar *n.* county
kotar *n* district
kotlar *n.* tinker
kotrljati *v.i.* roll
kotrljati *v.t.* wheel
kotur *n.* pulley
kovač *n.* smith
kovač *n* blacksmith
kovačnica *n* forge
kovanica *n* coinage
kovati *v.t.* mint
kovati zavjeru *v. i.* conspire
kovčeg *n.* ark
kovčeg *n* casket
koverat *n* envelope
kovitlac *n.i.* whirl
kovnica *n* mint
koza *n.* goat
kozmetički *a.* cosmetic
kozmetika *n.* cosmetic
kozmički *adj.* cosmic
koža *n.* cutis
koža *n.* leather
koža *n.* skin
kožar *n.* tanner
kožara *n.* tannery
kožuh *n.* jerkin
kraba *n* crab
kradljivac stoke *n* abactor
krađa *n.* theft
krađa stoke *n* abaction

kraj *n.* end
kraj *n.* terminus
kraj *n.* tip
krajnik *n.* tonsil
krajnost *n* utmost
krajnji *a.* ultimate
krajnji *a.* utmost
kralj *n.* king
kraljevina *n.* kingdom
kraljevski *a.* regal
kraljevski *a.* royal
kraljevstvo *n.* royalty
kraljica *n.* queen
kraljoubojstvo *n.* regicide
krastavac *n* cucumber
krasuljak *n* daisy
kratak *a.* short
kratak *a.* brief
kratica *n* abbreviation
kratko *adv.* short
kratkovid *a.* myopic
kratkovidost *n.* myopia
krava *n.* cow
kravata *n* tie
krčag *n.* jug
krčag *n.* pitcher
krčkati *v.i.* simmer
krčma *n.* inn
krčma *n.* saloon
krčma *n.* tavern
krćiti *v.t.* pioneer
kreativan *adj.* creative
kredit *n* credit
kredo *n* creed
kreirati *v. t* create
kreker *n* cracker
krema *n* cream
kremiranje *n* cremation
kremirati *v. t* cremate
kresta *n.* aigrette

kreštav *a.* strident
kretanje *n.* motion
kretati se *v.t* ambulate
krevet *n* bed
krevetac *n.* cot
krevetac *n.* crib
krez *n.* croesus
krhak *a.* fragile
krhk *a.* brittle
krigla *n.* mug
krijes *n* bonfire
krilat *adj.* aliferous
krilo *n.* wing
kriminal *n* criminal
kripta *n* cist
kriptografija *n.* cryptography
kristal *n* crystal
krišom *adv.* stealthily
kriterij *n* criterion
kritičan *adj* censorious
kritičan *a* critical
kritičar *n* critic
kritika *n.* censure
kritika *n* criticism
kritikovati *v. t.* censure
kritizirati *v. t* criticize
kriv *a* culpable
kriv *a.* guilty
kriva *v. t* curve
krivac *n* culprit
krivica *n.* guilt
krivično *a* criminal
krivina *n* curve
kriviti *v. t* blame
krivokletstvo *n.* perjury
krivotvoren *a.* counterfeit
krivudav *adj* anfractuous
kriza *n* crisis
kriza *n.* slump
križ *n* cross

križarski pohod *n* crusade	**krvav** *a* bloody
krma *n.* stern	**krvni srodnik** *adj* cognate
krmača *n.* sow	**krvoproliće** *n* bloodshed
krojač *n.* tailor	**krzno** *n.* fur
krojiti *v.t.* tailor	**ksilofon** *n.* xylophone
krckodil *n* crocodile	**kucati** *v.t.* knock
krom *n* chrome	**kucati** *v.i.* pulsate
krom *a.* lame	**kucati** *v.i.* tick
kroničan *a.* chronic	**kuća** *n* house
kronograf *n* chronograph	**kućica** *n.* lodge
kronologija *n.* chronology	**kućište** *n.* casing
krotak *a.* meek	**kuda** *adv.* whither
krov *n.* roof	**kuditi** *v.t* upbraid
kroz *prep.* through	**kuga** *n.* pestilence
krpa *n.* rag	**kuga** *a.* plague
krpiti *v.t.* stitch	**kuglati se** *v.i* bowl
krstarica *n* cruiser	**kuhar** *n* cook
krstariti *v.i.* cruise	**kuhati** *v. t* cook
krstiti *v.t.* baptize	**kuhinja** *n.* cuisine
krš *n.* rubble	**kuhinja** *n.* kitchen
kršan *a.* robust	**kuja** *n* bitch
kršenje *n.* violation	**kuk** *n* hip
krštenje *n.* baptism	**kuka** *n.* crotchet
krtica *n.* mole	**kuka** *n.* hook
krug *n.* circle	**kukac** *n.* bug
krug *n* cycle	**kukavica** *n.* coward
kruh *n* bread	**kukavica** *n* cuckoo
krumpir *n.* potato	**kukavičluk** *n.* cowardice
kruna *n* crown	**kukolj** *v. i* cockle
krunisanje *n* coronation	**kukuruz** *n* corn
krunisati *v. t* crown	**kukuruz** *n.* maize
krupan *a.* massy	**kula** *n.* rook
krupan *a.* stout	**kulminirati** *v.i.* culminate
kruška *n.* pear	**kult** *n* cult
krut *n.* stiff	**kultura** *n* culture
kruženje *n.* circuit	**kulturni** *a* cultural
kružni *a* circular	**kuna** *n.* marten
kružni *a* cyclic	**kupac** *n* customer
krv *n* blood	**kupac** *n.* buyer
krvariti *v. i* bleed	**kupanje** *n* bath

kupati *se* *v. t* bathe
kupidon *n* Cupid
kupiti *v.t.* purchase
kupiti *v. t.* buy
kuplet *n.* couplet
kupola *n* dome
kupon *n.* coupon
kupovati *v.i.* shop
kupovina *n.* purchase
kupus *n.* cabbage
kurir *n.* courier
kurir *n.* messenger
kurkuma *n.* turmeric
kurtizana *n.* courtesan
kurva *n.* slut
kurziv *n.* italics
kurzivan *a.* italic
kut *n.* angle
kut *n* corner
kutak *n.* nook
kutija *n* box
kutlača *n.* ladle
kutni *a.* angular
kutnjak *n.* molar
kvačilo *n* clutch
kvadrat *n.* square
kvaka *n.* latch
kvalificirati **se** *v.i.* qualify
kvalifikacija *n.* qualification
kvalitativan *a.* qualitative
kvalitet *n.* quality
kvant *n.* quantum
kvantitativan *a.* quantitative
kvarenje *n.* adulteration
kvarljiv *a.* perishable
kvasac *n* ferment
kvasac *n.* yeast
kvašenje *n.* soak
kviz *n.* quiz
kvorum *n.* quorum

kvota *n.* quota

L

labav *a.* lax
labav *a.* loose
labavost *n.* laxity
labijalni *a.* labial
labirint *n.* labyrinth
labirint *n.* maze
laboratorija *n.* laboratory
laboratorijska **posuda** *n.* cuvette
labud *n.* swan
ladica *n* drawer
lagan dodir *n* graze
lagano *adv.* leisurely
lagati *v.i.* lie
laguna *n.* lagoon
laik *n.* layman
lajanje *n* yap
lajati *v.t.* bark
lajati *v.i.* yap
lak *a* facile
lak *n* lac, lakh
lak *n.* varnish
lakat *n* elbow
lakej *n.* lackey
laki galop *n* canter
lakirati *v.t.* varnish
lako *a* easy
lako *a* light
lakomislenost *n* flippancy
lakomislenost *n.* levity
lakomo *adv* avidly
lakonski *a.* laconic
lakovjernost *adj.* credulity
lakrdijaš *n* antic
lakrdijaš *n.* pantaloon
lakrdijaš *n* buffoon

laksativ *n.* laxative
laktoza *n.* lactose
lama *n.* lama
lampa *n.* lamp
lanac *n* chain
lanac *n.* tether
lanceta *a.* lancet
laneno sjeme *n.* linseed
lansiranje *n.* launch
lansirati *v.t.* launch
lapor *n.* marl
larmadžija *a.* rowdy
lascivan *a.* lascivious
laskanje *n* flattery
laskati *v.t* flatter
lasta *n.* swallow
latica *n.* petal
laureat *n* laureate
lauta *n.* lute
lav *n.* Leo
lav *n* lion
lava *n.* lava
lavanda *n.* lavender
lavica *n.* lioness
lavovski *a* leonine
laž *n* lie
lažan *a* false
lažan *a* sham
lažan *a.* spurious
lažljiv *a.* mendacious
lažna vest *n* canard
lažno se zakleti *v.i.* perjure
lažov *n.* liar
lebdjeti *v.t.* waft
leća *n.* lentil
led *n.* ice
leden *a.* icy
ledenica *n.* icicle
ledina *n.* lea
legalizovati *v.t.* legalize

legenda *n.* legend
legendaran *a.* legendary
legija *n.* legion
legionar *n.* legionary
legitiman *a.* legitimate
legitimitet *n.* legitimacy
leglo *n* brood
legura žive *n* amalgam
legura *n.* alloy
lekcija *n.* lesson
leksikografija *n.* lexicography
leksikon *n.* lexicon
lelujanje *n.* undulation
lemljenje *n.* solder
leopard *n.* leopard
lep *a* beautiful
lepak za ptice *n* birdlime
lepota *n* beauty
lepotica *n* belle
lepra *n.* leprosy
lepršanje *n* flutter
lepršati *v.t* flutter
leptir *n* butterfly
leš *n* corpse
lešinar *n.* vulture
let *n* flight
letak *n.* leaflet
letargičan *a.* lethargic
letargija *n.* lethargy
letimičan pogled *n.* glimpse
letjelica *n.* aircraft
letjeti *v.i* fly
letopis *n.* chronicle
letva *n.* lath
ležaj *n* bearing
ležati *v.i* lie
ležeran *a.* casual
ležerno *a.* leisurely
liberalan *a.* liberal
liberalizam *n.* liberalism

lice *n* face
lice *n.* visage
licemerje *n.* hypocrisy
licemjer *n.* hypocrite
licemjeran *a.* hypocritical
licitacija *n* auction
licitirati *v.t.* auction
ličiti *v.t.* resemble
ličnost *n.* personality
liga *n.* league
lignit *n.* lignite
liječiti *v. t.* cure
liječiti *v.i.* heal
liječiti *v.t.* physic
liječiti *v.t.* treat
liječnik *n* doctor
liječnik *n.* physician
liječnik koji cijepi *n.* vaccinator
lijek *n* cure
lijek *n* drug
lijek *n.* medicament
lijek *v.t* remedy
lijen *a.* indolent
lijen *n.* lazy
lijen *n.* slothful
lijen *a.* sluggish
lijenost *n.* laziness
lijenost *n.* sloth
lijep *a* fair
lijep *a.* nice
lijep *a* pretty
lijevo *a.* left
likovati *v. i* exult
likvidacija *n.* liquidation
likvidirati *v.t.* liquidate
limenka *n.* can
limeta *n.* lime
limun *n.* lemon
limunada *n.* lemonade
limunski *adj.* citric

linč *v.t.* lynch
lingvista *n.* linguist
lingvistika *n.* linguistics
linija *n.* line
lira *n.* lyre
liričar *n.* lyricist
lirika *n.* lyric
lirski *a.* lyric
lirski *a.* lyrical
lisica *n.* fox
lisica *n.* vixen
lisice *n.* handcuff
lisnat *a.* leafy
list *n.* leaf
list *n.* sheet
listopad *n.* October
lišaj (oboljenje kože) *n.* ringworm
lišće *n* foliage
lišen *a* devoid
lišiti *v. t* deprive
litar *n.* litre
literatura *n.* litterateur
litica *n.* cliff
liturgijski *a.* liturgical
livada *n.* meadow
livnica *n.* foundry
livreja *n.* livery
lizalica *n.* lollipop
lizanje *n* lick
lizati *v.t.* lick
locirati *v.t.* locate
logaritam *n.* logarithim
logičan *a.* logical
logičar *n.* logician
logika *n.* logic
loj *n.* tallow
lojalan *a.* loyal
lojalnost *n.* loyalty
lokacija *n.* location
lokalizirati *v.t.* localize

lokalni akt *n* bylaw, bye-law
lokalno *a.* local
lokomotiva *n.* locomotive
lom *n* breakage
lomača *n.* pyre
lonac *n.* pot
lopata *n.* shovel
lopata *n.* spade
lopov *n.* thief
lopovski *a.* roguish
lopta *n.* ball
loptica za badminton *n.* shuttlecock
losion *n.* lotion
loš *a.* vile
loša procijena *n.* miscalculation
loše *adv.* ill
loše poslovanje *n.* maladministration
loše pristajati *n.* misfit
loše procijeniti *v.t.* miscalculate
loše spojiti *v.t.* mismatch
loše upravljanje *n.* mismanagement
loše varenje *n.* indigestion
loše vladanje *n.* misconduct
loše *adv.* amiss
loše *a.* bad
lotos *n.* lotus
lov *n* hunt
lovac *n.* hunter
lovac *n.* huntsman
lovački pas *n.* hound
lovački rog *n* bugle
loviti *v.t.* hunt
lovor *n.* laurel
loza *n.* lineage
lozinka *v. t.* countersign
lozinka *n.* watchword
ložač *n.* stoker
ložiti *v.t.* stoke
lubanja *n.* skull
lubenica *n.* water-melon

lucidnost *n.* lucidity
lučenje *n.* secretion
lučiti *v.t.* secrete
lud *a* crazy
lud *adj.* daft
lud *a.* insane
lud *a.* lunatic
ludak *n.* lunatic
ludilo *n.* insanity
ludilo *n.* lunacy
ludiranje *n.* romp
luk *n.* onion
luk *n.* arc
luk *n* bow
luka *n.* harbour
luka *n.* haven
luka *n.* port
lukav *a* crafty
lukav *a* cunning
lukav *a.* politic
lukav *a.* shrewd
lukav *a.* sly
lukav *a.* tricky
lukav *a.* wily
lukavost *n* cunning
lukavstvo *n.* guile
lukavstvo *n.* strategem
lukavstvo *n.* wile
luksuz *n.* luxury
luksuzan *a.* luxurious
lunjati *v.i.* rove
lupanje *n.* throb
lupati *v.i.* throb
lupiti *v.t.* bang
lupiti *v.t.* thump
lutalica *n.* rover
lutalica *n.* straggler
lutalice *n* stray
lutanje *n.* vagary
lutati *v.t* maroon

lutati *v.i.* roam
lutati *v.i.* straggle
lutati *v.i.* wander
lutka *n* doll
lutrija *n.* lottery

LJ

ljekovit *a* curative
ljenjivac *n.* sluggard
ljepilo *n.* glue
ljepiti *v.t.* paste
ljepljiv *n.* sticky
ljepljiva materija *n.* adhesive
ljepljiva materija *a.* adhesive
ljepota *n.* prettiness
ljestve *n.* ladder
ljetni *adj* aestival
ljeto *n.* summer
ljetopisac *n.* annalist
ljetopisi *n.pl.* annals
ljevica *n.* left
ljevičar *n* leftist
ljiljan *n.* lily
ljubav *n* love
ljubavna afera *n* amour
ljubavni *adj* amatory
ljubavnik *n.* lover
ljubavnik *n.* paramour
ljubazan *a.* affable
ljubazan *a.* amiable
ljubazno *adv.* kindly
ljubaznost *n.* amiability
ljubičast, ljubičasta *adj./n.* purple
ljubičica *n.* violet
ljubimac *n.* minion
ljubimac *n.* pet
ljubomora *n.* jealousy
ljubomoran *a.* jealous

ljudožderi *n.* androphagi
ljuljaška *n* swing
ljuljati *v.t.* rock
ljuljati *v.i.* swing
ljuljati *v.t.* dandle
ljuska *n.* husk
ljuštiti *v.t.* shell
ljut *a.* spicy
ljut *a.* angry
ljutina *n* acrimony
ljutnja *n.* ire

M

ma kako *adv.* however
ma ko *pron.* whoever
ma koji *adv.* any
mač *n.* sword
mačak *n.* tomcat
mačić *n.* kitten
mačka *n.* cat
madrac *n.* mattress
mađioničar *n.* magician
magacin *v.t* warehouse
magarac *n* donkey
magarac *n.* ass
magijski *a.* magical
magistrat *n.* magistracy
magla *n* fog
maglina *n.* nebula
maglovit *a.* hazy
maglovit *a.* misty
magnat *n.* magnate
magnet *n.* loadstone
magnet *n.* magnet
magnetizam *n.* magnetism
magnetski *a.* magnetic
mahagoni *n.* mahogany
mahanje *n* wag

mahati *v.i.* wag
mahati *v.i.* waver
mahati *v.t.* whisk
mahovina *n.* moss
mahuna *n.* pod
majčinski *a.* motherlike
majka *n* mother
majmun *n.* monkey
majmun *n* ape
majmunski *a.* apish
major *n* major
majstorija *n.* sleight
majstorija *n* stunt
majstorski *a.* masterly
majstorstvo *n.* mastery
maksima *n.* maxim
maksimalni *a.* maximum
maksimalno povećati *v.t.* maximize
maksimum *n* maximum
malarična groznica *n.* ague
malarija *n.* malaria
male boginje *n* measles
malen *a.* little
malenkost *n.* modicum
mali *n* small
mali *a.* small
mali *dio n.* pittance
malignitet *n.* malignity
malo *a* few
malo *adv.* little
malobrojnost *n.* paucity
malokrvnost *n* anaemia
maloljetnik *a.* juvenile
maloljetnik *n* minor
maloprodaja *n.* retail
maloprodajni *a* retail
maloprodajno *adv.* retail
maltertirati *v.t.* manhandle
maltretirati *v.t.* mistreat
malvazija *n.* malmsey

malj *n.* maul
mama *n* mum
mamac *n.* lure
mamac *n* bait
mamica *n* mummy
mamon *n.* mammon
mamut *n.* mammoth
mamuza *n.* spur
mana *n* blemish
mana *n* flaw
mana *n.* manna
mana *n.* shortcoming
manastir *n.* monastery
mandat *n.* mandate
mandat *n.* tenure
maneken *n.* mannequin
manevar *n.* manoeuvre
manevrirati *v.i.* manoeuvre
mangan *n.* manganese
mango *n* mango
mangup *n.* reveller
manifest *n.* manifesto
manifestacija *n.* manifestation
manifestirati *v.t.* manifest
manija *n* mania
manijak *n.* maniac
manikur *n.* manicure
manipulacija *n.* manipulation
manipulirati *v.t.* manipulate
manirizam *n.* mannerism
manjak *n.* shortage
manje *adv.* less
manje *prep.* less
manje *prep.* minus
manjeta *n* cuff
manji *a.* less
manji *a.* lesser
manji *a.* minor
manjina *n.* minority
mapa *n* map

marama *n.* kerchief
maramica *n.* handkerchief
maraton *n.* marathon
margarin *n.* margarine
margina *n.* margin
marginalni *a.* marginal
marioneta *n.* marionette
marioneta *n.* puppet
mariti *v.i.* matter
mariti *v.t.* mind
marka *n* brand
marker *n.* marker
marljiv *a* diligent
marljiv *a.* studious
marljivost *n* diligence
marmelada *n.* marmalade
mars *n* Mars
marš *n.* march
maršal *n* marshal
marširati *v.i* march
masa *n.* mass
masakr *n.* massacre
masakrirati *v.t.* massacre
masaža *n.* massage
maser *n.* masseur
masirati *v.t.* massage
masivan *a.* massive
masivan *a* molar
maska *n.* mask
maskarada *n.* masquerade
maskirati *v.t.* mask
maskirati se *v. t* bemask
maskota *n.* mascot
maslac *n* butter
maslačak *n.* dandelion
maslina *n.* olive
masnica *n.* weal
mast *n* fat
mast *n* grease
mast *n.* ointment

mastan *a.* greasy
mastan *a.* oily
mastilo *n.* ink
masturbirati *v.i.* masturbate
mašta *n* fancy
mašta *n.* imagination
maštovit *a.* imaginative
mat *n* checkmate
matador *n.* matador
matematičar *n.* mathematician
matematički *a.* mathematical
matematika *n* mathematics
materica *n.* uterus
materijal *n* material
materijal *n.* stuff
materijalan *a.* material
materijalizam *n.* materialism
materijalizovati *v.t.* materialize
materinski *a.* maternal
materinski *a.* motherly
materinstvo *n.* maternity
materinstvo *n.* motherhood
maternica *n.* womb
maternji *a.* native
materoubojstveni *a.* matricidal
materoubojstvo *n.* matricide
matičar *n.* registrar
matine *n.* matinee
matirati *v.t.* mate
matrica *n* matrix
matrica *n.* stencil
matrijarh *n.* matriarch
matrona *n.* matron
matura *n.* matriculation
mauzolej *n.* mausoleum
mazarija *n.* daub
mazati *v.t.* anoint
mazga *n.* mule
maziti *v. t* cocker
mazivo *n.* lubricant

meander v.i. meander
meč n. match
mećava n blizzard
med n. honey
medalja n. medal
medaljon n. locket
medeni mjesec n. honeymoon
medicina n. medicine
medicina n. physic
medicinska sestra n. nurse
medicinski a. medical
medicinski a. medicinal
medij n medium
meditirati v.t. meditate
medovina n. mead
medvjed n bear
međa n boundary
među prep. amid
među prep. among
međuvrijeme n. interim
međuzavisan a. interdependent
međuzavisnost n. interdependence
megafon n. megaphone
megalitski a. megalithic
mehaničar n. mechanic
mehanički a mechanic
mehanika n. mechanics
mehanizam n. mechanism
mehurić n bubble
mekan a. pulpy
melanholičan a. melancholic
melanholija n. melancholia
melasa n molasses
melem n. balm
melez a mongrel
melodičan a. melodious
melodija n. melody
melodija n. tune
melodrama n. melodrama
melodramatičan a. melodramatic

membrana n. membrane
memoari n. memoir
memorandum n memorandum
memorija n. memory
menadžer n. manager
menadžerski a. managerial
mene pron. me
meningitis n. meningitis
menopauza n. menopause
menstruacija n. menstruation
menstrualni a. menstrual
mentalitet n. mentality
mentalni a. mental
mentor n. mentor
menzis n. menses
mercerizirati v.t. mercerise
meridijan a. meridian
merkur n. mercury
mermer n. marble
mesar n butcher
mesečar n. somnambulist
mesija n. messiah
mesing n. brass
meso n flesh
meso n. meat
mešati se v.i. meddle
meta n bull's eye
metabolizam n. metabolism
metafizički a. metaphysical
metafizika n. metaphysics
metafora n. metaphor
metak n bullet
metal n. metal
metalni a. metallic
metalurgija n. metallurgy
metamorfoza n. metamorphosis
metar n. meter
metar n. metre
metarski a. metrical
meteor n. meteor

meteorolog *n.* meteorologist
meteorologija *n.* meteorology
meteorski *a.* meteoric
metež *n* babel
metež *n* commotion
metež *n.* tumult
metež *n.* uproar
metla *n.* mop
metla *n* broom
metod *n.* method
metodičan *a.* methodical
metrički *a.* metric
metropola *n.* metropolis
metropolit *n.* metropolitan
metropolitski *a.* metropolitan
metvica *n.* mint
mezalijansa *n.* misalliance
mezanin *n.* mezzanine
mig *n.* beck
mig *n* wink
migracija *n.* migration
migrant *n.* migrant
migrena *n.* migraine
migrirati *v.i.* migrate
mijalgija *n.* myalgia
mijenjati *v.t.* shift
miješanje *n* amalgamation
miješati *v.t.* mingle
miješati *v.i* mix
miješati *v.t.* temper
miješati sa živom *v.t.* amalgamate
mijoza *n.* myosis
mikrofilm *n.* microfilm
mikrofon *n.* microphone
mikrologija *n.* micrology
mikrometar *n.* micrometer
mikroskop *n.* microscope
mikroskopski *a.* microscopic
mikrovalna peć *n.* microwave
milicija *n.* militia

milijarda *n* billion
milijun *n.* million
milijuner *n.* millionaire
militant *n* militant
milosrđe *n.* charity
milost *n.* grace
milost *n.* mercy
milostinja *n.* alms
milostiv *a.* gracious
milostiv *a.* merciful
milovanje *n* stroke
milovati *v.t* fondle
milovati *v.t.* pet
milovati *v.t.* stroke
milovati *v. t.* caress
milja *n.* mile
miljaža *n.* mileage
mimičar *n* mimic
mimika *n.* mime
mimikrija *n.* mimesis
mimikrija *n* mimicry
minaret *n.* minaret
mineral *n.* mineral
mineralni *a* mineral
mineralog *n.* mineralogist
mineralogija *n.* mineralogy
minijatura *a.* miniature
minijaturan *n.* miniature
minimalan *a.* minimal
minimalan *a* minimum
minimum *n.* minimum
ministar *n.* minister
ministarstvo *n.* ministry
ministrant *a.* ministrant
minus *n* minus
minut *a.* minute
miomirisan *a.* odorous
mir *n.* calm
mir *n.* peace
mir *n.* quiet

mir *n.* still
mir *n.* tranquility
miran *a.* mum
miran *a.* peaceful
miran *a.* placid
miran *a.* quiet
miran *a.* still
miran *a.* tranquil
miraz *n* dowry
miris *n.* fragrance
miris *n.* odour
miris *n.* savour
miris *n.* scent
miris *n.* smell
mirisan *a.* fragrant
mirisati *v.t.* savour
mirisati *v.t.* scent
mirisati *v.t.* smell
mirisna smola *n.* myrrh
miroljubiv *a.* pacific
miroljubiv *a.* peaceable
mirovina *n.* pension
mirovina *n.* retirement
mirta *n.* myrtle
misao *n* thought
misija *n.* mission
misionar *n.* missionary
mislilac *n.* thinker
misliti *v.t.* opine
misliti *v.i.* reason
misliti *v.t.* think
misterija *n.* mystery
misteriozan *a.* mysterious
misticizam *n.* mysticism
mističan *a.* mystic
mistifikovati *v.t.* mystify
mistik *n* mystic
mistrija *n.* trowel
miš *n.* mouse
mišić *n.* muscle

mišićav *a.* muscular
mišljenje *n.* opinion
mit *n.* myth
mitariti se *v.i.* moult
mito *n* bribe
mitologija *n.* mythology
mitološki *a.* mythological
mitra *n.* mitre
mitski *a.* mythical
mizantrop *n.* misanthrope
mjaukati *v.i.* mew
mjeh *n.* bellows
mjehur *n* bladder
mjera *n.* measure
mjera *n.* measurement
mjeriti *v.t* measure
mjerljiv *a.* measurable
mjerodavan *a.* magisterial
mjesec *n.* month
mjesec *n.* moon
mjesečarenje *n.* somnambulism
mjesečev *a.* lunar
mjesečni *a.* monthly
mjesečnik *n* monthly
mjesečno *adv* monthly
mjesto *n.* locus
mjesto *n.* place
mjesto *n.* position
mjesto *n.* spot
mješavina *n* blend
mješavina *n* compound
mješavina *n.* mixture
mješovit *a.* miscellaneous
mješovit žargon *n.* lingua franca
mlaćenica *n* buttermilk
mlad *a.* adolescent
mlad *a.* young
mladalački *a.* youthful
mladenka *n* bride
mladi *n* young

mladi *n.* youth
mladić *n.* youngster
mladica *n.* offshoot
mladica *n.* sapling
mladica *n* sprout
mladost *n.* adolescence
mladoženja *n.* groom
mladoženja *n.* bridegroom
mladunče *n* cub
mlađi *a.* junior
mlak *a.* lukewarm
mlatiti *v.t.* thrash
mlaz *n* spurt
mlaznica *n.* nozzle
mlaznjak *n.* jet
mlekomer *n.* lactometer
mliječan *a.* milky
mliječni *a.* mammary
mliječni *a.* milch
mlijeko *n.* milk
mlin *n.* grinder
mlin *n.* mill
mlinar *n.* miller
mlitav *a* flabby
mljekara *n* dairy
mljeti *v.i.* grind
mljeti *v.t.* mill
mnogo *a.* many
mnogo *a* much
mnogo *n.* plenty
mnogonog *n.* multiped
mnogostruk *a.* manifold
mnogostruk *a.* multiple
mnogostrukost *n.* multiplicity
mnoštvo *n.* lot
mnoštvo *n.* multitude
mnoštvo *n* shoal
množenik *n.* multiplicand
množenje *n.* multiplication
množina *a.* plural

mobilizirati *v.t.* mobilize
moć *n.* leverage
moćan *adj.* mighty
moćan *a.* powerful
močiti *v.t.* steep
močvara *n.* marsh
močvara *n.* slough
močvara *n.* swamp
močvara *n* bog
močvaran *a.* marshy
moć *n.* might
moći *v* may
moći *v.* can
moda *n* fashion
moda *n.* vogue
modalitet *n.* modality
model *n.* model
moderan *a* fashionable
moderan *a.* modern
modernizirati *v.t.* modernize
modernost *n.* modernity
modificirati *v.t.* modify
modifikacija *n.* modification
modiskinja *n.* milliner
modist *n.* milliner
modrica *n* bruise
modulirati *v.t.* modulate
moguć *a.* possible
mogućnost *n.* possibility
moguć *a* able
moguć *a.* potential
mogućnost *n.* potential
moj *pron.* mine
moj *a.* my
mokar *a.* wet
mokrenje *n.* urination
molba *n.* plea
molekul *n.* molecule
molekularni *a.* molecular
molilac *n.* petitioner

moliti *v. t.* beg
moliti *v.t.* petition
moliti *v.i.* pray
molitva *n.* prayer
moljac *n.* moth
momak *n* carl
momak *n.* lad
monah *n.* monk
monarh *n.* monarch
monarhija *n.* monarchy
monaštvo *n* monasticism
monetarni *a.* monetary
monitor *n.* monitor
monodija *n.* monody
monogamija *n.* monogamy
monografija *n.* monograph
monogram *n.* monogram
monokl *n.* monocle
monokromatski *a.* monochromatic
monolit *n.* monolith
monolog *n.* monologue
monolog *n.* soliloquy
monopol *n.* monopoly
monopolist *n.* monopolist
monopolizirati *v.t.* monopolize
monoteist *n.* monotheist
monoteizam *n.* monotheism
monoton *a.* monotonous
monotonija *n* monotony
monstrum *n.* monstrous
monstruozan *a.* monstrous
monsun *n.* monsoon
monter *n* fitter
monumentalan *a.* monumental
moral *n.* morale
moralan *a.* moral
moralisati *v.t.* moralize
moralist *n.* moralist
moralnost *n.* morality
morati *v.* must

morbidan *a.* morbid
morbidnost *n* morbidity
more *n.* sea
morfij *n.* morphia
morgantski *a.* morganatic
mornar *n.* mariner
mornar *n.* sailor
mornarica *n.* navy
morski *a.* marine
mortalitet *n.* mortality
morž *n.* walrus
moskovljanin *n.* muscovite
most *n* bridge
mošt *n* must
mošus *n.* musk
motač *n.* winder
motel *n.* motel
motiv *n.* motif
motiv *n.* motive
motivacija *n.* motivation
motivirati *v* motivate
motka *n* bat
moto *n.* motto
motor *n* engine
motor *n.* motor
motovilo *v.t.* windlass
mozaik *n.* mosaic
mozak *n* brain
možda *adv.* perhaps
moždani *adj* cerebral
mrak *n* dark
mrav *n* ant
mraz *n.* frost
mrdnuti *v. i. & n* budge
mreža *n.* mesh
mreža *n.* web
mreža *n.* net
mreža *n.* network
mreže *n. pl.* toils
mrežnica *n.* retina

mrijest *n.* spawn
mrijestiti *se v.i.* spawn
mrk pogled *n.* scowl
mrko gledati *v.i.* scowl
mrkva *n.* carrot
mrlja *n.* smear
mrlja *n.* stain
mrlja *n.* taint
mrlja *n.* blot
mrlja *n* blur
mrljati *v.t.* stain
mrmljati *v.i.* mumble
mrmljati *v.t.* murmur
mrskost *n.* odium
mršav *a.* lank
mršavo *n.* lean
mrštenje *n.* frown
mrštiti *se v.i* frown
mrtav *a* dead
mrtvačka nosila *n* bier
mrtvački sanduk *n* coffin
mrtvačnica *n.* morgue
mrtvačnica *n.* mortuary
mrvica *n* crumb
mrzak *a.* odious
mrziti *v.t.* hate
mrzovoljan *a.* morose
mrzovoljan *a.* petulant
mržnja *n.* hate
mucanje *n* stammer
mucati *v.i.* stammer
mučan *a.* laborious
mučan *a.* troublesome
mučenik *n.* martyr
mučeništvo *n.* martyrdom
mučenje *n.* torture
mučiti *v.t.* rack
mučiti *v.t.* tantalize
mučiti *v.t.* torment
mučiti *v.t.* torture

mučiti *se v.i.* moil
mučiti *v.t.* agonize
mučnina *n.* nausea
mućkalica *v. t. & i.* churn
mućkati *n.* churn
mudar *a.* sagacious
mudar *a.* wise
mudrac *n.* sage
mudrost *n.* sagacity
mudrost *n.* wisdom
mudrost *n.* wisdom-tooth
muha *n* fly
muka *n.* torment
mukanje *v.i* moo
mukati *v.i.* low
mula *n.* mullah
mulat *n.* mulatto
multilateralan *a.* multilateral
multiparan *a.* multiparous
mulj *n.* silt
mulj *n.* slime
muljav *a.* slimy
mumija *n.* mummy
mungos *n.* mongoose
municija *n.* munitions
municija *n.* ammunition
munja *n.* lightening
mural *n.* mural
musketar *n.* musketeer
muslin *n.* muslin
mustang *n.* mustang
musti *v.t.* milk
mušketa *n.* musket
muški *a.* male
muški *a.* manly
muški *a.* masculine
muški *a.* virile
muški *rod n* male
muškost *n.* manhood
muškost *n* manliness

mutacija *n.* mutation
mutan *a.* lacklustre
mutativan *a.* mutative
muza *n* muse
muzej *n.* museum
muž *n* husband
muževan *a.* manlike
muževnost *n.* virility

N

na *prep.* on
na *prep* upon
na drugoj strani *adv.* overleaf
na kopnu *adv.* ashore
na kraju *adv.* lastly
na kraju *adv.* ultimately
na prvi pogled *adv. prima* facie
na umoru *a.* moribund
na vrijeme *a.* timely
na, po *prep.* per
nabaviti *v.t.* procure
nabavka *n.* procurement
nabob *n.* nabob
nabor *n* fold
nabor *n.* frill
nabor *n* ply
naborati *v.t.* crimple
nabrajati *v. t.* enumerate
nabrati *v.t.* ruffle
nabreknuti *v.i.* swell
nacija *n.* nation
nacionalista *n.* nationalist
nacionalizacija *n.* nationalization
nacionalizam *n.* nationalism
nacionalizirati *v.t.* nationalize
nacionalni *a.* national
nacrt *n* draught
načelo *n.* tenet

način *n.* manner
način *n.* mode
način *n.* way
način fotokopiranja *n.* xerox
način govora *n.* parlance
načiniti četvorokutim *v.t.* square
načiniti paralelnim *v.t.* parallel
načitan *a.* well-read
način *v.t.* overhear
naći prosječnu vrijednost *v.t.* average
nada *n* hope
nadalje *adv.* onwards
nadaren *a.* gifted
nadati *se v.t.* hope
nadčovjek *n.* superman
nadglasati *v.t.* overrule
nadgledanje *n.* invigilation
nadgledati *v.t.* oversee
nadgledati *v.t.* supervise
nadimak *n.* nickname
nadir *n.* nadir
nadiranje *n.* onrush
nadjačati *v.t.* overpower
nadležan *a* amenable
nadležnost *n.* jurisdiction
nadljudski *a.* superhuman
nadmašiti *v.i* excel
nadmašiti *v.t.* outdo
nadmašiti *v.t.* surpass
nadmašiti u brojnosti *v.t.* outnumber
nadmašiti u trčanju *v.t.* outrun
nadmetati se *v.t.* rival
nadmetati se *v.i.* vie
nadmoćan *a.* pre-eminent
nadmoćnost *n.* pre-eminence
nadmoćan *a.* predominant
nadmoćan *a.* superior
nadmudriti *v.t* gull
nadmudriti *v.t.* outwit
nadmudriti *v.t.* trump

nadničar *n.* jobber
nadničar *n.* peon
nadoknaditi *v.t* compensate
nadoknaditi *v.t.* recompense
nadoknaditi *v.t.* recoup
nadoknaditi *v.t.* reimburse
nadrilek *n.* nostrum
nadrliječnišvo *n.* quackery
nadsijati *v.t.* outshine
nadsvoditi *v.i.* vault
nadvoje *adv.* asunder
nadvratink *n.* lintel
nadživjeti *v.i.* outlive
nadzirati *v.t.* invigilate
nadzor *n.* oversight
nadzor *n.* supervision
nadzor *n.* surveillance
nadzornik *n* foreman
nadzornik *n.* invigilator
nadzornik *n.* overseer
nadzornik *n.* superintendent
nadzornik *n.* supervisor
naelektrisati *v. t* electrify
nafta *n.* petroleum
nag *a.* bare
nag *a.* naked
nagao *a.* impetuous
nagib *n* slant
nagib *n.* slope
nagib *n.* tilt
naginjati ukoso *v. t* bias
naglas *adv.* aloud
naglasak *n* accent
naglasak *n* emphasis
naglasiti *v.t* accent
naglasiti *v. t* emphasize
naglasiti *v.t.* punctuate
naglašavati *v.t* stress
naglo *a* abrupt
nagnati *v.t* urge

nagnut *a* downward
nagnuti *v.t.* slant
nagnuti *v.i.* slope
nagnuti se *v.i.* incline
nagnuti se *v.i.* tilt
nagodba *n* compromise
nagoditi se *v. t* compromise
nagomilati *v.t.* aggregate
nagomilati *v.t.* amass
nagomilati *v.t.* bank
nagomilati *v. i.* cluster
nagomilati *v.t.* lump
nagomilati se *v.i.* accrue
nagon *n.* appetite
nagon *n* urge
nagore *adv.* upwards
nagost *n* nude
nagovaranje *n.* abetment
nagoveštaj *n.* inkling
nagovijestiti *v.t.* intimate
nagovijestiti *v.t.* portend
nagoviještaj *n.* intimation
nagovjestiti *v.i* hint
nagovještaj *n* allusion
nagovještaj *n.* hint
nagrada *n.* prize
nagrada *n.* reward
nagrada *n.* award
nagraditi *v.t.* award
nagraditi *v.t.* remunerate
nagraditi *v.t.* reward
naime *adv.* namely
naivan *a.* naive
naivnost *n.* naivete
naivnost *n.* naivety
naizmjenično *a.* alternate
najam *n.* hire
najamnik *n.* hireling
najaviti *v.t* herald
najfiniji *a.* superfine

najgori *a* worst
najgušći dio *n.* thick
najlon *n.* nylon
najmanje *adv.* least
najmanji *a.* least
najniža plima *a.* neap
najskriveniji *a.* inmost
najviše *adv.* most
najzad *adv.* last
nakit *n.* jewellery
naklon *n* bow
naklon *n.* obeisance
naklonost *n* favour1
naklonost *n.* like
naklonjen *a* fond
naklonjenost *n.* affection
naknada *n.* recompense
naknadni izbori *n* by-election
nakon *prep.* past
nakon *adv.* post
nakon čega *conj.* whereupon
nakon *prep.* after
nakon *adv* after
nakovanj *n.* anvil
nalet *n.* gust
nalet *n* rush
nalik *a.* alike
nalog *n.* warrant
naljepnica *n.* sticker
namamiti *v.t.* bait
namamiti *v. t.* entice
namamiti *v.t.* lure
namazati *v.t* lime
namazati maslacem *v. t* butter
nametanje *n.* imposition
nametanje *n.* levy
nametati *v.t.* impose
nametnuti *v.t.* levy
namigivati *v.i.* wink
namiguša *n.* minx

namirisati *v.t.* perfume
namjera *n.* intention
namjeran *a* deliberate
namjeran *a.* intentional
namjeravati *v.t.* intend
namjeravati *v.t.* purpose
namjerni *a.* intent
namjerno *adv.* purposely
namjesnički *a.* vicarious
namještaj *n.* furniture
namotati *v.t.* convolve
namotati *v.i.* reel
namotati *v.t.* wind
namrštiti *v.t.* purse
nanijeti *v.t.* inflict
nanijeti štetu *v.t.* wrong
naočit *a.* sightly
naoružanje *n.* armament
naoružati *v.t.* arm
napad *n* fit
napad *n* offensive
napad *n.* seizure
napad *n.* assault
napad *n.* attack
napadački *a.* offensive
napasti *v.t.* invade
napasti iz zasjede *v.t.* waylay
napasti *v.t.* assault
napasti *v.t.* attack
napet *n.* intent
napet *a.* tense
napisati *v.t.* write
napitak *n* beverage
napojnica *n.* gratuity
napolje *adv* outwards
napolju *adv.* outwardly
napomena *n.* note
napomena *n.* remark
napomenuti *v.t.* remark
napon *n.* voltage

napor *n* effort
naporan *a.* laboured
naporan *a.* strenuous
naprasit *a.* waspish
naprašiti *v.t.* powder
napraviti *v.t.* make
napraviti od kruha *v. t. & i* breaden
napraviti salto *v.i.* somersault
napredak *n.* progress
napredovanje *n.* advancement
napredovati *v.i.* progress
napredovati *v.i.* prosper
napredovati *v.i.* thrive
napregnut *a.* intense
naprezanje *n* strain
naprezati *v.t.* strain
naprijed *adv.* forth
naprijed *adv* forward
naprijed *a.* onward
naprstak *n.* thimble
napuniti *v.t.* replenish
napuniti, ispuniti *v.t.* stuff
napunjen *a.* replete
napustiti *v.t.* abandon
napustiti *v. t.* desert
napustiti *v.t.* forsake
napustiti *v.t.* vacate
napustiti logor *v. i* decamp
naracija *n.* narration
naramak pruća *n* faggot
naranča *n.* orange
narandžast *a* orange
narcis *n* narcissus
narcisizam *n.* narcissism
naredba *n* command
narediti *v. t* command
narediti *v. i* decree
narediti *v.t.* instruct
narednik *n.* sergeant
naricanje *n.* lamentation

narkotik *n.* narcotic
narkoza *n.* narcosis
narod *n.* people
narodni *a.* vernacular
naručiti *v.t* order
narukvica *a.* armlet
narukvica *n.* bangle
narukvica *n* bracelet
narušiti *v.t.* infringe
naruśivanje *n.* infringement
nasapunjati *v.t.* soap
nasekirati *v.t.* vex
naseliti *v.t.* people
naseliti *v.t.* populate
naseliti *v.i.* settle
naselje *n.* settlement
naselje od baraka *n.* cantonment
naseljen *a.* populous
naseljenik *n.* settler
nasilan *a.* violent
nasilno odvajanje *n.* avulsion
nasilje *n.* outrage
nasilje *n.* violence
nasip *n* causeway
nasip *n* embankment
naslaga *n.* stratum
naslanjati se *v* abutted
naslijeđenost *n.* hereditary
naslijediti *v.t.* inherit
naslijeđen *a.* ancestral
naslikati *v.t.* picture
nasloniti *v.i.* lean
naslov *n.* heading
naslov *n.* title
naslov *n.* caption
nasljedan *a.* heritable
nasljednik *n.* heir
nasljednik *n.* successor
nasljednost *n.* heredity
nasljedstvo *n.* succession

nasljeđe *n.* heritage
nasljeđe *n.* inheritance
nasljeđe *n.* legacy
nasrnuti *v.* assail
nasrnuti *v.t.* mob
nastaniti *v.t.* inhabit
nastavak *n.* sequel
nastaviti *v. i.* continue
nastaviti *v.i.* proceed
nastavljanje *n.* continuation
nastavljanje *n.* resumption
nastavni plan *n* curriculum
nastojanje *n* endeavour
nastojati *v.i* endeavour
nastran *a.* queer
nastranost *n.* oddity
nastup *n* bout
nasukati *v.i.* strand
nasuprot *prep.* against
naš *pron.* our
nateći *v. i.* bag
nategnuti *v.t.* string
natjecanje *n.* competition
natjecanje *n.* contest
natjecatelj *n* agonist
natjecati se *v. i* compete
natjecati se *v. t* contest
natjecati se *v. t* emulate
natovariti *v. t* burden
natovariti *v.t.* lade
natovariti *v.t.* load
natovariti *v.t.* stow
natovariti *v.t.* incur
natpis *n.* inscription
natprirodan *a.* supernatural
natrpati *v. t* cram
naučiti *v.i.* learn
nauka *n.* science
nautički *a.* nautic(al)
navala *n* dash

navesti *v. t* coax
navesti *v.t.* induce
navesti *v.t.* specify
navesti *v.t.* adduce
navigacija *n.* navigation
navigator *n.* navigator
navijati *v.t.* wind
navika *n.* habit
navika *n* wont
naviknut *a.* accustomed
naviknut *a.* wont
naviknuti *v. t.* habituate
navlažiti *v.t.* leach
navod *n.* allegation
navoditi *v.t* state
navodnjavanje *n.* irrigation
navodnjavati *v.t.* irrigate
navođenje *n.* inducement
nazad *n.* back
nazal *n* nasal
nazalni *a.* nasal
nazdraviti *v.t.* toast
nazirati se *v.i.* loom
nazvati *v.t.* term
ne *n* no
ne *adv.* not
ne slagati se *v. i* disagree
ne sviđati se *v. t* displease
ne uspjeti *v.i* fail
ne voleti *v. t* dislike
ne zadovoljiti *v. t.* dissatisfy
neaktivan *a.* inactive
neaktivnost *n.* inaction
nebeski *a.* heavenly
nebeski *adj* celestial
nebesko tijelo *n.* orb
nebitan *a.* irrelevant
nebo *n.* heaven
nebo *n.* sky
nećak *n.* nephew

nečist *a.* impure
nečistoća *n* dirt
nečistoća *n* filth
nečistoća *n.* impurity
nečitak *a.* illegible
nečitkost *n.* illegibility
nečovek *n* brute
nečujan *a.* inaudible
nećaka *n.* niece
nedavni *a.* recent
nedavno *adv.* late
nedavno *adv.* recently
nedisciplina *n.* indiscipline
nedjelo *n.* misdeed
nedjelotvoran *a.* inoperative
nedjelja *n.* Sunday
nedjelja *n.* week
nedjeljiv *a.* indivisible
nedolično ponašanje *n.* misbehaviour
nedolično se ponašati *v.i.* misbehave
nedopustiv *a.* inadmissible
nedopušten *a.* prohibitive
nedostajati *v.t.* lack
nedostatak *n* defect
nedostatak *n* demerit
nedostatak *n* disadvantage
nedostatak *n.* lack
nedostižan *a* elusive
nedovoljan *adj.* deficient
nedovoljan *a.* insufficient
nedovoljno razviti *v.t.* depauperate
nedovršen *a.* sketchy
neefikasan *a.* ineffective
nefleksibilan *a.* inflexible
neformalan *a.* informal
negacija *n.* negation
negativ *n.* negative
negativan *a* minus
negativan *a.* negative
negde *adv.* somewhere

negdje *adv.* whereabout
negodovanje *a.* outcry
negostoljubiv *a.* inhospitable
negovati *v. t.* cherish
negovati *v.t.* nurture
nehotice *adv.* unawares
nehuman *a.* inhuman
neiskren *a.* insincere
neiskrenost *n.* insincerity
neiskustvo *n.* inexperience
neispravan *a* faulty
neizbježan *a.* inevitable
neizlječiv *a.* incurable
neizmjeran *a.* measureless
neizračunljiv *a.* incalculable
neizvesnost *n.* abeyance
neizvjesnost *n.* suspense
neizvjestan *a.* uncertain
neizvodljivost *n.* impracticability
neizvršiv *a.* impracticable
nejasan *a* dim
nejasan *a.* indistinct
nejasan *a.* obscure
nejasan *a.* vague
nejasnost *n.* obscurity
nejednak *a* unlike
nejednakost *n* disparity
nekako *adv.* somehow
nekažnjen *a.* scot-free
nekažnjivost *n.* impunity
neki *a.* some
neko *pron.* one
neko *n.* somebody
neko *pron.* somebody
neko *pron.* someone
nekritički *a.* indiscriminate
nektar *n.* nectar
nelagodan *a.* uneasy
nelagodnost *n* discomfort
nelogičan *a.* illogical

nelojalan *a* disloyal
neljubazan *a.* impolite
nem *a.* mute
nema osoba *n.* mute
nemar *n.* negligence
nemaran *a.* negligent
nemaran *a.* reckless
nemaran *a.* slack
nemaran *a.* slipshod
nematerijalni *a.* immaterial
nemilosrdan *adj.* merciless
nemilosrdan *a.* pitiless
nemilosrdan *a.* relentless
nemilosrdan *a.* ruthless
nemir *n.* turmoil
nemir *n* unrest
nemjerljiv *a.* immeasurable
nemoć *n.* infirmity
nemoćan *a.* unable
nemoguć *a.* impossible
nemogućnost *n.* impossibility
nemoralan *a.* immoral
nemoralan *a.* amoral
nemoralnost *n.* immorality
nenadmašan *a.* transcendent
nenamjerno *adv.* unwittingly
nenormalan *a* abnormal
nenormalnost *n.* aberrance
neobavezan *a.* optional
neobjašnjiv *a.* inexplicable
neobrazovan *a.* ignorant
neočekivana sreća *n.* godsend
neodbranjiv *a.* indefensible
neodgovoran *a.* irresponsible
neodlučan *a.* hesitant
neodlučnost *n.* indecision
neodobravanje *n* disapproval
neodobravati *v. t* disapprove
neodoljiv *a.* adorable
neodređen *a.* indefinite

neodređen *a* pending
neodređeni član *art* an
neodređenost *n.* vagueness
neodvojiv *a.* inseparable
neograničen *a.* limitless
neokaljan *a.* spotless
neolitski *a.* neolithic
neon *n.* neon
neophodan *a.* indispensable
neopipljiv *a.* intangible
neopisiv *a.* indescribable
neopisiv *a.* nefandous
neoprezan *a.* careless
neosjetljiv *a.* insensible
neosjetljivost *n.* insensibility
neosnovan *a.* baseless
neosporan *a.* indisputable
neotesanost *n.* rusticity
neovisan *a.* independent
neovisnost *n.* independence
neozbiljan *a.* frivolous
neparan *a.* odd
nepažljiv *a.* inattentive
nepce *n.* palate
nepčano *a.* palatal
nepismen *a.* illiterate
nepismenost *n.* illiteracy
nepobitan *a.* irrefutable
nepobjediv *a.* invincible
nepodmitljiv *a.* incorruptible
nepodnošljiv *a.* intolerable
nepodnošljivost *n.* intolerance
nepogrešiv *a.* infallible
nepokretan *a.* immovable
nepokretan *a.* motionless
nepokretan *a.* stagnant
nepomirljiv *a.* irreconcilable
nepopravljiv *a.* incorrigible
nepopustljiv *a.* adamant
neposlušan *a.* insubordinate

neposlušnost *n.* insubordination
neposredan *a* immediate
neposredan *a.* proximate
nepostojanje *n.* nonentity
nepošten *a* dishonest
nepošten *a.* fraudulent
nepošten *a.* underhand
nepošteno zarađivati *v.i.* profiteer
nepoštenje *n.* dishonesty
nepoštivanje *n* disrespect
nepotizam *n.* nepotism
nepotpun *a .* incomplete
nepotreban *a.* needless
nepouzdan *a.* unreliable
nepovezan *a.* incoherent
nepovjerenje *n* distrust
nepovjerenje *n.* mistrust
nepovoljnost *v.i.* skid
nepovrativ *a.* irrecoverable
nepoznat *a.* anonymous
nepoznat *a.* uncouth
nepravda *n.* injustice
nepravedan *a* unfair
nepravedan *a.* unjust
nepravilan *a* anomalous
nepravilan *a.* irregular
nepravilnost *n* anomaly
nepravilnost *n.* irregularity
neprekidan *a* continuous
neprelazni *a.* intransitive
nepremostiv *a.* insurmountable
neprestan *a.* ceaseless
neprestan *adj.* continual
neprestano ponavljanje *n.* reiteration
neprestano ponavljati *v.t.* reiterate
neprijatan *a.* disagreeable
neprijatelj *n* enemy
neprijatelj *n* foe
neprijateljski *a.* hostile
neprijateljski *a.* inimical

neprijateljstvo *n* enmity
neprijateljstvo *n.* hostility
neprijateljstvo *n* animosity
neprikladan *a.* improper
neprikladan *a.* inconvenient
neprikladan *a.* undue
neprikladnost *n.* impropriety
neprikosnoven *a.* inviolable
neprilagodljivost *n.* maladjustment
neprilika *n* fix
neprilika *n.* nuisance
neprilika *n.* predicament
neprimjenjiv *a.* inapplicable
neprincipijelan *a.* unprincipled
nepristojan *a.* indecent
nepristojan *a.* rude
nepristojnost *n.* indecency
nepristran *a.* impartial
nepristranost *n.* impartiality
neprobavljiv *a.* indigestible
neprobojan *a.* impenetrable
neprocjenjiv *a.* invaluable
neprohodan *a.* impassable
neprolazan *a.* imperishable
nepromišljen *a.* imprudent
nepromišljen *a.* inconsiderate
nepromišljen *a.* mindless
nepromočiv *a.* watertight
neproziran *a.* opaque
neprozirnost *n.* opacity
neptun *n.* Neptune
nerad *a.* reluctant
neraspoložen *a.* indisposed
nerastvoriv *n.* insoluble
neravan *a.* rugged
neravan *adj* bumpy
nerazborit *a.* injudicious
nered *n.* mess
nerotkinja *n* barren
nervozan *a.* nervous

nesavladiv *a.* indomitable
nesavršen *a.* imperfect
nesavršenost *n.* imperfection
nesebičan *a.* selfless
nesiguran *a.* insecure
nesigurnost *n.* insecurity
neskladan *adj* absonant
nesklon *a.* loath
neskroman *a.* immodest
neskromnost *n.* immodesty
nesloga *n* discord
nesmotrenost *n.* imprudence
nesnosan *a.* insupportable
nesporazum *n.* disagreement
nesporazum *n* misapprehension
nesporazum *n.* misunderstanding
nesposoban *a* disabled
nesposoban *a.* incapable
nesposoban *a.* incompetent
nesposobnost *n* disability
nesposobnost *n.* inability
nesposobnost *n.* incapacity
nespretan *a* clumsy
nespretan *a.* maladroit
nesreća *n.* misfortune
nesrećan *a.* unfortunate
nesrećan *a.* unhappy
nesrećan slučaj *n.* mischance
nesrećan slučaj *n.* mishap
nesreća *n* accident
nesreća *n.* adversity
nesreća *n.* calamity
nesrećan *a.* woebegone
nesretan *a.* luckless
nesretan *a.* miserable
nestabilan *adj.* astatic
nestabilnost *n.* instability
nestajati *v. t* dwindle
nestalnost *n.* vicissitude
nestanak *n* disappearance

nestašica *n* dearth
nestaško *n.* tomboy
nestašluk *n* mischief
nestašluk *n.* prank
nestašnost *n.* petulance
nestati *v. i* disappear
nestrpljenje *n.* impatience
nestrpljiv *a.* impatient
nestrpljiv *adj.* agog
nestručan *a.* lay
nesvijest *n.* swoon
nesvjestan *a.* oblivious
nesvjestan *a.* unaware
nesvrstanost *n.* non-alignment
nešto *pron.* some
nešto *adv.* something
nešto *pron.* something
nešto *adv.* somewhat
netaknut *a.* intact
neto *a* net
netočan *a.* inaccurate
netočan *a.* incorrect
netočan *a.* inexact
netolerantan *a.* intolerant
neučtiv *a* discourteous
neugodan *a.* awful
neugodan *a.* uncanny
neuhranjenost *n.* malnutrition
neumjetnički *a.* artless
neumoljiv *a.* inexorable
neumrljan *a.* stainless
neuporediv *a.* incomparable
neuporediv *a.* nonpareil
neurolog *n.* neurologist
neurologija *n.* neurology
neuroza *n.* neurosis
neuspio *adv* abortive
neuspjeh *n* failure
neustrašiv *a* dauntless
neustrašiv *a.* interpid

neustrašivost *n.* intrepidity
neutralan *a.* neutral
neutralisati *v.t.* neutralize
neutron *n.* neutron
nevaljalost *n.* roguery
nevaljao *a.* naughty
nevaspitan *a* unmannerly
nevažeći *a.* invalid
neven *n.* marigold
neveseo *a* cheerless
nevidljiv *a.* invisible
nevin *a.* chaste
nevin *a.* innocent
nevinost *n.* chastity
nevinost *n.* innocence
nevinost *n.* virginity
nevjerojatan *a* fabulous
nevjerojatan *a.* incredible
nevjerojatan *a.* unlikely
nevolja *n* ill
nevolja *n.* need
nevolja *n.* trouble
nezaboravan *a.* memorable
nezadovoljan *a.* malcontent
nezadovoljstvo *n* discontent
nezadovoljstvo *n* displeasure
nezadovoljstvo *n* dissatisfaction
nezadovoljstvo *n* malcontent
nezahvalan *a.* thankless
nezahvalnost *n.* ingratitude
nezakonit *a.* illegal
nezakonit *a.* illegitimate
nezakonit *a.* lawless
nezakonit *a.* wrongful
nezasit *a.* insatiable
nezgoda *n.* misadventure
nezgodan *a.* awkward
nezgrapan *a.* ungainly
neznanje *n.* ignorance
neznanje *n.* nescience

nezrelost *n.* immaturity
nezreo *a.* immature
nezreo *adj* callow
nežan *a.* affectionate
neženja *n* agamist
neženja *n.* bachelor
neživ *a.* inanimate
ni *conj.* neither
ni jedan *a.* no
nicati *v.i.* sprout
nigdje *adv.* nowhere
nihilizam *n.* nihilism
nijansa *n.* nuance
nijansa *n.* tinge
nijansirati *v.t.* tinge
nikada *adv.* never
nikako *adv.* no
nikako *adv.* none
nikl *n.* nickel
niko *pron.* nobody
nikotin *n.* nicotine
nimfa *n.* nymph
nisko *adv.* low
niša *n.* niche
ništa *adv.* nothing
ništa *n.* nothing
ništa *n.* nought
nit *n.* thread
niti *adv.* either
niti *conj* nor
nitko *pron.* none
nitkov *n* cad
nitkov *n.* miscreant
nitkov *n.* rascal
nitkov *n.* scoundrel
niz *prep* down
niz *n.* tier
nizak *a.* low
nizak položaj *n.* low
nizati *v.i.* file

niže *adv* beneath
niže *v.t.* lower
niže *adv* under
niže plemstvo *n.* gentry
niži *a.* nether
niži *a* under
noć *n.* night
noćna mora *n.* nightmare
noćni *a.* nocturnal
noću *adv.* nightly
noćni *a* overnight
noga *n.* leg
noj *n.* ostrich
nomad *n.* nomad
nomadski *a.* nomadic
nomenklatura *n.* nomenclature
nominalan *a.* nominal
nominirati *v.t.* nominate
nonparel *n.* nonpareil
nonšalantan *a.* nonchalant
nonšalantnost *n.* nonchalance
norma *n.* norm
normalan *a.* normal
normalizirati *v.t.* normalize
normalnost *n.* normalcy
nos *n.* nose
nosač *n.* carrier
nosač *n* coolie
nosač *n.* girder
nosat *a.* nosey
nosila *n.* stretcher
nosiljka *n.* sedan
nositelj medalje *n.* medallist
nositi *v.t* bear
nositi *v. t.* carry
nosorog *n.* rhinoceros
nostalgija *n.* nostalgia
nošen *adj.* borne
nošenje *n.* portage
notacija *n.* notation

nov *a.* new
nov *a.* novel
novac *n.* lucre
novac *n.* money
novčan *a.* pecuniary
novčana pošiljka *n.* remittance
novčanik *n.* purse
novčanik *n.* wallet
novčić *n* coin
novčić *n.* mite
novela *n.* novelette
novinar *n.* journalist
novinar *n.* reporter
novinarstvo *n.* journalism
novine *n.* gazette
novost *n.* novelty
nozdrva *n.* nostril
nož *n.* knife
nož pluga *n* colter
nožni prst *n.* toe
nuklearna *a.* nuclear
nula *n.* nil
nula *a.* null
nula *n.* zero
numerički *a.* numerical
nusproizvod *n* by-product
nutritivan *a.* nutritive
nužda *n.* necessity
nužnik *n.* latrine

NJ

njakanje *n* bray
njakati *v. i* bray
njega *pron.* him
njegov *pron.* his
njegovatelj *n* tender
njegovati *v.t* nurse
njen *a* her

nježan *a.* dainty
nježan *a* tender
nježno *a.* gentle
nježnost *n.* endearment
njih *pron.* them
njihanje *n* sway
njihati *v.i.* sway
njihov *a.* their
njihov *pron.* theirs
njoj *pron.* her
njušiti *v.t* nose
njuška *n.* muzzle
njuškalo *a.* nosy
njuškati *v.* nuzzle
o *prep* about

O

oaza *n.* oasis
oba *a.* either
oba *a* both
oba *pron* both
oba *conj* both
obad *n.* gadfly
obala *n* coast
obala *n.* shore
obala *n* strand
obasipati *v.t.* lavish
obaveza *n.* must
obaveza *n.* obligation
obavezan *a* compulsory
obavezan *a* incumbent
obavezan *a.* mandatory
obavezan *a.* obligatory
obavezati *v.t.* oblige
obavezati se *v. t.* commit
obavijest *n.* notification
obavijestiti *v.t.* apprise
obavijestiti *v.t.* inform

obavijestiti *v.t.* notify
obaviti *v.t.* transact
obazriv *adj.* circumspect
obazriv *a.* precautionary
obdanište *n.* kindergarten
obdariti *v. t* endow
obdukcija *n.* post-mortem
obdukcioni *a.* post-mortem
obećanje *n* promise
obećati *v.t* promise
obećavajući *a.* promising
obeshrabriti *v.i.* dehort
obeshrabriti *v. t.* discourage
obeshrabriti *v. t* dishearten
obesmrtiti *v.t.* immortalize
obeštećenje *n* redress
obezbediti *v. t* ensure
obezbediti *v.i.* provide
obezvrijediti *v.t.i.* depreciate
običaj *n.* custom
obično *adv.* usually
obijeleti *v.t.* whitewash
obilan *a* abundant
obilan *a.* profuse
obilovati *v.i.* abound
obilje *n* abundance
obilje *n.* profusion
obilje *n.* redundance
obilježiti *v.t.* sign
obilježiti inicijalima *v.t* initial
obim *n.* scope
obiman *a.* voluminous
objasniti *v. t* elucidate
objasniti *v. t.* explain
objašnjenje *n* explanation
objava *n.* announcement
objaviti *v.t.* announce
objaviti *v.t.* post
objaviti *v.t.* publish
objekat *n.* object

objektiv *n.* lens
objektivan *a.* objective
objesiti *v.t.* hang
oblačan *a.* overcast
oblačenje *n* dressing
oblačiti *v. t* dress
oblačno *a* cloudy
oblaganje *n* coating
oblagati *v.t.* panel
oblak *n.* cloud
oblik *n.* shape
oblikovati *v.t.* model
oblikovati *v.t.* mould
oblikovati *v.t* shape
obložiti *v.t.* pad
obložiti daskama *v.t.* plank
obložiti jastucima *v. t* cushion
obmana *n.* delusion
obmanuti *v. t* beguile
obmanuti *v. t* deceive
obmanuti *n.t.* delude
obmanjivati *v.t.* misguide
obnova *n.* renewal
obnova *n.* renovation
obnoviti *v.t.* renew
obnoviti *v.t.* restore
obod *n* brim
obod *n.* rim
obogatiti *v. t* enrich
obojiti *v.t.* tincture
obojiti *v.t.* tint
oboljenje *n.* ailment
oboriti *v.t.* prostrate
obožavalac *n.* idolater
obožavanje *n.* apotheosis
obožavanje *n.* worship
obožavanje *n.* adoration
obožavatelj *n.* worshipper
obožavati *v.t.* worship
obožavati *v.t.* adore

obraćati se *v.i.* plead
obradiv *a.* workable
obradiv *adj.* arable
obradovati *v.t.* gladden
obrađivati *v. t* cultivate
obrađivati *v.t.* till
obratiti se *v.t.* address
obraz *n* cheek
obrazac *n.* norm
obrazac *n.* pattern
obrazloženje *n.* rationale
obrazovanje *n* education
obrazovati *v. t* educate
obred *n.* ordinance
obred *n.* rite
obredni *a.* ceremonious
obrezivanje *n.* lop
obrisati spužvicom *v.t.* sponge
obrnuti *v.t.* invert
obrnuti *v.t.* reverse
obrnuto *adv.* vice-versa
obrok *n.* meal
obrok *n.* ration
obrt *n.* twist
obrtati se *v.i.* revolve
obrubiti *v.t* fringe
obrubiti *v.t.* list
obrva *n* brow
obućar *n* cobbler
obući *v.t.* apparel
obući *v. t* clothe
obući *v.t* garb
obući *v.t.* vest
obuhvaćanje *n* comprehension
obuhvatati *v.t.* implicate
obuhvatiti *v. t* comprehend
obujam *n.* volume
obuka *n.* training
obustava *n* stop
obustava *n.* suspension

obuti *v.t.* shoe
obuzdati *v.t.* restrain
obuzdati *v.t.* subdue
obuzdatu *v. t* curb
obvezujuć *a* binding
ocat *n* alegar
ocean *n.* ocean
oceanski *a.* oceanic
oceniti *v.t* grade
oceubojstvo *n.* patricide
ocijeniti *v. t* evaluate
očajan *a* desperate
očajanje *n* despair
očajavati *v. i* despair
očekivanje *n.* expectation
očekivati *v. t* expect
očevidan *a.* manifest
očevina *n.* patrimony
očigledan *a.* evident
očigledan *a.* obvious
očigledno *adv* clearly
očijukanje *n* ogle
očijukati *v.t.* ogle
očinski *a.* paternal
očistiti *v. t* cleanse
očistiti *v.t.* purge
očistiti *v.t.* purify
očna jabučica *n* eyeball
očni *a.* ocular
očuvati *v. t* conserve
očvrsnuti *v.t.* toughen
od *prep.* from
od *prep.* since
od sada *adv.* henceforth
od sada *adv.* hereafter
oda *n.* ode
odakle *adv.* whence
odan *a.* staunch
odan *a.* whole-hearted
odande *adv.* thence

odašiljač *n.* transmitter
odbaciti *v. t* discard
odbaciti *v. t.* dismiss
odbaciti *v.t.* rebuff
odbacivanje *n.* rebuff
odbegao *a.* fugitive
odbijanje *n.* rebound
odbijanje *n.* refusal
odbijanje *n.* rejection
odbijanje *n.* repulse
odbijanje dojenčeta *n* ablactation
odbiti *v.t.* deduct
odbiti *v.t.* negative
odbiti *v.i.* rebound
odbiti *v.t.* refuse
odbiti *v.t.* reject
odbiti *v.t.* repel
odbiti *v.t.* repulse
odbiti *v.t.* stud
odbiti dojenče *v. t* ablactate
odbojan *a.* repulsive
odbojno *adv.* recoil
odbojnost *n.* repulsion
odbor *n* committee
odbor *n* board
odbrambeno *adv.* defensive
odbrana *n* defence
odcjepljenje *n.* secession
odeća *n.* garb
odeća *n.* garment
odenuti *v.t.* attire
oderati *v.t* skin
odežda *n.* vestment
odgajati *v.t.* foster
odgajati *v.t.* mother
odgajivačnica zečeva *n.* warren
odgoditi *v.t.* adjourn
odgoj *n.* nurture
odgovarati *v. i* correspond
odgovarati *v.i.* match

odgovarati *v.t.* suit
odgovor *n.* rejoinder
odgovor *n* reply
odgovor *n.* response
odgovor *n.* retort
odgovor *n* answer
odgovoran *a.* liable
odgovoran *a.* responsible
odgovoran *a* accountable
odgovoriti *v.i.* reply
odgovoriti *v.i.* respond
odgovoriti *v.t.* retort
odgovoriti *v.t* answer
odgovorljiv *a.* answerable
odgovornost *n* blame
odgovornost *n.* liability
odgovornost *n.* responsibility
odijelo *n.* suit
odjeća *n.* clothes
odjeća *n* clothing
odjeća *n.* apparel
odjek *n* echo
odjekivati *v. t* echo
odjeknuti *v.i.* resound
odjel *n.* compartment
odjel *n* department
odjeljak *n.* section
odjenuti *v.t.* robe
odkad *conj.* since
odlaganje *n.* postponement
odlaganje *n.* adjournment
odlazak *n* departure
odličan *a.* excellent
odlika *n* feature
odložiti *v.t. & i.* delay
odložiti *v.t.* postpone
odlučan *a.* resolute
odlučan *a.* stalwart
odlučan zagovornik *n* stalwart
odlučiti *v. t* decide

odlučiti se *v.i.* opt
odlučnost *n.* determination
odlučujući *a* decisive
odluka *n* decision
odmah *adv.* forthwith
odmah *adv.* instantly
odmah *adv.* anon
odmarati se *v.i.* repose
odmazda *n.* retaliation
odmetnik *n.* outlaw
odmjeriti *v.t* mete
odmor *n.* holiday
odmor *n.* repose
odmor *n* rest
odmor *n.* vacation
odmor *n* break
odmoriti se *v.i.* rest
odnos *n.* intercourse
odnos *n.* ratio
odnos *n.* relation
odnosan *a.* respective
odnositi se *v.i.* pertain
odnositi se *v.t.* relate
odobravanje *n* acclaim
odobrenje *n* grant
odobrenje *n.* approbation
odobrenje *n.* approval
odobriti *v.t* acclaim
odobriti *v. t.* endorse
odobriti *v.t.* grant
odobriti *v.t.* vouchsafe
odobriti *v.t* approbate
odobriti *v.t.* approve
odoljeti *v.t.* resist
odoljeti *v.t.* weather
odomaćiti *v.t.* naturalize
odonda *adv.* since
odrasla osoba *n.* adult
odrastao *a* adult
odraz *n.* reflection

odraziti *v.t.* reflect
odražavati *v.t.* mirror
odreći se *v.t* forgo
odreći se *v.t.* relinquish
odreći se *v.t.* renounce
odredba *n.* provision
odredba *n.* stipulation
odrediti *v.t.* allot
odrediti *v. t* determine
određen *a* definite
određen *a* express
određen *a* set
određeni *a* certain
odricanje *n.* renunciation
odriješiti *v.t.* loose
održati *v.t.* sustain
održavanje *n.* maintenance
održavanje *n* upkeep
održavati *v.t.* maintain
održiv *a.* tenable
održiv *a.* viable
odsečan *a* curt
odsjeći glavu *v. t.* behead
odstupanje *n* deviation
odstupati *v. i* deviate
odsustvo *n* absence
odsutan *a* absent
odšteta *n.* indemnity
odšteta *n.pl.* amends
odučiti *v.t.* wean
odugovlačenje *n.* procrastination
odugovlačiti *v.i.* linger
odugovlačiti *v.i.* procrastinate
odustati *v.t.* waive
odušak *n.* vent
oduševljen *a* enthusiastic
oduzeti *v.t.* subtract
oduzimanje *n.* subtraction
odvajanje *n* detachment
odvažan *a.* mettlesome

odvjetnik *n.* attorney
odvjetnik *n.* barrister
odvjetnik *n.* lawyer
odvjetnik *n.* solicitor
odvod *n* drain
odvoditi *v. t* drain
odvodni kanal *n.* culvert
odvodni kanal *n* sewer
odvodni sustav *n.* sewage
odvojen *a.* separate
odvojeno *adv.* apart
odvojiti *v. t* detach
odvojiti *v.t.* segregate
odvojiv *v.t.* separate
odvratan *a.* hideous
odvratan *a.* obnoxious
odvratan *a.* repellent
odvratan *a.* repugnant
odvratiti *v.t. & i.* deflect
odvratiti *v. t* dissuade
odvratnost *n.* repugnance
oglas *n.* handbill
oglas *n* advertisement
oglasiti *v. t* denounce
oglašavati *v.t.* advertise
ogledalo *n* mirror
ognjište *n.* hearth
ogoliti *v.t.* denude
ogovaranje *n.* gossip
ogovaranje *v.t.* backbite
ograda *n.* close
ograda *n* fence
ograda *n.* hurdle1
ograda *n.* raling
ograditi *v.t* fence
ograditi *v.t* hedge
ograditi *v.t* hurdle2
ograditi *v.t.* rail
ograditi kolcima *v.t.* picket
ograničen *a.* limited

ograničen *a.* terminable
ograničenost *n.* insularity
ograničenje *n.* confinement
ograničenje *n.* limitation
ograničenje *n.* restriction
ograničiti *v. t* confine
ograničiti *v.t.* limit
ograničiti *v.t.* restrict
ogrlica *n.* necklace
ogroman *a* enormous
ogroman *a.* huge
ogroman *a.* immense
ogroman *a* mammoth
ogroman *a.* tremendous
ogroman *a.* vast
ogrozd *n.* gooseberry
ogrtač *n.* cloak
ogrtač *n.* overall
ohol *a.* arrogant
ohol *a.* haughty
oholo *a.* lordly
oholost *n.* arrogance
ohrabriti *v. t.* embolden
ohrabriti *v. t* encourage
ojačati *v.t.* strengthen
okaljati *v.t.* spot
okidač *n.* trigger
oklada *n* bet
oklevetati *v.t.* libel
oklijevanje *n* demur
oklijevanje *n.* hesitation
oklijevati *v. t* demur
oklijevati *v. t.* halt
oklijevati *v.i.* hesitate
okliznuće *n.* slip
okliznuti se *v.i.* slip
oklop *n* mail
oklop *n.* armour
oklopiti *v.t.* plate
oklopna rukavica *n.* gauntlet

okno *n.* pane
oko *n* eye
oko *prep.* around
okolnost *n* circumstance
okolo *adv.* round
okolo *adv.* around
okončati *v.t.* terminate
okoreo *a.* callous
okoštati *v.t.* ossify
okovati *v.t.* iron
okovati *v.t.* shackle
okovati *v.t.* tip
okovi *n.* shackle
okovratnik *n* collar
okrečiti *v.t.* plaster
okrenut uvis *a.* upward
okrenuti *v.i.* turn
okret *n* turn
okretan *a.* versed
okretanje *n.* spin
okretati se *v.t.* pivot
okretni *a.* nimble
okriviti *v.t.* impeach
okriviti *v.t.* incriminate
okrugao *a.* round
okruglost *n.* round
okrutan *a.* atrocious
okrutan *a* cruel
okrutnost *n* cruelty
okruženje *n.* environment
okruženje *n.* surroundings
okružiti *v. t.* encircle
okružiti *v.t.* ring
okruživati *v.t.* surround
oksidisati *v.* acetify
oktava *n.* octave
okular *n.* oculist
okultan *a.* occult
okupator *n.* occupier
okupiti *v.t.* gather

okus *n* flavour
okus *n.* smack
okus *n.* taste
okusiti *v.t.* taste
okutnost *n* atrocity
okvir *n* frame
okvir kamina *n.* mantel
olabaviti *v.t.* loosen
olabaviti *v.t.* slacken
olako *adv.* lightly
olakšanje *n.* alleviation
olakšati *v.t.* alleviate
olakšati *v.t* facilitate
olakšati *v.i.* lighten
olakšati *v.t.* relieve
olakšica *n* concession
oličavati *v.t.* impersonate
oličavati *v.t.* personify
oligarhija *n.* oligarchy
olimpijada *n.* olympiad
olovka *n.* pencil
olovni *a.* leaden
olovo *n.* lead
oltar *n.* altar
oluja *n.* gale
oluja *n.* storm
oluja *n.* tempest
olujni *a.* stormy
oluk *n.* gutter
olupina *n.* wrack
olupina *n.* wreck
olupina *n.* wreckage
oljuštiti *v.t.* peel
omalovažavanje *n.* slight
omalovažavati *v.t.* slight
omamiti *v.t.* stupefy
omašiti *v.i* blunder
omaška *n* blunder
omaž *n.* homage
omča *n* bight

omega *n.* omega
ometati *v.t.* hinder
ometati *v.t.* impede
ometati *v.t.* obstruct
omiljen *a* favourite
omladina *n. pl.* teens
omogućiti *v. t* enable
omotač *n* mantle
omotač *n.* wrapper
omplet *n.* omelette
on *pron.* he
ona *pron.* she
onaj *dem. pron.* that
onaj koji ima licencu *n.* licensee
onda *adv.* then
oneraspoložiti *v. t* deject
onesposobiti *v. t* disable
onesposobljen *a.* invalid
onesvijestiti se *v.i* faint
onesvijestiti *se v.i* swoon
ono što je glavno *n.* paramount
ono što je malo *n.* little
ono što je manje *n* less
ono što je najgore *n.* worst
onomatopeja *n.* onomatopoeia
opadanje *n.* decrement
opadanje *n* wane
opadati *v. i* ebb
opadati *v.i.* wane
opak *n.* arrant
opak *a.* vicious
opakost *n.* malignancy
opal *n.* opal
opasač *n.* waistband
opasan *a* dangerous
opasan *a.* perilous
opasan *a.* venturous
opasan *n* breakneck
opasati *v.t.* gird
opasati *v.t.* strap

opasati šancem *v.t.* moat
opasati zidom *v.t.* wall
opasati *v.t.* begird
opasivati *v.t* girdle
opasnost *n.* danger
opasnost *n.* jeopardy
opasnost *n.* peril
opasti *v.i.* subside
opatija *n.* abbey
opaziti *v. t* behold
opaziti *v.t.* perceive
opcija *n.* option
opčiniti *v. t* bedevil
opčiniti *v. t* enchant
opčinjenost *n* spell
opći *a.* general
općina *n.* municipality
općinski *a.* municipal
općinski *a.* township
opeći koprivom *v.t.* nettle
opeka *n* brick
opeklina *n* singe
opekotina *n.* burn
opera *n.* opera
operacija *n.* operation
operativan *a.* operative
operator *n.* operator
opet *adv.* again
opijum *n.* opium
opipati palcem *v.t.* thumb
opipljiv *a.* palpable
opipljiv *a.* tangible
opiranje *n.* reluctance
opis *n* description
opisati *v. t* describe
opisni *a* descriptive
opkoliti *v. t* encompass
oplakivanje *n* lament
oplakivanje *n.* mourning
oplakivati *v. t* bewail

oplakivati *v.i.* lament
oplemeniti *v. t.* ennoble
oploditi *v.t* fertilize
opljačkati *v.t.* depredate
opljačkati *v.t.* rifle
opljačkati *v.t.* rob
opljačkati *v.t.* sack
opojno sredstvo *n.* intoxicant
oponašati *v.t.* ape
opor *a.* pungent
oporavak *n.* recovery
oporaviti se *v.t.* recover
oporba *n.* opposition
oporeziv *a.* taxable
oporezivanje *n.* taxation
oporezovati *v.t.* tax
oporost *n.* pungency
oportunizam *n.* opportunism
opovrgnuti *v.t.* confute
opovrgnuti *v. t* disprove
opoziv *n.* recall
opoziv *n.* revocation
opozivan *a.* revocable
opozivanje *n* repeal
opozvati *v.t.* countermand
opozvati *v.t.* recall
opozvati *v.t.* repeal
opozvati *v.t.* revoke
opraštanje *n.* remission
oprati *v.t.* launder
opravdan *a.* justifiable
opravdanje *n.* justification
opravdanje *n.* vindication
opravdati *v.t* excuse
opravdati *v.t.* justify
opravdati *v.t.* vindicate
opravljiv *a.* repairable
oprema *n* equipment
oprema *n.* gear
oprema *n.* kit

oprema *n.* outfit
opremiti *v. t* equip
opremiti *v.t.* furnish
oprez *n.* caution
oprezan *a.* provident
oprezan *a.* vigilant
oprezan *a.* wary
oprezan *a.* alert
oprezan *a* careful
oprezan *a.* cautious
opreznost *n.* alertness
oprljiti *v.t.* scorch
oprljiti *v.t.* singe
oprostiti *v.t.* assoil
oprostiti *v.t* forgive
oprostiti *v.t.* pardon
oprostiti *v.t.* remit
oprostiv *a.* pardonable
oprostiv *a.* venial
oproštaj *n* farewell
oproštenje *n.* condonation
oproštenje *n.* pardon
opsada *n.* siege
opscen *a.* obscene
opsedati *v. t* besiege
opseg *n.* extent
opservatorija *n.* observatory
opsesija *n.* obsession
opsežan *a.* ample
opsjednuti *v.t.* obsess
opskrba *n* supply
opskrbiti *v.t.* stock
opskrbiti predgovorom *v.t.* preface
opskrbljivati *v.t.* supply
opstajati *v.i.* subsist
opstanak *n.* subsistence
opstanak *n.* survival
opstati *v.i.* survive
opstrukcija *n.* obstruction
opstruktivan *a.* obstructive

opšta tuča *n.* melee
opteretiti *v. t.* encumber
optičar *n.* optician
optički *a.* optic
optimalan *a* optimum
optimista *n.* optimist
optimistički *a.* optimistic
optimizam *n.* optimism
optimum *n.* optimum
optužba *n.* impeachment
optužba *n* accusation
optuženi *n* defendant
optuženik *n.* respondent
optuženik *n.* accused
optužiti *v.* arraign
optužiti *v.t.* indict
optužiti *v.t.* accuse
optužnica *n.* indictment
opunomoćenik *n.* warrantee
opunomoćenik *n.* assignee
opunomoćiti *v.t.* accredit
opustiti *v.t.* relax
opuštanje *n.* relaxation
orač *n.* ploughman
orah *n* nut
orah *n.* walnut
orao *n* eagle
orati *v.i* plough
oratorij *n.* oratory
orbita *n.* orbit
oreol *n.* nimbus
orezati *v.t.* prune
organ *n.* organ
organizacija *n.* organization
organizam *n.* organism
organizirati *v.t.* organize
organski *a.* organic
Orient *n.* orient
original *n* original
originalan *a.* original

originalnost *n.* originality
orijentalan *a.* oriental
orijentirati *v.t.* orient
orijentirati *v.t.* orientate
orkestar *n.* orchestra
orkestralni *a.* orchestral
orman *n* cupboard
ormar *n.* ambry
ormar *n.* locker
ornament *n.* ornament
ornamentni nož *n.* baslard
oružarnica *n.* armoury
oružje *n.* weapon
osa *n.* wasp
osakatiti *v.t.* lame
osam *n* eight
osamdeset *n* eighty
osamdesetogodišnje *a* octogenarian
osamdesetogodišnji *a.* octogenarian
osamiti *v.t.* seclude
osamljen *a.* secluded
osamljenost *n.* seclusion
osamnaest *a* eighteen
oscilacija *n.* oscillation
oscilirati *v.i.* oscillate
osedlati *v.t.* saddle
oseka *n* ebb
osigurač *n* fuse
osiguranje *n.* insurance
osigurati *v.t.* insure
osigurati *v.t.* secure
osim *prep* except
osim da *conj.* but
osion *a.* rampant
osip *a.* rash
osiromašiti *v.t.* impoverish
osjećaj *n* feeling
osjećaj *n.* sentience
osjećanje *n.* sentiment
osjećati *v.t* feel

osjećaj *n.* sense
osjećajan *a.* sentient
osjetiti *v.t.* sense
osjetljiv *a.* sensitive
osjetljiv *a.* touchy
osjetljivost *n.* sensibility
oskudan *a.* meagre
oskudan *a.* scant
oskudan *a.* scanty
oskudan *a.* sparse
oslabiti *v. t.* enfeeble
oslabiti *v.t. & i* weaken
oslikati *v.t.* portray
oslobađajuća presuda *n.* acquittal
oslobađanje roba *n.* manumission
oslobodilac *n.* liberator
osloboditi *v.t* absolve
osloboditi *v. t.* exempt
osloboditi *v.t* free
osloboditi *v.t.* liberate
osloboditi *v.t.* rid
osloboditi ropstva *v.t.* manumit
osloboditi *v.t.* acquit
oslobođen *adj.* exempt
oslobođenje *n.* liberation
oslonac *n.* backbone
osloniti *v.i.* rely
osmatrač *n.* on-looker
osmerokut *n.* octagon
osmijeh *n.* smile
osmina milje *n.* furlong
osmougli *a.* octangular
osnivač *n.* founder
osnivanje *n* establishment
osnov *n.* rudiment
osnova *n.* basis
osnovni *a.* fundamental
osnovni *a.* primary
osnovni *a.* rudimentary
osnovni *adj.* basal

osnovni *a.* base
osnovni *a.* basic
osoba *n.* person
osobina *n.* trait
osoblje *n.* personnel
osoblje *n.* staff
osobni *a* facial
osobni *a.* personal
osokoliti *v.t.* man
osovina *n.* axis
osovina *n.* axle
osposobiti *v. t* empower
osramotiti *v.t.* attaint
osramotiti *v. t.* debase
osramotiti *v. t* dishonour
osrednji *a.* mediocre
osrednji *a.* middling
osrednjost *n.* mediocrity
ostaci *n.* remains
ostario *a.* aged
ostatak *n.* remainder
ostatak *n.* residue
ostati *v.i.* remain
ostati *v.i.* stay
ostava *n.* pantry
ostaviti *v.t.* leave
ostaviti *v.t.* pot
ostaviti razmak *v.t.* space
ostavka *n.* resignation
ostriga *n.* oyster
ostvaren *a* accomplished
ostvariti *v.t.* accomplish
osuda *n* condemnation
osuda *n* conviction
osuditi *v. t.* condemn
osuditi *v. t.* convict
osuditi *v. t.* doom
osuditi *v.t.* sentence
osuditi *v.t.,* umpire
osuđenik *n* convict

osujetiti *v.t.* thwart
osumnjičen *a.* suspect
osumnjičeni *n* suspect
osumnjičiti *v.t.* suspect
osušiti *v. i.* dry
osvajanje *n* conquest
osveta *n.* revenge
osveta *n.* vengeance
osvetiti *v.t.* revenge
osvetiti *v.t.* sanctify
osvetiti se *v.i.* retaliate
osvetnik *n.* nemesis
osvetoljubiv *a.* revengeful
osvijetliti *v.t.* illuminate
osvijetliti *v.t.* light
osvijetljen *v.i.* alight
osvijetljenje *n.* illumination
osvježenje *n.* refreshment
osvježiti *v.t.* refresh
osvojiti *v. t* conquer
ošamariti *v.t.* slap
ošamutiti *v.t.* stun
ošišati *v.t* fleece
ošišati *v.t.* shear
oštar *a.* acute
oštar *a.* caustic
oštar *a.* poignant
oštar *a.* severe
oštar *a.* sharp
oštar bol *n* smart
oštetiti *v. t.* damage
oštetiti *v.t* harm
oštrica *n.* blade
oštrina *n.* poignancy
oštro *adv.* sharp
oštrokondža *n.* shrew
oštrouman *adj.* argute
otac *n* father
otapalo *n* solvent
otcepiti se *v.i.* secede

oteklina *n* swell	**otrov** *n*. venom
oteti *v.t.* abduct	**otrovan** *a*. poisonous
otići *v. i.* depart	**otrovan** *a*. venomous
otirač *n*. mat	**otrovati** *v.t.* intoxicate
otisak *n*. imprint	**otrovati** *v.t.* poison
otisak *n* print	**otud** *adv*. hence
otkazati *v. t.* cancel	**otuđiti** *v.t.* alienate
otkazivanje *n* cancellation	**otvaranje** *n*. opening
otkriće *n*. discovery	**otvor** *n*. aperture
otkriti *v. t* detect	**otvoren** *a*. open
otkriti *v. t* disclose	**otvoren** *a*. outspoken
otkriti *v. t* discover	**otvoren** *a*. overt
otkriti *v. t* divulge	**otvoreno** *adv*. openly
otkrovenje *n*. revelation	**otvoriti** *v.t.* open
otkucaj *n*. tick	**otvoriti** *v.t.* unfold
otkup *n*. ransom	**ova noć** *n*. to-night
otkupiti *v.t.* ransom	**ovacija** *n*. ovation
otmica *n* abduction	**ovakav** *a*. such
otmjenost *n*. sublimity	**oval** *n* oval
otočni *a*. insular	**ovalan** *a*. oval
otok *n*. island	**ovamo** *adv*. hither
otok *n*. isle	**ovan** *n*. ram
otoman *n*. ottoman	**ovan** *n*. aries
otpaci stakla *n*. cullet	**ovaploćenje** *n*. incarnation
otpad *n*. waste	**ovaplotiti** *v.t.* incarnate
otpadak *n*. scrap	**ovca** *n* ewe
otplata *n*. instalment	**ovca** *n*. sheep
otplata *n*. repayment	**ovčetina** *n*. mutton
otpor *n*. resistance	**ovdje** *adv*. here
otporan *a* proof	**ovdje u okolini** *adv*. hereabouts
otporan *a*. resistant	**ovenčati** *v.t.* garland
otpremiti *v.t* outfit	**ovisan** *a* dependent
otprilike *adv* about	**ovisiti** *v. i.* depend
otprilike *adv*. thereabouts	**ovisnik** *n*. addict
otpust *n*. conge	**ovisnik** *n* dependant
otpuštanje *n* dismissal	**ovisnost** *n*. addiction
otrcan *a*. shabby	**ovisnost** *n* dependence
otrcan *a*. threadbare	**ovisnost od drugih** *n* anaclisis
otrgnuti *v.t.* pluck	**ovjekovečiti** *v.t.* perpetuate
otrov *n*. poison	**ovjenčan lovorom** *a*. laureate

ovlastiti *v. t* depute
ovlastiti *v. t.* entitle
ovlastiti *v.t.* authorize
ovlaštenje *n* deputation
ovršitelj *n.* bailiff
ozakoniti *v. t* enact
ozbiljan *a* earnest
ozbiljan *a.* grave
ozbiljan *a* serious
ozbiljan *a.* stern
ozbiljnost *n.* gravity
ozbiljnost *n.* severity
ozloglašen *a.* infamous
ozloglašen *a.* notorious
ozloglašenost *n* disrepute
ozloglašenost *n.* notoriety
ozlojeđen *a.* indignant
ozlojeđenost *n.* indignation
ozlojeđenost *n.* resentment
označavati *v. i* denote
označavati *v.t.* signify
označiti *v.t* mark
označiti *v.t.* tag
oznaka *n.* book-mark
oznaka *n.* tag
ozračiti *v.i.* irradiate
ožalostiti *v. t* distress
ožalostiti *v.t.* afflict
ožalostiti *v.t.* aggrieve
ožalošćeni *n.* mourner
ožiljak *n* scar
oživjeti *v.t.* animate
oživjeti *v. t.* enliven
oživjeti *v.i.* revive
oživjeti *v.t.* zip
oživljavanje *n.* revival
oživljavati *v.t.* vitalize
ožujak *n* march

P

pa *conj.* so
pacijent *n* patient
pad *n.* tumble
padati *v.i* hail
padati *v.i.* rain
padobran *n.* parachute
padobranac *n.* parachutist
pagoda *n.* pagoda
pajalica *n* duster
pakao *a.* hell
paket *n.* pack
paket *n.* package
pakiranje *n.* packing
pakirati u bale *v.t.* bale
paklen *a.* infernal
pakost *n.* meanness
pakost *n.* virulence
pakostan *a.* virulent
pakt *n.* pact
palac *n.* thumb
palača *n.* mansion
palača *n.* palace
palankin *n.* palanquin
paleta *n.* palette
palež *n* arson
palica *n* baton
palma *n.* palm
paluba *n* deck
pametan *a.* clever
pametan *a.* smart
pamflet *n.* pamphlet
pamfletista *n.* pamphleteer
pamuk *n.* cotton
panaceja *n.* panacea
panegirik *n.* panegyric
panika *n.* panic

panorama *n.* panorama
pantalone *n.* breeches
panteista *n.* pantheist
panteizam *n.* pantheism
panter *n.* panther
pantomima *n.* pantomime
pantomimičar *n.* mummer
panj *n.* stub
panj *n.* stump
panj *n* block
papa *n.* pope
papagaj *n.* parrot
papazjanija *n.* hotchpotch
papinstvo *n.* papacy
papir *n.* paper
paprika *n* capsicum
paprikaš *n.* stew
papski *a.* papal
papuča *n.* slipper
papučar *a.* henpecked
par *n* couple
par *n.* pair
para *n* steam
para *n.* vapour
parabola *n.* parable
parada *n.* pageant
parada *n.* parade
paradajz *n.* tomato
paradirati *v.t.* parade
paradoks *n.* paradox
paradoksalan *a.* paradoxical
parafin *n.* paraffin
parafraza *n.* paraphrase
parafrazirati *v.t.* paraphrase
paragraf *n.* paragraph
paralelan *a.* parallel
paralelizam *n.* parallelism
paralelogram *n.* parallelogram
paralitički *a.* paralytic
paraliza *n.* palsy

paraliza *n.* paralysis
paralizirati *v.t.* paralyse
parazit *n.* parasite
parcela *n.* parcel
parče *n.* slice
parfem *n.* perfume
pariranje *n.* parry
parirati *v.t.* parry
paritet *n.* parity
pariti *v.t.* mate
pariti *v.i.* steam
pariti se *v.i.* copulate
park *n.* park
parkirati *v.t.* park
parlament *n.* parliament
parlamentarac *n.* parliamentarian
parlamentaran *a.* parliamentary
parni *a.* vaporous
parničar *n.* litigant
parničenje *n.* litigation
parničiti *v.t.* litigate
parobrod *n.* steamer
parodija *n.* parody
parodirati *v.t.* parody
paroh *n.* parson
parohija *n.* parish
parola *n.* slogan
partiotizam *n.* partiotism
partizan *n.* partisan
partizanski *a.* partisan
partner *n* co-partner
partner *n.* partner
partnerstvo *n.* partnership
pas *n* dog
pasivan *a.* passive
pasmina *n* breed
pasta *n.* paste
pastel *n.* pastel
pasti *v.i.* fall
pasti *v.t* fell

pasti *v.i.* graze
pasti *v.t.* pasture
pasti *v.i.* tumble
pasti u krizu *v.i.* slump
pastir *n.* herdsman
pastir *n.* shepherd
pastirski *a.* pastoral
pastuh *n.* stallion
pasus *n.* passage
pašnjak *n.* pasture
pat *n.* stalemate
patent *n* patent
patentan *a.* patent
patentni *v.t.* patent
patetičan *a.* pathetic
patiti *v.t.* suffer
patka *n.* duck
patos *n.* pathos
patriota *n.* patriot
patriotski *a.* patriotic
patrola *n* patrol
patrolirati *v.i.* patrol
patrona *n.* cartridge
patuljak *n* dwarf
patuljak *n* elf
patuljak *n.* midget
paučina *n* cobweb
pauk *n.* spider
paun *n.* peacock
paunica *n.* peahen
pauza *n.* pause
paviljon *n.* pavilion
paziti *v.t.* heed
pažljiv *a.* mindful
pažljiv *a.* thoughtful
pažljiv *a.* attentive
pažnja *n* heed
pčela *n.* bee
pčelarstvo *n.* apiculture
pčelinjak *n.* apiary

peć *n.* furnace
peć *n.* oven
peć *n.* stove
pecati *v.i.* dap
pecati *v.i* fish
pečat *n.* seal
pečat *n.* stamp
pečat *n* cachet
pečen *a* roast
pečenje *n* roast
peći *v.t.* roast
pedagog *n.* pedagogue
pedagogija *n.* pedagogy
pedala *n.* pedal
pedant *n.* pedant
pedantan *n.* pedantic
pedanterija *n.* pedantry
pedeset *n.* fifty
pedigre *n.* pedigree
pehar *n.* goblet
pehar *n* beaker
pejzaž *n.* landscape
pejzaž *n.* scenery
pekar *n.* baker
pekara *n* bakery
pelen *n.* wormwood
pelud *n.* pollen
penetracija *n.* penetration
peni *n.* penny
penis *n.* penis
pentagon *n.* pentagon
pentrati se *v. i* clamber
penjanje *n.* climb1
penjanje *n* scramble
penjati se *v.t.* ascend
penjati se *v.i* climb
penjati se *v.i.* shine
pepeo *n.* ash
perač *n.* washer
peraje *n* fin

percepcija *n.* perception
perceptivan *a.* perceptive
periferija *n.pl.* outskirts
periferija *n.* periphery
perika *n.* wig
period *n.* period
periodičan *a.* periodical
perla *n* bead
permutacija *n.* permutation
pero *n* feather
pero *n.* nib
pero *n.* pen
personifikacija *n.* personification
perspektiva *n.* perspective
perut *n* dandruff
perverzan *a.* perverse
perverzija *n.* perversion
pesimista *n.* pessimist
pesimističan *a.* pessimistic
pesimizam *n.* pessimism
pesnica *n* fist
pesticid *n.* pesticide
pet *n* five
peta *n.* heel
petak *n.* Friday
peticija *n.* petition
petlja *n.* loop
petljanje *n* bungle
petnaest *n* fifteen
piće *n* drink
pigmej *n.* pigmy
pigmejac *n.* pygmy
pijaca *n.* mart
pijanac *n* bibber
pijančenje *n* debauch
pijančiti *v. t.* debauch
pijančiti *v.i.* revel
pijančiti *v. i* booze
pijanica *n* drunkard
pijanista *n.* pianist
pijanka *n.* revel
pijanka *n.* spree
pijanka *n.* wassail
pijavica *n.* leech
pijesak *n.* sand
pijetao *n* cock
pijuk *v.t.* hack
pijuk *n.* mattock
pijukati *v. i* cheep
pikantan *a.* piquant
piknik *n.* picnic
pila *n.* saw
piliti *v.t.* saw
pilot *n.* pilot
pilotirati *v.t.* pilot
pilula *n.* pill
pionir *n.* pioneer
pipati *v.t.* grope
piramida *n.* pyramid
piratstvo *n.* piracy
pisac *n.* writer
pisač *n.* printer
pisak posude *n.* spout
pisati *v.t.* pen
piskav *a.* shrill
pismen *a.* literate
pismena izjava *n* affidavit
pismenost *n.* literacy
pismo *n* letter
pisoar *n.* urinal
pištolj *n.* pistol
pitalica *n.* conundrum
pitanje *n.* issue
pitanje *n.* query
pitanje *n.* question
pitati *v.t* query
pitati *v.t.* question
pitati *v.t.* ask
piti *v. t* drink
pitom *a.* tame

piton *n.* python
pivo *n* ale
pivo *n* beer
pivovara *n* brewery
pjena *n* foam
pjena *n.* lather
pjeniti se *v.t* foam
pjeskovit *a.* sandy
pjesma *n.* poem
pjesma *n.* song
pjesma *n* carol
pjesma *n* chant
pjesnik *n.* poet
pjesnikinja *n.* poetess
pješadija *n.* infantry
pješak *n.* pedestrian
pješice *adv.* afoot
pjevač *n.* singer
pjevač *n.* songster
pjevač *n.* vocalist
pjevati *v.i.* sing
plaćanje *n.* payment
plačljiv *a.* lachrymose
plaća *n* pay
plaća *n.* remuneration
plaća *n.* stipend
plaća *n.* wage
plaćenički *a.* mercenary
pladanj *n.* tray
plafon *n.* ceiling
plahovitost *n.* impetuosity
plakar *n.* closet
plakat *n.* placard
plakat *n.* poster
plakati *v.i.* weep
plamen *n* flame
plameno *adv.* ablaze
plamtjeti *v.i* flame
plana *n.* plan
planeta *n.* planet

planetarni *a.* planetary
planina *n.* mountain
planinar *n.* mountaineer
planinski *a.* mountainous
planinski vrh *n.* alp
planirati *v.t.* plan
plantaža *n.* plantation
planuti *v.i* flare
plast *n.* rick
plašenje *n.* shy
plašiti se *v.i* fear
plašiti se *v.i.* shy
plašljiv *a.* timorous
platan *n* plane
platforma *n.* platform
platiti *v.t.* pay
plativ *a.* payable
platno *n.* linen
platno *n.* canvas
plato *n.* plateau
platonski *a.* platonic
plav *a.* blue
plava boja *n.* blue
plaža *n* beach
plebiscit *n.* plebiscite
pleme *n.* tribe
plemenit *a.* noble
plemenit *n.* noble
plemenski *a.* tribal
plemić *n.* nobleman
plemić *n.* peer
plemstvo *n.* nobility
plemstvo *n.* aristocracy
ples *n* dance
plesati *v. t.* dance
plesti *v.t.* knit
pleviti *v.t.* weed
plićak *n.* shoal
plijen *n.* prey
plijen *n* spoil

plijen *n* booty
plijesan *n.* mildew
plijesan *n* mould
plik *n* blain
plik *n* bleb
plima *n.* tide
plimski *a.* tidal
plitak *a.* shallow
plivač *n.* swimmer
plivajući *a.* natant
plivanje *n* swim
plivati *v.i.* swim
ploča *n.* plate
ploča *n.* slab
pločnik *n.* pavement
plodan *a* fertile
plodan *a.* fruitful
plodan *a.* prolific
plodnost *n* fertility
plombirati *v.t.* lead
plovan *a.* navigable
ploveći *adv.* afloat
ploviti *v.i* boat
ploviti *v.i* float
pluća *n* lung
plug *n.* plough
pluralitet *n.* plurality
plus *n* plus
pluta *n.* cork
plutača *n* buoy
pljačka *n.* loot
pljačka *n.* robbery
pljačkanje *v.t.* plunder
pljačkaš *n.* marauder
pljačkaš *n.* robber
pljačkati *v.i.* loot
pljačkati *v.i.* maraud
pljačkati *n* plunder
pljeskanje *n* clap
pljeskati *v. i.* clap

pljoska *n* flask
pljunuti *v.i.* spit
pljusak *n* downpour
pljuvačka *n.* saliva
pljuvačka *n* spit
pljuvaonica *n.* spittoon
po strani *adv.* aside
pobaciti *v.i.* miscarry
pobačaj *n* abortion
pobačaj *n.* miscarriage
pobeći *v. i* elope
pobeći *v.i* flee
pobediti *v.t.* vanquish
pobednički *a.* triumphant
pobijanje *n.* refutation
pobijediti *v.t.* win
pobijediti *v.t.* worst
pobiti *v.t.* refute
pobjeći *v.i* escape
pobjeći *v.i* scamper
pobjeći od zakona *v.i* abscond
pobjeda *n.* victory
pobjeda *n* win
pobjednik *n.* victor
pobjednik *n.* winner
pobjedonosan *a.* victorious
poblijedeti *v.i.* pale
poboljšanje *n.* improvement
poboljšanje *n.* amelioration
poboljšanje *n* betterment
poboljšati *v. t* better
poboljšati *v.t.* improve
poboljšati *v.t.* meliorate
poboljšati *v.t.* ameliorate
pobornik *n* bigot
pobornik *a.* combatant
pobožan *a.* pious
pobožnost *n.* piety
pobratim *n* chum
pobrkan *a.* topsy turvy

pobrkano *adv* topsy turvy
pobrkati *v.i* mess
pobrkati *v. t* bungle
pobuditi *v.t.* arouse
pobuđivanje *n.* solicitation
pobuna *n.* insurrection
pobuna *n.* mutiny
pobuna *n.* rebellion
pobuna *n.* revolt
pobuna *n.* riot
pobuna *n.* sedition
pobuniti se *v. i* mutiny
pobuniti se *v.i.* revolt
pocepati u dronjke *v.t* tatter
pocrniti *v. t.* blacken
pocrvenio *adv* ablush
počasni *a.* honorary
početak *n* commencement
početak *n.* inception
početak *n.* onset
početak *n.* prime
početak *n.* beginning
početi *v. t* commence
početi *v.t.* start
početi *n* begin
početni *a.* initial
početnik *n.* novice
počiniti grijeh *v.i.* sin
počiniti nasilje *v.t.* outrage
počistiti *v.t.* tidy
počovječiti *v.t.* humanize
pod *n* floor
pod *prep.* underneath
podbosti *v.t.* spur
poderati *v.t.* tear
poderotina *n.* tear
podesiti *v.t* fit
podesiti *v.t.* proportion
podići *v. t* elevate
podići *v.t.* uplift

podijeliti *v. t* divide
podijeliti na četiri dijela *v.t.* quarter
podijum *n.* dais
podizanje *n* boost
podizanje *n.* lift
podizati *v.t.* lift
podjela *n* division
podjela *n.* partition
podjeliti *v.t.* partition
podlac *n.* knave
podlaktica *n* forearm
podleći *v.i.* succumb
podlost *n.* knavery
podložan *a* subject
podmazati *v.t* grease
podmazati *v.t.* lubricate
podmazivanje *n.* lubrication
podmiti *v. t.* bribe
podmitljiv *a.* venal
podmitljivost *n.* venality
podmladiti *v.t.* rejuvenate
podmlađivanje *n.* rejuvenation
podmornica *n.* submarine
podmorski *a* submarine
podmuklost *n.* perfidy
podne *n.* midday
podne *n.* noon
podnijeti *v.t.* submit
podnositi *v.t.* stomach
podnošljiv *a.* tolerable
podobnost *n.* suitability
podrazumijevati *v.t.* imply
podređen *a.* subordinate
podređeni *n* subordinate
podređenost *n.* subordination
podrhtavati *v.i.* palpitate
podrigivanje *v. t* belch
podrignuti *n* belch
podriti *v.t.* subvert
podriti *v.t.* undermine

podrška n. support
područje n area
podrugivanje n sneer
podrugivanje n taunt
podrugivati se v.i sneer
podrugivati se v.t. taunt
podrum n. basement
podrum n cellar
podružnica a. subsidiary
podržati v.t. support
podržati v.t uphold
podsjetiti v.t. remind
podsjetnik n. reminder
podstaći v.t. galvanize
podstaći v.t. instigate
podstrekač ns. barrator
podstrekivanje n. instigation
podsuknja n. petticoat
podudarati v. i coincide
podudarati v.t. tally
podugačak a. lengthy
podupirač n. corbel
podupirač n. prop
podupirač n. seconder
podupirati v.t. prop
podupirati v.t. second
poduzeća adj. corporate
poduzeće n enterprise
poduzeti v.t. undertake
poduzetnik n businessman
podvala n. hoax
podvala n. imposture
podvaliti v.t hoax
podvezica n. garter
podvig n feat
podvodačica n. bawd
podvodna struja n. undercurrent
podvrgnuti v.t. subject
podvući v.t. underline
podzemlje n. underworld

podzemni a. subterranean
poðoniti v.t sole
poetika n. poetics
poetski a. poetic
poezija n. poesy
poezija n. poetry
pogaziti v.t. trample
poginuti v.i. perish
poglavica n. chieftain
poglavlje n. chapter
pogled n. glance
pogled n. sight
pogled n. view
pogledati v.i. glance
pognuti se v.i. stoop
pognutost n stoop
pogodak n hit
pogodan a convenient
pogodan a. handy
pogodan a. suitable
pogodan za stanovanje a. habitable
pogodan za stanovanje a. inhabitable
pogoditi v.t. hit
pogodnost n. convenience
pogoršati v.t. worsen
pogoršati v.t. aggravate
pogoršavanje n. aggravation
pogrešan a erroneous
pogrešan a. wrong
pogrešno adv. wrong
pogrešno liječenje n. malpractice
pogrešno nazvati v.t. miscall
pogrešno odštampati v.t. misprint
pogrešno predstaviti v.t. misrepresent
pogrešno procijeniti v.t. misjudge
pogrešno razumjeti v.t. misapprehend
pogrešno razumjeti v.t. misconceive
pogrešno razumjeti v.t. misconstrue
pogrešno razumjeti v.t. misunderstand

pogrešno shvatanje *n.* misconception
pogrešno upućivanje *n.* misdirection
pogrešno uputiti *v.t.* misdirect
pogrešno vjerovanje *n.* misbelief
pogrešno voditi *v.t.* mislead
pogriješiti *v. i* err
pogriješiti *v.t.* mistake
poguban *a.* baleful
poguban *a* malign
pohabati *v.t.* wear
pohađanje *n.* attendance
pohlepa *n* cupidity
pohlepa *n.* greed
pohlepan *adj.* avid
pohlepan *a.* greedy
pohlepno *adv.* avidity
pohotan *a.* lustful
pohotan *a.* voluptuous
pohotljivac *n.* voluptuary
pohvala *n* commendation
pohvala *n* laud
pohvala *n.* praise
pohvalan *a.* laudable
pohvalan *a.* praiseworthy
pohvaliti *v. t* commend
pohvaliti *v.t.* laud
poigravati *v.t.* trip
pojačalo *n* amplifier
pojačanje *n.* reinforcement
pojačanje *n* amplification
pojačati *v.t.* intensify
pojačati *v.t.* reinforce
pojačati *v.t.* amplify
pojačati *v. t* boost
pojam *n.* notion
pojas *n.* girdle
pojas *n.* strap
pojas *n* belt
pojava *n.* advent
pojaviti se *v.i.* appear

pojaviti se *v. i* emerge
pojedinačan *a.* singular
pojedinačni *a.* individual
pojedinačno *adv.* singularly
pojedinačnost *n.* singularity
pojedinost *n.* particular
pojednostaviti *v. t* ease
pojednostaviti *v.t.* simplify
pojeftiniti *v. t.* cheapen
pojmovni *a.* notional
pokajanje *n.* remorse
pokajanje *n.* repentance
pokajanje *n.* atonement
pokajati se *v.i.* repent
pokajnički *a.* repentant
pokazati *v. t* demonstrate
pokazati *v. t* display
pokazivanje *n.* demonstration
pokazivanje *n* display
poklapati se *v.t.* correlate
poklon *n.* gift
poklon *n.* present
pokloniti *v. t* donate
pokloniti se *v. t* bow
poklopac *n.* cover
poklopac *n.* lid
poklopiti *v. t.* cap
pokolj *n.* slaughter
pokolj *n* carnage
pokop *n* burial
pokoran *a.* submissive
pokoravanje *n.* subjugation
pokoravati se *v.t.* obey
pokornost *n.* submission
pokositi *v.t.* scythe
pokrenuti *v.t.* propel
pokret *n.* movement
pokretač *n.* mover
pokretan *a.* mobile
pokretan *a.* movable

pokretan a. portable
pokretna imovina n. movables
pokretnost n. mobility
pokriti v. t. cover
pokriti v.t mantle
pokriti v.t. top
pokriti crijepom v.t. tile
pokriti krov v.t. thatch
pokriti krovom v.t. roof
pokriti plaštom v.t. shroud
pokriti slamom v.t. litter
pokrivač n blanket
pokrivač n wrap
pokrov n. shroud
pokrovitelj n. patron
pokroviteljstvo n. patronage
pokušaj n try
pokušaj n. attempt
pokušati v.t. attempt
pokušati v.i. try
pokvareno adj. addle
pokvarenjak v.t. pervert
pokvariti v.t. mar
pokvariti v.t. spoil
pokvariti v.i. tamper
pokvariti v.t. vitiate
pokvasiti v. t drench
pokvasiti v.t. wet
pol n. gender
pol n. pole
pol n. sex
pola a half
polako adv. slowly
polarni n. polar
polazak n. outset
polemika n controversy
polet n. zest
polica n. shelf
policajac n constable
policajac n. policeman

policajac n. trooper
policija n. police
policijski sat n curfew
poligamija n. polygamy
poligamski a. polygamous
poliglota n. polyglot1
poliglotski a. polyglot2
polirati v.t. polish
politehnički a. polytechnic
politehnika n. polytechnic
politeista n. polytheist
politeistički a. polytheistic
politeizam n. polytheism
političar n. politician
politički a. political
politika n. policy
politika n. politics
polo n. polo
polomiti v.t fracture
polovina n. half
položaj n. locality
položiti v.t. lay
poiožiti v.t. pillow
poluga n. lever
polumjer n. radius
poluslep n. purblind
polje n field
poljoprivreda n. agriculture
poljoprivredni a. agricultural
poljoprivrednik n farmer
poljoprivrednik n. agriculturist
poljski klozet n. outhouse
poljubac n. kiss
poljubiti v.t. kiss
pomagati v.t aid
pomagati v.t favour
pomagati v.i. minister
pomaknuti v. t displace
pomaknuti v.t. move
pomama n craze

pomama *n.* frenzy
pomaman *a.* frantic
pomen *v. t.* commemorate
pomiješati *v.t.* intermingle
pomirenje *n.* acquiescence
pomiriti *v.t.* reconcile
pomiriti se *v.t.* conciliate
pomoć *n* help
pomoć *n.* succour
pomoći *v.t.* help
pomoći *v.t.* succour
pomoćnik *n.* helpmate
pomoć *n.* aid
pomoć *n.* assistance
pomoći *v.t.* assist
pomoći *v.t.* avail
pomoćni *a.* auxiliary
pomoćnik *n.* auxiliary
pomorski *a.* maritime
pomorski *a.* naval
pompezan *a.* pompous
pompeznost *n.* pomposity
pomračenje *n* eclipse
ponašanje *n* behaviour
ponašati se *v. i.* behave
ponavljanje *n.* repetition
ponavljati se *v.i.* recur
ponedjeljak *n.* Monday
ponekad *adv.* sometimes
poni *n.* pony
poništenje *n.* nullification
poništiti *v. t.* abrogate
poništiti *v.t.* invalidate
poništiti *v.t.* nullify
poništiti *v.t.* undo
poništiti *v.t.* void
poništiti *v.t.* annul
poniziti *v.t.* abase
poniziti *v.t.* humiliate
poniziti *v.t.* mortify

poniznost *n.* humility
ponižavanje *n.* humiliation
poniženje *n* abasement
ponoć *n.* midnight
ponor *n* abyss
ponos *n.* pride
ponosan *a.* proud
ponositi se *v.t.* pride
ponoviti *v.t.* repeat
ponovno postaviti *n.* reinstatement
ponovno postavljanje *v.t.* reinstate
ponovno pridružiti *v.t.* rejoin
ponovo *adv.* afresh
ponovo štampati *v.t.* reprint
ponovo zapasti u grijeh *v.i.* backslide
ponuda *n* offer
ponuda *n* tender
ponuda *n* bid
ponuditelj *n* bidder
ponuditi *v.t* bid
ponuditi *v.t.* offer
ponuditi *v.t.* tender
poplava *n* flood
poplaviti *v.t* flood
poplaviti *v.t.* swamp
poplaviti *v.t.* whelm
popločati *v.t* floor
popločati *v.t.* pave
popodnevni odmor *n.* siesta
popraviti *v.t.* amend
popraviti *v.i.* atone
popraviti *v.t* fix
popraviti *v.t.* mend
popraviti *v.t.* redress
popraviti *v.t.* repair
popravka *n.* repair
popravni *a* reformatory
popravni *a.* remedial
popravni dom *n.* reformatory
poprijeko *prep.* athwart

poprište *n.* locale
poprskati *v.i.* splash
popularan *a.* popular
popularizirati *v.t.* popularize
popularnost *n.* popularity
popuniti *v.t* fill
popust *n* discount
popustiti *v.i.* relent
popustljiv *adj.* compliant
popustljiv *a.* indulgent
popustljiv *a.* lenient
popustljivost *n.* connivance
popustljivost *n.* lenience, leniency
poput *prep* like
poput čestice *a.* particle
pora *n.* pore
porast *n* increase
porasti *v.t.* increase
poravnanje *n.* alignment
poravnati *v.t.* align
poravnati *v.i* surface
poraz *n* defeat
poraziti *v. t.* defeat
porcelan *n* bisque
porculan *n.* porcelain
pored toga *adv.* nonetheless
pored *prep.* beside
porediti *v.t.* liken
poređati *v.t.* line
poređati *v.t.* tabulate
poređenje *n.* simile
poremećaj *n* disorder
poremetiti *v.t.* perturb
porez *n.* tax
porez na uvezenu robu *n.* octroi
poricanje *n* abnegation
poricanje *n* denial
poricati *v. t* abnegate
poricati *v. t.* deny
poricati *v.t.* gainsay

porijeklo *n.* ancestry
porijeklo *n.* origin
porodica *n* family
porok *n.* vice
porota *n.* jury
porotnik *n.* juror
porotnik *n.* juryman
portal *n.* portal
portfolio *n.* portfolio
portret *n.* portrait
portret *n.* portrayal
portretisanje *n.* portraiture
porub *n.* welt
poručnik *n.* lieutenant
poruka *n.* message
porumeneti *v.i* blush
porumeneti *v.t.* redden
poružnjavati *v.t.* uglify
posada *n.* crew
posaditi *v.t.* seed
posaditi na prijestolje *v.t.* throne
posao *n* business
posao *n.* job
poseban *a* distinct
poseban *a* especial
poseban *a.* particular
poseban *a.* special
poseban porez na dohodak *n.* supertax
posipati *v. t.* sprinkle
posjeći sabljom *v.t.* sabre
posjedovanje *n.* possession
posjedovati *v.t.* own
posjedovati *v.t.* possess
posjet *n.* visit
posjetitelj *n.* visitor
posjetiti *v.t.* visit
poslanica *n.* missive
poslastica *n.* comfit
poslastica *n.* dainty
poslati *v.t* forward

poslati *v.t.* send	**postaviti** *v.t.* mount
poslati poštom *v.t.* mail	**postaviti** *v.t.* post
posle toga *adv.* thereafter	**postaviti** *v.t.* right
poslednji *a* after	**postaviti** *v.t* set
poslednji *a.* last	**postaviti dijagnozu** *v. t* diagnose
poslodavac *n* employer	**posteljina** *n.* bedding
poslovanje *n.* dealing	**postepen** *a.* gradual
poslovica *n.* proverb	**postići** *v.t.* achieve
poslovica *n.* adage	**postići** *v.t.* attain
poslovičan *a.* proverbial	**postiti** *v.i* fast
posluga *n* domestic	**postizanje** *n.* acquirement
poslušan *a* docile	**posto** *adv. per* cent
poslušan *a.* obedient	**postojan** *a.* steadfast
poslušnost *n.* obedience	**postojanost** *n.* steadiness
poslužitelj *n.* beadle	**postojanje** *n* existence
poslužiti *v.t.* serve	**postojati** *v.i* exist
posljedica *n* consequence	**postojeći** *n* being
posljedica *n.* repercussion	**postolje** *n.* mount
posmrtni *a.* obituary	**postolje** *n.* pedestal
posmrtni *a.* posthumous	**postotak** *n.* percentage
pospan *a.* sleepy	**postrojenje** *n* facility
pospan *n.* somnolent	**postrojiti** *v.t* marshal
pospanost *n.* somnolence	**postrojiti** *v.t.* range
posramiti *v.t.* abash	**postupak** *n.* proceeding
posramiti *v. t* embarrass	**postupati** *v.i.* act
posramljen *a.* ashamed	**posuditi** *v.t.* lend
posrebriti *v.t.* silver	**posuditi** *v.t.* loan
posredan *a.* oblique	**posuti** *v.t.* strew
posrednik *n.* intermediary	**posvećivanje** *n.* sanctification
posrednik *n.* mediator	**posveta** *n* dedication
posrednik *n.* middleman	**posvetiti** *v.t.* consecrate
posredovanje *n.* mediation	**posvetiti** *v. t.* dedicate
posredovanje *n.* mediation	**posvetiti** *v. t* devote
posredovati *v.i.* mediate	**posvetiti** *v.t.* hallow
posrnuti *v.i* falter	**pošiljka** *n.* consignment
post *n* fast	**pošiljka** *n.* shipment
post skriptum *n.* postscript	**pošta** *n.* mail
postati vitak *v.i.* slim	**pošta** *n.* post-office
postati *v. i* become	**poštanski** *a.* postal
postava *n* lining	**poštar** *n.* postman

poštarina *n.* postage
pošten *a.* honest
pošteno *adv.* fairly
poštenje *n.* honesty
pošto *conj.* after
pošto *conj.* whereas
poštovanje *n* esteem
poštovanje *n.* regard
poštovanje *n.* respect
poštovanje *n.* reverence
poštovati *v. t* esteem
poštovati *v. t* honour
poštovati *v.t.* profane
poštovati *v.t.* respect
poštovati *v.t.* venerate
pošumiti *v.t.* afforest
pošumljen *a.* sylvan
potaknuti *v.t.* abet
potaknuti *v.t.* prompt
potamnjeti *v. t* dim
potamnjeti *v.t.* obscure
potamnjeti *v.t* shadow
potapanje *n.* immersion
potaša *n.* potash
potcjenjivanje *n* disregard
potcjenjivati *v. t* disregard
potčiniti *v.t.* subjugate
potčiniti *v.t.* subordinate
potčinjenje *n.* subjection
potencijal *n.* pontentiality
potencijalan *a.* prospective
potentan *a.* potent
potentnost *n.* potency
potera *n.* chase2
potez *n.* move
pothvat *n.* venture
poticaj *n.* goad
poticaj *n.* incentive
poticaj *n.* stimulus
poticati *v.t* goad

potiljak *n.* nape
potisak *n* thrust
potisnuti *v.t.* repress
potjera *n.* pursuit
potka *n.* woof
potkazivanje *n.* denunciation
potkopavati *v.t.* sap
potkralj *n.* viceroy
potkrijepiti *v.t.* corroborate
potkrovlje *n.* loft
potočić *n.* rivulet
potočić *n.* streamlet
potok *n.* creek
potok *n.* stream
potok *n.* brook
potom *adv.* next
potomak *n* descendant
potomak *n.* offspring
potomstvo *n.* posterity
potomstvo *n.* progeny
potonuti *v.i.* sink
potopiti *v.t.* soak
potopiti *v.i.* submerge
potpaliti *v.t.* kindle
potpis *n.* signature
potpisati *v.t.* subscribe
potpisnik *n.* signatory
potpun *a* absolute
potpun *adj.* crass
potpun *a* downright
potpun *a.* sheer
potpun *adv.* stark
potpun *a* utter
potpuno *adv* absolutely
potpuno *adv* downright
potpuno *adv* entirely
potpuno *adv.* fully
potpuno *adv.* utterly
potpunost *n.* stark
potraživanje *n* claim

potreba n. necessary
potreba n requisite
potreba n want
potreban a necessary
potreban a. needful
potreban a. requisite
potres n earthquake
potres n quake
potres n shake
potrostručiti v.t. triplicate
potrošiti v. t expend
potroš'.ja n consumption
potvrda n affirmation
potvrda n confirmation
potvrdan a affirmative
potvrditi v. t. certify
potvrditi v. t confirm
potvrditi v.t. substantiate
potvrditi v.t. validate
potvrditi v.t. affirm
potvrditi v.t. attest
potvrđivanje n. substantiation
pouka n. moral
pouzdan a. reliable
pouzdan a. trustworthy
pouzdanje n. reliance
povećanje n. augmentation
povećati v.t. augment
povelik a. sizable
povelja n charter
povelja n. muniment
povezati v. t. connect
povezati v.t. rope
povijesni a . historic
povijesni a. historical
povijesničar n. historian
povijest n. history
povik n. shout
povisiti v.t. heighten
povjerenik n. commissioner

povjerenik n confidant
povjerenik n. trustee
povjerenje n confidence
povjerenje n. trust
povjeriti v. i confide
povjeriti v. t. consign
povjeriti v. t entrust
povjerljiv a. confidential
povjerljiv a. trustful
povjetarac n breeze
povlačenje n drag
povlačenje n. pull
povlačenje n. withdrawal
povlačiti v. t drag
povlačiti se v.i. retreat
povlašten a. preferential
povoljan a favourable
povoljan a. providential
povoljan a. advantageous
povoljan a. auspicious
povorka n. procession
povraćaj n. refund
povraćanje n vomit
povraćati v.t. vomit
povratak n. relapse
povratak n. return
povratak u domovinu n. repatriation
povratan a. reversible
povratiti v.t. refund
povratiti v.t. retrieve
povratni a. recurrent
povratni a reflexive
povratnik n repatriate
povrće n. vegetable
povreda n hurt
povreda n. injury
povremen a. occasional
povremeno adv. occasionally
povrh adv above
povrijediti v.t. hurt

povrijediti v.t. injure
povrijediti v.t. violate
površan a cursory
površan a. superficial
površina n. surface
površina u jutrima n. acreage
površnost n. superficiality
povrtni a. vegetable
povući v.t. pull
povući v.t. withdraw
povučen a. reticent
povučenost n. reticence
poza n. pose
pozadina n. rear
pozadina n. background
pozajmiti v. t borrow
pozamašan a bulky
pozdrav n. salutation
pozdrav n salute
pozdraviti v.t. greet
pozdraviti v.t hail
pozdraviti v.t. salute
pozdraviti v.t welcome
pozdraviti se n. adieu
pozicija u kriketu n. mid-off
pozicija u kriketu n. mid-on
pozirati v.i. pose
pozitivan a. positive
poziv n. calling
poziv v. invitation
poziv n. summons
poziv n. call
pozivatelj n caller
pozlata a. gilt
pozlatiti v.t. gild
poznanici n. kith
poznanstvo n. acquaintance
poznat a familiar
poznat a famous
poznat a. renowned

poznat a. well-known
pozornica n. stage
pozornost n. attention
pozvati v.t. invite
pozvati v.t. summon
pozvati v. t. call
poželjan a desirable
poželjan a eligible
požuda n. appetence
požuda n. lust
požuriti v. t. expedite
požutjeti v.t. yellow
praćka n. sling
prag n. threshold
pragmatičan a. pragmatic
pragmatizam n. pragmatism
prah n. powder
praksa n. practice
praktičan a. practical
praktičar n. practitioner
pralja n. laundress
pranje n ablution
pranje n wash
praotac n forefather
prapovijesni a. prehistoric
pras a snap
prasak n crack
prasak n pop
prasak n snap
prasak n. bang
praska n burst
prasnuti v. i. burst
prastar a. primeval
prastari a. immemorial
prašina n dust
prati v.t. wash
pratilac n. attendant
pratiti v.t. accompany
pratiti v. t dog
pratiti v. t escort

pratiti *v.t* follow
pratnja *n* accompaniment
pratnja *n* escort
pratnja *n.* retinue
prav *a.* straight
pravac *n* direction
pravda *n.* justice
pravedan *a* equitable
prav ˌdan *a.* just
pravedan *a.* righteous
pravedno *adv.* aright
pravedno *adv.* justly
pravi *a.* genuine
pravi *a.* proper
pravi *a.* real
pravi *a.* right
pravi *a.* true
pravi *a.* veritable
pravilno *adv* aright
pravilnost *n.* regularity
pravilo *n.* precept
pravilo *n.* rule
praviti akrobacije *v.t.* stunt
praviti dosjetke *v.i.* quibble
pravni *a.* legal
pravni lijek *n.* remedy
pravnik *n.* jurist
pravo *n* right
pravo *adv.* straight
pravo glasa *n.* suffrage
pravo zaloge *n.* lien
pravokutni *a.* rectangular
pravoslavan *a.* orthodox
pravoslavlje *n.* orthodoxy
pravosuđe *n.* judicature
pravoukutnik *n.* rectangle
pravovaljanost *n.* validity
pravovremen *a.* seasonable
prazan *a* empty
prazan *a.* vacant

prazan *a.* void
prazan *a* blank
praziluk *n.* leek
praznina *n* blank
praznina *n.* lacuna
praznina *n.* void
prazniti *v. t* discharge
prazniti *v* empty
praznovjeran *a.* superstitious
praznovjerje *n.* superstition
pražnjenje *n.* discharge
pre podne *n* forenoon
prebivalište *n* domicile
prebivalište *n* dwelling
prebivalište *n.* residence
precijeniti *v.t.* overrate
preciznost *n.* precise
preciznost *n.* precision
prećutan *a.* tacit
prečasni *a.* venerable
prečišćavanje *n.* purification
prečišćavanje *n.* refinement
prečka *n.* spoke
prećutna saglasnost *v.i.* acquiesce
predaja *n* surrender
predak *n.* ancestor
predati se *v.t.* surrender
predavač *n.* lecturer
predavanje *n.* lecture
predavati *v* lecture
predbračni *a.* premarital
predbračni *adj.* antenuptial
predenje *n.* purr
predgovor *n* foreword
predgovor *n.* preamble
predgovor *n.* preface
predgrađe *n.* suburb
predikat *n.* predicate
predivan *a.* wonderful
predivo *n.* yarn

predjelo *n* appetizer
predložiti *v.t.* propose
predložiti *v.t.* propound
predložiti *v.t.* suggest
prednost *n.* precedence
prednost *n.* advantage
prednja noga *n* foreleg
prednjak *n* limber
prednji *a* foremost
prednji *a.* forward
prednji *a* front
predodrediti *v.t.* predetermine
predodređenje *n.* predestination
predosećanje *n.* premonition
predosećanje *n.* prescience
predostrožnost *n.* precaution
predozirati *v.t.* overdose
predrasuda *n.* prejudice
predsjedatelj *n* chairman
predsjedavati *v.i.* preside
predsjednički *a.* presidential
predsjednik *n.* president
predsoblje *n.* lobby
predstaviti *v.t.* present
predstaviti *v.t.* typify
predstavljanje *n.* impersonation
predstavljanje *n.* representation
predstavljati *v.t.* represent
predstavnik *n.* representative
predstojeći *a.* forthcoming
predstojeći *a.* imminent
predstraža *n.* outpost
preduhitriti *v.t* forestall
predujam *n.* advance
predumišljaj *n.* premeditation
preduslovan *a.* prerequisite
preduvjet *n* prerequisite
predvidjeti *v.t* foresee
predvidjeti *v.t.* predict
predvidjeti *v.t.* anticipate

predviđanje *n.* anticipation
predviđanje *n* forecast
predviđanje *n.* foreknowledge
predviđanje *n* foresight
predviđanje *n.* prediction
predviđati *v.t* forecast
predvorje *n.* lounge
prefekt *n.* prefect
preferirati *v.t.* prefer
prefiks *n.* prefix
prefinjenost *n.* sophistication
pregača *n.* rung
pregled *n.* conspectus
pregled *n.* digest
pregled *n.* overhaul
pregled *n.* perusal
pregled *n* review
pregled *n.* survey
pregled *n.* syllabus
pregledati *v.t.* inspect
pregledati *v.t.* overhaul
pregledati *v.t.* peruse
pregledati *v.t.* review
pregledati *v.t.* scrutinize
pregledati *v.t.* survey
pregledavanje *n* browse
pregovarač *n.* negotiator
pregovaranje *n.* negotiation
pregovaranje *n.* parley
pregovarati *v.t.* negotiate
pregovarati *v.i* parley
pregovor *n.* treaty
pregršt *n.* handful
pregrupisati *v.t.* deploy
prehrana *n.* nutrition
preispitivati se *v.i.* introspect
prekid *n* abruption
prekid *n.* interruption
prekidač *n.* switch
prekinuti *v.i* abort

prekinuti *v. t* break
prekinuti *v. t* discontinue
prekinuti *v. t* disrupt
prekinuti *v.t.* interrupt
prekinuti *v.t.* sever
preklapanje *n* overlap
preklapati *v.t.* overlap
preklinjanje *n.* entreaty
preklinjanje *n* adjuration
preklinjati *v. t.* entreat
preklinjati *v.t.* implore
preko *prep.* over
preko *prep.* via
preko noći *adv.* overnight
preko palube *adv.* overboard
preko *adv.* across
preko puta *prep.* across
prekomjeran *rad n.* overwork
prekoračenje *n.* demurrage
prekoračenje računa *n.* overdraft
prekoračiti *v.t* exceed
prekoračiti *v.t.* transcend
prekoračiti račun *v.t.* overdraw
prekovremeni *rad n* overtime
prekovremeno *adv.* overtime
prekretnica *n.* milestone
prekriti *v.t.* veil
prekrivač *n.* coverlet
prekrstiti *v. t* cross
prekršaj *n.* default
prekršaj *a.* foul
prekršaj *n.* misdemeanour
prekršiti *v.t.* transgress
prekršiti zakletvu *v.t.* forswear
prelat *n.* prelate
preliminaran *a.* preliminary
prelomiti *v.t.* page
prelja *n.* spinner
preljuba *n.* adultery
prema gore *prep.* up

prema tome *adv.* accordingly
premašivati *v.i.* preponderate
premazati katranom *v.t.* tar
premda *conj.* notwithstanding
premda *conj.* though
premija *n.* premium
premijer *a.* premier
premijer *n* premier
premijera *n.* premiere
preminuti *v. i* decease
premostiti *v.t.* span
premostiv *a.* negotiable
prenatalni *adj.* antenatal
prenemaganje *n* whine
prenemaganje *n* affectation
prenemagati se *v.i.* whine
prenoćiti *v.i.* roost
prenositi *v. t.* convey
prenositi *v.t.* relay
prenositi *v.t.* telecast
prenositi *v.t.* transfer
prenositi *v.t.* transmit
prenosiv *a.* removable
prenosiv *a.* transferable
preobilan *a.* superabundant
preobilje *n.* superabundance
preobraćenik *n* convert
preobraziti *v.t.* transfigure
preobraženje *n.* transfiguration
preokret *n.* reversal
preokret *n.* upheaval
preokupacija *n.* preoccupation
preopširan *a.* verbose
preopširnost *n.* verbosity
preopterećenje *n* overload
preopterećenje *n.* surcharge
preopterećenje *n* overcharge
preopteretiti *v.t.* overburden
preopteretiti *v.t.* overcharge
preopteretiti *v.t.* overload

preopteretiti *v.t.* surcharge
preopteretiti radom *v.i.* overwork
preosjetljiv *a* maudlin
preostali *a.* residual
preovlađivati *v.i.* predominate
preovlađivati *v.i.* prevail
preovlađujući *a.* prevalent
prepad *n* swoop
prepelica *n.* quail
prepirati *se v. i* dispute
prepirati *se v.i.* wrangle
prepirati *se v. t* bicker
prepirka *n.* altercation
prepirka *v. t* brangle
prepirka *n.* wrangle
prepisati *v.t.* transcribe
prepiska *n.* correspondence
preplanulost *n., a.* tan
preplanuti *v.i.* tan
preplašiti *v.t.* overawe
prepoloviti *v.t.* halve
prepoloviti *v. t* bisect
preporod *n.* rebirth
preporod *n.* resurgence
preporučiti *v.t.* recommend
preporučiv *a.* advisable
preporučivost *n* advisability
preporuka *n.* recommendation
prepoznati *v.t.* recognize
prepoznavanje *n.* recognition
prepraviti *v.t.* revise
prepreden *a* arch
prepreka *n.* hindrance
prepreka *n.* impediment
prepreka *n.* obstacle
preraditi *v.t.* refine
prerasti *v.t.* outgrow
prerušen *n* disguise
prerušiti *se v. t* disguise
presađivati *v.t.* transplant

presedan *n.* precedent
preskakivanje *n* skip
preskočiti *v.i.* skip
presrećan *a* overjoyed
presresti *v.t.* intercept
presretanje *n.* interception
prestati *v.t.* quit
prestati *v. i.* cease
presti *v.i.* purr
prestići *v.t.* overtake
prestiž *n.* prestige
prestižan *a.* prestigious
prestraviti *v.t.* terrify
prestravljen *a.* aghast
presuda *n.* judgement
presuda *n.* verdict
presudan *adj.* crucial
presuditi *v.t.* arbitrate
preštampavanje *n.* reprint
pretegnuti *v.t.* outweigh
pretenciozan *a.* pretentious
pretendent *n.* aspirant
pretenzija *n.* pretension
prethoditi *v.* precede
prethoditi *v.t.* antecede
prethodni *a.* antecedent
prethodni *a* former
prethodni *a.* previous
prethodnik *n* forerunner
prethodnik *n.* precursor
prethodnik *n.* predecessor
pretilost *n.* obesity
pretjerano čedna žena *n.* prude
pretjerano laskanje *n* adulation
pretjerano uslužan *a.* officious
pretjerati *v.t.* overdo
pretjerivati *v.t.* overact
pretplata *n.* subscription
pretpostaviti *v.i* guess
pretpostaviti *v.t.* presume

pretpostaviti *v.t.* presuppose
pretpostaviti *v.t.* suppose
pretpostaviti *v.t.* surmise
pretpostaviti *v.t.* assume
pretpostavka *n* conjecture
pretpostavka *n.* guess
pretpostavka *n.* presumption
pretpostavka *n.* supposition
pretpostavka *n.* surmise
pretpostavka *n.* assumption
pretpostavljanje *n.* presupposition
pretpostavljati *v. t* conjecture
pretraga *n.* search
pretrčati *v.t* overrun
pretresti *v.t.* ransack
pretrpjeti *v.t.* undergo
preturanje *n* rummage
preturati *v.i.* fumble
pretvaranje *n.* pretence
pretvarati se *v.t* feign
pretvarati se *v.t.* pretend
pretvarati se *v.i.* sham
pretvorbe *n* conversion
pretvoriti *v. t* convert
pretvoriti u kašu *v.t.* pulp
pretvoriti u stihove *v.t.* versify
preuveličavanje *n.* exaggeration
preuveličavati *v. t.* exaggerate
preuzeti *v.t.* shoulder
prevaga *n.* preponderance
prevagnuti *v.t.* out-balance
prevara *n* deception
prevara *n* eyewash
prevara *n.* fraud
prevara *n.* ruse
prevara *n.* bam
prevarantski *a* crook
prevariti *v.t.* hoodwink
prevariti *v.t.* swindle
prevariti *v.t.* trick

prevariti *v. t.* bilk
prevazići *v.t.* overcome
prevelik *a.* outsize
prevelika doza *n.* overdose
prevencija *n.* prevention
preventivan *a.* preventive
previdjeti *v.t.* overlook
prevlast *n.* predominance
prevlast *n.* prevalence
prevlast *n.* supremacy
prevodilac *n.* interpreter
prevoditi *v.t.* translate
prevođenje *n.* translation
prevoziti *v.t* ferry
prevoziti *v.t.* transport
prevremen *a.* premature
prevrnuti *v.t.* tip
prevrnuti *v. i.* capsize
prezasićenost *n* glut
prezasićenost *n.* surfeit
prezasititi *v.t.* glut
prezentacija *n.* presentation
prezervativ *n.* preservative
prezime *n.* surname
prezir *n* contempt
prezir *n* disdain
prezir *n.* scorn
prezirati *v. t* despise
prezirati *v. t.* disdain
prezirati *v.t.* loathe
prezirati *v.t.* scorn
prezriv *a* contemptuous
preživač *n.* ruminant
preživanje *v.i.* rummage
preživati *v.i.* ruminate
pribjeći *v.i.* resort
pribježište *n* resort
približan *a.* approximate
pribor *n* accessory
pribor *n. pl* paraphernalia

pribor *n.* tackle	**prijateljstvo** *n.* amity
pribor *n.* utensil	**prije** *prep* before
pribosti *v.t.* pin	**prije nego** *conj* before
pribranost *n.* composure	**prije** *prep.* afore
priča *n.* story	**prije** *adv.* ago
priča *n.* tale	**prijedlog** *n.* preposition
pričati *v.i.* talk	**prijedlog** *n.* proposal
pričljiv *a.* talkative	**prijedlog** *n.* proposition
pričvrstiti *v.t* fasten	**prijedlog** *n.* suggestion
pričvrstiti *v.t* key	**prijekor** *n.* reproach
pričvrstiti *v.t.* limber	**prijelaz** *n.* crossing
pričvrstiti klinom *v.t.* wedge	**prijelaz** *n.* transition
pričvrstiti *v.t.* affix	**prijelazni** *n.* transitive
pričvrstiti *v.t.* attach	**prijelom** *n.* fracture
pridev *n.* adjective	**prijem** *n.* reception
pridruženje *n.* affiliation	**prijemčiv** *a.* receptive
pridružiti *v.t.* join	**prijemnik** *n.* receiver
pridržavanje *n.* observance	**prijenos** *n* conveyance
prigodan *a.* pertinent	**prijenos** *n.* telecast
prigovarati *v.t.* reproach	**prijenos** *n.* transfer
prigovor *n.* objection	**prijestup** *n.* transgression
prigovoriti *v.t.* object	**prijestup** *n.* trespass
prigradski *a.* suburban	**prijestupnik** *n.* offender
prigrušeno se smijati *v. i* chuckle	**prijetiti** *v.t* menace
prigušen glas *n.* undertone	**prijetiti** *v.t.* threaten
prigušiti *v.t.* muffle	**prijetnja** *n* menace
prigušivač *n.* muffler	**prijetnja** *n.* threat
prigušivač *n.* silencer	**prijevara** *n* deceit
prihod *n* emolument	**prijevara** *n.* swindle
prihod *n.* income	**prijevoz** *n.* transport
prihod *n.* revenue	**prikazati** *v.t.* show
prihvaćanje *n* acceptance	**prikazati u profilu** *v.t.* profile
prihvatiti & accept	**prikazivanje** *n.* show
prihvatljiv *a* acceptable	**prikazivati** *v. t.* depict
prihvatljiv *a.* admissible	**prikladan** *a* expedient
prijatan *a* kind	**prikladan** fit
prijatan *a.* pleasant	**prikladan** *a.* opportune
prijatelj *n.* friend	**prikladan** *a.* seemly
prijatelj *n.* mate	**prikladan** *adj* apposite
prijateljski *adj.* amicable	**prikladan** *a.* appropriate

prikladno *adv* appositely
priklanjanje *n* deference
priključenje *n.* incorporation
priključiti *v.t.* incorporate
prikolica *n.* trailer
prikovati *v.t.* peg
prikradati *se v.i.* stalk
prikriti *v. t.* conceal
prikriven *a.* latent
prikriven *a.* ulterior
prikupiti *v. t* collect
prikupiti *v.t.* muster
prilagodba *n.* adjustment
prilagoditi *se v.t* acclimatise
prilagoditi *v.t.* adapt
prilagoditi *v.t.* adjust
prilagodljiv *a.* malleable
prilagođavanje *n.* adaptation
prilično *adv.* pretty
prilijepiti se *v. i.* cling
prilika *n.* occasion
prilika *n.* opportunity
priliv *n.* influx
prilog *n.* attachment
prilog *n.* enclosure
prilog *n.* adverb
priložiti *v. t* enclose
priložni *a.* adverbial
priljubljen *adj* cohesive
primatelj *n.* payee
primatelj *n.* recipient
primatelj *n.* addressee
primijećen *a.* notice
primijeniti *v. t.* enforce
primijeniti *v.t.* appropriate
primijetiti *v.t.* notice
primirje *n.* truce
primirje *n.* armistice
primitivan *a.* primitive
primjena *n.* usage

primjena *n.* application
primjeniti *v.t.* apply
primjenjiv *a.* applicable
primjer *n* example
primjer *n.* instance
primjerak *n.* specimen
primjeran *a.* apposite
primjetan *adj* perceptible
primjetan *a.* appreciable
primorski *a.* littoral
princ *n.* prince
princeza *n.* princess
princip *n.* principle
prinos *n* yield
prinuda *n* compulsion
prionuti *v.t.* tackle
priopćenje *n.* communiqué
priopćiti *v.t.* impart
prioritet *n.* priority
pripadanje *n* appurtenance
pripadati *v. i* belong
pripajanje *n* annexation
pripisati *v.t.* impute
pripisati *v.t.* ascribe
pripit *a.* mellow
pripit *a.* tipsy
pripitomiti *v.t.* tame
pripovijedati *v.t.* narrate
pripovijest *n.* narrative
pripovjedač *n.* narrator
pripovjedački *a.* narrative
pripravnik *n.* probationer
pripravnik *n.* trainee
priprema *n* preliminary
priprema *n.* preparation
pripremiti *v.t.* prepare
pripremni *a.* preparatory
priraštaj *n.* increment
prirediti *v.t.* stage
priroda *n.* nature

prirodni *a.* natural
prirodno *adv.* naturally
prirodnjak *n.* naturalist
priručnik *n.* handbook
priručnik *n* manual
prisilan *a* forcible
prisiliti *v. t* compel
prisnost *n.* rapport
pristajanje *n.* landing
pristalica *n.* stickler
pristanak *n.* consent
pristanak *n.* assent
pristanište *n.* dock
pristati *v.i.* assent
pristati *v. i* consent
pristati uz jednu stranu *v.i.* side
pristojan *a* becoming
pristojan *a* decent
pristojba *n.* toll
pristojba za vaganje *n.* weighage
pristojnost *n* decency
pristojnost *n* decorum
pristrasnost *n.* partiality
pristup *n* access
pristup *n.* admission
pristup *n.* approach
pristupanje *n* accession
pristupanje *n.* admittance
pristupiti *v.t.* accede
pristupiti *v.t.* approach
prisustvo *n.* presence
prisustvovati *v.t.* attend
prisutan *a.* present
prisvajanje *n.* appropriation
pritegnuti *v.t.* tighten
pritisak *n.* pressure
pritisnite *v.t.* press
pritisnuti *v. t* depress
pritoka *n.* tributary
pritvoren *adv.* ajar

priuštiti *v.t.* afford
privatni *a.* private
privatnost *n.* privacy
privezati *v.t.* tether
privići se *v.t.* accustom
prividan *a.* apparent
prividan *a* bogus
privilegija *n.* prerogative
privilegija *n.* privilege
privlačan *a.* attractive
privlačan *n.* sexy
privlačiti *v.t.* allure
privlačnost *n* allurement
privlačnost *n.* attraction
privoljeti *v.t.* consent3
privremen *a.* provisional
privremen *a.* temporary
privrženik *n* devotee
privrženik *n.* loyalist
privrženost *n.* adherence
privrženost *n* devotion
privući *v.t.* attract
prizivač duhova *n.* necromancer
prizivanje *n.* invocation
prizivati *v.t.* conjure
prizivati *v.t.* invoke
priznanica *n* bill
priznanje *n.* acknowledgement
priznanje *n* confession
priznati *v. t.* confess
priznati *v.* acknowledge
priznati *v.t.* admit
prkos *n* defiance
prljav *a* dirty
prljav *a* filthy
prljav *a.* sordid
proba *n.* probation
proba *n.* rehearsal
probati *v.t.* rehearse
problem *n.* problem

problematičan a. problematic

probni a. tentative

probosti v.t. jab

probosti kopljem v.t. spear

probuditi v.t. awake

probuditi v.t. wake

probuditi se v.i. rouse

probušiti v.t hole

probušiti v.t. perforate

probušiti v.t. puncture

procedura n. procedure

proces n. process

proći v.i. pass

procijeniti v.t. rate

procijeniti v.t. appraise

procijeniti v.t. assess

procjena n. estimate

procjena n estimation

procjena n. valuation

procjena n. assessment

procjeniti v. t estimate

procvat n blossom

pročišćenje n. purgation

pročišćavajući a laxative

prodaja n. sale

prodavac knjiga n book-seller

prodavaonica n. store

prodavatelj n. monger

prodavatelj n. salesman

prodavatelj n. seller

prodavatelj n. vendor

prodavati v.t. sell

prodavati robu na malo v.t. retail

prodavnica n. shop

prodor n breach

prodrijeti v.t. penetrate

produkt n. product

produktivan a. productive

produktivnost n. productivity

produljiti v.t. lengthen

produženje n. prolongation

produžiti v.t. prolong

profesija n. profession

profesionalan a. professional

profesor n. professor

profil n. profile

profitabilan a. profitable

profiter n. profit

profiter n. profiteer

profitirati v.t. profit

proganjanje n. persecution

proglas n. proclamation

proglasiti v. t. declare

proglasiti v.t. proclaim

prognati v. t exile

prognati v.t. ostracize

progoniti v.t. haunt

progoniti v.t. persecute

progoniti v.t. pursue

progonstvo n. exile

program n. programme

programirati v.t. programme

progresivan a. progressive

progutati v.t engulf

progutati v.t. swallow

prohladno a chilly

proizilaziti v.i ensue

proizlaziti v.i. result

proizvod n. produce

proizvoditi v.t fabricate

proizvoditi v.t. manufacture

proizvoditi v.t. produce

proizvodnja n fabrication

proizvodnja n manufacture

proizvodnja n. production

proizvođač n manufacturer

proizvoljno a. arbitrary

projekat n. project

projekcija n. projection

projektil n. missile

projektil *n.* projectile
projektirati *v.t.* project
projektor *n.* projector
proklet *a.* accursed
prokleti *v. t* curse
prokleti *v. t.* damn
prokletstvo *n.* damnation
prokletstvo *n.* malediction
prokrijumčariti *v.t.* smuggle
prokurator *n.* proctor
prolaz *n* pass
prolaz *n.* thoroughfare
prolazan *n.* transitory
prolaziti *v. t* elapse
proleće *n* spring
prolivanje *n* spill
prolog *n.* prologue
proljetni *a.* vernal
promašaj *n.* miss
promašiti *v.t.* miss
promatrački *a.* observant
promatranje *n.* observation
promatrati *v.t.* observe
promijena *n.* change
promijeniti *v. t.* change
promišljen *a.* considerate
promišljen *a.* prudential
promišljenost *n* forethought
promjena *n.* variance
promjenljiv *a* fickle
promjer *n* diameter
promocija *n.* promotion
promovirati *v.t.* promote
promrmljati *v.i.* mutter
promukao *a.* hoarse
pronalazač *n.* inventor
pronalazački *a.* inventive
pronalazak *n.* invention
pronevjera *n.* misappropriation
pronevjeriti *v.t.* misappropriate

pronicljiv *a.* apprehensive
proniknuti *v.t* fathom
propadanje *n* decline
propadati *v. t.* decline
propaganda *n.* propaganda
propagator *n.* propagandist
propagirati *v.t.* propagate
propast *n* doom
propast *n.* rack
propast *n.* ruin
propis *n.* regulation
propisati *v.t.* prescribe
propisno *adv* duly
proporcija *n.* proportion
proporcionalan *a.* proportional
propovijed *n.* sermon
propovijedati *v.i.* preach
propovijedati *v.i.* sermonize
propovjedaonica *a.* pulpit
propovjednik *n.* preacher
propust *n* lapse
propustiti *v.i.* lapse
proračun *n.* calculation
proreći *v.t.* prophesy
proreći *v.t* foretell
proricanje *n.* auspice
proricati *v.t.* auspicate
proročanski *a.* oracular
proročanstvo *n.* oracle
proročanstvo *n.* prophecy
proročki *a.* prophetic
prorok *n.* prophet
prosijati *v.i.* riddle
prosijati *v.t.* sieve
prosilac *n.* suitor
prosinac *n* december
prosjačiti *v. i* cadge
prosjak *n* beggar
prosječan *a.* average
prosjek *n.* average

proso *n.* millet
prospekt *n* brochure
prospekt *n.* prospectus
prost *čovjek n.* commoner
prostitucija *n.* prostitution
prostituirati *v.t.* prostitute
prostitutka *n.* prostitute
prostitutka *n.* whore
prostor *n.* space
prostorni *a.* spatial
prostran *a.* roomy
prostran *a.* spacious
prostran *a.* capacious
prosuti *v.i.* spill
prosvijetliti *v. t.* enlighten
prosvjetitelj *n.* luminary
proširenje *n.* expansion
proširiti *v.t.* expand
proširiti *v. t* extend
proširiti *v.t.* widen
prošli *a.* past
prošlost *n.* antecedent
prošlost *n.* past
protagonista *n.* protagonist
protein *n.* protein
protektirana guma *n.* retread
protektirati gumu *v.t.* retread
protest *n.* protest
protest *n.* protestation
protestovati *v.i.* protest
protiv *pref.* contra
protiv *prep.* versus
protivan *a.* averse
protiviti se *v.t.* antagonize
protivljenje *n.* antagonism
protivnik *n.* antagonist
protivnik *n.* opponent
protivnik *n.* rival
protivnik *n.* adversary
protjerati *v. t* evict

protjerati *v.t.* banish
protjerivanje *n.* banishment
protjerivanje *n* eviction
protok *n* flow
prototip *n.* prototype
protuavionski *a.* anti-aircraft
protumačiti *v.t.* interpret
protuotrov *n.* mithridate
protuotrov *n.* antidote
proturječiti *v. t* contradict
protutužba *n.* countercharge
protuzakonit *a.* illicit
prouzrokovati *v.t* occasion
provala *n.* irruption
provala *n* burglary
provalnik *n* burglar
provera *n* check
proveriti *v. t.* check
provesti *v.t.* spend
provesti *v.t.* while
proviđenje *n.* providence
provincija *n.* province
provincijalizam *n.* provincialism
provincijski *a.* provincial
provizija *n.* commission
provocirati *v.t.* provoke
provokacija *n.* provocation
provokativan *a.* provocative
proza *n.* prose
prozaičan *a.* prosaic
prozivka *n.* roll-call
prozodija *n.* prosody
prozor *n.* window
proždirati *v. t* devour
proždrljiv *a.* voracious
proždrljivac *n.* glutton
proždrljivost *n.* gluttony
prožimati *v.t.* pervade
prsa *n* chest
prskanje *n* splash

prskati *v.t.* spray	**pubertet** *n.* puberty
prsluk *n.* vest	**publicitet** *n.* publicity
prsluk *n.* waistcoat	**pucanje** *n* shoot
prsluk *n* bodice	**pucati** *v.i.* pop
prst *n* finger	**pucati** *v.t.* shoot
prsten *n.* ring	**pucketati** *v. t* brustle
prstenčić *n.* ringlet	**pucketati** *v. i* crack
prstenčić *n* annulet	**pucketati** *v.t.* crackle
prtljag *n.* luggage	**pučina** *n.* offing
prtljag *n.* baggage	**puding** *n.* pudding
pruga *n.* stripe	**puhanje** *n* blow
prut *n.* withe	**puhati** *v.i.* blow
pružanje *n.* offering	**puk** *n.* regiment
pružiti utočište *v.t* harbour	**puki** *a.* mere
prvak *n.* champion	**pukotina** *n* fissure
prvenstveno *adv.* primarily	**pukotina** *n* gap
prvi *a* first	**pukotina** *n.* rift
prvi *n* first	**pukotina** *n* split
prvo *adv* first	**pukovnik** *n.* colonel
prvoklasan *a.* sterling	**pulover** *n.* pullover
pržiti *v.t.* fry	**pulpa** *n.* pulp
psalm *n.* psalm	**puls** *n.* pulse
pseudonim *n.* pseudonym	**puls** *n* pulse
pseudonim *n.* alias	**pulsacija** *n.* pulsation
psiha *n.* psyche	**pulsirati** *v.i.* pulse
psihički *a.* psychic	**pumpa** *n.* pump
psihijatar *n.* psychiatrist	**pumpati** *v.t.* pump
psihijatrija *n.* psychiatry	**pun** *a.* full
psiholog *n.* psychologist	**pun nade** *a.* hopeful
psihologija *n.* psychology	**pun poštovanja** *a.* respectful
psihološki *a.* psychological	**pun poštovanja** *a.* reverent
psihopata *n.* psychopath	**pun poštovanja** *a.* reverential
psihoterapija *n.* psychotherapy	**pun šavova** *a.* seamy
psihoza *n.* psychosis	**puna žlica** *n.* spoonful
psovati *v. t.* chide	**punč** *n.* punch
psovati *v.t.* swear	**punionica** *n* bottler
pšenica *n.* wheat	**puniti** *v. t.* charge
ptica pjevačica *n.* warbler	**puno** *adv.* full
ptica *n* bird	**punoća** *n.* fullness
ptičar *n.* fowler	**punjenje** *n.* charge

punjenje *n.* padding
puplin *n.* poplin
pupoljak *n* bud
purgativ *n.* purgative
purgativan *a* purgative
purista *n.* purist
puritanac *n.* puritan
puritanski *a.* puritanical
pust *a.* waste
pustinja *n* desert
pustinjačka stanica *n.* hermitage
pustinjak *n.* hermit
pustinjak *n.* recluse
pustiti *v.t.* release
pustolovan *a.* adventurous
pustoš *n.* havoc
pustošenje *n.* ravage
pustošiti *v.t.* ravage
pustošiti *v.t.* waste
pušiti se *v.i.* smoke
puška *n* rifle
puškarnica *n.* loop-hole
puštanje *n* release
put *n.* path
put *n.* road
put *n.* route
putarina *n.* cartage
putnik *n.* passenger
putnik *n.* traveller
putnik *n.* voyager
putnik *n.* wayfarer
putovanje *n.* journey
putovanje *n* travel
putovanje *n.* trek
putovanje *n.* trip
putovanje *n.* voyage
putovati *v.i.* journey
putovati *v.i.* tour
putovati *v.i.* travel
putovati *v.i.* voyage

putovnica *n.* passport
putujući *adj* ambulant
puzanje *n* crawl
puzati *v. i* creep
puzati *v. i.* cringe
puzati *v.t.* trail
puzavac *n* creeper
puziti *v. t* crawl
puž *n.* snail

R

rabat *n.* rebate
racija *n.* raid
racionalan *a.* rational
racionalizirati *v.t.* rationalize
racionalnost *n.* rationality
račun *n.* count
račun *n.* receipt
račun *n.* account
računanje *n.* computation
računati *v.t.* compute
računati *v. t.* count
računati *v.t.* reckon
računovodstvo *n.* accountancy
računovođa *n.* accountant
rad *n.* labour
rad *n.* work
radan *a.* painstaking
radij *n.* radium
radije *adv.* rather
radikalan *a.* radical
radio *n.* radio
radio *n* wireless
radionica *n.* workshop
raditi *v.i.* labour
raditi *v.t.* operate
raditi *v.t.* work
radna soba *n.* study

radni sto n desk
radnik n. labourer
radnik n. worker
radnik n. workman
radno odijelo n. smock
radnja modistkinje n. millinery
radost n. glee
radost n. joy
radostan a. glad
radostan a. jolly
radostan n. joyful, joyous
radovati se v.i. rejoice
radoznalost n curiosity
radoznao a curious
radoznao a. inquisitive
rađanje n. nativity
rafinerija n. refinery
rahitičan a. rickety
rahitis n. rickets
raj n. paradise
rak n. cancer
raketa n. rocket
rakija n brandy
rame n. shoulder
ran adv early
rana n sore
rana n. wound
randevu n. rendezvous
rang n. rank
rangirati v.t. rank
ranije adv. before
ranije adv formerly
raniji a. prior
raniji datum n. antedate
raniti v.t. wound
rano a early
rano djetinjstvo n. infancy
ranjiv a. sore
ranjiv a. vulnerable
rapir n. rapier

rascepiti v.t. splinter
rascepiti v.i. split
rascjep n cleft
rashladiti v.t. refrigerate
rashod n expenditure
rasipan a. prodigal
rasipan a. profligate
rasipan a. wasteful
rasipanje n. wastage
rasipnik n. spendthrift
rasipnost n. prodigality
rasizam n. racialism
raskalašan a. wanton
raskalašnost n. profligacy
raskid n. rupture
raskinuti v.t. rupture
raskol n. schism
raskoš n. luxuriance
raskoš n. pomp
raskošan a. lavish
raskošan a. luxuriant
raskošan a. sumptuous
raskrsnica n. intersection
raskrsnica n. junction
rasni a. racial
rasol n brine
raspadanje decay
raspadati v. i decay
raspaliti v.t. inflame
raspaljiv a. inflammatory
raspeće n. rood
raspitati se v.t. inquire
raspodijeliti v.t. apportion
raspodjela n. allocation
raspojasan a. licentious
raspolaganje n disposal
raspolagati v. t dispose
raspoloženje n. mood
raspoloživ a available
raspon n. circumference

raspon *n.* span
raspor *n.* slit
raspored *n.* schedule
rasporediti *v.t.* array
rasporediti *v. t* co-ordinate
rasporediti *v.t.* regiment
rasporediti *v.t.* schedule
rasporiti *v.t.* slit
rasprava *n.* argument
rasprava *n.* treatise
raspraviti *v. t.* canvass
raspravljati *v.t.* argue
rasprostranjen *a.* widespread
raspustiti *v.t.* prorogue
rast *n.* growth
rastaviti *v.t.* sunder
rastavljanje *n.* decomposition
rasteretiti *v.t.* unburden
rastezanje *n* stretch
rastezati *v.t.* stretch
rasti *v.t.* grow
rasti *v.t.* wax
rastojanje *n* distance
rastopiti *v.t.* fuse
rastopiti *v.t.* liquefy
rastopiti *v.i.* melt
rastrgnuti *v.t.* lacerate
rasturiti *v.t.* scatter
rastužiti *v.t.* sadden
rastvoriti *v.t* dissolve
rastvorljivost *n.* solubility
rasuti *v. t* disperse
raščlanjen *a.* articulate
rat *n.* war
ratarstvo *n.* husbandry
ratificirati *v.t.* ratify
ratnik *n.* warrior
ratoboran *a.* militant
ratoboran *a.* warlike
ratoboran *a* bellicose

ratoboran *a* belligerent
ratovanje *n.* warfare
ratovati *v.i.* militate
ratovati *v.i.* war
ravan *a* even
ravan *a* flat
ravan *n.* plain
ravan *a.* plane
ravnica *n.* plane
ravnina *n* flat
ravnodušan *a.* indifferent
ravnodušnost *n.* indifference
ravnopravnost *n* equal
ravnoteža *n* poise
ravnoteža *n.* balance
razaranje *n* destruction
razbacati *v.t.* winnow
razbesneti *v. t* enrage
razbijanje *n* smash
razbiti *v.t.* rout
razbiti *v.t.* shatter
razbiti *v.t.* smash
razbjesneti *v.t.* infuriate
razboj *n* loom
razbojnik *n.* bandit
razbojnik *n.* dacoit
razbojnik *n.* thug
razbojništvo *n.* dacoity
razborit *a.* judicious
razborit *a.* prudent
razborit *a.* sage
razboritost *n.* prudence
razdijeliti *v.t.* parcel
razdoblje *n.* innings
razdragan *a.* mirthful
razdraganost *n.* mirth
razdražljiv *a.* irritable
razdvajanje *n.* separation
razdvajanje *n.* severance
razglasiti *v.t.* rumour

razgledati *v.t.* view
razgolititi *v.t.* bare
razgovarati *v.t.* converse
razgovor *n* conversation
razgovor *n* talk
razgraničenje *n.* demarcation
razina *n.* level
razjasniti *v. t* clarify
razjasniti *v. t* clear
razjašnjenje *n* clarification
različit *a* different
različit *a* dissimilar
različit *a* diverse
različit *a.* various
razlika *n* difference
razlika *n* distinction
razlikovati *v. t.* discriminate
razlikovati *v. i* distinguish
razlikovati se *v. i* differ
razlog *n.* reason
razložiti *v. t.* decompose
razmatranje *n* consideration
razmatranje *n* deliberation
razmatrati *v. i* deliberate
razmaziti *v.t.* pamper
razmeniti *v. t* exchange
razmetanje *n* strut
razmetati se *v.i.* strut
razmijeniti *v.* interchange
razmišljanje *n* contemplation
razmišljanje *n.* rumination
razmišljati *v. t* contemplate
razmišljati *v.i.* muse
razmišljati *v.t.* ponder
razmjena *n* exchange
razmjena *n.* interchange
razmjeran *a.* proportionate
razmnožavanje *n.* proliferation
razmnožiti se *v.i.* proliferate
razmotriti *v. t* consider

raznolik *a.* multifarious
raznolik *n.* multiform
raznolik *a.* varied
raznovrsnost *n.* variety
razočarati *v. t.* disappoint
razonoda *n.* pastime
razoriti *v.i* blast
razoružanje *n.* disarmament
razoružati *v. t* disarm
razraditi *v. t* elaborate
razrađen *a* elaborate
razred *n.* grade
razrokost *n·* squint
razrokost *v.i.* squint
razrušiti *v.t.* raze
razum *n.* sanity
razuman *a.* reasonable
razuman *a.* sane
razuman *a.* sensible
razumijevanje *n.* apprehension
razumjeti *v.t.* understand
razvedriti *v. t* brighten
razvesti *v. t* divorce
razvesti se *v.t.* repudiate
razviti *v. t.* develop
razvod *n* divorce
razvod *n.* repudiation
razvodniti *v. t* dilute
razvodnjen *a* dilute
razvoj *n.* development
razvrat *n* debauchery
razvratan *a.* lewd
razvratnik *n* debauchee
razvratnost *n.* obscenity
razvrstati *v. t* classify
raž *n.* rye
rđa *n.* rust
rđati *v.i* rust
reagirati *v.i.* react
reakcija *n.* reaction

reakcionaran a. reactionary
realista n. realist
realističan a. realistic
realizacija n. realization
realizam n. realism
realizirati v.t. realize
realnost n. reality
rebreni adj. costal
rebro n. rib
recept n. prescription
recept n. recipe
recesija n. recession
reći n. say
reći v.t. tell
recipročan a. reciprocal
recitacija n. recitation
recital n. recital
recitovati v.t. recite
rečenica n. sentence
rečnik n dictionary
red n. array
red n. order
red n. queue
red n. row
red n trim
redovan a. ordinary
redovan a. regular
redovito adv. ordinarily
referenca n. reference
referendum n. referendum
refleks n. reflex
refleksan a reflex
refleksivan a. meditative
reflektor n. reflector
reflektujuće a. reflective
reforma n. reform
reformacija n. reformation
reformator n. reformer
reformirati v.t. reform
refren n. chorus

refren n refrain
regeneracija n. regeneration
regenerirati v.t. regenerate
regij n. region
regionalni a. regional
registar n. register
registar n. registry
registracija n. registration
registrirati v.t. register
regres n. recourse
regrut n. recruit
regrutirati v. t enlist
regrutovati v.t. recruit
regulator n. regulator
regulirati v.t. regulate
rehabilitacija n. rehabilitation
rehabilititati v.t. rehabilitate
reket n. racket
rekla-kazala n. hearsay
reklamacija n reclamation
rekreacija n. recreation
rektum n. rectum
rekvijem n. requiem
relativan a. relative
relej n. relay
relevantan a. relevant
relevantnost n. relevance
religija n. religion
relikvija n. relic
reljef n. relief
remek-djelo n. masterpiece
remi n. rummy
rendgen n. x-ray
rendgenski a. x-ray
renesansa n. renaissance
renome n. renown
renovirati v.t. renovate
renta n. annuity
rentijer n annuitant
rep n. tail

repa *n.* turnip
repa *n* beet
replika *n.* replica
reprezentativan *a.* representative
reproducirati *v.t.* reproduce
reprodukcija *n* reproduction
reproduktivan *a.* reproductive
reptil *n.* reptile
republika *n.* republic
republikanac *n* republican
republikanski *a.* republican
resa *n.* fringe
restauracija *n.* restoration
restoran *n.* restaurant
restriktivan *a.* restrictive
resurs *n.* resource
rešetka *n.* grate
rešetka *n.* lattice
retardiranost *n.* retardation
retorički *a.* rhetorical
retorika *n.* rhetoric
retorta *n.* crevet
retrospekcija *n.* retrospection
retrospektiva *n.* retrospect
retrospektivan *a.* retrospective
retuširati *v.t.* retouch
reumatizam *n.* rheumatism
reumatski *a.* rheumatic
revidirati *v.t.* audit
revizija *n.* revision
revizija *n.* audit
revizor *n.* auditor
revnost *n* bigotry
revnost *n.* zeal
revnostan *a.* zealous
revolucija *n.* revolution
revolucionar *n* revolutionary
revolucionaran *a.* revolutionary
revolver *n.* revolver
rez *n* cut

reza *n* bolt
rezač *n.* sharpener
rezati *v. t* cut
rezati *v.t.* lop
rezati *v.t.* trench
rezbariti *v. t.* carve
rezervat *n.* reservation
rezervisati *v.t.* reserve
rezervni *a* spare
rezervni dio *n.* spare
rezervoar *n.* reservoir
rezervoar *n.* tank
rezidentan *a.* resident
rezime *n* abstract
rezimirati *v.t.* resume
rezimirati *v.t.* summarize
rezolucija *n.* resolution
rezonanca *n.* resonance
rezonantan *a.* resonant
rezultat *n.* result
režanje *n* growl
režanje *n.* snarl
režati *v.i.* growl
režati *v.i.* snarl
režim *n.* regime
riba *n* fish
ribar *n* fisherman
ribizla *n.* currant
ribnjak *n.* pond
ricinusovo ulje *n.* castor oil
rigidan *a.* rigid
rigorozan *a.* rigorous
riječ *v.t.* say
riječ *v.t* word
riječ *n.* word
rijedak *a.* rare
rijedak *a.* scarce
rijeka *n.* river
riješiti *v.t.* resolve
riješiti *v.t.* solve

rijetko *adv.* seldom
rika *n.* roar
rikati *v.i.* roar
rikša *n.* rickshaw
rilo *n.* snout
rima *n.* rhyme
rimovati se *v.i.* rhyme
rintanje *n.* toil
rintati *v.i.* toil
ris papira *n.* ream
riskantan *a.* venturesome
riskiranje *n* nap
riskirati *v.t* hazard
riskirati *v.t.* risk
ritam *n.* rhythm
riti *v. t.* bury
ritmičan *a.* rhythmic
ritual *n.* ritual
ritualni *a.* ritual
rivalstvo *n.* rivalry
rizičan *a.* risky
rizik *n.* hazard
rizik *n.* risk
riža *n.* paddy
riža *n.* rice
rječit *a* eloquent
rječitost *n* eloquence
rječnik *n.* glossary
rječnik *n.* vocabulary
rješenje *n.* solution
rob *n.* slave
rob *n.* thrall
roba *n.* commodity
roba *n.* merchandise
roba *n.* ware
robot *n.* robot
robovati *v.i.* slave
roda *n.* stork
rodbina *n.* kin
roditelj *n.* parent

roditeljoubojstvo *n.* parricide
roditeljski *a.* parental
roditeljstvo *n.* parentage
roditi *v.* born
roditi *v.t* breed
rodni *a.* natal
rođak *n.* cousin
rođak *n.* relative
rođen bogat *adj.* born rich
rođenje *n.* birth
rog *n.* horn
rog *n.* antler
rogonja *n.* cuckold
roj *n.* swarm
rojalistički *n.* royalist
rojiti se *v.i.* swarm
rok *n.* term
roktanje *v.i.* grunt
roktati *n.* grunt
rolna *n.* roll
roman *n* novel
romanopisac *n.* novelist
romantičan *a.* romantic
romantika *n.* romance
rominjati *v. i* drizzle
roniti *v. i* dive
ronjenje *n* dive
ronjenje *n* plunge
ropski *a.* slavish
ropstvo *n.* slavery
ropstvo *n.* thraldom
ropstvo *n* bondage
rosa *n.* dew
rotacija *n.* rotation
rotacijski *a.* rotary
rotirati *v.i.* rotate
rotkvica *n.* radish
rov *n.* sap
rov *n.* trench
rožnica *n* cornea

rt *n.* cape
rub *n.* list
rub *n.* verge
rub *n.* brink
rubin *n.* ruby
rublja *n.* rouble
rublje *n.* laundry
ručak *n.* lunch
ručati *v.i.* lunch
ručka *n.* handle
ručna burgija *n.* wimble
ručni rad *n.* handiwork
ručni zglob *n.* wrist
ručnik *n.* towel
ručno *a.* manual
ruda *n.* ore
rudar *n.* miner
rudnik *n* mine
ruganje *n* gibe
ruganje *n.* scoff
rugati se *v.i.* gibe
rugati se *v.i.* jeer
rugati se *v.i.* scoff
ruho *n.* attire
rujan *n.* September
ruka *n.* arm
rukav *n* sleeve
rukavica *n.* glove
rukavica bez prstiju *n.* mitten
rukopis *n.* manuscript
rukotvorina *n.* handicraft
rukovati *v.t* handle
rukovati *v.t.* wield
rukovoditi *v.t.* superintend
rum *n.* rum
rumen *a.* rosy
rumenilo *n* flush
rumenilo *n* blush
runo *n* fleece
rupa *n* hole

rupa *n.* puncture
rupica *n* eyelet
rupija *n.* rupee
rušenje *n* overthrow
ruševina *n* debris
rutina *n.* routine
rutinski *a* routine
ruža *n.* rose
ružan *a.* ugly
ružičast *a* pink
ružičast *a.* pinkish
ružičast *a.* roseate
ružičnjak, brojanice *n.* rosary
ružnoća *n.* ugliness
rvanje *n.* grapple
rvati se *v.i.* grapple
rzanje *n.* neigh
rzati *v.i.* neigh

S

sa *prep.* with
sabat *n.* sabbath
sablast *n* bogle
sablja *n.* sabre
sabotaža *n.* sabotage
sabotirati *v.t.* sabotage
saće *n.* honeycomb
sačuvati *v.t.* preserve
sačuvati *v.t.* save
sada *conj.* now
sada *adv.* now
sadista *n.* sadist
saditi *v.t.* plant
sadizam *n.* sadism
sadržaj *n* content
sadržati *v.t.* contain
sadržitelj *n* multiple
safir *n.* sapphire

saharin *n.* saccharin
sahrana *n.* funeral
sahrana *n.* sepulture
sajam *n.* fair
sakaćenje *n.* mutilation
sakatiti *v.t.* mutilate
sakrament *n.* sacrament
sakriti *v.t* hide
sakriti se *v.i.* cower
sakriti se *v.i.* darkle
sakrivanje *n.* hide
salata *n.* salad
salo *n.* lard
salon *n* drawing-room
salto *n.* somersault
salveta *n.* napkin
sam am
sam *a.* solo
sam *a.* alone
samac *n.* single
samo *adv.* only
samo što *conj.* only
samoglasnik *n.* vowel
samoispitivanje *n.* introspection
samostan *n.* cloister
samostan *n.* nunnery
samoubilački *a.* suicidal
samoubojstvo *n.* suicide
samouvjeren *a.* confident
samozadovoljan *adj.* complacent
samozadovoljan *a.* smug
san *n* dream
san *n.* sleep
sanatorij *n.* sanatorium
sandala *n.* sandal
sandalovina *n.* sandalwood
sanduk *n.* crate
sangviničan *a.* sanguine
sanitarni *a.* sanitary
sankcija *n.* sanction

sankcionirati *v.t.* sanction
santa leda *n.* iceberg
sanjalački *a.* shadowy
sanjarenje *n.* reverie
sanjati *v. i.* dream
saobraćaj *n.* traffic
saosećajan *a.* sympathetic
sapun *n.* soap
sapunast *a.* soapy
sarađivati *v.t.* associate
sarkastičan *a.* sarcastic
sarkazam *n.* sarcasm
saslušavanje *n.* interrogation
saslušavati *v.t.* interrogate
sastanak *n.* meeting
sastanak *n.* tryst
sastanak u četiri oka *n.* tete-a-tete
sastav *n* composition
sastav *n* compound
sastav *n.* texture
sastaviti *v. t* compile
sastaviti *v. t* compose
sastaviti *v. i* compound
sastaviti *v.t.* piece
sastaviti *v.t.* assemble
sastavljač *n.* compounder
sastavni *adj.* component
sastavni *adj.* constituent
sastojak *n.* ingredient
sastojati se *v. i* consist
sasvim *adv.* quite
sat *n.* clock
sat *n.* hour
sat *n.* watch
satelit *n.* satellite
satira *n.* lampoon
satira *n.* satire
satiričan *a.* satirical
satiričar *n.* satirist
satirizovati *v.t.* satirize

saučesnik *n* accomplice
saučešće *n* condolence
sav *a.* all
savez *n.* alliance
saveznik *n.* ally
savijanje *n* bend
savijati *v.t.* crankle
saviti *v.t* fold
saviti *v. t* bend
savitljiv *a.* supple
savjest *n* conscience
savjestan *a* dutiful
savjet *n.* council
savjet *n.* counsel
savjet *n.* tip
savjet *n* advice
savjetnik *n.* counsellor
savjetovati *v. t.* counsel
savjetovati *v.t.* tip
savjetovati *v.t.* advise
savladati *v.t.* master
savladati *v.t.* overwhelm
savladati *v.t.* surmount
savršen *a.* perfect
savršenstvo *n.* perfection
sazivač *n* convener
sazivanje *n.* convocation
sazivati *v.t.* convoke
sazrijevati *v.i.* ripen
sazvati *v. t* convene
sazvježđe *n.* asterism
sažaljenje *n.* pity
sažaljevati *v.t.* pity
sažaljiv *a.* pitiful
sažet *a* summary
sažet *a.* terse
sažetak *n.* resume
sažetak *n.* summary
sažeti *v.t* abstract
sažeti *v. t.* compress

sažetost *n* brevity
scena *n.* scene
scenski *a.* scenic
sebe *pron.* myself
sebičan *a.* selfish
sećanje *n.* remembrance
secesionista *n.* secessionist
seciranje *n* dissection
secirati *v. t* dissect
seći *v. t* chop
seći *v.t.* intersect
seći *v.t.* poll
seći *v.t.* slice
sedam *n.* seven
sedamdeset *n., a* seventy
sedamdeseti *a.* seventieth
sedamnaest *n., a* seventeen
sedamnaesti *a.* seventeenth
sedativ *n* sedative
sedlo *n.* saddle
sedmi *a.* seventh
sedmo- *a* seven
segment *n.* segment
segmentirati *v.t.* segment
segregacija *n.* segregation
seizmički *a.* seismic
sejati *v.t.* sow
sekiracija *n* vexation
seksualan *a.* sexual
seksualnost *n.* sexuality
sekta *n.* sect
sektaški *a.* sectarian
sektor *n.* sector
sekunda *n* second
sekundaran *a.* secondary
sekvenca *n.* sequence
selektivan *a.* selective
seliti se *v.i.* trek
selo *n.* village
seljak *n.* peasant

seljak *n* rustic
seljak *n.* villager
seljaštvo *n.* peasantry
sem ako *conj.* unless
sem toga *adv.* withal
sem toga *adv* besides
semestar *n.* semester
seminar *n.* seminar
senat *n.* senate
senator *n.* senator
senatorski *a.* senatorial
senatski *a* senatorial
sendvič *n.* sandwich
senf *n.* mustard
senilan *a.* senile
senilnost *n.* senility
senior *n.* senior
senka *n.* shadow
seno *n.* hay
sentimentalan *a.* sentimental
senzacija *n.* sensation
senzacionalan *a.* sensational
senzualan *a.* sensual
seoba *n.* transmigration
seoce *n.* hamlet
seoski *a.* rural
seoski *a.* rustic
seosko dvorište *n.* barton
separabilan *a.* separable
sepsa *n.* sepsis
septičan *a.* septic
septička jama *n.* cesspool
serija *n.* series
serija *n* batch
serijski *a.* serial
serpentina *n.* serpentine
servilan *a.* menial
servilan *a.* servile
servilnost *n.* servility
servis *n.* serve

servisirati *v.t* service
serž *n.* serge
sestra *n.* sister
sestrinski *a.* sisterly
sestrinstvo *n.* sisterhood
sezona *n.* season
sezonski *a.* seasonal
sfera *n.* sphere
sferni *a.* spherical
shema *n.* scheme
shvatiti *v.t.* apprehend
shvatljiv *a.* intelligible
sićušnost *adv.* smallness
sićušan *a.* tiny
sidrište *n.* moorings
sidro *n.* anchor
signal *n.* signal
signalizirati *v.t.* signal
siguran *a.* safe
siguran *a.* secure
siguran *a.* sure
sigurno *adv.* certainly
sigurno *adv.* surely
sigurnost *n.* safe
sijati *v.i.* glitter
sijati *v.i.* glow
sijati *v.t.* sift
siktanje *n* hiss
siktati *v.i* hiss
sila *n* force
silazak *n.* descent
siledžija *n* bully
siledžija *n.* ruffian
siliti *v.t* force
silom *adv.* perforce
silovanje *n.* rape
silovati *v.t.* rape
silueta *n.* silhouette
simbol *n.* symbol
simboličan *a.* symbolic

simbolizam *n.* symbolism
simbolizirati *v.t.* symbolize
simetričan *a.* symmetrical
simetrija *n.* symmetry
simfonija *n.* symphony
simpatičan *a.* lovable
simpatija *n.* sympathy
simpozijum *n.* symposium
simptom *n.* symptom
simptomatičan *a.* symptomatic
sin *n.* son
singlirati *v.t.* single
sinonim *n.* synonym
sinoniman *a.* synonymous
sinopsis *n.* synopsis
sintaksa *n.* syntax
sintetički *a.* synthetic
sintetika *n* synthetic
sinteza *n.* synthesis
sipati *v.i.* pour
sir *n.* cheese
sirće *n.* vinegar
sirena *n.* mermaid
sirena *n.* siren
siroče *n.* orphan
siromah *n.* pauper
siromašan *a.* needy
siromaštvo *n.* poverty
sirotinjski kraj *n.* slum
sirotište *n.* orphanage
sirov *a* crude
sirov *a.* raw
sirup *n.* syrup
sisa *n.* teat
sisanje *n.* suck
sisar *n.* mammal
sisati *v.t.* suck
sistem *n.* system
sistematičan *a.* systematic
sistematizirati *v.t.* systematize

sitan *a.* petty
sitnica *n.* jot
sitnica *n.* trifle
sito *n.* sieve
sitost *n.* satiety
situacija *n.* situation
siva *a.* grey
sjaj *n* glitter
sjaj *n.* gloss
sjaj *n* glow
sjaj *n.* lustre
sjaj *n* polish
sjaj *n.* radiance
sjaj *n.* refulgence
sjaj *n* shine
sjaj *n.* sparkle
sjaj *n.* splendour
sjajan *a.* glossy
sjajan *a.* lustrous
sjajan *a.* radiant
sjajan *a.* refulgent
sjajan *a.* resplendent
sjajan *a.* splendid
sjajiti *v.i.* sparkle
sjećanje *n.* recollection
sjedeći *a.* sedentary
sjediniti *v.t. & i.* conjugate
sjedište *n.* seat
sjediti *v.i.* sit
sjednica *n.* session
sjekira *n.* hatchet
sjekira *n.* axe
sjeme *n.* seed
sjeme *n.* semen
sjenica *n* bower
sjesti *v.t.* seat
sjetiti se *v.t.* recollect
sjever *n.* north
sjeverni *a* north
sjeverni *a.* northerly

sjeverni *a.* northern
sjeverno *adv.* north
sjeverno *adv.* northerly
skakanje *n* hop
skakati *v.i.* romp
skakavac *n.* locust
skala *n.* scale
skalp *n* scalp
skandal *n* scandal ·
skandalizovati *v.t.* scandalize
skeč *n.* skit
skele *n.* scaffold
skelet *n.* skeleton
skenirati *v.t.* scan
skepticizam *n.* scepticism
skeptičan *a.* sceptical
skeptik *n.* sceptic
skica *n* draft
skica *n.* outline
skica *n.* sketch
skicirati *v. t* draft
skicirati *v.t.* outline
skicirati *v.t.* sketch
skiptar *n.* sceptre
skitalački *a* vagabond
skitanje *v.t.* ramble
skitati *n* ramble
skitnica *n.* ranger
skitnica *n.* vagabond
sklad *n.* conformity
sklad *n.* consonance
skladan *a.* shapely
skladatelj compositor
skladište *n* cache
skladište *n.* godown
skladište *n.* repository
skladištenje *n.* storage
skladištiti *v.t.* store
sklon *a.* prone
sklonište *n.* shelter

sklonost *n* bent
sklonost *n.* inclination
sklonost *n.* preference
sklonost *n.* proclivity
sklonost *n* affinity
skočiti *v. i* hop
skočiti *v.i* jump
skočiti *v.i.* leap
skočiti *v.i.* spring
skok *n.* jump
skok *n* leap
skok *n.* vault
skolastičar *a.* scholastic
skoro *adv.* nearly
skorojević *n.* upstart
skraćivanje *n* abridgement
skratiti *v.t.* abbreviate
skratiti *v.t* abridge
skratiti *v. t* curtail
skratiti *v.t.* shorten
skrbništvo *n.* wardship
skrenuti *v. t* divert
skrenuti *v.t.* shunt
skrenuti *v.t.* switch
skrenuti pažnju *v.* advert
skresati *v.t* volley
skripte *n.* script
skriven *a.* allusive
skroman *a.* humble
skroman *a.* lowly
skroman *a.* modest
skromnost *n.* lowliness
skromnost *n* modesty
skroz *adv.* through
skroz *adv.* throughout
skulptura *n.* sculpture
skup *a* expensive
skup *n.* social
skupina *n* cluster
skupljač trofeja *n.* scavenger

skupljanje *v.t.* rally
skupljanje *n.* shrinkage
skupljati se *v.i* troop
skupo *a.* costly
skut *n.* lap
skuter *n.* scooter
slab *a* faint
slab *a* feeble
slab *a.* frail
slab *a.* infirm
slab *a.* weak
slabašan *a.* puny
slabić *n.* weakling
slabina *n.* loin
slabost *n.* malaise
slabost *n.* weakness
slad *n.* malt
sladak *a.* sweet
sladunjav *a.* mawkish
slagalica *n.* puzzle
slagati se *v.t.* accord
slajd *n* slide
slama *n.* litter
slama *n.* straw
slama *n.* thatch
slan *a.* saline
slan *a.* salty
slanina *n.* bacon
slanoća *n.* salinity
slanje u selo *n.* rustication
slast *n* relish
slastičar *n* confectioner
slastičarnica *n* confectionery
slatkiš *n.* candy
slatkiš *n* sweet
slatkiš *n.* sweetmeat
slatkoća *n.* sweetness
slava *n* fame
slava *n.* glory
slavan *a.* glorious

slavina *n.* tap
slaviti *v. t. & i.* celebrate
slavlje *n.* jubilation
slavlje *n.* celebration
slavljenje *n.* glorification
slavna osoba *n* celebrity
slavuj *n.* nightingale
sledeći *a.* subsequent
sleganje ramenima *n* shrug
slegnuti ramenima *v.t.* shrug
sleng *n.* slang
siepilo *n* ablepsy
slezina *n.* spleen
sličan *a.* like
slične *a.* similar
sličnost *n.* likeness
sličnost *n.* resemblance
sličnost *n.* semblance
sličnost *n.* similarity
sličnost *n.* similitude
slijediti *v.t.* track
slijep *a* blind
slijepiti *v.t.* conglutinate
slijepo crevo *n.* appendix
slika *n* effigy
slika *n.* image
slika *n.* painting
slika *n.* picture
slikar *n.* painter
slikarev potporni štap *n.* maulstick
slikarski *a.* pictorical
slikati *v.t.* pencil
slikovit *a.* picturesque
slikovito izlaganje *n.* imagery
sloboda *n.* freedom
sloboda *n.* liberty
slobodan *a.* free
slobodan *a* leisure
slobodno vrijeme *n.* leisure
slobodnjak *n.* yeoman

slobodoumnik *n.* libertine
slog *n.* syllable
sloga *n.* concord
slogovni *n.* syllabic
sloj *n.* layer
slom *n* breakdown
slom *n* downfall
slon *n* elephant
slonovača *n.* ivory
složen *a* complex
složen *a* compound
složiti se *v.i.* agree
slučaj *n.* case
slučajan *a* accidental
slučajan *a.* haphazard
slučajan *a.* incidental
slučajan *a.* random
slučajnost *n.* contingency
sluga *n* menial
sluga *n.* servant
slušalac *n.* listener
slušati *v.i.* listen
slušni *adj.* auditive
slutiti *v.t.* misgive
slutnja *n.* hunch
slutnja *n.* misgiving
slutnja *n.* omen
sluz *n.* mucus
sluzav *a.* mucous
sluznica *n.* conjunctiva
služavka *n.* maid
služba *n.* service
službeni *a.* official
službenik *n* clerk
službenik *n* employee
službeno *adv.* officially
službovati *v.i.* officiate
služiti se polugom *v.t.* lever
služiti vojsku *v.i.* soldier
sljedbenik *n* follower

sljedbenik *n.* henchman
sljedeći *a.* next
sljepoća *n* blindness
sljepoočnica *n* temple
smanjenje *n.* abatement
smanjenje *n* decrease
smanjenje *n.* reduction
smanjiti *v.t.* abate
smanjiti *v. t* decrease
smanjiti *v. t* diminish
smanjiti *v.t* lessen
smanjiti *v.t.* reduce
smanjiti izdatke *v.t.* retrench
smanjiti se *v.i* shrink
smaragd *n* emerald
smatrati *v.i.* deem
smatrati *za v.t.* repute
smeće *n.* garbage
smeće *n.* trash
smeće *n.* refuse
smelost *n.* daring
smetnja *n* drawback
smicalica *n.* artifice
smijanje *n.* laugh
smijati *se v.i* laugh
smijeh *n.* laughter
smiješan *n.* funny
smiješan *a.* hilarious
smiješan *a.* laughable
smiješan *a.* ridiculous
smiješan *a.* zany
smiješiti se *v.i.* smile
smio *a* daring
smiriti *v. t.* calm
smišljati *v.t.* plot
smjelost *n* boldness
smjena *n* shift
smjer *n* lay
smjesta *adv.* straightway
smjestiti *v.t* accommodate

smjestiti *v.t* house
smjestiti *v.t.* place
smještaj *n.* accommodation
smog *n.* smog
smokva *n* fig
smola *n.* pitch
smotati *v.t.* furl
smotra *n* muster
smrad *n.* stench
smrad *n* stink
smrdjeti *v.i.* stink
smrt *n* death
smrt *n* decease
smrtan *a.* mortal
smrtnik *n* mortal
smrtno *adj.* alamort
smrtonosan *a* deadly
smrtonosan *a.* lethal
smutiti *v. t* bemire
snabdevati hranom *v. i* cater
snabdjeti osobljem *v.t.* staff
snaga *n* main
snaga *n.* power
snaga *n.* strength
snalažljiv *a.* resourceful
snalažljiv *a.* shifty
snažan *a* forceful
snažan *a.* hefty
sneg *n.* snow
snežiti *a.* snowy
sniježiti *v.i.* snow
snimati *v.t* film
snob *n.* snob
snobizam *n.* snobbery
snobovski *v* snobbish
snop *n* bundle
snop *n.* sheaf
snop *n* beam
so *n.* salt
soba *n.* room

soba za posjete *n.* parlour
socijalistički *n,a* socialist
socijalizam *n* socialism
sociologija *n.* sociology
sočan *a.* juicy
sočan *a.* luscious
sočan *a.* lusty
sodomija *n.* sodomy
sodomit *n.* sodomite
sofa *n.* sofa
sofista *n.* sophist
sofisticiran *a.* sophisticated
sofisticirati *v.t.* sophisticate
sofizam *n.* sophism
sojka *n.* jay
sok *n* juice
sokak *n.* lane
soko *n* falcon
sokolar *n* hawker
sokolovski *adj* accipitral
solarni *a.* solar
solidarnost *n.* solidarity
solista *n.* soloist
soliti *v.t* salt
solo *adv.* solo
solo *n* solo
solventan *a.* solvent
solventnost *n.* solvency
somot *n.* velvet
sonda *n* probe
sonet *n.* sonnet
sortirati *v.t.* size
sortirati *v.t* sort
sos *n.* sauce
sotona *n.* satan
sova *n.* owl
spajalica *n.* staple
spajanje žicom *n.* wiring
spakovati *v. t* encase
spanać *n.* spinach

sparan *a.* muggy	**spoljašnjost** *n* outside
sparan *a.* sultry	**spomenik** *n.* monument
spariti *v.t.* pair	**spominjanje** *n.* mention
spasavanje *n.* salvage	**spominjati** *v.t.* mention
spasenje *n.* salvation	**spona** *n* brace
spasitelj *n.* saviour	**spona** *n.* link
spasiti *v.t.* rescue	**spontan** *a.* spontaneous
spasiti *v.t.* salvage	**spontanost** *n.* spontaneity
spašavanje *n* rescue	**sponzor** *n.* sponsor
spavaćica *n.* nightie	**sponzorirati** *v.t.* sponsor
spavač *n.* sleeper	**spor** *n* dispute
spavati *v.i.* sleep	**spor** *a* slow
specifičan *a.* specific	**sporadičan** *a.* sporadic
specifikacija *n.* specification	**sporan** *n.* moot
specijalista *n.* specialist	**sporazum** *n.* compact
specijalitet *n.* speciality	**sporazum** *n.* agreement
specijalizacija *n.* specialization	**sporost** *n.* slowness
specijalizirati se *v.i.* specialize	**sport** *n.* sport
spektakl *n.* spectacle	**sportaš** *n.* athlete
spektakularan *a.* spectacular	**sposoban** *a.* apt
spekulacija *n.* speculation	**sposoban** *a.* competent
spekulirati *v.i.* speculate	**sposoban za brak** *a.* marriageable
spelovati *v.t.* spell	**sposoban za jemstvo** *a.* bailable
sperma *n.* sperm	**sposoban** *a.* capable
spirala *n.* spiral	**sposobnost** *n* ability
spiralni *a.* spiral	**sposobnost** *n* competence
spiritista *n.* spiritualist	**sposobnost** *n.* acumen
spiritualizam *n.* spiritualism	**sposobnost** *n.* aptitude
spis *n.* writ	**sposobnost** *n.* capability
spletkariti *v.i.* scheme	**spotaći se** *v.i.* stumble
spljoštiti *v.t.* laminate	**spoticanje** *n.* stumble
spoj *n.* juncture	**spotraš** *n.* sportsman
spojiti *v. t* couple	**spoznaja** *n* cognizance
spojiti *v.t* link	**sprati** *v.i* flush
spojiti *v.t.* merge	**sprečiti** *v.t.* avert
spojiti se *v.t.* interlock	**sprej** *n.* spray
spojni *adj.* annectant	**spreman** *a.* ready
spokoj *n.* calm	**spreman** *a.* stock
spokoj *n.* serenity	**spremno** *adv.* readily
spokojan *a.* serene	**spremnost** *n.* readiness

spremnost *n.* willingness
spretan *adj.* deft
sprijateljiti *se v. t.* befriend
spriječiti *v.t.* prevent
sprint *n* sprint
sprintati *v.i.* sprint
spržiti *v.t.* parch
spustiti se *v.i.* perch
spuštati se *v. i.* descend
sputati *v.t* fetter
sputnik *n.* sputnik
spužva *n.* sponge
sraman *a.* shameful
sramota *n* dishonour
sramota *n.* infamy
sramota *n.* shame
sramotan *a* flagrant
sramotiti *v.t.* shame
sramotiti *v.t.* vilify
srastanje *n.* concrescence
srasti *v.t.* accrete
srce *n.* heart
srcolik *adj.* cordate
srčani *adjs* cardiacal
srdačan *a* cordial
srdačno *adv.* heartily
srdit *a.* irate
srebrn *a* silver
srebro *n.* silver
sreća *n.* fortune
sreća *n.* happiness
sreća *n.* luck
srećan *a.* fortunate
srećan *a.* lucky
srećom *adv.* luckily
srećan *a.* happy
sreda *n.* Wednesday
sredina *n.* mean
sredina *n* middle
sredina *n.* midst

sredina ljeta *n.* midsummer
srednjeg roda *a.* neuter
srednji *a.* intermediate
srednji *a.* median
srednji *a* medium
srednji *a.* mid
srednji *a.* middle
srednji rod *n* neuter
srednjovjekovni *a.* medieval
sredovječan *a.* medieval
sredstvo *n* means
sredstvo za umirenje *adj* calmative
sredstvo protiv insekata *n* repellent
sresti *v.t.* meet
srna *n* doe
srna *n.* roe
srodan *a* congenial
srodan *a.* akin
srodnik *n.* in-laws
srodstvo *n.* kinship
srp *n.* sickle
srušiti *v.t.* overthrow
srušiti se *v.i.* topple
stabilan *a.* stable
stabilizacija *n.* stabilization
stabilizirati *v.t.* stabilize
stabilnost *n.* stability
stabla *n.* stem
stablo *n.* trunk
stabljika *n.* stalk
stacionaran *a.* stationary
stacionirati *v.t.* station
stadion *n.* stadium
stado *n* flock
stado *n.* herd
stagnacija *n.* stagnation
stagnirati *v.i.* stagnate
staja *n.* cote
stajanje *n.* standing
stajati *v.i.* stand

staklo *n.* glass
staklorezac *n.* glazier
stalan *a* constant
staložen *a.* sedate
staložen *a.* staid
stampedo *n.* stampede
stan *n.* apartment
stanar *n.* inmate
stanar *n.* occupant
stanar *n.* tenant
standard *n.* standard
standardan *a* standard
standardizacija *n.* standardization
standardizirati *v.t.* standardize
stanica *n.* cell
stanica *n.* station
stanište *n.* habitat
stanovanje *n.* habitation
stanovanje *n.* occupancy
stanovati *v. i* dwell
stanovište *n* angle
stanovište *n.* standpoint
stanovnik *n.* inhabitant
stanovnik *n* resident
stanovništvo *n.* populace
stanovništvo *n.* population
stanje *n.* plight
stanje, država *n.* state
star *a.* old
staratelj *n* custodian
starateljstvo *v* custody
starešinstvo *n.* seniority
starije *a* elderly
stariji *a* elder
stariji *a.* senior
starinar *n.* antiquary
starinski *a.* antiquarian
starinski *a.* antique
starješina *n* elder
starješina *n.* martinet

starješina *n.* principal
staromodan *a.* outmoded
starosjedilački *a* aboriginal
starosjedioci *n. pl* aborigines
start *n* start
stas *n.* physique
stas *n.* stature
stasala za udaju *a.* nubile
statičnost *n.* static
statika *n.* statics
statističar *n.* statistician
statistički *a.* statistical
statistika *n.* statistics
statua *n.* statue
status *n.* status
statut *n.* statute
statutarne *a.* statutory
stav *n.* attitude
stavak *n.* posture
staviti *v.t.* position
staviti *v.t.* put
staviti kasniji datum *v.t.* post-date
staviti lisice *v.t* handcuff
staviti na policu *v.t.* shelve
staviti pod pritisak *v.t.* pressurize
staviti povez preko očiju *v. t* blindfold
staviti u džep *v.t.* pocket
staviti u jamu *v.t.* pit
staviti van zakona *v.t* outlaw
staviti veto *v.t.* veto
stavka *n.* item
staza *n.* track
stažirati *v.t.* intern
stečaj *n.* bankruptcy
steći *v.t.* acquire
stega *n* clamp
stegnuti *v.t.* constrict
stena *n* boulder
stenograf *n.* stenographer
stenografija *n.* stenography

stenjanje *v.i.* groan
stenjanje *n.* moan
stenjati *n* groan
stenjati *v.i.* moan
stepa *n.* steppe
stepenik *n.* stair
stereotip *n.* stereotype
stereotipizirati *v.t.* stereotype
sterilan *a.* sterile
sterilitet *n.* sterility
sterilizacija *n.* sterilization
sterilizirati *v.t.* sterilize
sterling *n.* sterling
stetoskop *n.* stethoscope
stidljiv *a.* timid
stidljiv *a.* bashful
stigma *n.* stigma
stih *n.* verse
stihoklepac *n.* poetaster
stihopisac *n.* rhymester
stihotvorstvo *n.* versification
stijena *n.* rock
stil *n.* style
stimulans *n.* stimulant
stimulisati *v.t.* stimulate
stipendija *n.* scholarship
stipendista *n.* scholar
stisak *n* grip
stiskati *v.t* wring
stisnuti *v.t.* grip
stisnuti *v.* pinch
stišati *v.t.* tranquillize
stjuard *n.* steward
sto *n.* hundred
sto *n.* table
sto stepeni *a.* centigrade
stočna hrana *n* fodder
stoga *adv.* thus
stogodišnjak *n* centenarian
stogodišnji *adj.* centennial

stogodišnjica *n.* centenary
stoik *n.* stoic
stolar *n.* joiner
stolar *n.* carpenter
stolarija *n.* carpentry
stolica *n.* chair
stolica *n* chaise
stolica *n.* stool
stoljeće *n.* century
stomačni *a.* abdominal
stomak *n* abdomen
stomak *n.* stomach
stomatolog *n* dentist
stonoga *n.* centipede
stonoga *n.* millipede
stopa *n.* rate
stopalo *n* foot
stostruk *n. & adj* centuple
stovarište *n* depot
stožer *n.* pivot
straćara *a.* shanty
stradanje *n.* tribulation
strah *n* dread
strah *n* fear
strah *n.* fright
strah *n.* scare
strahopoštovanje *n.* veneration
strahopoštovanje *n.* awe
strahovati *v.t* dread
strana *n.* aside
strana *n.* page
strana *n.* side
stranac *n* foreigner
stranac *n.* stranger
stranac *a.* alien
stranački *a* factious
strani *a* foreign
stranka *n.* party
strast *n.* passion
strastven *a.* passionate

strašan *a* dire
strašan *a* dread
strašan *a.* horrible
strašan *a.* terrific
strašno *a.* fearful
strateg *n.* strategist
strategija *n.* strategy
strateški *a.* strategic
straža *n.* sentry
stražʔr *n.* guard
stražar *n.* sentinel
stražnjica *n* buttock
strela *n.* arrow
strelast koren *n.* arrowroot
strelica *n.* dart
stres *n.* stress
stric, tetak, ujak *n.* uncle
strijelac *n.* marksman
strijelac *n.* archer
strm *adj.* declivous
strm *a.* steep
strmina *n* bluff
strmoglav *adv.* headlong
strnjika *n.* stubble
strofa *n.* stanza
strog *a.* strict
strog *a.* stringent
strog *a.* austere
strogost *n.* rigour
strojno *a.* mechanical
strpljenje *n.* patience
strpljiv *a.* patient
stršljen *n.* hornet
stručan *a* expert
stručnjak *n* expert
strug *n.* lathe
strugar *n.* turner
strugati *v.t* grate
strugati *v.t.* whittle
struja *n* current

struk *n.* waist
struktura *n.* structure
strukturni *a.* structural
studeni *n.* november
student *n.* student
student *n.* undergraduate
student medicine *n.* medico
studio *n.* studio
stup *n.* pillar
stupanj *n* degree
stvar *n.* matter
stvar *n.* thing
stvaran *a.* actual
stvaranje *n* creation
stvarno *adv.* really
stvor *n.* wight
stvorenje *n* creature
stvrdnuti *v.t.* harden
sub *n.* post
subjekat *n.* subject
subjektivan *a.* subjective
sublimirati *v.t.* sublimate
subota *n.* Saturday
subvencija *n.* subsidy
subvencionirati *v.t.* subsidize
subverzija *n.* subversion
subverzivan *a.* subversive
sud *n.* court
sud *n.* tribunal
sudac *n.* judge
sudac *n.* referee
sudac *n.* umpire
sudac za prekršaje *n.* magistrate
sudar *n.* clash
sudar *n* collision
sudar *n* crash
sudariti se *v. t.* clash
sudariti se *v. i.* collide
sudariti se *v. i* crash
sudbina *n* destiny

sudbina *n* fate	**sunčan** *a.* sunny
sudija *n.* arbiter	**sunčati** *v.t.* sun
suditi *v.i.* judge	**suočenje** *n.* confrontation
sudjelovati *v.i.* partake	**suočiti** *se v.t* face
sudjelovati *v.i.* participate	**suosećanje** *n* compassion
sudopera *n* sink	**suosjećati** *v. t* commiserate
sudski *a.* judicial	**suosjećati** *v.i.* sympathize
sudski nalog *n.* injunction	**superiornost** *n.* superiority
sudski *progon n.* prosecution	**superlativ** *n.* superlative
sudstvo *n.* judiciary	**superlativan** *a.* superlative
suđenje *n.* trial	**supersoničan** *a.* supersonic
sufiks *n.* suffix	**suprotan** *a* adverse
sufler *n.* prompter	**suprotan** *a.* opposite
sugestivan *a.* suggestive	**suprotan** *a.* reverse
suglasan *a.* agreeable	**suprotno** *a* contrary
suglasnik *n.* consonant	**suprotnost** *n* reverse
suglasnost *n.* accord	**suprotstaviti** *v.t.* contrapose
suglasnost *n.* conformity	**suprotstaviti** *v. t* contrast
suh *adj.* arid	**suprotstaviti** *v.t.* counteract
suh *a.* torrid	**suprotstaviti** *v.t.* oppose
suho *a* dry	**supruga** *n.* wife
sujeta *n.* vanity	**supstanca** *n.* substance
suknar *n* draper	**suptilan** *n.* subtle
suknja *n.* skirt	**suptilnost** *n.* subtlety
sukob *n.* strife	**suradnik** *n.* companion
sukobiti se *v. i* conflict	**suradnik** *n.* associate
suma *n.* sum	**suradnja** *n* collaboration
sumirati *v.t.* sum	**suradnja** *n* co-operation
sumnja *n* doubt	**surađivati** *v. i* collaborate
sumnja *n.* suspicion	**surađivati** *v. i* co-operate
sumnjati *v. t.* distrust	**surf** *n.* surf
sumnjati *v. i* doubt	**surutka** *n* curd
sumnjiv *a.* questionable	**susjedni** *a.* adjacent
sumnjiv *a.* suspicious	**susjedski** *a.* neighbourly
sumoran *a.* gloomy	**susjedstvo** *n.* neighbourhood
sumoran *a.* sullen	**suspendirati** *v.t.* suspend
sumornost *n.* gloom	**susresti** *v. t* encounter
sumpor *n.* sulphur	**susret** *n.* encounter
sumporni *a.* sulphuric	**suša** *n* drought
sunce *n.* sun	**sušara** *n.* kiln

suština *n* essence
suština *n.* gist
suština *n.* quintessence
suštinski *a* essential
suton *n* dusk
suton *n* twilight
sutra *adv.* tomorrow
sutrašnji dan *n.* tomorrow
suvenir *n.* souvenir
suveren *a* sovereign
suverenost *n.* sovereignty
suvišan *a* excess
suvišan *a.* redundant
suviše *adv.* too
suvišno *a.* superfluous
suvremen *a* contemporary
suvremen *a.* up-to-date
suza *n.* tear
suzan *a.* tearful
suzbijanje *n.* repression
suzbijanje *n.* suppression
suzbijati *v.t.* suppress
suzdržan *a.* taciturn
suzdržati se *v.i.* abstain
suziti *v.t.* narrow
suziti *v.t.* straiten
svadba *n.* nuptials
svadba *n.* spousal
svadbeni *a.* nuptial
svadljiv *a.* quarrelsome
svađa *n.* quarrel
svađa *n.* row
svađa *v. i. & n* brawl
svađati se *v.i.* quarrel
svakako *adv.* needs
svaki *a.* any
svaki *pron.* each
svaki *a* each
svaki *a* every
svaki čas *adv.* minutely

svakidašnji *a.* commonplace
svakidašnji *a.* workaday
svariti *v. t.* digest
svečan *a.* ceremonial
svečan *a* festive
svečan *a.* solemn
svečanost *n* festivity
svečanost *n.* solemnity
svećenica *n.* priestess
svećenički *a* clerical
svećenik *n.* priest
svećenstvo *n* clergy
svećenstvo *n.* priesthood
svemir *n.* universe
svemoć *n.* omnipotence
svemoguć *a.* omnipotent
svemoguć *a.* almighty
sveobuhvatan *a* comprehensive
sveprisutan *a.* omnipresent
sveprisutnost *n.* omnipresence
svestran *a.* versatile
svestranost *n.* versatility
svetac *n.* saint
svetački *a.* saintly
sveti *a.* holy
svetinja *n.* shrine
svetište *n.* sanctuary
svetiti se *v.t.* avenge
svetkovati *v.t.* solemnize
svetogrdan *a.* sacrilegious
svetogrđe *n.* sacrilege
svetost *n.* sanctity
svetovan *a.* profane
sveučilište *n.* university
sveukupno *adv.* altogether
svezati trakom *v.t* tape
svezati žicom *v.t.* wire
sveznajući *a.* omniscient
sveznanje *n.* omniscience
svi *pron.* all

svibanj *n.* May
svijeća *n.* candle
svijet *n.* globe
svijet *n.* world
svijetao *a* bright
svijetao *a.* lucent
svijeti *a.* sacred
svijeti *a.* sacrosanct
svila *n.* silk
svilen *a.* silken
svilenkast *a.* silky
svinja *n.* pig
svinja *n.* swine
svinjac *n.* sty
svinjsko meso *n.* pork
svirati flautu *v.i* flute
svirati na fruli *v.i* pipe
svirep *a* ferocious
svitak *n.* scroll
svitati *v. i.* dawn
svjedočanstvo *n.* testimony
svjedočiti *v.i.* testify
svjedočiti *v.i.* witness
svjedok *n.* deponent
svjedok *n.* witness
svjestan *a* conscious
svjestan *a.* aware
svjetionik *n* beacon
svjetleći *a.* luminous
svjetlo *n.* light
svjetlucanje *n.* scintillation
svjetlucanje *n.* twinkle
svjetlucati *v.i.* scintillate
svjetlucati *v.i.* twinkle
svjetovni *a.* mundane
svjetovni *a.* worldly
svjetski čovek *n.* worldling
svjež *a.* fresh
svlačiti *v.t.* slough
svlačiti *v.t.* strip

svo *adv.* all
svod *n.* vault
svod *n* arcade
svod *n.* arch
svoja ličnost *n.* self
svoje *a.* own
svojevoljan *a.* wayward
svojina *n.* belongings
svojstvenost *n.* peculiarity
svojstvo *n.* ownership
svrab *n.* itch
svraka *n.* magpie
svrbeti *v.i.* itch
svrdlo *n.* auger
svrgnuti *v. t* depose
svrha *n.* purpose
svrstavati *v.t.* assort
svršena učenica *n* alumna

Š

šafran *n.* saffron
šah *n.* chess
šaht *n.* manhole
šaka *n* hand
šakal *n.* jackal
šal *n.* scarf
šal *n.* shawl
šala *n.* jest
šala *n.* pleasantry
šaliti se *v.i.* jest
šamar *n.* slap
šamar *n* smack
šampon *n.* shampoo
šamponirati *v.t.* shampoo
šanac *n.* moat
šansa *n.* chance
šapa *n.* paw
šapat *n* whisper

šaputati *v.t.* whisper	**širina** *n.* width
šara *n.* mottle	**širina** *n* breadth
šarlatan *n* quack	**širiti** *v.i.* spread
šarm *n.* charm	**širok** *a.* wide
šarmirati *v. t.* charm	**širok** *a* broad
šarolik *a.* motley	**široko** *adv.* wide
šator *n.* tent	**širom** *prep.* throughout
šav *n.* seam	**šišarka** *n.* cone
šav *n.* stitch	**šišmiš** *n* bat
ščepati *v.t.* grasp	**šiti** *v.t.* seam
ščepati *v.t.* nab	**šiti** *v.t.* sew
ščepati *v.t.* snap	**škare** *n.* scissors
šećer *n.* sugar	**škare** *n. pl.* shears
šećerni *a.* saccharine	**škljocaj** *n.* click
šef *n* boss	**škodljiv** *a.* maleficent
šegrt *n.* apprentice	**škodljiv** *a.* pernicious
šepurenje *n* swagger	**škola** *n.* school
šepuriti se *v.i.* swagger	**školarina** *n.* tuition
šesnaest *n., a.* sixteen	**školjka** *n.* conch
šesnaesti *a.* sixteenth	**školjka** *n.* shell
šest *n., a* six	**školjke** *n* barnacles
šesti *a.* sixth	**škorpija** *n.* scorpion
šešir *n.* hat	**škot** *n.* Scot
šetati *v.i.* walk	**škotski** *a.* scotch
šetkati se *v.i.* lounge	**škrabanje** *n.* scribble
šetnja *n* walk	**škrabati** *v.t.* scrawl
ševa *n.* lark	**škrabati** *v.t.* scribble
šezdeset *n., a.* sixty	**škrabotina** *n* scrawl
šezdeseti *a.* sixtieth	**škriljevac** *n.* slate
šibati *v. t.* cane	**škripanje** *n* creak
šibati *v.t* flog	**škripati** *v. i* creak
šibica *n* match	**škrob** *n.* starch
šiling *n.* shilling	**škrt** *a.* niggardly
šiljak *n.* spike	**škrt** *a.* stingy
šiljat *adj.* cultrate	**škrtica** *n.* niggard
šina *n.* rail	**škrtost** *n.* avarice
šipka *n.* bar	**šljiva** *n.* plum
širenje *n.* propagation	**šljokica** *n.* tinsel
širenje *n.* spread	**šljunak** *n.* pebble
širina *n.* latitude	**šmrkanje** *n* sniff

šmrkati *v.i.* sniff
šofer *n.* chauffeur
šok *n.* shock
šokirati *v.t.* shock
šolja *n.* cup
šorts *n. pl.* shorts
španijel *n.* spaniel
španjloski jezik, španjolac *n.* Spanish
španjolac *n.* Spaniard
španjolski *a.* Spanish
špijun *n.* spy
špijunirati *v.i.* spy
špilja *n.* cave
špilja *n.* cavern
špric *n.* syringe
špricati *v.i.* spurt
šta *pron.* what
šta *interj.* what
štagod *pron.* whatever
štaka *n* crutch
štakor *n.* rat
štala *n.* barn
štala *n.* bawn
štala *n* stable
štala *n.* stall
štala *n* byre
štampa *n* press
štamparska greška *n.* misprint
štand *n.* stand
štap *n.* rod
štap *n.* stick
štapić *n.* wand
štedjeti *v.t.* spare
štedljiv *a.* frugal
štedljiv *a.* thrifty
štednja *n.* retrenchment
štednja *n.* thrift
štednjak *n* cooker
štenara *n.* kennel
štene *n.* puppy

štene *n.* whelp
šteta *n.* damage
šteta *n.* harm
štetan *a.* injurious
štetan *a.* noxious
štetan uticaj *n* blight
štetočina *n.* pest
štićenik *n.* ward
štirkati *v.t.* starch
štit *n.* shield
štititi *v.t.* patronize
štititi *v.t.* shelter
štoviše *adv.* moreover
štrajk *n* strike
štrajkač *n.* striker
štrcnuti *v.t.* syringe
štucanje *n.* hiccup
štula *n.* stilt
šuga *n.* scabies
šuma *n* forest
šuma *n.* woods
šumar *n* forester
šumarak *n.* coppice
šumarstvo *n* forestry
šumovit *kraj n.* woodland
šunjati se *v.i.* sneak
šupalj *a.* hollow
šupljina *n.* hollow
šuškanje *n* lisp
šuškati *v.t.* lisp
šut *n.* kick
šutirati *v.t.* kick
švercer *n.* smuggler
švicarska *n.* swiss
švicarski *a* swiss

T

tabak za pisanje *n* foolscap

tabati *v.t* stump	**Talijanski** *a.* Italian
tabelarni *a.* tabular	**talijanski jezik, Talijan** *n.* Italian
tabelisanje *n.* tabulation	**talisman** *n.* talisman
tabla *n.* panel	**talog** *n.* sediment
tableta *n.* tablet	**taman** *a* dark
tabu *n.* taboo	**tamjan** *n.* incense
tabulator *n.* tabulator	**tamničar** *n.* jailer
tačka *n* dot	**tamno-crven** *n* crimson
tadašnji *a* then	**tamo** *adv.* there
taj *a.* that	**tamo** *adv.* thither
tajan *adj.* clandestine	**tamo** *adv.* yonder
tajanstven *a.* secretive	**tamošnji** *a.* yonder
tajfun *n.* typhoon	**tanak** *a* flimsy
tajna *n.* secret	**tanak** *a.* thin
tajni *a.* secret	**tangenta** *n.* tangent
tajni sporazum *n* collusion	**tanka voštana svijeća** *n* taper
tajnik *n.* secretary	**tanker** *n.* tanker
tajništvo *n.* secretariat (e)	**tanjiti** *v.t.* thin
tajnost *n.* secrecy	**tanjurić** *n.* saucer
tak *n* cue	**tapiserija** *n.* tapestry
takav *pron.* such	**tapkanje** *n* pat
tako *adv.* as	**tapkati** *v.t.* pat
tako *adv.* so	**tapkati** *v.t.* tap
tako *adv.* that	**tarifa** *n.* tariff
također *adv.* also	**tata** *n* dad, daddy
također *adv.* likewise	**tečaj** *n.* course
taksa za vezivanje broda *n.* wharfage	**tečan** *a* fluent
taksi *n.* taxi	**tečan** *a.* liquid
taksi *n.* cab	**teći** *v.i* flow
takt *n.* tact	**teći** *v.i.* stream
taktičan *a.* tactful	**tegla** *n.* jar
taktičar *n.* tactician	**teglenica** *n.* barge
taktika *n.* tactics	**tegoban** *a.* onerous
taktilni *a.* tactile	**tegoban** *a* burdensome
talac *n.* hostage	**tehničar** *n.* technician
talasanje *n.* ripple	**tehnički** *n.* technical
talasati *v.t.* ripple	**tehnika** *n.* technique
talasati se *v.i* billow	**tehnolog** *n.* technologist
talasati se *v.i.* undulate	**tehnologija** *n.* technology
talenat *n.* talent	**tehnološki** *a.* technological

teista *n.* theist
teizam *n.* theism
tekovina *n* acquest
tekst *n.* text
tekstil *n* textile
tekstilni *a.* textile
tekstualni *n.* textual
tekući *a* fluid
tekućina *n* fluid
tekućina *n* liquid
tele *n.* calf
telefon *n.* phone
telefon *n.* telephone
telefonirati *v.t.* telephone
telegraf *n.* telegraph
telegrafija *n.* telegraphy
telegrafisati *v.t.* telegraph
telegrafista *n.* telegraphist
telegrafski *a.* telegraphic
telegram *n.* telegram
telekomunikacije *n.* telecommunications
telepata *n.* telepathist
telepatija *n.* telepathy
telepatski *a.* telepathic
teleskop *n.* telescope
teleskopski *a.* telescopic
televizija *n.* television
telo *n* body
tema *n.* theme
tema *n.* topic
tematski *a.* thematic
tematski *a.* topical
temeljan *a* thorough
temperament *n.* mettle
temperament *n.* temper
temperament *n.* temperament
temperamentan *a.* temperamental
temperatura *n.* temperature
ten *n* complexion
tendencija *n.* tendency

tenis *n.* tennis
tenzija *n.* tension
teokracija *n.* theocracy
teolog *n.* theologian
teologija *n.* theology
teološki *a.* theological
teorema *n.* theorem
teoretičar *n.* theorist
teoretizirati *v.i.* theorize
teorija *n.* theory
teorijski *a.* theoretical
tepih *n.* carpet
terapija *n.* therapy
terasa *n.* terrace
teret *n.* load
teret *n.* onus
teret *n* burden
teret *n.* cargo
terevenka *n.* revelry
terijer *n.* terrier
teritorija *n.* territory
teritorijalni *a.* territorial
termalni *a.* thermal
terminal *n* terminal
terminologija *n.* terminology
terminološki *a.* terminological
termometar *n.* thermometer
termos (boca) *n.* thermos (flask)
teror *n.* terror
terorisati *v.t.* terrorize
terorista *n.* terrorist
terotizam *n.* terrorism
terpentin *n.* turpentine
tesati *v.t.* hew
test *n* test
testament *n.* testament
testirati *v.t.* test
testis *n.* testicle
teško koračati *v.i.* plod
teškoća *n* difficulty

teškoća *n.* hardship
tetka, strina, ujna *n.* aunt
tetoviranje *n.* tattoo
tetovirati *v.i.* tattoo
teturanje *n.* stagger
teturati se *v.i.* stagger
teza *n.* thesis
težak *a* difficult
težak *a* gross
težak *a.* hard
težak *a.* tough
težak *a.* trying
težak hod *n.* shuffle
težina *n.* weight
težiti *v.i.* strive
težiti ka *v.i.* gravitate
težiti *v.t.* aspire
težnja *n.* aspiration
tifozan *n.* typhoid
tifus *n.* typhus
tigar *n.* tiger
tigrica *n.* tigress
tih *a.* silent
tijara *n.* tiara
tijekom *prep.* pending
tijesto *n* dough
tik *n.* teak
tikva *n.* gourd
tikvan *n.* loggerhead
tim *n.* team
timariti *v.t* groom
time *adv.* thereby
tinejdžer *n.* teenager
tinjac *n.* mica
tinjati *v.i.* smoulder
tip *n.* type
tipičan *a.* typical
tipkati *v.t.* type
tirada *n.* tirade
tiranija *n.* tyranny

tiranin *n.* tyrant
tiranski *a.* oppressive
tiskati *v.t.* print
tisuća *n.* chiliad
tisuća *n.* thousand
tisućljeće *n.* millennium
tisuću *a* thousand
tišina *n* hush
tišina *n.* silence
tišina *n.* stillness
titanski *a.* titanic
titularni *a.* titular
tjedni *a.* weekly
tjednik *n.* weekly
tjedno *adv.* weekly
tjelesni *a* corporal
tjelesni *a* bodily
tjelohranitelj *n.* bodyguard
tjesnac *n.* defile
tjesnac *n.* ravine
tjesnac *n.* strait
tkač *n.* weaver
tkanina *n* cloth
tkanina *n* fabric
tkati *v.t.* weave
tkivo *n.* tissue
tlačitelj *n.* oppressor
tlo *n.* ground
tlo *n.* soil
tmuran *a.* sombre
to *pron.* it
toalet *n.* lavatory
toalet *n.* toilet
tobolac *n.* quiver
tobožnji *a.* would-be
točan *a* correct
točan *a* exact
točan *a.* punctual
točan *a.* accurate
točka *n.* point

točno *adv* due	**trag** *n.* trail
točnost *n.* punctuality	**trag** *n.* vestige
točnost *n.* accuracy	**traganje** *n.* quest
toga *n.* toga	**tragati** *v.t.* quest
tolerancija *n.* tolerance	**tragati** *v.t.* trace
tolerancija *n.* toleration	**tragedija** *n.* tragedy
tolerantan *a.* tolerant	**tragičan** *a.* tragic
tolerirati *v.t.* tolerate	**tragičar** *n.* tragedian
toljaga *n* cudgel	**trajan** *a* abiding
tom *n.* tome	**trajan** *a.* lasting
tona *n.* ton	**trajan** *a.* permanent
tona *n.* tonne	**trajanje** *n* duration
toničan *a.* tonic	**trajati** *v.i.* last
tonik *n.* tonic	**trajekt** *n* ferry
tonzura *n.* tonsure	**trajnica** *n.* perennial
top *n.* cannon	**trajnost** *n.* permanence
topao *v.t.* warm	**traka** *n.* ribbon
topaz *n.* topaz	**traka** *n.* streamer
topiti se *v.i* thaw	**traka** *n.* strip
topiv *a.* soluble	**traka** *n.* tape
toplota *n.* heat	**trakt** *n.* tract
toplota *n.* warmth	**traktat** *n* tract
topljenje *n* thaw	**traktor** *n.* tractor
topograf *n.* topographer	**trampa** *n.* barter2
topografija *n.* topography	**trampiti** *v.t.* barter1
topografski *a.* topographical	**tramvaj** *n.* tram
topola *n.* poplar	**trans** *n.* trance
toranj *n.* tower	**transakcija** *n.* transaction
torba *n.* satchel	**transformacija** *n.* transformation
torba *n.* bag	**transformirati** *v.* transform
torbar *n.* marsupial	**transkripcija** *n.* transcription
tornado *n.* tornado	**transmisija** *n.* transmission
torpedo *n.* torpedo	**transparentan** *a.* transparent
torpedovati *v.t.* torpedo	**transport** *n.* transportation
torta *n.* cake	**tranzit** *n.* transit
tovar *n.* freight	**trava** *n* grass
traćiti *v.t.* squander	**travnjak** *n.* lawn
tradicija *n.* tradition	**traženje** *n.* requirement
tradicionalan *a.* traditional	**tražiti** *v.t.* require
trag *n.* trace	**tražiti** *v.t.* search

tražiti *v.t.* seek
trbuh *n* belly
trčanje *n.* run
trčati *v.i.* run
trčati za ženama *v.t.* womanize
trebati *v.t.* need
trebovanje *n.* requisition
trebovati *v.t.* requisition
treće *adv.* thirdly
treći *a.* third
trećina *n.* third
trend *n.* trend
trenirati *v.t.* train
trenutak *n.* instant
trenutak *n.* moment
trenutan *a.* momentary
trenutni *a* current
trenutni *a.* instant
trenje *n.* friction
trepavica *n* eyelash
treperenje *n* flicker
treperenje *n.* palpitation
treperenje *n* warble
treperiti *v.t* flicker
treperiti *v.i.* warble
treptati *v. t. & i* blink
tresak *n* slam
treset *n.* turf
tresnuti *v.t.* slam
tresti *v.i.* shake
tresti se *v.i.* quake
tretman *n.* treatment
trezan *a.* sober
trezvenost *n.* sobriety
trezvenjački *a.* teetotal
trezvenjak *n.* teetotaller
trgovac *n* dealer
trgovac *n.* merchant
trgovac *n.* trader
trgovac *n.* tradesman

trgovac konjima *n.* coper
trgovac na malo *n.* retailer
trgovac pisaćim priborom *n.* stationer
trgovački *a* commercial
trgovački *a.* mercantile
trgovati *v.t* market
trgovati *v.i* trade
trgovati *v.i.* traffic
trgovina *n* commerce
trgovina *n.* trade
tri *a* three
tri *n.* three
tricikl *n.* tricycle
tričav *a.* paltry
trideset *a* thirty
trideset *n.* thirty
trideseti *a.* thirtieth
tridesetina *n* thirtieth
trijem *n.* portico
trijumf *n.* triumph
trijumfalan *a.* triumphal
trijumfovati *v.i.* triumph
trik *n* trick
trinaest *n.* thirteen
trinaest *a* thirteen
trinaesti *a.* thirteenth
trio *n.* trio
triplikat *n* triplicate
triput *adv.* thrice
triton *n.* merman
trivijalan *a.* trivial
trkač *n.* runner
trljanje *n* rub
trljati *v.t.* rub
trn *n.* thorn
trnovit *a.* thorny
trobojni *a.* tricolour
trobojnica *n* tricolour
trodelan *a.* tripartite
trofej *n.* trophy

trojstvo *n.* trinity
trokratan *a.* triplicate
trokut *n.* triangle
trokutni *a.* triangular
trom *n.* laggard
trom *a.* listless
tromjesečni *a.* quarterly
tromo se kretati *v.t.* maunder
tron *n.* throne
tronožac *n.* tripod
tropski *a.* tropical
tropski pojas *n.* tropic
trostruk *a.* triple
trošak *n.* expense
trošarina *n* excise
trošiti *v. t* consume
trpeti *v.i* abide
trska *n.* cane
truba *n.* trumpet
trubiti *v.i* hoot
trubiti *v.i.* trumpet
trubiti *v. t* blare
trubljenje *n.* hoot
trudna *a.* pregnant
trudnoća *n.* pregnancy
trulež *n.* rot
truliti *v.i.* rot
trunčica *n.* mote
truo *adj* carious
trupa *n* rout
trzaj *n.* jerk
trzaj *n.* lurch
trzanje *n* pluck
trzati *v.t.* tug
trzati se *v.i.* wince
tržište *n* market
tuberkuloza *n.* tuberculosis
tuce *n* dozen
tuča *n* fray
tući se *v.i.* scuffle

tuga *n.* grievance
tuga *n.* melancholy
tuga *n.* sorrow
tugovati *v.t.* grieve
tugovati *v.i.* mourn
tumač *n* exponent
tumaranje *n* stroll
tumarati *v.i.* loiter
tumarati *v.t.* saunter
tumarati *v.i.* stroll
tumor *n.* tumour
tunel *n.* tunnel
tup *a* dull
tup *a.* obtuse
tup udarac *n.* thump
tup *a* blunt
tupiti *v. t.* dull
tura *n.* tour
turban *n.* turban
turbina *n.* turbine
turbulencije *n.* turbulence
turbulentan *a.* turbulent
turista *n.* tourist
turizam *n.* tourism
turnir *n.* tournament
turšija *n.* pickle
tuš *n.* shower
tuširati *v.t.* shower
tutnjava *n.* rumble
tutnjava *n.* thud
tutnjiti *v.i.* rumble
tutnjiti *v.i.* thud
tutor *n.* tutor
tužan *adj* melancholy
tužan *a.* sad
tužan *n.* woeful
tužitelj *n* claimant
tužitelj *n.* plaintiff
tužitelj *n.* prosecutor
tužiti *v.t.* sue

tvorac *n* creator
tvorac *n.* maker
tvorac *n.* originator
tvorevina *n* make
tvornica *n* factory
tvrdica *n.* miser
tvrditi *v.t.* assert
tvrdnja *n* contention
tvrdoća *n.* adamant
tvrdoglav *adj.* asinine
tvrdoglav *a.* headstrong
tvrdoglav *a.* mulish
tvrdoglav *a.* obstinate
tvrdoglav *a.* stubborn
tvrdoglavost *n.* obstinacy
tvrdokoran *a.* obdurate
tvrđava *n.* citadel
tvrđava *n.* fortress
tvrtka *n.* company
tvrtka *n.* firm

U

u *prep.* in
u *prep.* into
u *prep.* within
u *prep.* at
u blizini *adv.* near
u celosti *adv.* bodily
u dobroj nameri *a* bonafide
u gomili *adv.* aheap
u inozemstvu *adv* abroad
u izobilju *adv.* galore
u kome *adv.* wherein
u krivi čas *a.* inopportune
u međuvremenu *adv.* meanwhile
u obliku uha *adj.* auriform
u okviru *adv.* within
u pokretu *adv.* astir

u poređenju sa *prep* besides
u posljednje vrijeme *adv.* lately
u postelji *adv.* abed
u*i adv.* wholly
u samoj unutrašnjosti *a.* innermost
u snu *adv.* asleep
u svakom slučaju *adv.* anyhow
u unutrašnjosti *a.* inland
ubediti *v. t* convince
ubedljiv *adj.* cogent
ubijanje *n.* kill
ubilački *a.* murderous
ubilježiti *v.t* file
ubiti *v.t.* kill
ubiti *v.t.* murder
ubiti *v.t.* slay
ubiti *v.t.* assassinate
ublažavanje *n.* mitigation
ublažiti *v.t.* mince
ublažiti *v.t.* mitigate
ublažiti *v.t.* moderate
ublažiti *v.t.* soften
ublažiti *v.t.* soothe
ublažiti *v.t.* allay
ublažiti *v.t.* assuage
ubod *n.* prick
ubod *n.* stab
ubod *v.t.* sting
ubojica *n.* assassin
ubojica *n.* murderer
ubojstvo *n.* homicide
ubojstvo *n.* murder
ubosti *v.t.* lance
ubosti *v.t.* prick
ubosti *v.t.* stab
ubrizgati *v.t.* inject
ubrizgavanje *n.* injection
ubrzanje *n* acceleration
ubrzati *v.t* accelerate
ubrzati *v.i.* hasten

ubrzati *v.i.* speed
ubuduće *adv.* henceforward
ucjena *n* blackmail
ucjeniti *v.t* blackmail
ucrtati *v.t.* map
ucvijeliti *v. t.* bereave
ucvijeljenost *n* bereavement
učen *a.* learned
učenik *n* disciple
učenik *n.* learner
učenik *n.* pupil
učenje *n.* learning
učenje napamet *n.* rote
učesnik *n.* participant
učestalost *n.* frequent
učešće *n.* participation
učetvorostručiti *v.t.* quadruple
učiniti *v.t.* render
učiniti dragim *v.t* endear
učiniti imunim *v.t.* immunize
učiniti nepromočivim *v.t.* waterproof
učiniti siročetom *v.t* orphan
učiniti udovicom *v.t.* widow
učiniti vitezom *v.t.* knight
učinkovit *a* effective
učinkovitost *n* efficiency
učitelj *n.* preceptor
učitelj *n.* teacher
učiteljski *a.* tutorial
učiti *v.i.* study
učiti *v.t.* teach
učtiv *a.* mannerly
učtiv *a.* polite
učtiv *a.* urbane
učtivost *n.* courtesy
učtivost *n.* politeness
učtivost *n.* urbanity
učvrstiti *v.t.* steady
ud *n.* limb
udaljen *a* distant

udar *n.* coup
udar *n.* impact
udarac *n* beat
udarac *n.* jostle
udarac *n.* stroke
udarac bičem *n* lash
udarac bičem *n* slash
udarati *v. t.* beat
udarati u bubanj *v.i.* drum
udariti *v.t.* punch
udariti *v.t.* strike
udariti *v.t.* whack
udariti da poleti visoko *v.t.* sky
udariti motkom *v. i* bat
udariti o *v.t.* jostle
udariti šapom *v.t.* paw
udati *v.t.* marry
udenuti *v.t* thread
udio *n.* share
udisati *v.i.* inhale
udoban *a* comfortable
udoban *a.* cosy
udoban *adj.* cozy
udoban *n.* snug
udostojiti *v.t* dignify
udovac *n.* widower
udovica *n.* widow
udovoljavanje *n.* compliance
udovoljiti *v. i* comply
udružen *a.* associate
udruženje *n.* association
udruživanje *n.* merger
udubljen *adj.* concave
udubljenje *n.* recess
udvaranje *n.* courtship
udvarati se *v. t.* court
udvarati se *v.t.* woo
udvostručiti *v. t.* double
udvostručiti *v. t* duplicate
udvostručiti *v.t.* redouble

ugađanje *n.* indulgence
ugađati *v.t.* indulge
ugađati *v.t.* tune
uganuće *n.* sprain
uganuti *v.t.* sprain
ugar *n* fallow
ugasiti *v.t* extinguish
ugasiti *v.t.* quench
uglađen *a.* sleek
uglađenost *n.* nicety
uglavnom *adv.* generally
uglavnom *adv.* mainly
ugled *n.* reputation
ugled *n.* repute
ugledati *v.t.* sight
ugledna ličnos*t n.* personage
ugljen *n* coal
ugljik *n.* carbon
ugnijezditi *v.t.* nest
ugnjetavanje *n.* oppression
ugnjetavati *v.t.* oppress
ugoditi *v.t.* please
ugostiti *v.t.* banquet
ugovor *n* contract
ugovor *n.* covenant
ugovoriti *v. t* contract
ugravirati *v. t* engrave
ugristi *v. t.* bite
ugriz *n* bite
ugroziti *v. t.* endanger
ugroziti *v.t.* imperil
ugroziti *v.t.* jeopardize
ugroziti *v.t.* peril
ugrušak *n.* clot
ugušiti *v.t.* quell
ugušiti *v.t.* smother
ugušiti *v.t.* stifle
ugušiti *v.t.* strangle
ugušiti *v.t* suffocate
uhapsiti *v.t.* imprison

uhapsiti *v.i.* lag
uhićenje *n.* arrest
uhititi *v.t.* arrest
uhvatiti *v. t.* capture
uhvatiti u mrežu *v.t* mesh
uhvatiti u zamku *v.t.* noose
uhvatiti u zamku *v.t.* snare
uhvatiti u zamku *v.t.* trap
ujarmiti *v.t.* yoke
ujediniti *v.t.* unite
ujediniti se *v.t.* ally
ujedinjenje *n.* unification
ukalupljen *a.* stereotyped
ukaljati *v.* asperse
ukazati *v.t.* indicate
ukidanje *v* abolition
ukinuti *v.t* abolish
ukinuti ograničenje *v.t.* decontrol
ukiseliti *v.t* pickle
ukiseliti *v.t.* sour
uklanjanje *n.* removal
ukloniti *v.t.* remove
uključen *a.* incorporate
uključiti *v.t.* involve
uključivanje *n.* inclusion
uključivati *v.t.* include
uključivo *a.* inclusive
uknjižiti *v. t.* book
ukočen *a.* numb
ukonačiti *v.t.* lodge
ukor *n.* rebuke
ukor *n.* reprimand
ukor *n.* reproof
ukorijeniti *v.i.* root
ukorijenjen *a.* ingrained
ukoriti *v.t.* reprimand
ukras za nogu *n* anklet
ukras za vrat *n.* necklet
ukrasiti *v.t.* bedight
ukrasiti *v. t* deck

ukrasiti *v. t* decorate
ukrasiti *v.t.* grace
ukrasiti *v.t.* ornament
ukrasiti draguljima *v.t.* jewel
ukrasiti zvijezdama *v.t.* star
ukrasna palma *n* areca
ukrasni *a.* ornamental
ukrasti *v.t.* pilfer
ukrasti *v.i.* steal
ukrašavanje *n.* ornamentation
ukratko *adv.* summarily
ukrcano *adv* aboard
ukrcati *v. t.* board
ukrcati *v. t* embark
ukrcati *v.t.* ship
ukršten *a* cross
ukrutiti *v.t.* stiffen
ukuhano voće *n.* preserve
ukupan *a* overall
ukupan *a.* total
ukusan *a* delicious
ukusan *a.* palatable
ukusan *a.* tasteful
ukusan *a.* tasty
ukusan *a.* toothsome
ulaz *n* entrance
ulazak *n* entry
ulaziti *v. t* enter
ulazni *n.* input
ulepšati *v. t* beautify
ulica *n.* street
uličarka *n.* strumpet
ulijevati *v.t.* instil
uliti *v.t.* infuse
ulizica *n.* sycophant
ulizivanje *n.* sycophancy
ulog *n* stake
ulog *n.* wager
uloga *n.* role
ulov *n.* catch

uloviti *v. t.* catch
uložiti *v.t.* stake
ultimatum *n.* ultimatum
ulje *n.* oil
uljepšavati *v.t.* adorn
uljiti *v.t* oil
uljudan *a.* courteous
um *n.* mind
umakanje *n.* dip
umakati *v. i.* dabble
umalo *adv.* almost
umanjiti *v.t.* avale
umanjivati *v.t.* minimize
umarati *v.t* fatigue
umejtnost *n.* art
umetak *n.* parenthesis
umetanje *n.* insertion
umetnuti *v.t.* insert
umetnuti *v.t.* sandwich
umiranje *n* die
umirati od gladi *v.i.* starve
umiriti *v.t.* pacify
umiriti *v.t.* quiet
umiriti *v.t.* still
umiriti *v.t.* appease
umiroviti *v.t.* pension
umiroviti *v.i.* retire
umirovljenik *n.* pensioner
umirujući *a.* sedative
umjeren *a.* moderate
umjeren *a.* temperate
umjerenost *n.* moderation
umjerenost *n.* temperance
umjesto *n.* lieu
umješati *v. t* blend
umjetni *a.* artificial
umjetnički *a.* artistic
umjetnik *n.* artist
umnožavati na ciklostilu *v. t* cyclostyle
umnožiti *v.t.* multiply

umnožiti matricom *v.i.* stencil
umočiti *v. t* dip
umor *n* fatigue
umoran *a.* weary
umoriti *v.t. & i* weary
umotati *v.t.* sheet
umreti *v. i* die
umrljati *v. t* blot
unaprijed oružati *v.t* forearm
unaprijed smisliti *v.t.* premeditate
unaprijed *adv.* beforehand
unaprijediti *v.t.* advance
unaprijediti *v.t* further
unatoč *prep.* notwithstanding
unazad *adv.* aback
unazad *adv.* back
unazad *a.* backward
unazad *adv.* backward
unca *n.* ounce
unezveren *a.* haggard
unija *n.* union
unijeti u zapisnik *n.* minute
unionista *n.* unionist
uništenje *n* annihilation
uništiti *v. t* destroy
uništiti *v.t.* obliterate
uništiti *v.t.* wreck
uništiti *v.t.* annihilate
univerzalan *a.* universal
univerzalnost *n.* universality
unosan *a.* lucrative
unosan *a.* remunerative
unovčiti *v. t.* cash
unutar *prep.* inside
unutarnji *a.* indoor
unutarnji *adv.* inland
unutarnji *a.* inner
unutarnji *a.* intrinsic
unutarnji *a.* inward
unutra *adv.* indoors

unutra *adv.* inside
unutra *adv.* inwards
unutrašnji *a* inside
unutrašnji *a.* interior
unutrašnjost *n.* inside
unutrašnjost *n.* interior
unutrašnjost *n.* midland
unutrašnjost *n.* within
uobičajen *a* customary
uobičajen *a.* usual
uobičajen *a.* wonted
uobličiti *v.t* figure
uobraženost *n* conceit
upad *n.* intrusion
upadljiv *a.* conspicuous
upakirati *v.t.* pack
upala slijepog creva *n.* appendicitis
upaljač *n.* lighter
upasti *v.t.* intrude
upasti *v.t.* raid
upetljati *v. t* entangle
upisati *v. t* enrol
upisati *v.t.* inscribe
upisati visoku školu *v.t.* matriculate
upiti *v.t* absorb
upitni *a.* interrogative
upitnik *n* interrogative
upitnik *n.* questionnaire
uplašen *a.* afraid
uplašiti *v. t* daunt
uplašiti *v.t.* frighten
uplašiti *v.t.* scare
uplesti *v.t.* wreathe
uplitanje *n.* interference
uplitati se *v.i.* interfere
uporan *a.* insistent
uporan *a.* persistent
uporan *a.* tenacious
uporan *a.* untoward
uporište *n.* stronghold

uposliti *v.t.* task	**uramiti** *v.t.* frame
upotreba *n.* use	**uravnotežiti** *v.t.* balance
upotrebljavati *v.t.* ply	**uravnotežiti** *v.t.* sedate
upotrijebiti *v.t.* use	**urbani** *a.* urban
upoznat *a* conversant	**ured** *n.* office
upoznati *v.t.* acquaint	**uredan** *a.* neat
upozorenje *n.* admonition	**uredan** *a.* orderly
upozorenje *n.* warning	**uredan** *a.* tidy
upozoriti *v.t.* admonish	**uredan** *a.* trim
upozoriti *v. t.* caution	**urediti** *v. t* edit
upozoriti *v.t* forewarn	**urediti** *v.t.* trim
upozoriti *v.t.* warn	**urediti** *v.t.* arrange
uprava *n.* administration	**urednički** *a* editorial
uprava *n.* governance	**urednik** *n* editor
upravitelj zatvora *n.* warden	**uredno** *n.* orderly
upravljanje *n* conduct	**urednost** *n.* tidiness
upravljanje *n.* management	**uređaj** *n* device
upravljanje *n.* ruling	**uređaj** *n.* appliance
upravljati *v. t* conduct	**uređenje** *n.* arrangement
upravljati *v.t.* govern	**urez** *n.* scotch
upravljati *v.t.* manage	**urezati** *v.t.* score
upravljati *v.i.* navigate	**urin** *n.* urine
upravljati *v.t.* steer	**urinarni** *a.* urinary
upravljati *v.t.* administer	**urinirati** *v.i.* urinate
upravni *a.* administrative	**urlati** *v. i* bellow
upravnik pošte *n.* postmaster	**urna** *n* urn
upravo *adv.* just	**urnebes** *n.* pandemonium
upravo *adv* pat	**urođen** *a.* inborn
upražnjeno mesto *n.* vacancy	**urođen** *a.* innate
upregnuti *v.t* harness	**urođenički** *a.* indigenous
uprljati *n.* slur	**urođenik** *n* native
uprljati *v.t.* taint	**uručiti** *v.t* hand
upropastiti *v.t.* ruin	**usamljen** *a* forlorn
uprošćavanje *n.* simplification	**usamljen** *a.* lone
upućen *adj.* conversant	**usamljen** *a.* lonely
uputa *n.* tutorial	**usamljen** *a.* lonesome
uputiti *v.i.* motion	**usamljen** *a.* solitary
uputiti *v.t.* refer	**usamljenost** *n.* loneliness
ura *interj.* hurrah	**usamljenost** *n.* solitude
uragan *n.* hurricane	**usavršiti** *v.t.* perfect

usedelica *n.* spinster
ushićen *a.* jubilant
ushićen *a.* rapt
ushititi *v. t* enrapture
usidrenje *n* anchorage
usidriti brod *v.t* moor
usjev *n* crop
uska ulica *n.* alley
uskladiti *v. t* equate
usklađen *a.* co-ordinate
uskomešati se *v.i.* stir
uskoro *adv.* presently
uskoro *adv.* shortly
uskoro *adv.* soon
uskratiti *v. t.* debar
uskrs *n* easter
uslužan *adj.* complaisant
uslužan *a.* serviceable
uslužnost *n.* complaisance
usmen *a.* oral
usmen *a* viva-voce
usmeni ispit *n* viva-voce
usmeno *adv.* orally
usmeno *adv.* verbally
usmeno *adv.* viva-voce
usmjeriti *v. t* direct
usna *n.* lip
uspavanka *n.* lullaby
uspjeh *n.* success
uspjeh *n.* achievement
uspješan *a.* prosperous
uspješan *a* successful
uspjeti *v.i.* succeed
uspomena *n.* keepsake
uspomena *n.* memento
uspomena *n.* reminiscence
uspon *n.* ascent
usporedba *n* comparison
usporediti *v. t* compare
usporedo *adv* abreast

usporiti *v.t.* retard
usporiti *v.i.* slow
uspostaviti *v. t.* establish
uspraviti *v. t* erect
uspravljen *a* erect
usredtočenost *n.* concentration
usredtočiti *v. t* concentrate
usta *n.* mouth
ustajao *a.* mouldy
ustajao *a.* stale
ustanak *n.* uprising
ustanoviti *v. t* constitute
ustanoviti *v. t.* essay
ustanoviti *v.t.* stipulate
ustati *v.i.* arise
ustav *n* constitution
ustoličiti *v. t* enthrone
ustuknuti *v.i.* recoil
ustupiti *v.t.* concede
usuditi se *v. i.* dare
usuditi se *v.t.* venture
usvajanje *n* adoption
usvojiti *v.t.* adopt
ušće *n* confluence
ušna mast *n* cerumen
ušna resa *n.* lobe
uštinuti *v.t* nip
uštinuti *v.t.* pinch
ušutkati *v.t* muzzle
utakmica *n.* meet
utaknuti *v.t.* jack
utemeljenje *n.* foundation
utemeljiti *v.t.* found
uticaj *n.* influence
utičnica *n.* jack
utičnica *n.* socket
utikač *n.* plug
utilitaristički *a.* utilitarian
utisnuti *v.t.* imprint
utišati *v.i* hush

utišati *v.t.* lull	uvesti *v.t.* prelude
utišati *v.t.* silence	uvesti *v.t.* usher
utjecaj *v.t.* influence	uvid *n.* insight
utjecati *v.t.* affect	uvijek *adv.* always
utjecati *a.* influential	uviti *v.t.* twist
utjeha *n.* comfort	uvjeravanje *n.* persuasion
utjeha *n* consolation	uvjeravati *v.t.* reassure
utjeha *n.* solace	uvjerenje *n* belief
utjeloviti *v. t.* embody	uvjerenje *n.* certificate
utjelovljen *a.* incarnate	uvjerenje *n.* testimonial
utjelovljenje *n* embodiment	uvjeriti *v.t.* persuade
utjerivanje u rupu *n.* gobble	uvjet *n.* proviso
utješiti *v. t* comfort	uvjet, stanje *n* condition
utješiti *v.t.* solace	uvjetni *a* conditional
utočište *n* haunt	uvjetni otpust *n.* parole
utočište *n.* refuge	uvjetno otpustiti *v.t.* parole
utoliti *v.t.* slake	uvježbavati *v.t.* practise
utonuti *v.t.* immerse	uvo *n* ear
utopija *n .* utopia	uvod *n.* introduction
utopijski *a.* utopian	uvod *n.* prelude
utopiti *v.i* drown	uvodni *a.* inaugural
utrka *n.* race	uvodni *a.* introductory
utrkivati se *v.i* race	uvodnik *n* editorial
utroba *n.* entrails	uvođenje *n.* induction
utrostručenje *n.* triplication	uvojak *n.* curl
utrostručiti *v.t.,* triple	uvojak *n* forelock
utučenost *n* dejection	uvojak *n* lock
utuviti *v.t.* inculcate	uvoz *n.* import
utvara *n.* wraith	uvoziti *v.t.* import
utvrda *n.* fort	uvreda *n.* insult
utvrditi *v.t.* fortify	uvreda *n.* offence
utvrditi *v.t.* ascertain	uvreda *n* affront
uvećanje *v. t* enlarge	uvredljiv *a* abusive
uveličati *v.t.* magnify	uvrijediti *v.t.* affront
uvenuti *v.i.* wither	uvrijediti *v.t.* insult
uverenje *n.* assurance	uvrijediti *v.t.* offend
uveriti *v.t.* assure	uzajamno djelovanje *n.* interplay
uvertira *n.* overture	uzak *a.* narrow
uvesti *v.t.* induct	uzalud *adv.* vainly
uvesti *v.t.* introduce	uzaludan *a.* futile

uzaludan *a.* vain	**uzrečica** *n* byword
uzaludnost *n.* futility	**uzročnost** *n* causality
uzastopan *a.* successive	**uzrok** *n.* cause
uzastopni *adj.* consecutive	**uzrokovati** *v.t* cause
uzastopno *adv* consecutively	**uzrujanost** *n* agitation
uzbuditi *v. t* excite	**uzrujanost** *n.* fret
uzbuditi *v.t.* thrill	**uzrujati** *v.t.* agitate
uzbuđenje *n.* thrill	**uzrujati se** *v.t.* fret
uzbuna *n* alarm	**uzurpacija** *n.* usurpation
uzbuniti *v.t* alarm	**uzurpirati** *v.t.* usurp
uzburkati *v.t.* trouble	**uzvik** *n* cry
uzda *n.* rein	**uzvik** *n* exclamation
uzda *n* bridle	**uzvik** *n.* interjection
uzdah *n.* sigh	**uzviknuti** *v.i* exclaim
uzdahnuti *v.i.* sigh	**uzvišen** *a.* lofty
uzdignuće *n* elevation	**uzvišen** *a.* sublime
uzdignuće *n* uplift	**uzvišenost** *n* sublime
uzdržavati se *v.i.* refrain	**uzvraćati** *v.t.* reciprocate
uzduž *adv.* along	**uzvratiti** *v. t* counter
uzengija *n.* stirrup	**užaren** *adv.* aglow
uzeti *v.t* take	**užaren** *a.* ardent
uzeti žlicom *v.t.* spoon	**užaren** *a* fiery
uzgajivač *n.* grower	**užas** *n.* horror
uzgon *n* buoyancy	**užasan** *a.* terrible
uzica biča *n.* whipcord	**uže** *n.* rope
uzimajući u obzir *prep.* considering	**užina** *n.* snack
uzmaći *v.i.* recede	**uživanje** *n* delight
uznemiravanje *n.* harassment	**uživanje** *n* enjoyment
uznemiravati *v. t* disturb	**uživati** *v. t.* delight
uznemiravati *v.t.* harass	**uživati** *v. t* enjoy
uznemiren *a* anxiety	**uživati** *v.t.* relish
uznemirenost *n* disquiet	**uživati** *v.i.* bask
uznemiriti *v. t* commove	**užlebiti** *v.t* groove
uznemiriti *v.t.* unsettle	**užurban** *a.* hasty
uznemiriti *v.t.* upset	
uznemiriti se *v.i* fuss	
uzor *n.* paragon	
uzorak *n.* sample	
uzoran *a.* commendable	**vagati** *v.t.* scale
uzorkovati *v.t.* sample	**vagati** *v.t.* weigh

vagina *n.* vagina
vagon *n.* wagon
vajar *n.* sculptor
vajarski *a.* sculptural
vakuum *n.* vacuum
val *n* billow
val *v.i.* surge
val *n.* surge
val *v.t.* wave
val *n.* wave
validan *a.* valid
valuta *n* currency
valjak *n.* roller
valjanost *n* good
valjati rublje *v.t.* mangle
valjati se *v.i.* wallow
van *adv.* out
van *adv* outward
vanbračan *a* bastard
vani *adv.* afield
vani *a.* outdoor
vani *adv* outside
vanjski *a* external
vanjski *a.* outer
vanjski *a.* outside
vanjski *a.* outward
vapno *n.* lime
varalica *n.* impostor
varalica *n.* sharper
varalica *n.* swindler
varalica *n.* trickster
varanje *n.* cheat
varanje *n.* trickery
varati *v. t.* cheat
varati *v.t.* rook
varenje *n* digestion
varijabla *a.* variable
varijacija *n.* variation
varirati *v.t.* vary
variti *v. t.* brew

varka *n* sham
varnica *n.* spark
varničiti *v.i.* spark
vaška *n.* louse
vat *n.* watt
vatra *n* fire
vatren *a* fervent
vatreno oružje *n.* gun
vaučer *n.* voucher
vazdušast *adj.* aeriform
vazdušast *a.* airy
vazektomija *n.* vasectomy
vazelin *n.* vaseline
važan *a* considerable
važan *a.* weighty
važno *a.* important
većina *n.* majority
večer *n* evening
večera *n* dinner
večera *n.* supper
večeras *adv.* tonight
večerati *v. t.* dine
večit *a.* perpetual
već *adv.* already
većina *n* most
većinom *a.* most
vegetacija *n.* vegetation
vegetarijanac *n.* vegetarian
vegetarijanski *a* vegetarian
vekna *n.* loaf
velelepnost *n.* festivity
veleposlanik *n.* ambassador
veleprodaja *n.* wholesale
veleprodajni *a* wholesale
veleprodajno *adv.* wholesale
veletrgovac *n.* wholesaler
veličanstven *a.* magnificent
veličanstven *a.* majestic
veličanstven *a.* marvellous
veličanstven *a.* palatial

veličanstven *a.* stately
veličanstvenost *n.* grandeur
veličanstvo *n.* majesty
veličati *v. t* exalt
veličati *v. t.* extol
veličati *v.t.* glorify
veličina *n.* magnitude
veličina *n.* size
velignton *n.* wellignton
velik *a.* grard
velik *a* great
velik *a.* large
velik *a* big
velike boginje *n.* smallpox
velikodušan *a.* generous
velikodušan *a.* magnanimous
velikodušnost *n.* generosity
velikodušnost *n.* liberality
velikodušnost *n.* magnanimity
veljača *n* February
vena *n.* vein
ventil *n.* valve
ventilacija *n.* ventilation
ventilator *n.* ventilator
ventilirati *v.t.* ventilate
veo *n.* veil
veoma *adv* much
veoma *a.* very
vepar *n* boar
veranda *n.* porch
veranda *n.* verendah
verati *se v.i.* scramble
verbalni *a.* verbal
verificirati *v.t.* verify
verifikacija *n.* verification
vertikala *n.* perpendicular
vertikalan *a.* perpendicular
vertikalan *a.* vertical
verzija *n.* version
veseliti se *v.i.* frolic

veselost *n.* gaiety
veselost *n.* joviality
veseljak *n.* spark
veselje *n.* hilarity
veselje *n.* jollity
veselje *n.* merriment
veseo *a.* cheerful
veseo *a.* gay
veseo *a.* jovial
veseo *a* merry
veseo *a.* sportive
veslač *n.* oarsman
veslanje *n* row
veslati *v.i.* paddle
veslati *v.t.* row
veslo *n.* oar
veslo *n* paddle
vestern *a.* western
veteran *n.* veteran
veteranski *a.* veteran
veterinarski *a.* veterinary
veto *n.* veto
veverica *n.* squirrel
vez *n* embroidery
vez *n* berth
veza *n* bond
veza *n* connection
veza *n.* liaison
vezati *v.t.* knot
vezati *v.t.* lace
vezati *v.t.* tie
vezati kablom *v. t.* cable
vezati *v.t* bind
vezivanje *n* deligate1
vibracija *n.* vibration
vibrirati *v.i.* vibrate
vic *n.* joke
vidik *n.* vista
vidikovac *n* belvedere
vidjeti *v.t.* see

vidljiv *a.* visible
vidljivost *n.* visibility
vidokrug *n.* purview
vidovnjak *n.* seer
vidra *n.* otter
vigvam *n.* wigwam
vihor *n.* whirlwind
vijak *n.* screw
vijećnik *n.* councillor
vijenac *n.* coronet
vijenac *n* festoon
vijenac *n.* garland
vijenac *n.* wreath
vijenac za glavu *n* anadem
vijesti *n.* news
vijesti *n. pl.* tidings
vijuganje *n* wriggle
vijugati *v.i.* wriggle
vijugati se *v.i.* zigzag
vijugav *a.* sinuous
vijugav *a.* zigzag
vika *n.i.* bawl
vikanje *n* yell
vikar *n.* vicar
vikati *v. i* cry
vikati *v.i.* shout
vikati *v.i.* yell
vila *n* fairy
vila *n.* villa
vilica *n.* jaw
vime *n.* mamma
vime *n.* udder
vino *n.* wine
vinova loza *n.* vine
vinuti se *v.i.* soar
violina *n* fiddle
violina *n.* violin
violinista *n.* violinist
virenje *n* peep
viriti *v.i.* peep

virtuelan *a* virtual
virus *n.* virus
visak *n.* lead
visina *n.* height
visina *n.* altitude
visinomjer *n* altimeter
viski *n.* whisky
visok *a.* high
visok *a.* tall
visoko *adv.* aloft
visoko *adv.* highly
Visost *n.* Highness
višak *n* excess
višak *n* over
višak *n.* superfluity
višak *n.* surplus
više *adv* more
više *adv* over
više *a* several
više ponuditi *v.t.* outbid
višegodišnji *a.* perennial
višestruk *a.* multiplex
vitak *n.* slender
vitak *a.* slim
vitalan *a.* vital
vitalnost *n.* vitality
vitamin *n.* vitamin
viteški *a.* chivalrous
viteštvo *n.* chivalry
vitez *n.* knight
vizija *n.* vision
vizionar *n.* visionary
vizionarski *a.* visionary
vizualizovati *v.t.* visualize
vizualni *a.* visual
vječan *adj.* eternal
vječan *a.* everlasting
vječnost *n* eternity
vjenčanje *n.* wedding
vjenčati *v.t.* wed

vjera *n.* creed
vjera *n* faith
vjeran *a* faithful
vjeran *n.* trusty
vjernost *n* fidelity
vjernost *n.* allegiance
vjerodostojan *a* credible
vjerojatan *a.* probable
vjerojatno *a.* likely
vjerojatno *adv.* probably
vjerojatnost *n.* likelihood
vjerojatnost *n.* probability
vjerojatnost *n.* verisimilitude
vjerovati *v.t* trust
vjerovati *v. t* believe
vjerovnik *n* creditor
vjerski *a.* religious
vješala *n.* gallows
vješt *a.* artful
vješt *a.* proficient
vješt *a.* skilful
vješt *a.* adept
vještica *n.* hag
vještica *n.* witch
vještina *n.* adept
vještina *n.* proficiency
vještina *n.* skill
vjetar *n.* wind
vjetrenjača *n.* windmill
vjetrovit *a.* windy
vježba *n.* exercise
vježbati *v. t* exercise
Vlada *n.* government
vladar *n.* ruler
vladar *n.* sovereign
vladati *v.i.* reign
vladati *v.t.* rule
vladavina *n* reign
vlaga *n* damp
vlaga *n.* moisture

vlakno *n* fibre
vlasnički *a.* proprietary
vlasnik *n.* owner
vlasnik *n.* proprietor
vlast *n* dominion
vlast *n.* authority
vlastelin *n.* squire
vlastelinski *a.* manorial
vlastelinstvo *n.* manor
vlažan *a* damp
vlažan *adj.* dank
vlažan *a.* humid
vlažan *a.* moist
vlažiti *v. t.* damp
vlažiti *v.t.* moisten
vlažnost *n.* humidity
vlažnost *n.* wetness
vo *n.* ox
voće *n.* fruit
voćnjak *n.* orchard
vod *n.* platoon
vod *n.* squad
vode *n.* water
vodeni *a.* watery
vodič *n.* guide
vodik *n.* hydrogen
voditi *v.t.* guide
voditi *v.t* head
voditi *v.t.* wage
voditi napad *v.t.* spearhead
voditi porijeklo *v.t.* originate
vodoinstalater *n.* plumber
vodolija *n.* aquarius
vodootporan *a.* waterproof
vodootpornost *n* waterproof
vodopad *n.* waterfall
vođa *n.* leader
vođstvo *n.* guidance
vođstvo *n.* leadership
vojni *a.* martial

vojni *a.* military	**vratilo** *n.* shaft
vojnik *n.* soldier	**vratiti** *v.t.* reclaim
vojska *n* military	**vratiti** *v.t.* requite
vojska *n.* army	**vratiti se** *v.i.* relapse
vojvoda *n* duke	**vratiti se** *v.i.* return
vokalni *a.* vocal	**vratiti se** *v.i.* revert
volej *n.* volley	**vratiti se istim putem** *v.t.* retrace
voleti *v.t.* love	**vratiti u domovinu** *v.t.* repatriate
volonter *n.* volunteer	**vratiti u pritvor** *v.t.* remand
volontirati *v.t.* volunteer	**vratnice** *n.* wicket
volovska koža *n* buff	**vrba** *n.* willow
volt *n.* volt	**vrbovnik** *n* crimp
volja *n.* volition	**vrebati** *v.i.* lurk
volja *n.* will	**vrebati** *v.i.* prey
voljan *a.* willing	**vreća** *n.* sack
voljen *a.* loving	**vreća** *n.* poke
vosak *n.* wax	**vrećica** *n.* pouch
voštana mast *adj.* cerated	**vreme za spavanje** *n.* bed-time
voz *n.* train	**vremenski** *a.* temporal
vozač *n* driver	**vremenski period** *n.* while
vozač *n.* motorist	**vreo** *a.* hot
vozilo *n.* vehicle	**vresište** *n.* moor
voziti *v. t* drive	**vreteno** *n.* spindle
voziti *v.t.* ride	**vrh** *n.* peak
voziti bicikl *v.t.* pedal	**vrh** *n.* summit
voziti se *v.i.* motor	**vrh** *n.* tip
voziti se na jahti *v.i* yacht	**vrh** *n.* top
voziti se u taksiju *v.i.* taxi	**vrh koplja** *n.* spearhead
vožnja *n* drive	**vrh** *n.* apex
vožnja *n* ride	**vrhovni** *a.* supreme
vrabac *n.* sparrow	**vrhovni nadzor** *n.* superintendence
vraćanje *n.* recurrence	**vrhunac** *n.* climax
vračanje *n.* witchcraft	**vrhunac** *n.* heyday
vraćanje u pritvor *n* remand	**vrhunac** *n.* pinnacle
vragolast *a.* mischievous	**vrijedan** *a.* industrious
vrana *n* crow	**vrijedan** *a.* valuable
vrat *n.* neck	**vrijedan** *a* worth
vrata *n* door	**vrijedan pažnje** *a.* noteworthy
vratar *n.* porter	**vrijednost** *n.* value
vratar *n.* usher	**vrijednost** *n.* worth

vrijeđati *v.t.* resent
vrijeme *n.* time
vrijeme *n* weather
vrisak *n* scream
vrisak *n.* shriek
vrištati *v.i.* scream
vrištati *v.i.* shriek
vrli *a.* virtuous
vrlina *n.* virtue
vrpca *n.* string
vrsta *n.* kind
vrsta *n.* sort
vrsta *n.* species
vrsta baruta *n.* amberite
vrsta biljke *n.* cardamom
vrsta cigare *n* cheroot
vrsta konja *n.* bayard
vrsta krojača *n.* cosier
vrsta organa *n.* cornicle
vrsta ponošanja *v.t.* condite
vršalica *n.* thresher
vršati *v.t.* thresh
vrtlog *n* whirl
vrtlog *n.* whirlpool
vrtoglav *a.* giddy
vruć *a.* warm
vrućina *n.* ardour
vrveti *v.i.* teem
vuča *n.* traction
vući *v.t* draw
vući noge *v.i.* shuffle
vuk *n.* wolf
vulgaran *a.* vulgar
vulgarnost *n.* vulgarity
vulkan *n.* volcano
vulkanski *a.* volcanic
vuna *n.* wool
vunena tkanina *n* woollen
vuneni *a.* woollen

Z

za *prep* for
za divljenje *a.* admirable
za razliku od *prep* unlike
za vrijeme *prep* during
zabava *n.* entertainment
zabava *n.* frolic
zabava *n.* fun
zabava *n* amusement
zabaviti *v. t* entertain
zabavljati se *v.i.* sport
zabavljati *v.t.* amuse
zabilježiti *v.t.* jot
zabilježiti *n.* log
zabiti *v.t.* nail
zabluda *n* fallacy
zaborav *n.* oblivion
zaboravan *a* forgetful
zaboraviti *v.t* forget
zabosti *v.t.* stick
zabrana *n.* prohibition
zabrana *n.* ban
zabraniti *v.t* bar
zabraniti *v.t* forbid
zabraniti *v.t.* prohibit
zabraniti *v.t.* taboo
zabranjen *a* taboo
zabranjujući *a.* prohibitory
zabraviti *v. t* bolt
zabrinut *a.* solicitous
zabrinut *a.* anxious
zabrinutost *n.* solicitude
zabrljati *v.t.* mull
zabuna *n* confusion
zabušant *n.* shirker
zabušavati *v.t.* shirk
začarati *v.t* bewitch

začepiti *n.* gag
začepiti *v.t.* plug
začeti *v. t* conceive
začeti *v. t* beget
začin *n.* spice
začiniti *v.t.* season
začiniti *v.t.* spice
začuditi *v.t.* astonish
zadatak *n* errand
zadatak *n.* task
zaderati *v.t.* scar
zadesiti *v. t* befall
zadimljen *a.* smoky
zadirati *v. i* encroach
zadirkivanje *n.* banter
zadirkivanje *n.* raillery
zadirkivati *v.t.* banter
zadirkivati *v.t.* rag
zadirkivati *v.t.* tease
zadiviti *v.t.* amaze
zadivljenost *n.* amazement
zadovoljan *a.* content
zadovoljavajući *a.* satisfactory
zadovoljavati *v.i.* suffice
zadovoljiti *v. t* content
zadovoljiti *v.t.* satisfy
zadovoljstvo *n.* content
zadovoljstvo *n* contentment
zadovoljstvo *n.* gratification
zadovoljstvo *n.* pleasure
zadovoljstvo *n.* satisfaction
zadružni *a* co-operative
zadržati *v. t* detain
zadržati *v.t.* retain
zadržati *v.t.* withhold
zadržavanje *n.* retention
zadubljen u misli *a.* pensive
zadužen *a.* indebted
zaduženje *n* debit
zadužiti *v. t* debit

zagaditi *v.t.* pollute
zagađenje *n.* pollution
zagledano *adv.* agaze
zaglibiti *v.i* bog
zagonetka *n.* riddle
zagorčati *v. t* embitter
zagrijati *v.t* heat
zagrliti *v. t.* embrace
zagrljaj *n* embrace
zagubiti *v.t.* misplace
zagušljiv *a.* stuffy
zahtijevati *v. t* claim
zahtijevati *v.t.* necessitate
zahtijevati *v.t.* request
zahtjev *n* demand
zahtjev *n* request
zahtjevati *v. t* demand
zahvalan *a.* grateful
zahvalan *a.* thankful
zahvaliti *v.t.* thank
zahvalnost *n.* gratitude
zahvalnost *n.* thanks
zahvalnost *n.* appreciation
zahvat *n* grasp
zainteresiran *a.* interested
zaista *adv.* indeed
zajam *n.* loan
zajažljiv *a.* satiable
zajednica *n.* community
zajednički *a.* common
zajednički *a.* mutual
zajedničko *adv.* jointly
zajedno *adv.* together
zajedno živjeti *v. t* cohabit
zakašnjeli *adj.* belated
zakašnjelo *a.* overdue
zaklanjati *v.t.* screen
zaklati *v.t.* slaughter
zakletva *n.* oath
zaklon *n.* lee

zaključak *n.* conclusion	**založni verovnik** *n.* mortagagee
zaključati *v.t* lock	**zaluđivati** *v.t.* infatuate
zaključiti *v. t* conclude	**zalutao** *a* stray
zaključiti *v.t.* infer	**zalutao** *adv.* astray
zaključivanje *n.* inference	**zalutati** *v.i.* stray
zaključni *a* conclusive	**zaljev** *n.* gulf
zakon *n.* law	**zaljubiti se** *v. t* enamour
zakonit *a.* lawful	**zaljubljiv** *a.* amorous
zakonitost *n.* legality	**zamagliti** *v. t* blear
zakonodavac *n.* legislator	**zamah** *n.* lunge
zakonodavan *a.* legislative	**zamah** *n.* sweep
zakonodavstvo *n.* legislature	**zamah** *n* whisk
zakopčati *v. t.* button	**zamazati** *v. t.* daub
zakovati *v.t.* rivet	**zamazati** *v.t.* smear
zakovica *n.* rivet	**zamijeniti** *v. t* commute
zakrčiti *v. t* clutter	**zamijeniti** *v.t.* replace
zakrčiti *v.t.* ram	**zamijeniti** *v.t.* substitute
zakrpa *n* patch	**zamijeniti** *v.t.* supersede
zakrpiti *v. t* botch	**zamisliti** *v.t* fancy
zakrpiti *v.t.* patch	**zamisliti** *v.t.* imagine
zakucati *v.t.* jam	**zamišljen** *a.* wistful
zakup *n.* lease	**zamjena** *n.* replacement
zakup *n.* tenancy	**zamjena** *n.* substitute
zakupac *n.* lessee	**zamjena** *n.* substitution
zakupiti *v.t.* lease	**zamjenica** *n.* pronoun
zalazak *n* set	**zamjenik** *n* deputy
zalemiti *v.t.* solder	**zamjenjivati** *v.t.* alternate
zalet *n* pounce	**zamjerka** *n.* stricture
zaleteti se *v.i.* pounce	**zamka** *n.* noose
zaliha *n.* stock	**zamka** *n.* pitfall
zalijevati *v.t.* water	**zamka** *n.* snare
zaliti *v.t.* pitch	**zamka** *n.* trap
zaliv *n* bay	**zamoran** *a.* irksome
zaloga *v.t.* pledge	**zamoran** *a.* tiresome
zaloga *n.* pledge	**zamotati** *v. t* envelop
zalogaj *n.* morsel	**zamotati** *v.t.* wrap
zalogaj *n.* mouthful	**zamrsiti** *v.t.* tangle
založiti *v. t* deposit	**zamrznuti** *v.i.* freeze
založiti *v.t.* mortgage	**zamuljiti** *v.t.* silt
založni dužnik *n.* mortgagor	**zanat** *n* craft

zanatlija *n.* artisan
zanatlija *n* craftsman
zanemariti *v.t.* neglect
zanemarivanje *n* neglect
zanemarljiv *a.* negligible
zanesenost *n.* rapture
zanimanje *n.* occupation
zanimanje *n.* vocation
zanimljiv *a.* interesting
zanovetati *v.i.* grumble
zanovijetanje *n.* nag
zanovjetalo *v.t.* nag
zao *a* evil
zao *a.* malignant
zao *a.* nefarious
zao *a.* wicked
zaobilaznica *n* bypass
zaobliti *v.t.* round
zaokupiti *v.t* engross
zaokupiti *v.t.* preoccupy
zaoštriti *v.t.* point
zapad *n.* occident
zapad *n.* west
zapadni *a.* west
zapadni *adv.* westerly
zapadno *adv.* west
zapadno *a.* westerly
zapadnjački *a.* occidental
zapaliti *v.t* fire
zapaljeno *adv.* aflame
zapaljenje *n.* inflammation
zapaljenje pluća pneumonia
zapaljiv *a.* inflammable
zapamtiti *v.t.* remember
zapanjeno *adv.* agape
zapanjenost *n* daze
zapanjiti *v.t* daze
zapanjiti *v.t* astound
zapečatiti *v.t.* seal
zapečatiti *v.i.* stamp

zapetljan *a.* intricate
zapisati *v.t.* note
zapisati *v.t.* record
zapisničar *n.* recorder
zapisničar *n.* scorer
zapisnik *n.* record
zaplet *n.* plot
zaplet *n.* tangle
zaplijeniti *v.t.* sequester
započeti *v.t.* initiate
zaposlenje *n* employment
zaposliti *v. t* employ
zaposliti *v.t* hire
zapovednički *a.* authoritative
zapovjednik *n* commandant
zaprašiti *v.t.* dust
zapravo *adv.* actually
zapreka *n.* hitch
zaprepastiti *v.t.* horrify
zaptivač *n.* gasket
zaraćena strana *n* belligerent
zaraćenost *n* belligerency
zarada *n.* salary
zaraditi *v.t.* net
zarazan *a* contagious
zarazan *a.* infectious
zaraziti *v.t.* plague
zarđao *a.* rusty
zarez *n* comma
zarez *n.* notch
zarobiti *v.t.* enslave
zarobiti *v. t.* entrap
zarobiti *v. t.* captivate
zaroniti *v.i.* duck
zaroniti *v.t.* plunge
zaručiti *v. t* betroth
zaruka *n.* betrothal
zasićenje *n.* saturation
zasijati *v.t* flash
zasipati *v. t* bestrew

zasititi *v.t.* satiate	**zaštitni** *a.* preservative
zasititi *v.t.* saturate	**zaštitni** *a.* protective
zasjeda *n.* ambush	**zaštitnik** *n.* protector
zasjeniti *v. t.* dazzle	**zašto** *adv.* why
zasjeniti *v.t.* overshadow	**zatajiti** *v.i.* misfire
zasjeniti *v.t.* shade	**zateturati se** *v.i.* lurch
zasladiti *v. t.* candy	**zatišje** *n.* lull
zasladiti *v.t.* sugar	**zatočen** *a.* captive
zaslijepljenost *n.* infatuation	**zatočenik** *n.* captive
zasluga *n.* merit	**zatočeništvo** *n.* captivity
zaslužan *a* creditable	**zatvarač** *n.* shutter
zaslužan *a.* meritorious	**zatvaranje** *n.* closure
zaslužiti *v. t.* deserve	**zatvor** *n.* constipation
zaslužiti *v. t* earn	**zatvor** *n.* jail
zaslužiti *v.t* merit	**zatvor** *n.* prison
zasnovati *v.t.* base	**zatvoren** *a.* close
zastario *a.* obsolete	**zatvorenik** *n.* prisoner
zastario *a.* outdated	**zatvoriti** *v. t* close
zastario *a.* antiquated	**zatvoriti** *v.t.* pound
zastati *v.i.* pause	**zatvoriti** *v.t.* shut
zastava *n* flag	**zatvoriti u svetilište** *v. t* enshrine
zastava *n.* banner	**zaustaviti** *v.i.* stem
zastoj *n* halt	**zaustaviti** *v.t.* stop
zastoj *n.* standstill	**zauške** *n.* mumps
zastoj *n* stoppage	**zauvijek** *adv* forever
zastrašiti *v. t.* cow	**zauzdati** *v.t.* rein
zastrašiti *v.t.* intimidate	**zauzet** *a* busy
zastrašivanje *n.* intimidation	**zauzeti** *v.t.* occupy
zastrašivati *v. t.* bully	**zavada** *n.* feud
zastupati *v.t.* advocate	**zavaliti se** *v.i.* loll
zastupnik *n.* proxy	**zavarak** *n* weld
zasvoditi *v.t.* arch	**zavarivati** *v.t.* weld
zašećeriti *v.t.* sweeten	**zavežljaj** *n.* packet
zašiljiti *v.t.* spike	**zavidan** *a* enviable
zašiljiti *v.i.* taper	**zavidjeti** *v. t* envy
zašrafiti *v.t.* screw	**zavidljiv** *a* envious
zaštita *n.* protection	**zavidnik** *n* grudge
zaštita *n.* safeguard	**zavijanje** *n* howl
zaštititi *v.t.* protect	**zavijati** *v.t.* howl
zaštitne naočale *n.* goggles	**zaviještati** *v. t.* bequeath

zavirivati *v.i.* pry
zaviti *v.t* bandage
zavjera *n.* conspiracy
zavjesa *n* curtain
zavjet *n.* vow
zavjetovati *v.t.* vow
zavod *n.* bureau
zavoditi *n.* seduce
zavodljiv *a* seductive
zavođenje *n.* seduction
zavoj *n.* bandage
završetak completion
završetak *n* finish
završetak *n.* termination
završiti *v. t* end
završiti *v.t* finish
zavrtjeti *v.i.* spin
zbaciti *v. t* dethrone
zbaciti *v.t.* toss
zbacivanje *n* toss
zbijati šalu *v.i.* joke
zbirka *n.* miscellany
zbogom *interj.* bye-bye
zbogom *interj.* farewell
zbogom *interj.* good-bye
zbogom *interj.* adieu
zbor *n.* assembly
zbor *n* rally
zbrinuti *v. t* bestow
zbrka *n.* jumble
zbrka *n.* muddle
zbrka *n.* welter
zbrkano *adv.* pell-mell
zbrkati *v.t.* jumble
zbrkati *v.t.* muddle
zbrojiti *v.t.* total
zbuniti *v.t.* nonplus
zbuniti *v.t.* perplex
zbuniti *v.t.* puzzle
zbuniti *v. t.* baffle

zbuniti *v. t* bemuse
zbuniti *v. t* bewilder
zbunjenost *v. t* confuse
zbunjenost *n.* perplexity
zdjela *n* bowl
zdrav *a.* healthy
zdrav *a.* salutary
zdrav *a.* sound
zdrav *a.* wholesome
zdravica *n.* toast
zdravlje *n.* health
združeno *adj.* conjunct
zebra *n.* zebra
zec *n.* hare
zec *n.* rabbit
zefir *n.* zephyr
zelen *a.* green
zelen *a.* verdant
zelena boja *n* green
zelenaš *n.* usurer
zelenaštvo *n.* usury
zelenilo *n.* greenery
zelenkada *n.* daffodil
zemaljski *a* earthly
zemlja *n.* country
zemlja *n* earth
zemljan *a* earthen
zemljano posuđe *n.* crockery
zemljište *n.* land
zenit *n.* zenith
zerez *n.* nick
zgodan *a.* handsome
zgrabiti *v.t.* grab
zgrabiti *v.t.* seize
zgrabiti *v.t.* snatch
zgrada *n* building
zgriješiti *v.i.* trespass
zgrušati *v. t* clot
zgusnuti *v.i.* thicken
zid *n.* wall

zidar *n.* mason
zidarstvo *n.* masonry
zidni *a.* mural
zijevanje *n.* yawn
zijevati *v.i.* gape
zijevati *v.i.* yawn
zima *n.* winter
zimovati *v.i* winter
zimski *a.* wintry
zimzelen *a* evergreen
zlatan *a.* golden
zlatar *n.* goldsmith
zlato *n.* gold
zlikovac *n.* villain
zlo *n* evil
zloba *n.* malice
zloba *n.* rancour
zloban *a.* sardonic
zločin *n* crime
zločinac *n.* malefactor
zlokoban *a.* inauspicious
zlokoban *a.* sinister
zlonamjeran *a.* malicious
zlonamjernost *n* animus
zloslustan *a.* ominous
zlostavljanje *n* abuse
zlostavljanje *n.* mal-treatment
zlostavljanje *n.* molestation
zlostavljati *v.t.* abuse
zlostavljati *v.t.* molest
zloupotreba *n.* misapplication
zloupotreba *n.* misuse
zloupotrebiti *v.t.* misuse
zmaj *n* dragon
zmaj *n.* kite
zmija *n.* serpent
zmija *n.* snake
značaj *n.* importance
značaj *n.* significance
značajan *a.* meaningful

značajan *a.* momentous
značajan *a.* notable
značajan *a.* significant
značajnost *n.* notability
značenje *n.* meaning
značenje *n.* purport
značenje *n.* signification
značiti *v.t* mean
značiti *a.* mean
značiti *v.t.* purport
značka *n.* badge
znak *n.* mark
znak *n.* sign
znak *n.* token
znamenit *a.* signal
znanstveni *a.* scholarly
znanstveni *a.* scientific
znanstvenik *n.* scientist
znanje *n.* knowledge
znanje *n.* lore
znatan *a* formidable
znatan *a.* substantial
znati *v.t.* know
znoj *n.* sweat
znojenje *n.* perspiration
znojiti se *v.i.* perspire
zob *n.* oat
zodijak *n* zodiac
zona *n.* zone
zonski *a.* zonal
zoolog *n.* zoologist
zoologija *n.* zoology
zoološki *a.* zoological
zoološki vrt *n.* zoo
zora *n* dawn
zora *n* aurora
zračenje *n.* radiation
zračiti *v. i* beam
zračiti *v.t.* radiate
zračni *a.* aerial

zračni duh *n.* sylph
zrak *n.* air
zrak *n.* ray
zrakoplovstvo *n.* aviation
zrelost *n.* maturity
zreo *a.* mature
zreo *v.i* mature
zreo *a* ripe
zrno *n.* grain
zub *n.* tooth
zubac *n* cog
zubobolja *n.* toothache
zujanje *n.* buzz
zujanje *n* hum
zujanje *n.* whir
zujanje *v.i.* whiz
zujati *v. i* hum
zujati *v. i* buzz
zum *n.* zoom
zumirati *v.i.* zoom
zurenje *n* gaze
zuriti *v.t.* gaze
zvano *adv.* alias
zvat *v.t.* beckon
zveckanje *n.* jingle
zveckati *v.i.* jingle
zveckati *v.i.* rattle
zvečka *n* rattle
zvekan *n.* soft
zveket *n.* clink
zveknuti *v.i.* smack
zvezdan *a.* starry
zvezdan *a.* stellar
zvijer *n* beast
zvijezda *n.* star
zvijezda vodilja *n.* loadstar
zviježđe *n.* constellation
zviždati *v.i.* whistle
zvižduk *n* whistle
zvjerski *a* beastly

zvjezdica *n.* asterisk
zvjezdolik *adj.* asteroid
zvonik *n.* steeple
zvoniti *v.t.* toll
zvono *n* bell
zvonjava *n* toll
zvrk *n.* whirligig
zvučati *v.i.* sound
zvučni *a.* sonic
zvučnik, govornik *n.* speaker
zvučnost *n.* sonority
zvuk *n* sound
zvuk *n.* tone
zvuk trube *n.* clarion

Ž

žaba *n.* frog
žaba krastača *n.* toad
žacnuti *v.i* smart
žad *n.* jade
žalba *n.* appeal
žalba *n* complaint
žaliti *v.i.* regret
žaliti *v.t.* rue
žaliti *v.i.* sorrow
žaliti se *v.t.* appeal
žaliti se *v. i* complain
žalost *n.* affliction
žalost *n.* grief
žalostan *a.* grievous
žalostan *a.* lamentable
žalostan *n.* mournful
žalostan *a.* rueful
žalostan *a.* sorry
žaljenje *n* regret
žamor *n.* murmur
žaoka *n.* sting
žargon *n.* jargon

žargon *n.* lingo
žarišni *a* focal
žarulja *n.* bulb
žbuka *v.t.* mortar
žbun *n.* shrub
žedan *a.* thirsty
žedan *adj.* athirst
žeđ *n.* thirst
žele *n.* jelly
želudačni *a.* gastric
želja *n* desire
želja *n.* wish
željan *a* desirous
željan *a* eager
željan *a.* wishful
željeti *v.t* desire
željeti *v.t.* want
željeti *v.t.* wish
željeznica *n.* railway
željezo *n.* iron
željno *adj.* appetent
žena *n* female
žena *n.* woman
ženska košulja *n* chemise
ženski *a* female
ženski *n.* womanish
ženski manastir *n* convent
ženskog roda *a* feminine
ženstven *a* effeminate
ženstvenost *n.* womanhood
žestina *n* fervour
žestina *n.* vehemence
žestok *a* fierce
žestok *a.* vehement
žetelac *n.* haverster
žetelac *n.* reaper
žeti *v.t.* reap
žetva *n.* harvest
žica *n.* wire
židov *n.* Jew

žig *n.* hallmark
žiganje *n.* pang
žir *n.* acorn
žirafa *n.* giraffe
žitarica *n.* cereal
žitni *a* cereal
živ *a.* live
živ *a.* vivid
živ *a.* alive
živa *n.* quicksilver
živa ograda *n.* hedge
živac *n.* Nerve
živac *n* quick
živahan *adj* alacrious
živahan *a.* animate
živahan *a.* living
živahan *a.* spirited
živahan *a.* sprightly
živahnost *n.* alacrity
živahnost *n.* vivacity
živi pijesak *n.* quicksand
živin *a.* mercurial
živina *n.* fowl
živina *n.* poultry
živjeti *v.i.* live
živjeti na selu *v.t.* rusticate
živo *a.* lively
život *n* life
život *n* living
životinja *n.* animal
životopisac *n* bioscope
žižak *n.* weevil
žlica *n.* spoon
žlijeb *n.* groove
žlijezda *n.* gland
žongler *n.* juggler
žonglirati *v.t.* juggle
žrtva *n.* oblation
žrtva *n.* victim
žrtva nesreće *n.* casualty

žrtveni *a.* sacrificial
žrtveni jarac *n.* scapegoat
žrtvovanje *n.* sacrifice
žrtvovati *v.t.* sacrifice
žrtvovati *v.t.* victimize
žućkast *a.* yellowish
žuč *n* bile
žudjeti *v.t.* covet
žudjeti *v.t.* crave
žudjeti *v.i.* hanker
žudjeti *v.i.* yearn
žudnja *n.* yearning
žulj *n* blister

žumance *n.* yolk
žurba *n.* haste
žurba *n* hurry
žurba *n.* rush
žuriti *v.t.* hurry
žuriti *v.t.* rush
žuriti *v. t* bustle
žustar *adj* brisk
žut *a.* yellow
žut poput šafrana *a* saffron
žuta boja *n* yellow
žutica *n.* jaundice
žvakati *v. t* chew
žvakati *v.t.* masticate